Incentives and Choice in Health Care

Incentives and Choice in Health Care

edited by Frank A. Sloan and
Hirschel Kasper

The MIT Press
Cambridge, Massachusetts
London, England

MIT Press books may be purchased at special quantity discounts for business or sales promotional use. For information, please email <special_sales@mitpress.mit.edu> or write to Special Sales Department, The MIT Press, 55 Hayward Street, Cambridge, MA 02142.

This book was set in Palatino by SNP Best-set Typesetter Ltd., Hong Kong. Printed and bound in the United States of America.

Library of Congress Cataloging-in-Publication Data
Incentives and choice in health care / edited by Frank A. Sloan and Hirschel Kasper.
    p. cm.
Includes bibliographical references and index.
ISBN 978-0-262-19577-5 (hardcover : alk. paper)—ISBN 978-0-262-69365-3 (pbk. : alk. paper) 1. Medical economics. 2. Medical economics—United States. I. Sloan, Frank A. II. Kasper, Hirschel.
RA410.I53 2008
338.4'73621—dc22

2007039861

Contents

Preface

This book is a collection of essays by many of the preeminent scholars in the field of health economics. The authors describe the development of research on some of today's most important issues in health care, and add their own recent findings and perspectives, to aid the reader in gaining a better understanding of the role of incentives in choices by patients and providers in health care.

The purpose of the book is to evaluate the role of incentives and markets in a variety of health contexts, ranging from demand decisions—individuals who make choices about the health care services they consume and the health insurance policies they purchase as well as their personal health more generally—to supply decisions—by students who are considering a career in medicine practicing physicians, hospitals, and pharmaceutical manufacturers.

Preliminary versions of most of the chapters were presented on the second and third days of a conference held September 8–10, 2006, at Oberlin College in Oberlin, Ohio. This conference assembled the distinguished academic researchers of the chapters that are included here, but in addition, nearly every discussant of the papers was a graduate of Oberlin, as were most of the expert panelists, demonstrating that, as one of us experienced personally (Frank Sloan, 1964), liberal arts colleges are the home to rising scholars and crucial research on issues at the top of the nation's agenda. Academic and research economists came together at the conference with people with everyday experience in many different aspects of the nation's health care. The roundtable on the first day of the conference included panelists from a wide array of health care providers and organizations. The chief executive officer of the Cleveland Clinic, one of the nation's foremost research hospitals, opened the conference, and his remarks were followed by those of an administrator of a nonprofit multihospital chain, economists in and outside the government who evaluate health policies, and experts from venture capital funds that help finance new providers of medical devices and pharmaceutical drugs. A manufacturer of generic pharmaceutical drugs offered his perspective on one panel.

In organizing this project, we viewed the conference as an important vehicle for assembling the authors, discussants of the papers, health care practitioners and administrators, Oberlin students, faculty, and alumni, and persons in the community who have a general interest in health care and policy. The authors substantially revised their chapters based on the comments they received at the conference as well as through general discussion, subsequent reviews, and further reflection and research.

Much discussion of the issues contained in this book ordinarily takes place among specialists in the field. Some excellent technical summaries have appeared, such as the *Handbook of Health Economics.*[1] The *Handbook*, however, is oriented to professional economists— faculty, graduate students, and other researchers. In organizing the conference and ultimately this book, our goal has been to address a general audience. This book is appropriate as a supplement to a text in health economics. It is also aimed at readers who may have a limited background in economics, but have an interest in health policy, either as a health care provider, public policy maker, or consumer-patient-citizen. Each author is well aware of the other chapters, and there is referencing across chapters. The subject matter is quite diverse, and readers may wish to concentrate on individual chapters according to their interests rather than read the book sequentially from cover to cover.

This book focuses on the health care system in the United States. Yet there is much in the book that applies to other countries as well. Patient behavior is fairly universal. Innovation in pharmaceuticals and medical devices is a global concern. The issue of how to best compensate health care professionals is relevant, to a greater or lesser extent, to all countries. While pay for performance is still in its infancy, the issues pertinent to the United States also apply to other countries. Although polls often indicate that people like their own health care system, policy makers in few countries are entirely satisfied with their existing system, and most are considering new ideas to improve what they now have.

Finally, the book describes our current understanding, but also identifies what we do not know. Substantial progress has been made in health economics, but we have only scratched the surface. There is indeed much to be learned.

Note

1. Culyer and Newhouse (2000).

Acknowledgments

As mentioned in the preface, initial drafts of most of the chapters in this book were presented at the 2006 Health Economics Conference held September 8–10 at Oberlin College. The conference could not have been held without substantial financial and administrative support. College officers provided encouraging and generous support, and we expressly thank the president, the dean, and Oberlin's Alumni Office for their enthusiastic willingness to bring such a conference to Oberlin. The staff of the Development Office, and especially Jim Howard, went out of their way to make the conference a successful achievement. Oberlin alumnus Joshua Durst (1981) provided the base of our necessary funds, and took the time to make sure the conference was as good as he hoped. Geoffrey Harris (1983) and Jeffrey Weidenthal (1985) thoughtfully gave their personal and financial support when it was needed. The officers of the hospitals of Community Health Partners offered their generous commitment of funds and time to make this event happen in their "backyard."

The burden of arranging the conference was piled on the members and staff of the economics department, chaired by Luis Fernandez, but the detailed responsibility was cheerfully and proficiently shouldered by Terri Pleska, who everyone in attendance at the conference learned is more than the department's administrative assistant.

Since the conference, much of the administrative burden in preparing the book for publication has been capably borne by Khuwailah Beyah at the Center for Health Policy, Duke University. We owe her our thanks as well.

Contributors

Henry J. Aaron, The Brookings Institution

Ernst R. Berndt, Sloan School of Management, MIT

John Cawley, Cornell University

Julie M. Donohue, Graduate School of Public Health, University of Pittsburgh

Donna Gilleskie, University of North Carolina at Chapel Hill

Brian R. Golden, University of Toronto

Gautam Gowrisankaran, University of Arizona

Chee-Ruey Hsieh, Academia Sinica

Hirschel Kasper, Oberlin College

Thomas G. McGuire, Harvard Medical School, Harvard University

Joseph P. Newhouse, John F. Kennedy School of Government, Harvard University

Sean Nicholson, Cornell University

Mark V. Pauly, The Wharton School, University of Pennsylvania

Anna D. Sinaiko, Harvard University

Frank A. Sloan, Duke University

Incentives and Choice in Health Care

1 Introduction

Frank A. Sloan and
Hirschel Kasper

Health and health care are important to us as individual patients, health care providers, and the broader economy more generally.[1] Better health for more people takes resources: the skill of the surgeon, the creativity of the pharmaceutical researcher, and the time to exercise, among many others.

As its title implies, this book is about the role of incentives in health and health care decision making. Its central theme is that a vast body of empirical evidence has accumulated to demonstrate that incentives affect the choices of individual consumers as well as the suppliers of health care services, including students making choices about their careers, practicing physicians, hospitals, and pharmaceutical manufacturers. Government and private decision makers who seek to influence choices about health and health care should pay considerable attention to how people's behavior is affected by their "economic" incentives, both the financial and nonmonetary ones. To economists, any carrot or stick that affects resource allocation is an economic incentive or disincentive. The carrots and sticks are not limited to financial rewards and penalties.

While we know a lot about individuals' and organizations' responses to incentives, however, there is still much to be learned, which adds complexity to the design of appropriate incentives. For example, if Medicare were to cut the fees it pays to physicians by five percent—a type of proposal that reappears frequently—how would physicians respond? Would physicians reduce or increase their work hours and the number of services? Would certain disadvantaged populations among the elderly be disproportionately affected? How many fewer people would train to be physicians, two or two hundred? We have some answers to these questions, but there is still much to be learned.

Many concepts and empirical findings are presented in this book. To all but the health care experts, many of these concepts and findings will be unfamiliar, perhaps even provocative. The objective of this chapter is to provide the background and context for the discussion that follows as well as a road map to the book.

Incentives have long been a focus in the discipline of economics. Within economics there are applied topics that concentrate on a particular sector or situation, such as the behavior of organizations or the regulation of the environment. Most of the research on the role of incentives in health and health care, especially the financial ones, has been conducted by economists specializing in the field of health economics—a subfield of microeconomics. The vast majority of the authors in this book regard themselves as health economists, but economists from many fields have contributed to our understanding of health economics, including several Nobel laureates.

Applied microeconomics almost always involves the empirical analysis of data that are based on a conceptual framework provided by an underlying theory. The research questions may be broad, such as an analysis of hospital competition, or narrow, such as a cost-benefit analysis of a particular drug or an evaluation of a specific public policy change, but good theory leads the researcher to seek the requisite data needed to test hypotheses implied by the theory.

Health economics deals with both the allocation and financing of resources used to produce health services, and the role of health and other factors in improving personal well-being, often termed "utility" by economists. These researchers frequently study the effect of one variable on another, *all else* being equal. All else may be held equal either as a theoretical analysis or a statistical exercise. Sometimes one variable affects another by working through a third, a fourth, or many variables. In that event, no less than the simpler case, all the relevant variables must be explicitly considered.

Even the more theoretical studies in health economics incorporate the relevant institutional aspects of health care. Examples include the predominance of health insurance coverage, the large share of hospitals under not-for-profit ownership, the inherently asymmetrical relationship between physicians and their patients, and the various forms of regulation, such as the regulation of entry into the medical professions, including professional licensure; requiring certificates of need to allow hospitals, nursing homes, or outpatient surgery facilities to be built; and the government approval of new drugs.

As an academic field of inquiry, there was virtually no *sustained* health economics research before 1945 and relatively little until after 1965, the year that the law establishing the Medicare and Medicaid programs was enacted in the United States. Nonetheless, between the years 1945 and 1965, three pathbreaking studies were published. All dealt in one way or another with distinguishing institutional arrangements in the provision of health care.

The first, which analyzed incomes in various professions including dentistry and medicine, was Milton Friedman and Simon Kuznets's (1945), *Income from Independent Professional Practice*. In addition to assembling data on national income in the 1930s, Kuznets had gathered data on income in various occupations and completed a draft study in 1936. Friedman picked up the project, completing it as his PhD dissertation in 1945. The importance of this study for health economics was its focus on the entry barriers to occupations imposed by licensure and the resulting effect of increasing physicians' incomes above the level that would prevail under competition.

Reuben Kessel (1958) published an article in the first issue of the *Journal of Law and Economics* on price discrimination by physicians—a common practice before health insurance coverage was widespread. He argued that contrary to the conventional wisdom, multipart pricing of physicians' services (with poor families paying less) was not an act of charity. Rather, he asserted, such price discrimination reflected the exercise of market power by physicians to raise their incomes.

One implication of the work of Friedman and Kuznets as well as Kessel is that the effect of the institutional arrangements in markets for physicians' services was to some extent the physicians' financial gain rather than patients' protection. By contrast, an important article by Kenneth Arrow (1963) described the existing institutional arrangements in health care markets as "second-best" alternatives that ultimately serve the public interest. The first-best option for everyone would be to insure one's own health. Absent the feasibility of this, however, consumers require other protections, such as the not-for-profit ownership of hospitals.

Incentives, Private Choices, and Roles of Governments

Broadly speaking, health economics deals with issues related to the financing and delivery of health services as well as the effects of such services and other decisions in the production of health. Health economists investigate positive issues—that is, empirical relationships among variables and normative issues—that is, how resources should be optimally allocated to produce a level of health that maximizes the well-being of persons in a society.

People, firms, and health care organizations are motivated by incentives. Not all of the incentives that affect decisions are financial but many are. Prestige and personal satisfaction also motivate people. Financial incentives are often the most effective because they can be altered most easily. To achieve socially desirable outcomes, incentives must be structured appropriately. In most markets, prices perform a crucial role in providing inducements for suppliers to furnish the quantities and kinds of goods and services that consumers most desire, given the resources at their disposal. For many goods and services, governments are largely on the sidelines, sometimes policing abuses or imposing taxes to raise revenue, or monitoring performance, such as gas mileage standards on automobiles.

By contrast, governments in most high-income countries, even in the United States but to a lesser extent than in many others, are active participants in their countries' health sectors. One principal rationale is redistribution. Absent government intervention, market forces may lead to a situation in which less-affluent populations and populations disadvantaged for other reasons, such as the geographic remoteness of locations at which health services are delivered, may have "inadequate" access to health services. This is a common rationale for public provision of health insurance, subsidies to medical students and their universities, and low-interest loans for hospital construction.

While there is a broad consensus that some redistribution of resources is appropriate, there is no agreement on either the amount of redistribution that is appropriate or how it should be accomplished. Also, in seeking to redistribute resources, there has been a tendency on the part of some to view public policies as almost exclusively redistributional, as if there were no incentive effects. Returning to an example mentioned above, for example, there is a widespread perception among some observers that the government can cut fees to physicians by 5 percent in an attempt to reduce a government deficit without any effect on the supply of physicians' services. The explicit reason for such policies is largely to reduce public spending, coupled with a secondary, more implicit justification, that "rich" physicians can afford such fee reductions. The possibility that such cuts could affect incentives often takes a backseat in such discussions or is viewed as pleading on the part of special interests.

Another key rationale for government intervention is to correct "market failures," that is, when markets do not provide the "right" goods to the "right" people at the "right" time. Markets fail, for instance, when there are "externalities" in consumption. For example, vaccinating person B against a contagious disease may have health benefits for person A. Yet absent some government intervention, person B will not take account of the benefits to person A, unless perhaps A is a close relative. Governments also intervene to counter market power on the part of sellers, such as physicians and hospitals. As explained below, some abuses of market power are particularly critical in health care.

An alternative to government intervention is to implement private arrangements to cope with market failure. This is one rationale for the dominance of private nonprofit organizations in health care in the United States and other countries.[2]

The Important Institutional Features of Health Care

Health Insurance

In many industrialized countries, health insurance is provided by the government. In the United States, health insurance is provided both publicly and privately. The use of personal health services is to some extent random because the onset of illness is random—that is, often unpredictable. As a result, risk-averse individuals, presumably most people, seek to reduce the risk of unforeseen large expenditures, which is the major function of health insurance. Risk-averse people are better off with insurance for this reason.

While insurance is welfare enhancing—that is, it improves the personal well-being of society's members in the aggregate by providing protection against financial losses in the event of an illness—there is an important respect in which it could be welfare decreasing. In the popular view, it is not possible to have too much health insurance. After all, are people not better off if medical care is "free"? This view neglects the fact that resources are used and people pay for such care whether or not it is provided at no out-of-pocket cost at the point of service. Individuals are taxed to pay for public insurance. Most private insurance in the United States is employer based. But the general consensus among economists is that employees, not employers, foot most, if not all, of the bill of employer-supplied insurance premiums in the form of reduced wages and/or other fringe benefits.[3]

While health insurance reduces a person's expenditure risk—that is, their exposure to a large expenditure in the event that the person becomes severely ill—it also can distort a person's choice about how much health care to consume. The tendency to consume more medical care as a result of having insurance is termed "moral hazard." Moral hazard, which results from the provision of health insurance coverage, leads people to take *advantage* of their insurance, which is a misallocation of resources. Had people been required to pay the full cost of their care, they would have obtained less, but been better off on the *whole* because they would consume more of other goods and services, even spending more leisure time with their families.[4]

Both governments and private organizations employ various ways to reduce moral hazard. One alternative is to limit the supply of health resources by erecting barriers to entry. For example, before a new hospital can be built, most states require that its advocates demonstrate that a hospital is needed. Another approach for combating this moral hazard is to monitor the utilization of health services, disallowing insurance coverage for services considered to be of low marginal value. Still another way is to increase cost sharing—that is, raise the share of the payment to the provider that the insured consumer bears. While increased cost sharing also increases expenditure risk, it reduces moral hazard.

Moral hazard is only one problem that arises in health insurance markets. Another is "adverse selection," a phenomenon that can arise when health insurance is provided privately rather than by a government.

Adverse selection may arise when there is asymmetric information—that is, when consumers know more about their own health risks than do insurers. Adverse selection can lead healthier consumers to avoid high-cost complete health insurance coverage or eschew coverage altogether, leaving the market to individuals at higher risk for adverse health outcomes.

In theory, adverse selection can lead to the unraveling of insurance markets.[5] This process works as follows. Not knowing each insured person's health risk, insurers frequently do not charge different premiums to high- versus low-risk individuals. Thus, for any premium that allows the insurer to break even, insurance is an attractive purchase for high- but not low-risk individuals. Fewer low-risk persons demand insurance as a result. To break even on the remaining persons it covers, the insurer must raise premiums in the following year. And again, the lower-risk individuals among the higher-risk persons drop out of the insurance market. This process of unraveling continues until only a few high-risk individuals remain in the market. All the rest of the population is made worse off because they have lost a vehicle for reducing expenditure risk at actuarially fair premiums—that is, at premiums that cover the losses that may be anticipated from a person with a specific set of observable characteristics. Although conceptually plausible, the quantitative significance of adverse selection in health insurance markets is an empirical question. Among the currently uninsured in the United States are some healthy young men who prefer to buy health insurance.

Health insurance also has important effects on the decisions of the suppliers of health care. From the mid-1930s when private health insurance markets began to develop in the United States to the early 1980s, the amounts paid to hospitals and physicians depended on how much the services cost—for instance, how much the hospitals and physicians charged for their services. Cost- and charge-based reimbursement proved to be increasingly expensive. From a hospital's standpoint, increases in reported costs resulted in higher payments to the hospital.

These cost and charge pass-through systems were replaced by payment on a fixed-price basis. The public insurer Medicare, the largest one in the United States, pays hospitals a fixed price per case under its Prospective Payment System. Physicians are paid by Medicare under a fixed-pricing system based on the Resource-Based Relative Value Scale that seeks to account for the resource costs incurred in each patient encounter. Since the mid-1980s, private health insurance plans often negotiate fixed fees with providers. Changing from a cost and charge pass-through system of paying health care providers to fixed-fee systems has, not surprisingly, substantially altered the incentives that providers face. In particular, the fixed-fee systems offer an incentive for hospitals and physicians to operate more efficiently, but they may also have side effects such as affecting providers' willingness to accept patients covered by such fee arrangements for care.

There are other important information asymmetries as well. Physicians are more knowledgeable about medical issues than are their patients. Ideally, physicians would provide unbiased information to their patients. Professional norms are designed to combat any tendency that physicians might have to take advantage of their superior information, compared to the patient's knowledge, about the patient's health status.

Society has designed a wide variety of ways of dealing with the information asymmetry, such as implementing various forms of regulatory scrutiny ranging from policies that bar market entry to providers deemed to be of low quality or untrustworthy, to the imposition of tort liability, to employer and/or public or private insurer scrutiny of utilization and quality.

In recent years, an increasing emphasis has been placed on educating health care consumers about their options. This has taken the form of public health announcements as well as direct-to-consumer advertising by pharmaceutical companies and report cards on hospital performance. Even though information provision also has potential pitfalls—for example, direct-to-consumer advertising may give the seller more market power—such advertising may help consumers know more about their treatment options, perhaps leading to better health.

There have also been attempts, both extensive and expensive, to educate physicians on the efficacy of alternative treatments. Given the rapid rate of technological change, the evidence on efficacy is always changing too, and it is costly to get new information promptly to all the providers who can use it. Innovators such as research hospitals and private manufacturers often sponsor educational conferences.

The Dominance of Nonprofit Organizations in Some Parts of Health Care

Economists have attributed the dominance of the not-for-profit ownership in the hospital sector to the fact that it is so difficult to identify and purchase the specific "quality" of hospital care one wants. Some types of quality are easily monitored by consumers, such as the features of the hospital room and how quickly hospital employees respond to calls from patients. Other aspects of quality, however, are not observable by consumers. An example would be how well the radiologist reads the patient's X-ray or the accuracy of dispensing in the hospital pharmacy. The latter aspects of quality are noncontractible. When noncontractible quality is important, society may grant financial incentives to encourage entry of organizations that are not profit seeking. This is the theory. Whether or not not-for-profit hospitals indeed perform better than their for-profit counterparts is an empirical question to be examined later in this book.

Health and Health Behaviors

The ultimate goal of consuming health services is to improve one's personal health. Economists have made major strides in understanding the decisions people make that affect their health. One key theme of this research is to cast decisions about health within a standard microeconomic framework. In this framework, medical care along with other health "inputs" such as physical exercise and a good diet go into producing improvements in health. Recently, though, some economists have begun to question the validity of the standard assumptions that are generally made in their field about household decision makers.

The Production of Health

A framework developed by Michael Grossman (1972a, 1972b) views health as a "stock," a form in which wealth is held, much like an automobile, a house, or a financial asset. An individual's stock of health yields daily flows of healthy days, much like a house yields residential services and an automobile provides daily transportation. Like houses and cars, a person's health depreciates as one grows older. And like houses and cars, renovation and reconstruction is sometimes possible. But when health declines to certain point, the person dies.

Many factors go into the "production" of this health stock. Health is produced by medical care as well as various health behaviors such as good diet and nutrition, physical activity, not smoking, not consuming illicit drugs or alcohol to excess, washing one's hands, medical care, and so on. The demand for health services is derived from the individual's demand for health. In this framework, numerous prices, not only of medical care, ultimately affect personal health. Other prices relevant to health include the prices of cigarettes, beer, tennis shoes, and foods that are rich in calories and unsaturated fats.

In a standard economic model, individuals decide on health inputs based on prices, their views of the marginal products to them of various inputs (some of which, such as cigarettes, have negative marginal products), discount rates reflecting the trade-off between receiving benefits now versus receiving them later (think exercise), the value they attach to being in good health, and their perceived value of consuming more/less of the many nonhealth goods.

Technological improvements may increase the marginal product of health inputs. The invention of antibiotics made physicians far more

productive in treating strep throats and thereby avoiding the complication of rheumatic fever. Various scanners, such as CT scanners,
revolutionized the diagnosis of many conditions. Such technological
changes may not be neutral. That is, they may increase the marginal
products of some inputs relative to others. A flu vaccine, for example,
is a substitute for visits to physicians by persons with the flu. On the
other hand, the invention of new chemotherapeutic agents for treating
cancer plausibly increases the demand for physician time along with
an increase in the demand for such drug therapies.

Since health care contains an important probabilistic or stochastic
element, the value of the marginal product of any input varies for each
specific person. The random nature of one's future health introduces
uncertainty. Thus, an individual's risk preferences also affect that person's demand for health inputs.

Rationality, Irrationality, and Health Care Choices

A critical building block of economic analysis is the assumption that
people try to make rational decisions. Rationality does not require
omniscience but rather that individuals try to use all the information
at hand in making decisions, including those that have implications
for the future. Scholars in other social science disciplines are less
prone to rely on the assumption of rationality and often define it differently. A common retort by economists when criticized for employing
an assumption of rationality has been this: judge our models not
by their assumptions but by how well they predict actual observed
behavior.[6]

In recent years, many economists have begun to question the assumption of rationality and are exploring the implications of alternative
assumptions underlying decision making. Some are conducting empirical studies of this subject under the general heading of behavioral
economics and are discussed in some of the follwing chapters.

Overview of Book

The chapters following this one consider and report our understanding
of the effects of various incentives for many crucial issues in health
care.

Chapter 2, "To Find the Answer, One Must Know the Question," by
Henry Aaron provides another overview of health economics, but from

a policy perspective. In several of the areas that Aaron identifies, economists have made substantial progress, but public policy demands ever more precise answers, such as how to best structure cost sharing in health insurance plans as well as how to structure medical malpractice insurance to best achieve the goals of injury deterrence, compensation, and reducing the high administrative cost of tort liability. By contrast, while some important research has been conducted on the economics of epidemics, much remains to be done. Results could inform decisions about optimal resource allocation to cope with possible pandemics.

Aaron's report on the state of research reflects both his overview from the standpoint of a long-term health economics researcher and his practical experience employing existing research as Assistant Secretary of Planning and Evaluation in the U.S. Department of Health and Human Services in the 1970s.

Chapters 3 through 7 focus more specifically on issues about the demand for health and health care. Chapter 3, "Human Capital: Theory and Empirical Evidence," by Donna Gilleskie first describes the Grossman health capital model. From there, Gilleskie discusses theoretical extensions of the model—the most significant of which is to incorporate the effects of uncertainty. There are many empirical applications of the Grossman model, including empirical studies of demand for medical care and other inputs affecting health, such as diet, exercise, and tobacco and drug use. Several studies have focused on the relationship between health and education. Education has several potential effects on health, including but not limited to the individual's ability to process information. Gilleskie's own research has centered on developing structural models of household decision making about health and health care. She explains her own work on the use of medical care and absences from work during episodes of acute illness as well as three other applications of the structural approach to modeling: the use of mental health services during childhood, choices of prescription drugs when the effects of the drug can only be learned by trying it, and a study of annual smoking, exercise, alcohol consumer, and medical care use decisions over a lifetime.

Chapter 4, "What We Know and Don't Know about the Effects of Cost Sharing on the Demand for Medical Care," by Joseph Newhouse and Anna Sinaiko focuses on demand for medical care. Newhouse led the Rand Health Insurance Experiment (HIE) during the 1970s and 1980s. That experiment gathered substantial information about price elasticities of demand for various types of personal health services for families with different income levels, and separately for children and adults. The study also conducted pioneering research on the effect of health insurance coverage on health outcomes. The HIE started the movement to measure health outcomes—research that has mostly been conducted by noneconomists during the past two decades.

Several important changes identified in the chapter have occurred since the HIE was conducted. Nevertheless, it seems unlikely that another HIE will be conducted soon, since running a randomized experiment with hundreds of families over many years is so costly.

As explained above, two key issues in any insurance market are adverse selection and moral hazard. Chapter 5, "Adverse Selection and Moral Hazard: Implications for Health Insurance Markets," by Mark Pauly deals with the theory and empirical evidence on both issues. Pauly is widely recognized as the leader in economic research on health insurance.

First, Pauly characterizes ideal insurance to serve as a benchmark for comparing insurance in the presence of moral hazard and adverse selection. He concludes that moral hazard is indeed an important issue. Given moral hazard, there is a rationale for high-deductible plans, such as the typical Health Savings Accounts, but an impediment to the diffusion of such plans is the tax treatment of employer-provided health insurance benefits. These employee benefits are currently excluded from employees' income for the purposes of the U.S. federal personal income tax. A person paying a marginal tax rate of 25 percent, for example, obtains a twenty-five cents per dollar subsidy on personal health care spending. For this reason, it may make sense for individuals to demand health insurance, which covers highly predictable services, such as annual physical exams or even toothpaste (the latter is not covered in any plan, to our knowledge) rather than more cash income. For high-income families in particular, or even families that confront progressive state and local income taxes, the 35 to 40 percent marginal income tax rate may far exceed the administrative cost of the insurance policy, making complete insurance coverage a good deal.

In contrast to moral hazard, Pauly calls adverse selection a "paper tiger," more important in theory than in practice. Even if not critical in health insurance, however, adverse selection may be a significant phenomenon in other markets, depending on their specific characteristics.

As discussed above, consumer information is an important issue in health care. Two countries allow the direct-to-consumer advertising of prescription drugs: the United States and New Zealand. Ernst Berndt and Julie Donohue analyze the economic effects of this form of advertising in chapter 6, "Direct-to-Consumer Advertising in Health Care: An Overview of Economic Issues." Interestingly, before the passage of the U.S. Food and Drug Act in 1906, which established the Food and Drug Administration (FDA) to review the safety—and later also the efficacy—of prescription drugs, direct-to-consumer advertising was prevalent in the United States. Physicians and others were free to advertise their potions and elixirs to the general public. There was a widespread perception that consumers were easily duped by such ads, and would thus spend their money on potentially dangerous and ineffective products. Parallel to the professionalization of medicine, physicians were made the gatekeepers of prescription drugs, and the advertising of drugs by pharmaceutical manufacturers was directed at them, not the general public.

In the late 1990s, the FDA permitted direct-to-consumer advertising in the United States for the first time in the modern era. Such ads remain controversial. Some critics remain skeptical that consumers can adequately process the information in the ads, even given the regulatory restrictions as to ad content. Economists generally are suspicious of advertising that mainly has the effect of reducing the elasticity of the demand curves facing individual firms, thereby increasing the seller's market power to raise price. This is a concern for direct-to-consumer advertising as well. Alternatively, however, such advertising may remind persons with chronic diseases (or chronic diseases yet to be diagnosed) to visit their physicians to discuss the wide variety of available therapies. In that event, such advertising may be welfare increasing. Berndt has conducted a number of highly regarded empirical studies of pharmaceuticals in recent years and is probably the leading economic expert on direct-to-consumer advertising.

The final chapter on demand is "*Reefer Madness*, Frank the Tank, or *Pretty Woman*: To What Extent Do Addictive Behaviors Respond to Incentives?" by John Cawley. It looks at different kinds of human behavior. As noted previously, economists have long realized that some behaviors, not only medical care, are important inputs in the production of health. Those behaviors are hard to model, and often seem counter to economists' usual assumption that people are rational and forward-looking in their decision making.

There have been attempts to reconcile observed consumption of addictive goods with the assumptions of rationality and forward-looking behavior. The most notable study, "The Theory of Rational Addiction," is by Gary Becker and Kevin Murphy (1988). Another attempt is a theoretical study based on the notion that when people first try addictive goods, they do not know whether or not they are addictive types.[7] This is determined after some of the good is consumed. For those who learn that they are addictive types, it is too late, and they are hooked.

Other disciplines, such as social psychology, view addiction quite differently. The field of behavioral economics seeks to bridge the disciplines of economics and psychology, and addiction is proving to be a fertile area for such research. We leave it to readers to determine whether they are more like Frank the Tank or *Pretty Woman*. Interestingly, Cawley entered this field by studying the economics of obesity, which he began exploring as a student at the University of Chicago—a university regarded as seldom sympathetic to the perspectives of behavioral economics.

Chapters 8 through 12 focus on the supply of personal health services. The chronological order of the five chapters reflects a distinction often made in economics between the long run and the short run. In the short run, some factor of production is fixed. In the long run, all factors are variable. On the demand side, health capital is largely fixed in the short run. Among the supply chapters, chapters 8 and 9, which deal with career choice and biomedical research, are long-run oriented. People and firms are deciding whether or not to enter a market. Pricing and output decisions of physicians and hospitals in the remaining chapters are short-run decisions in that exit-entry decisions have already been made.

The decision of whether to become a physician is clearly a choice with personal and financial consequences to be realized over a span of four decades and in some cases more. Few physicians quit medicine entirely for other fields, though they may move to another "market" by changing their specialty, becoming administrators, or working in another region. In chapter 8, "Medical Career Choices and Rates of Return," Sean Nicholson investigates two related issues. First, are the rates of return on medical education in general and specialty training excessive? And second, do prospective rates of return affect career choices in medicine?

The first concern in particular is an old one. Friedman and Kuznets (1945) investigated this issue some six decades ago, clearly presuming that a barrier to entry such as a requirement that members of a profession be licensed would result in excess returns to education in the protected field, reflecting the excess supply of medical school applicants.

Actually determining whether or not returns are excessive is quite difficult since entrants are presumably motivated by many factors in deciding on an occupation or a job. For example, unless chefs like heat, they will demand a compensating differential for working in a hot kitchen. If doctors have to put up with bureaucratic managed care, medical malpractice suits, and telephone calls in the middle of the night, presumably their compensation would be higher than for those professionals with comparable investments in their human capital who do not have to put up with such disturbances.

Money may or may not be a powerful incentive in career choices. If it does not matter—that is, medical students decide on a particular specialty just for the love of it—then returns to practitioners just represent economic rents that serve no social purpose. Of course, even if "nonfinancial" factors dominate, economists still have contributions to make in thinking about this because the determinants of career choices is an important empirical issue for students, patients, and policymakers. It is possible that students may be quite rational and forward-looking in making career decisions, but irrational when it comes to the consumption of an addictive substance. One size may not fit all. Much of Nicholson's work is in labor economics, but he has done important work on the specific topic of his chapter in the recent past.

An entry decision for an existing firm is whether to invest in research and development in a new pharmaceutical product. In chapter 9, "Effects of Incentives on Pharmaceutical Innovation," Frank Sloan and Chee-Ruey Hsieh discuss the role of incentives in pharmaceutical innovation. Technological change in this field has led to dramatic improvements in population health. Yet there is probably no area in the health field in which the issue of the role of incentives is more controversial.

In one camp are those who view incentives as important. Companies undertake substantial investments in research to find and develop new and better drug products. Absent adequate returns anticipated in advance, companies will not undertake investments, which have potentially significant health benefits.

In the other camp are those who view much pharmaceutical research and development as investments in mostly "me-too" products that offer little or no therapeutic advantages over existing products, and believe that returns to such innovation are excessive. According to the second camp, certain controls are needed to prevent companies from earning economic rents by introducing new products that lead merely to substantial increases in health expenditures. These controls may take the form of price controls and/or stringent utilization standards.

A critical feature of the pharmaceutical sector is that there is a large initial fixed cost of research and development. Thereafter, the marginal cost of producing and distributing drugs is small. The low marginal cost itself may act to encourage price controls—a particular temptation in countries that generally import, rather than manufacture, drugs. The authors' empirical evidence supports the view that incentives are useful as a stimulus for research and development.

Obviously, "Me-toos" are not limited to drugs. After all, one could say that after the Toyota Prius was introduced, all other hybrid cars were me-toos. Just like a particular drug may be a better match for an individual, given its side effect profile, an alternative to the Prius may better satisfy a given consumer's wants. Perhaps that driver wants to haul material for a garden, or to be able to accelerate from a stoplight faster than most anyone else. Me-tooism is common, and not a unique characteristic of the pharmaceutical industry, though the regulatory authorities in some counties look askance at new brands that seem to replicate existing drugs.

Chapter 10, "Physician Fees and Behavior: Implications for Structuring a Fee Schedule," by Thomas McGuire discusses one of the major controversies in health economics: whether standard models apply to the physician market, or alternatively, whether physicians can and do induce demand for their products. To the extent that they do the latter, observed demand patterns for health reveal less about the satisfaction of patient wants.

After years of disputing this issue, McGuire and Pauly (1991) put an end to much of the controversy, at least within the economics profession, by developing a model that reconciles the two views of the markets for physicians' services. In Chapter 10, McGuire explores these views, but then goes a step further to recommend a pricing system that would be appropriate if induced demand is in fact a key empirical phenomenon. Under the proposed system, a patient's doctor would get a fixed payment per period—say, per month—for being that person's doctor. But in addition, the doctor would be paid less than the marginal cost for the surgical procedure. At least in theory, this approach would guarantee the patient's adequate access to physicians' services, but would make the doctor a lot less likely to recommend the surgical procedure. Even if the physician were to still recommend the procedure, the doctor would be more likely to frown than to "beam."

Chapter 11 by Brian Golden and Frank Sloan, "Physician Pay for Performance," addresses an issue gaining popularity in the health policy world: namely, paying more to physicians who perform better on some predetermined criteria. There is no open dispute about the principle of paying more for better service. Rather, the controversy is about whether the quality of physician services can be measured sufficiently accurately by an external body so that these incentives can really lead to improvements in patient care without wasting money and creating an environment in which gaming to attain higher payment is likely to occur. As of 2007, the pay-for-performance train had already left the station. Many health care providers are not happy about this, but the push to improve the quality of care and reduce medical errors is sufficient enough that many private and public decision makers are unwilling to wait for conclusive findings from empirical studies.

The chapter not only reviews economic evidence on pay for performance but also synthesizes relevant research findings from the fields of social psychology and sociology. This chapter includes the usual explanations that pay-for-performance systems often produce unanticipated and perverse incentives, yet also identifies the conditions under which pay for performance may be most and least effective.

In chapter 12, "Competition, Information Provision, and Hospital Quality," Gautam Gowrisankaran discusses issues related to the public provision of information about hospital quality. Perhaps in theory, given entry regulation of hospitals, including state licensure, every hospital is "good enough," but that is no longer the perception of health professionals or consumers. Traditionally, patients have largely relied on physicians to make the decision about which hospital is most appropriate for the patient. In recent years, however, at least in the United States, patients are increasingly having a role in this important decision. Hospitals are selected for various reasons, including their proximity to patients' residences, where patients' physicians have admitting privileges, and the physical features of the hospital itself, such as the size and ambience of the hospital rooms. Outcomes are also a factor in choice. Physicians can at least casually observe outcomes of care from a number of admissions to a given hospital, and they can discuss this with their colleagues. For most patients, by contrast, admission to a hospital is a rather rare event.

To the extent that consumers are substantively involved in the choice of a hospital, there is the issue of how they should make comparisons. At first glance, it would seem that one could simply examine various outcome measures, such as the percentage of patients admitted with a heart attack at the hospital who die during the stay. A problem with such simple comparisons is that some hospitals may have specialized facilities to care for patients with more serious heart attacks or patients with heart attacks who have other coexisting illnesses. If so, the comparisons will be biased. A good hospital may get more patients who are critically ill just because it is a good hospital. To make accurate comparisons, it is essential to adjust for the patient mix—a process called risk adjustment.

Risk adjustment is not a trivial exercise, particularly because certain characteristics of the patient that may be observable to the patient's physician and even to the patient may not be observable to the researcher. Unless risk adjustment is done properly, the dissemination of information on the outcomes of care may be highly misleading.

Chapter 13, by the coeditors, summarizes the other chapters. A substantial amount of research is described in this book. This body of research has important implications for the further development of theory (although no new theoretical findings are reported in this book), the empirical analysis of critical issues relating to individual and firm behavior, and public policy. This chapter's discussion is organized around these three themes.

Thus each chapter is self-contained so readers can explore, in accordance with their interests, how incentive affect the behavior of patients, physicians, hospitals, and other health care providers. The chapters in this book describe the economists' current understanding of many of the individual factors that determine health and health care. Anyone interested in good public policy will be able to use these chapters as the foundation to improve and widen access to health care in this country and elsewhere.

Notes

1. See, for example, Lopez-Casasnovas et al. (2006).

2. See, in particular, Arrow (1963).

3. Pauly (1997).

4. Mark Pauly (1968) wrote a brief article about the moral hazard resulting from insurance coverage as a comment on Arrow's (1963) article, introducing the concept and its relevance to the field of health economics. Generally brief comments, even to important articles, are not remembered, but Pauly's note is still widely cited today.

5. Rothschild and Stiglitz (1976).

6. Friedman (1953).

7. Suranovic, Goldfarb, and Leonard (1999).

2

To Find the Answer, One Must Know the Question: Health Economics and Public Policy

Henry J. Aaron

Public policy influences health care in numerous ways. Governments finance nearly half of all health care spending in the United States. Regulations shape who can practice medicine, what techniques they can use—or *must* use—how they can organize, and the terms of insurance. They establish rules under which patients, physicians, and shareholders can sue or be sued. Under these circumstances, policymakers need vast amounts of information to make their decisions intelligently.

This chapter describes a number of such questions. I indicate whether economists have contributed useful answers to those questions and suggest where additional research may be desirable. As will become apparent, important questions are often difficult. Not all are answerable. Many depend so heavily on value judgments about which reasonable people disagree that there can be little prospect of reliable answers.

The following list includes questions relevant not only to legislative or regulatory policy but also to managerial efficiency. The list is not screened to include only questions that are answerable given current methods, or even in principle. Rather, it includes anything that, it seemed to me, one would want to know in order to decide how much to spend on health care services or research, how to spend it, and on whom to spend it. This chapter omits some major issues. For example, I focus on health policy issues in the United States. The health policy issues facing the world's poor, who are denied the luxury of modern medical care, are not separately mentioned. The policy issues relevant to the developing world would overlap only a bit with this one and merit separate treatment.

Economists have spent a good deal of time trying to decide whether various participants in the health care market respond to traditional economic incentives, such as prices and incomes. Not surprisingly, incentives have been shown to matter. Though anticipated, this class of findings is perhaps the most important contribution that health economists have made to health care policy.

Demand

Effects of Price

Price influences demand for health insurance as well as demand for personal health care services. Any other finding about the effect of price on the quantity demanded would be shocking—the law of demand is, after all, a *law*. But the effects are large enough to matter. That means that deductibles and cost sharing can be used to influence how much care people consume. Insurance design is therefore a potentially powerful tool for controlling the level and composition, if not the rate of growth, of people's demand for care. Price sensitivity underlies the seminal observation that insurance promotes the overuse of medical care.[1] Overuse does not imply that the care is without benefit—merely that benefits are below production cost.

If out-of-pocket money costs influence demand for health care, it is a short step to linking demand to waiting times, travel distance, hassle, and red tape. Evidence that nonmonetary costs, such as travel time, influence demand is no less clear-cut.[2] These findings mean that access to care is not a "yes/no" variable. Rather, demand is smoothly continuous in a multidimensional "price." This finding means that the quantity and distribution of health care personnel and facilities affect use not just because it shifts supply but also because it changes demand by altering price (see below on induced demand).

Estimates of demand price elasticities are quite varied, especially when some of the estimates from empirical research in health economics' early years, the 1970s, are compared to more recent ones. This field has been blessed, however, by a random-assignment experiment, the RAND Health Insurance Experiment (HIE).[3] This study was state of the art in its day. Despite advances in theory and econometrics as well as large institutional changes, I doubt that the cost and effort of fielding a new demand experiment would be justified.

The fundamental finding—that variations in insurance provisions such as deductibles, stop loss, and cost sharing influence demand for care—is well established. To be sure, the precise results depended on conditions specific to the time. Those conditions have changed hugely in the roughly three decades since the HIE was carried out. The medical value of health care has increased enormously, and it seems clear that the perceived value of medical interventions per dollar of cost to the patient would directly affect the willingness to pay. Some areas of medicine—interventional radiology, for example—did not even exist as specialties when the HIE was done. The organization of physician practices has changed. Average per capita spending has more than doubled. Sizable deductibles have become commonplace. They are now linked to lavishly generous tax treatment of savings designated for health care.[4] Stop-loss provisions are now standard. The organization and administrative spending constraints in prepaid group plans have changed. As a result, there is no simple way to translate many of the findings from the HIE into estimates of the impact on spending today of such changes as a shift to high-deductible insurance.

But while there have been changes in insurance practices, the fundamental relationships between price and the quantity of care demanded, measured by the HIE, have not changed. More recently, published results based on nonexperimental approaches are similar to those from the HIE when comparisons can be made.[5] Social experiments are both costly and time-consuming—the cost of the HIE in 2007 dollars was approximately $200 million, and the study took more than a decade from start to finish. Economists had never doubted that insurance parameters powerfully influence the demand for care, but some noneconomists were skeptical. The HIE revealed these effects for all to see. But experience has shown that precise numerical results are guaranteed to become obsolete in short order as key aspects of health care and its financing evolve.

Implications of Empirical Evidence on Price Responsiveness of Demand for Insurance Design

The classic articles by Kenneth Arrow (1963) and Mark Pauly (1968), written roughly four decades ago, explained why insurance produces partly offsetting welfare gains and losses—the former by reducing risk, and the latter by reducing user price below marginal cost. Efforts to specify whether insurance produces these offsetting effects by directly changing consumer choice or indirectly by causing physicians to induce demand have generated a small library of studies. Peter Zweifel and Willard Manning (2000) and Thomas McGuire (2000) jointly include bibliographies with roughly four hundred somewhat overlapping entries. As the menu and cost of beneficial medical services has grown, both the benefit of insurance from reducing risk and the cost of insurance from inducing demand have probably also increased. Which has grown faster? A definitive answer may not be possible. We really do not know the slope of the utility function, and we do not know the full medical consequences of care induced by insurance.

The real choice, however, is not between insurance and no insurance. Every developed nation relies on health insurance. Only in the United States is coverage not approximately universal. Stripped of ideological overtones, the current debate is not about whether insurance is desirable but about which insurance arrangements will work best.

It is an oversimplification—but not much of one—to say that ordinary unmanaged fee-for-service insurance produces a system with no budget constraint. The current U.S. system contains budget constraints. In the public sector, they are manifest in managed Medicaid, Medicare Advantage, and the Veterans Administration (VA) health system. In the private sector, they comprise the residual trappings of managed care and the marginal incursions of traditional health maintenance organizations. With the exception of managed Medicaid and the VA, the constraints are quite weak.

Insurance with budget constraints comes in three flavors, depending on whether the budget constraint directly binds individuals, insurers, or a single (government) payer. The strength of individual budget constraints is in inverse proportion to the extent of insurance. High deductibles, large co-payments, and high coinsurance edge smoothly into an individual budget constraint, but they do so by uninsuring the individual. Individual budget constraints are not really a flavor but rather a dilution of insurance. Furthermore, as long as insurance is sufficient to prevent financial devastation for people with moderate incomes, full insurance will apply at the margin during episodes of care in which most health care spending occurs. The reason is that health care spending is highly concentrated. A small fraction of the population in any given year or small number of years accounts for most health care spending. Their expenditures are large relative to their incomes. Raising deductibles and cost sharing increases the *average* cost of all care that is even partially insured, which deters demand. It does not, however, increase the marginal cost of care above the stop-loss limit. (A stop-loss specifies the insured's maximum out-of-pocket payment for covered health services. For covered expenditures above the stop-loss, the insured person pays nothing.) With plausible stop-loss limits, most outlays will occur during episodes where marginal spending is still subject to moral hazard. For that reason, individual cost sharing cannot, by itself, fully counter moral hazard.

A second way to constrain moral hazard is through capitation, under which the individual agrees at the start of a period to sign a contract that obligates an insurer to cover broadly defined categories of medical services for a fixed fee. Individuals rely on broad terms along with the insurers' expertise and good will to allocate the agreed sum among contractually enumerated services to maximize benefits. Vendors who do a bad job will lose customers, or so it is assumed. I believe that the evidence that mobility will effectively discipline vendors is not strong, except in egregious cases. Whether it is desirable to encourage health insurance shoppers to be more mobile than they are, and if it is, how to help them to do so, merits study. Capitation is embodied in Medicare Advantage, or Medicare reform proposals designated "voucher" or "premium-support" plans. As experience under Medicare has demonstrated, adverse selection can be disruptive and costly.

Finally, it is possible to constrain moral hazard collectively through political processes. Legislators can set health budgets as in the United Kingdom or Canada. Or the budget-setting function can be performed, as in Sweden, through negotiations involving unions or employer groups.

Determining which of these approaches is the best way to control moral hazard, other than the individual budget constraint, which is used everywhere to a limited extent but cannot do the job alone, involves considerations that far transcend economics. Even if charges on individuals cannot control moral hazard, they will inevitably be used in two ways.

First, cost sharing reduces the need for both taxes, which produce economic distortions, and curtailing earnings, which distorts labor supply. Second, cost sharing influences demand for care.

Yet cost sharing does not affect demand for all forms of care identically. The health consequences of curtailing demand for personal health depend on the type of care that is involved. No health plan covers all health care products or services identically. Some services are not covered at all. Some are subject to deductibles or other forms of cost sharing. And some may be available free of all charges. In some cases, such as Medicare, the pattern of cost sharing is clearly irrational. But what patterns of differentiation are rational is less clear—and less analyzed. More work on this topic is in order.

Since cost sharing influences demand, it is important to know what the marginal impacts on health of reduced demand might be. The HIE produced some evidence on this subject. It suggested that high cost sharing damaged the health of the poor, but not of those with higher incomes, and saved money on all.[6] Because vaccinations provide large public-good benefits, they are free, and if not free, then mandatory. Some high-deductible health insurance plans stipulate that certain services, such as screening children for disease, will not be included in the deductible but will be fully covered. Since the elasticity of demand (to say nothing of cross elasticities) and the marginal benefits of health care differ by type of service and by such characteristics of the insured as age, income, or prior health status, optimal deductibles, cost sharing, and even stop-loss limits would vary.

While from some other perspectives more health insurance is to be preferred to less, economists argue that it is possible for people to be overinsured. In an economic framework, the choice of the optimal amount of health insurance involves a trade-off between risk reduction and the deadweight loss of moral hazard. Holding other factors constant, if people are more risk averse, the welfare gain from risk spreading through insurance is higher, implying more insurance coverage is desirable from society's standpoint. While risk reduction is a plus, the deadweight loss of moral hazard is a minus.

If certain extremely restrictive conditions are satisfied, the optimal amount of *medical care* would be that quantity at which individuals' willingness to pay for the marginal unit equals the marginal social cost of providing it. Those conditions include that income distribution satisfies some ethical ideal and that sick patients with limited savings are able to borrow at their personal rate of time preference enough to pay for any service they deem worth the cost. As extreme as those conditions may be, actual demand for care by insured patients will be excessive because moral hazard, brought about by the provision of health insurance, causes people to demand more care than is optimal because insurance shifts the cost of care at the time of illness to others. As a result, marginal social cost exceeds marginal willingness to pay for each extra unit.

The deadweight loss is the sum of the differences per unit between the marginal social cost and the marginal social value of services (which includes the value of care to the patient, the patient's family, and others). This loss varies with the price elasticity of demand for care. If demand is completely inelastic—that is, the quantity demanded is the same regardless of the price people pay for care out of pocket—then there is no deadweight loss. If demand is responsive to the out-of-pocket price, then deadweight loss is positive. If this loss exceeds the gain from risk reduction, then people are overinsured. Several empirical studies have concluded that in the United States, some cost sharing is optimal.[7] This conclusion has been subjected to some criticism.[8]

One weakness of the preceding analyses is the failure to incorporate administrative costs associated with cost sharing. Collecting money from patients as well as insurers is costly. "Optimal" cost sharing might not turn out to be optimal once account is taken of the costs of gathering the requisite information and administration. Those who argue for single-payer plans financed entirely by taxes, for example, do so partly because they believe that administrative savings would offset all added service costs from covering the currently uninsured or underinsured. Cost sharing is more or less costly, depending on how it is done. The more differentiated the system of cost sharing, the more costly it will be to administer. Income-related cost sharing is particularly costly to administer.[9]

Joseph Newhouse has summarized studies demonstrating that optimal cost sharing varies by illness as well as service.[10] Public finance analysts have shown that costs of administering and complying with taxes are of the same general magnitude as excess burdens that the taxes generate. For that reason, costs of administration and compliance must be considered in evaluating the impact of taxes on economic efficiency. By analogy, costs of administration and compliance should be incorporated formally and empirically into analyses of alternative methods of paying for health care, and even whether any cost sharing is desirable. Health economists have not, I believe, done such analyses. For example, I know of no study of the cost to households of filling out forms necessary to comply with private insurance and Medicare.

Some insurers cover particular services by subcontracting with specialist providers. Such carve-outs may be done because specialist providers do a better job. In other cases, such carve-outs may be a way to set a fixed budget for a particular class of services.

Broadening Insurance Coverage

Some believe that universal coverage is imperative for reasons that transcend the medical benefits of health care.[11] One rationale for universal coverage is that it has a leveling effect. It is argued that it puts everyone on an equal footing—what is sometimes termed the "solidarity principle." This position rests on the assumption that all benefit from fighting illness and that all, therefore, should pay for it.

But for those who are not persuaded by such arguments, evidence that insurance improves health status might tip the balance. As reviewed in some detail in chapter 4, there is some evidence that imposing cost sharing, particularly for pharmaceuticals, has a negative impact on health. Much more research on the topic remains to be done, however, and it is plausible that the effects of health insurance coverage differ by the type of service covered.

In that connection, the debate about how best to expand health insurance coverage is entering its eighth decade. During much of that period, some people have favored policies covering the population as a whole. Others have favored focusing on children first, in part because of a belief that covering children will be politically easier than covering everyone. But so too has the sense that additional health care expenditures will yield greater returns if spent on children than on adults. Children are physiologically more malleable than adults. The payoff period for expenditures that improve their health is longer for children than it is for adults, especially for older adults, on whom most health care dollars are now spent. Solid evidence is lacking, though. Once again, addressing this question is enormously difficult. Doing so would require, I believe, long-term epidemiological studies analogous in duration and size to the Framingham Heart Study, which has monitored three generations of enrollees starting in 1948 to identify the causes of heart disease.

Effect of Income

The demand for care is also positively related to income. An analysis of cross-sectional data from several countries reveals that health care spending rises at least proportionally with income.[12] These income elasticities do not control for the factors affecting health spending, such as differences in real labor costs per unit of service, which are difficult to quantify because they depend not only on labor compensation but also on productivity. And measuring service productivity remains problematic. Still, no amount of tinkering seems likely to upset the qualitative conclusion based on intercountry comparisons that health care is at least a normal and possibly a superior good—that is,

consumption rises with increases in personal income.[13] Despite considerable effort to estimate the relationship between income and
health care spending, perhaps the most careful review of outstanding
research on cross-country differences in spending concluded in 2000
that "research is still in its infancy and has raised more questions than
it has answered."[14] If valid in 2000, this observation still holds. Even
so, it seems unlikely that spending a lot more intellectual effort to pin
down the relationship of health care spending to income would
be justified. I doubt that any policy question would be answered
differently if the income elasticity of demand for health care were 1.0,
1.2, or 0.8?

Robert Hall and Charles Jones develop a conceptual framework for
understanding why health expenditures are commanding a rising
share of national income in the United States and other high-income
countries.[15] In their framework, as people become more affluent, and
their consumption of goods and services other than health care rises,
the marginal utility per dollar of non–health care consumption declines.
It is, after all, possible to drive only one car or take one vacation at a
time. But health care spending extends and improves the quality of
life, adding years during which to consume. In contrast to other
consumption, the marginal utility of life extension does not fall as
longevity increases, if health status is maintained. Because the marginal
utility of non–health care consumption declines but the utility of
spending on health care does not, nations spend an increasing share of
their income on health care as incomes rise. The authors predict that
by the middle of the twenty-first century, U.S. spending on health care
will be 30 percent of gross domestic product—more than double the
percentage at the turn of this century. This share is approximately
what one would calculate from a simple extrapolation of gaps between
the growth of income and the growth of health care spending that
have prevailed since 1970. The authors argue that empirical evidence
from one published and one unpublished study that the value of life
increases twice as fast as income, is consistent with the explanation for
the growing secular trend in health care spending as a share of
the national product in the United States and other high-income
countries.[16]

This line of argument raises more questions than it answers. First, it
is not clear how much of the improvement in longevity is traceable to
health care. Second, it is not apparent whether the absolute level of U.S.
spending now or projected into the future is optimal. The United States

spends twice as much per capita as the ten other richest countries and has slightly shorter longevity than they do on average. Should one infer that other countries spend too little or that the United States spends too much? More to the point, perhaps one should conclude that correlations do not establish optimality with respect to the consumption of a good whose cost is drastically reduced by insurance at the time of use.

Supply

Do Incentives Lead to a Misallocation of Services Supplied?

It is also well established that the supply of medical services responds to economic incentives.[17] The selection of specialty by physicians, the services they supply, their level of effort, and location of their practices all respond to economic incentives.[18] For example, specialty care is more highly reimbursed than is primary care; cardiac surgery is better reimbursed than is obstetric care. These pay differences raise the question of whether the price signals observed by physicians and other health care providers are distorted, and whether these distortions also skew what services they render. As Mark Pauly has observed, if physicians are willing to do more of certain things when paid well to do them, it is hard to see why the idea that physicians might induce demand was ever controversial. To be sure, even defining "physician-induced demand" is tricky and distinguishing it from simple moral hazard may be impossible.[19]

Pinning down motivation is never easy, of course, as physicians are as capable as the rest of us of giving high-minded rationalizations for self-serving actions. To make matters even worse, for most of what physicians do we have poor measures or none at all of actual benefits, and no metric for comparing benefit with cost. For all of these reasons, I believe that the effort to pin down whether and how much physicians induce demand was, to put it gently, not worth it.

That health care facilities such as hospitals and clinics also respond to economic incentives seems obvious, with the proliferation of specialty hospitals being a case in point. Budget limits clearly put ceilings on what hospitals can offer—one cannot, for example, do coronary artery surgery without a heart-lung machine or carry out MRI investigations without the requisite hardware.[20]

The Role of Professional Norms and Ethics

A distinguishing characteristic of medical care is that the provider normally knows more about the patient's condition than the patient does. If the patient were as skilled in diagnosing illness as the physician, many medical encounters could be avoided.

A problem arises under asymmetric information: namely, that a patient's relative lack of knowledge places the provider in a position to exploit the patient. For this reason, societies have relied on medical ethics and professional norms. The rationale is that an ethical physician will act as a perfect agent for the patient—that is, offer advice to patients that patients would offer for themselves if they were as well-informed as their physicians.

In reality, norms of practice differ widely within countries—more so than can be explained by variations in patient characteristics and preferences. Pioneering work by John Wennberg (in collaboration with many colleagues) established that the use of medical procedures varies enormously among small areas.[21] A huge volume of follow-on research both in the United States and elsewhere has ensued. The *Dartmouth Atlas of Health Care*, which is based on tabulations of Medicare data, has left no doubt about the pervasiveness of such variations. Physicians clearly have widely varying ideas about the right things to do to help patients. Some variations may arise because specialists are disposed to treat given conditions with techniques in which they were trained, and the distribution of specialists varies geographically. But specialty mix cannot fully explain the enormous differences in practice methods and may not even be a significant determinant. The fact is that we just do not understand why "Wennberg variations" exist. Nor do we have any idea about why they seem not to have narrowed in the three decades since they were first identified. Indeed, we are not even sure whether they have narrowed or widened.[22] We still do not know, except in a few areas, whether variations are evidence of overuse, underuse, or most likely both. And we do not know what interventions would be effective in moving actual practice to an average that is arguably more efficient than the status quo. The discovery of variations and, more recently, that heavy use of some therapies does no good—and may even do harm—is a huge challenge. But it is not a challenge that health economists or others have met.[23]

These questions comprise a juicy research target for economists and other social scientists. It is also a topic of enormous importance. We do not begin to understand what I think of as the "sociology of medicine." Why do doctors do what they do? What can be done to change what they do? The paucity of evidence regarding the efficacy of most of what physicians do suggests that physicians' firm adherence to particular practices rests on adherence to practices learned (inherited?) from mentors, peer example, or financial incentives.[24]

Physicians sometimes describe their adherence to such non-evidence-based patterns of practice as medical ethics. Medical ethics prevail when solid research on efficacy does not exist—or is ignored—as seems all too common. But even where such evidence is available, practice variations are large. That practice is resistant to research on efficacy has profound policy implications, but the whole question has attracted distressingly little research. This situation seems to call for managerial experiments and tests of different instructional methods. Experiments have shown, for example, that small changes in the framing of decisions can massively change behavior.[25] Even though disciplines other than economics may have to take the lead, the issue is too important for health economists to continue to ignore it.

Medical as well as patient ethics are also necessary when resource limits exist. In situations where limits on resources preclude treatment of all patients who might benefit from care, physicians develop rationales for why they should do what they must do. Similarly, patients develop norms for what sorts of treatment they should receive.[26] Thus, patients' demand for care and physicians' norms on how to practice are highly path dependent. Whether economists have the tools to study the formation of such norms or what changes them is not clear to me.

Medical Malpractice

Tort law provides remedies for patients when health care providers do not act in their interests. In this context, tort law should perform various functions, including assuring provision of beneficial care, avoiding medical error, avoiding wasteful care, appropriately compensating (and not overcompensating) victims of medical negligence and not compensating those who have not suffered medical negligence, encouraging providers to invest optimally in maintaining and improving medical knowledge, forcing substandard providers to find other work, and minimizing administrative costs.

On all scores, it performs miserably.[27] Most victims of medical negligence receive no compensation.[28] Incentives are weak for poor performers to mend their ways or shift occupations. Overhead is high. The public is intensely dissatisfied with the malpractice system and remarkably misinformed about it. The public believes that awards for noneconomic damages are excessive, but some empirical evidence suggests the opposite.[29] In addition, the public has been exposed to arguments by organized medicine and others that litigation induces huge amounts of wasteful "defensive" medicine. Yet the public's conception of what constitutes defensive medicine is primitive. The question is not whether malpractice insurance causes physicians to do more but whether such services are, on balance, not worth what they cost.

Measuring the extent of defensive medicine confronts the same obstacles that bedevil attempts to measure physician-induced demand. In both cases, it would be necessary to show that the marginal cost of care exceeded the marginal benefit, but that outcome is not sufficient to establish either behavior, as *marginal cost exceeding marginal* benefit is expected for some services when well-insured patients confront physicians who are being paid on a fee-for-service basis. How to distinguish among physician-induced demand, defensive medicine, and the behavior of patients and providers responding normally to the price incentives generated by insurance and fee-for-service reimbursement poses a formidable—perhaps an impossible—challenge.

Few rigorous empirical evaluations of defensive medicine have been conducted. One exception is a widely cited study by Daniel Kessler and Mark McClellan.[30] In a study of Medicare beneficiaries admitted to hospitals with heart disease, the authors found that tort reform that reduces the threat of medical malpractice suits to physicians reduced the cost of care, but did not lead to increased mortality. This study makes an excellent contribution to the study of defensive medicine. Nevertheless, the data are for one disease affecting one health outcome in one population—persons in the United States over age sixty-five. Further empirical analysis of defensive medicine is clearly needed.

Economists have done a good job of documenting the failure of malpractice to compensate the injured. They have also documented the exorbitant overhead cost of the system.[31] They have worked with lawyers and others on the strengths and weaknesses of alternative rules and institutions for compensating victims of negligence at reasonable administrative cost. Economists have done less work on the issue of incentives to providers to maintain and improve skills.[32] Careful study of systems adopted in other nations may provide guidance to desirable reforms for adoption in the United States.[33] The size of the gap between the professional and public understanding of the shortcomings of the malpractice system and ways to improve it is extraordinary.

Technological Change

Economic analysis has shown that returns on research and development (R & D) spending in general are quite high.[34] Other studies also indicate that applied and even basic research is responsive to economic incentives. That health care is technologically dynamic is a pallid understatement. Yet few studies have been done of the returns on investments specifically in medical technology. That health R & D is subject to economic incentives seems highly probable.

Health care is characterized by considerable static resource misallocation, often attributed to moral hazard. Insurance induces spending for services that provide benefits greater than costs directly incurred by patients but less than total production cost. The resulting insurance-induced spending should influence R & D incentives. Whether and how is critically important, yet extremely difficult to investigate. In particular, insurance renders consumers relatively price insensitive. If physicians act flawlessly as their patients' agents, they will prescribe with less attention to price than they would if patients were more price sensitive.

As a result, those investing in health R & D will find a better market for new products that improve quality even modestly and at high cost than they would if patients were more sensitive to price. A ready market for new products that are even a little bit better, even if much more expensive, than previously available services, should both spur research and distort it. To make matters worse, research on new medical products may overemphasize technical specifications and neglect their impact on patient outcomes or cost-effectiveness.[35]

For example, a count made in 2004 of studies of magnetic resonance spectroscopy for brain tumors revealed that eighty-five studies had been done on whether the test performed as intended in a physical sense. Eight studied sensitivity and specificity. Two studied whether the test affected diagnosis. Two studied whether the test affected treatment. None studied whether the test improved the patient's health or was cost-effective.[36] More generally, a few studies have tried to appraise the economic value of medical innovation and have generally concluded that the benefits far exceed the costs.[37]

The inducement of wasteful or the wrong sorts of research produces dynamic inefficiency. On the other hand, excess static consumption may induce added, highly beneficial research that would not have occurred had product markets been competitive and efficient.

If static resource misallocation so distorts research that technical advance is slowed, the dynamic welfare loss could well exceed that from static inefficiencies. Static losses from resource misallocation—for example, from moral hazard—are proportional to the capacity of the system to provide benefit. Dynamic loss lowers the growth of the capacity to supply benefits and is unbounded. Unless static inefficiency increases over time, dynamic losses are likely eventually to exceed them. Conversely, if static inefficiencies in health care (excessive demand resulting from moral hazard, for example) accelerate technical advance, reducing static inefficiencies will eventually lower welfare.

Which effect dominates? We may all have seat-of-the-pants views on which way the balance goes. But I do not know of any empirical research on this question. Although understanding the impact of static inefficiency on dynamic progress is enormously important, it is not clear to me how one would go about doing research on it. Nor is it clear to me how one would determine what incentives for research are optimal.[38] Answers to these questions are assuredly important, but are they discoverable?

The question of how to promote investment in knowledge poses a well-understood dilemma. Once knowledge is developed, the marginal cost of using it is zero. Efficiency requires a zero price for use. But developing knowledge is costly. Nonaltruistic investors will not voluntarily spend money to develop knowledge without the prospect of adequate economic return. Governments and foundations deal with part of the problem by supporting basic research. Patents and copyrights that award investors a temporary monopoly are the customary way for promoting applied research and development.

Although it is unlikely that the same incentives provide the best balance for research and efficient exploitation for all forms of research, incentives are currently roughly the same for all types of research. Sometimes patents are not the best way to protect intellectual property. Because those seeking patents must disclose information, concealment sometimes offers better protection than a patent. The value of patents is reduced further in the case of drugs because a part of the patent life must be used to meet regulatory requirements before a sale is permitted.

Current arrangements "socialize" the cost of drug research, but in a way that is quite weird. Patents create a monopoly, which permit patent holders to charge prices well above production cost, generating supernormal profits. Part of these profits fund research. The monopoly profits do not fund just research budgets, however. Some of those profits also go to enlarge shareholders' profits. Some also support advertising and other forms of marketing.

Patent-enabled monopoly profits are financed in diverse ways. Private and public health insurance spare the consumers of these drugs from having to pay these high prices out of pocket. Part comes from a lump-sum tax on earnings, if as most economists suppose, employer-financed insurance causes a reduction in other forms of compensation.[39] Part comes from payroll taxes and general revenues that finance publicly sponsored health benefits. And part comes from insured individuals who pay premiums and cost sharing. The market for drugs is worldwide. How much of patent-enabled monopoly profits each nation pays varies according to their buying strength. U.S. buyers pay most because they are among the most fragmented.

Is the current system the best that we can do? Should the duration or other terms of patents differ by type of discovery? Should the same patent protection be awarded to "rent-seeking" or "me-too" drugs introduced to capture some of the profits being earned by previously patented medications? Is it possible to design administratively feasible incentives that exact a smaller toll in static resource misallocation than patents do, but that provide comparable research incentives? Would it be better, for example, to pay those who develop new drugs a fee equal to the present discounted value of profits that they believe they could realize were the product patented? In return, the new technology would be freely available to any user within the country making the payment. This system would resemble that proposed by Aidan Hollis, but with a key difference.[40] Under the Hollis system, the choice between patent and lump-sum bonus lies with the private entity. If the choice rested instead with the public, the system would create incentives for the discoverer to disclose all (or more than all) potential uses of the new drug or device.[41]

Each system has difficulties. If discretion rests with the developer, how would one avoid adverse selection? If discretion rests with the public, how would one avoid a misrepresentation of the benefits of the discovery? And of course, drugs are sold worldwide, but bonuses must be paid by separate sovereign governments. The current system is so peculiar, and drugs and devices are so crucial in improving health and health care as well as driving health care spending, that alternatives merit increased attention.

The Measurement of Prices

Academic economists for a long time ignored the measurement of health care prices. The U.S. Bureau of Labor Statistics and the U.S. Department of Commerce supplied the package, and we economists opened it without reading the table of contents. Serious problems with health price statistics, especially the consumer price index, have been recognized for nearly two decades.[42] A large literature on the measurement of health care prices has since emerged.[43] The key finding is striking. Official measures of the price of treating selected illnesses—heart attacks and mental illness, for example—had the wrong sign: the statistics indicated rapid inflation. After correction for quality improvements, it turned out that prices of treating these two conditions had actually fallen.

Part of the problem is that the measurement of service prices is difficult—what is the product of a visit with a lawyer or a doctor, or for that matter, a professor of economics? In the case of health care, the measurement problem is critically important and extremely difficult, even for products. For example, what is the quantity of health care service provided by successive versions of statins, which reduce cholesterol by increasing amounts in varying proportions to those for whom they are prescribed, with perhaps varying side effects?

Because health care accounts for a steadily growing share of the gross domestic product, a more accurate measurement of health care prices is increasingly important. Insufficient correction for quality improvements indirectly aggravates public angst that the "problem" of rising health care spending is traceable to rising prices rather than increasing quantities. It is a short step from this perception to the belief that growing health care spending is traceable principally to rapacious drug companies, greedy insurers, and overcompensated managed care executives. Although the reality of rapacity, greed, and obscene overpayment should not be denied, they can divert attention from the primary cause: rapidly increasing consumption of health care services. For this reason, I think that a major effort to extend to other treatments and conditions the type of price research carried out on coronaries and mental illness is of some urgency. Only official agencies can support such research on an adequate scale, but research budgets have been shrinking.

The Organization of Health Care Delivery

Doctors were once expected to know "everything." The best doctors were those who knew most and processed that information most efficiently. Doctors now are expected to specialize—that is, *not* to know everything. The best medicine is that provided through collaborating teams whose members have a wide range of expertise and who exchange information easily through electronic means. Many patients, especially the chronically ill and the elderly, see many specialists. The U.S. population is highly mobile. Accordingly, the importance of making information about the patient accessible and portable is high—and has increased.

These developments seem to imply that the optimal size, organization, and activities of the medical "firm" have changed. Hospitals receive patients who have been under the care of scattered physicians, each of whom may have gathered information from tests and observation. Hospitals likewise discharge patients to independent physicians in private practice. Physicians and hospitals, once technologically distinct production units for the delivery of care, are increasingly part of what is functionally a single production unit. Such a change in technology does not necessarily mean that all stages should be jointly owned or managed. With few exceptions, those who deliver primary, secondary, and tertiary care are not jointly owned and managed. If the technology of health care delivery requires collaboration, does it also require joint ownership? And if so, how should the benefits of such agglomeration be balanced against the loss of competition, which economists traditionally prize for its efficiency-enhancing and price-reducing effects?[44]

One current issue relevant to this question arises from the design and financing of information technology. A reduction in the cost of exchanging information can enable decentralization or require concentration, depending on how property rights in that information are distributed. Yet, financial considerations seem to be pushing concentration. The capital requirements for investments in information technology are so large that small units, such as most physician practices, have found them unaffordable. The question is whether the emerging importance and high cost of information technology have, for financial reasons, increased the optimal size of the units that deliver health care. In particular, is the optimal concentration of ownership of these units now larger than antitrust policy permits? If so, current policies to "maintain price competition," including limits on hospital mergers and obstacles to subsidies offered by hospital groups to allied physicians for investments in information technology, may need to be reconsidered.

International data show that the ratios of physicians, nurses, and other professionals involved in rendering care varies enormously from country to country.[45] At the same time, the relative remuneration of health care providers also differs greatly among nations.[46] Differences among the relative remuneration may accurately reflect productivity and training. That is, labor markets may be functioning flawlessly and indicate that varying input combinations reflect cost minimization along the same production possibility surface. Given the role of licensure, which requires particular inputs, and the lack of sufficient research to support these combinations, such a happy outcome hardly seems likely. There is some research on whether particular services now provided by physicians can be produced as well and at lower cost by less highly trained personnel. Some research has been done on the relative productivity of specialists and general practitioners. Closed-panel health maintenance organizations—prepaid health plans that rely on a limited number of physicians, usually salaried, to provide all care to plan members—use different mixes of professionals than are found in the rest of the health care system. This seems to me to be an area of research for economists, in collaboration with health care professionals that might save a lot of money.

Looking to the Future: Challenges Facing Health Care in the United States

Perhaps the two most frequently stated facts about the U.S. health care system are that per capita spending vastly exceeds that in other developed nations, and that U.S. life expectancy and infant mortality are inferior to those of most other developed countries—and not a few middle-income nations. Regressions of health care spending on income and other variables consistently show the United States to be well north of the upward sloping regression line, which relates national income to health care expenditures, indicating that we spend more than our income on health care than do other countries with similar incomes. On the other hand, at least three studies suggest that the value of improvements in health outcomes approximates that of all currently measured economic growth and vastly exceeds increases in health care spending.[47] Do we spend too much? How could one tell?

National Income Accounting 101

Before turning to these questions, it is worth recalling the standard theory for measuring benefits. First, standard national income measures of the value of all products are based on their *marginal* valuation, which in turn approximates production cost if markets are competitive. This measure excludes consumer surplus.

The contribution of automobiles to gross domestic product, for example, is the number of automobiles produced multiplied by the sales price of automobiles. If competitive pricing is assumed, economists normally believe that people buy the welfare-maximizing number of automobiles unless there are queues. Anyone who values a car at more than its price is free to buy one, and no one who values a car at less than its price is forced to do so. That is, the gross domestic product statistics ignore consumer surplus. We do not ask what the maximum amount is that people would pay to retain their cars or how much they would be willing to offer to acquire them.

The national income accounting convention means that the subjective valuation of health care differs from market value for at least two partly offsetting reasons. Insured patients pay little of the production cost of most of the care they consume. Consequently, the *marginal* benefit is likely to be well under long-term production cost. On the other hand, health care typically provides enormous benefits for some patients, even if moral hazard means that it is overused. These large *inframarginal* benefits are not counted in market valuations. Whether they should be included depends on one's purposes. National income accounts measure the value of resources used in producing health care. Consumer surplus is relevant to a consideration of willingness to pay *in total* for the health care consumed.

Studies of the value of health care mostly use methods different from those employed in national income accounting.[48] They typically begin with estimates of the value of a human life. These estimates come from various sources, such as insurance purchases, surveys, and wage differentials associated with risky occupations. I believe that estimates from such sources are of doubtful relevance because the characteristics of the people involved in those studies are quite different from those who receive health care—and Jeffersonian ideals notwithstanding, not all lives are of equal value. Actual health care spending cannot provide information on the marginal value of lives because of insurance and moral hazard. Besides, it is unclear that marginal valuations, even if they were rock solid, are what one would want to use. Then there is the simple fact that no one has yet disentangled the contributions to improved health outcomes of income growth, personal habits, the environment, and health care. Despite all of these shortcomings, the various studies have, at a minimum, shifted the burden of proof on to those who would deny that the *total* benefit of health care spending much exceed its costs.

Collateral Damage

Even if true, this finding leaves room for a lot of waste. If half of health care spending uniformly produces benefits worth ten times its cost and the rest is worthless, total benefits would vastly exceed total cost. It would still pay to try to end the worthless spending, *provided that it can be cut without sacrificing too many beneficial services*. How much is too many? In my example, eliminating the half of health care spending that is useless inadvertently caused the loss of more than a tenth of the beneficial services, the campaign would reduce welfare and should not be undertaken. Because the benefits of health care are probabilistic, waste reduction must be sufficiently accurate to be beneficial. That means that counting consumer surplus among inframarginal users is an essential part of determining whether a procedure is beneficial. The widespread revulsion against the concept of health care rationing may rest in part on an inchoate sense that rooting out useless tests and needless surgeries will inevitably result in the loss of some high-value applications, and may discourage research investments that promise even more.

Information Provision to Improve Resource Allocation in Health Care

The notion that all health providers are equally excellent, once widely accepted as valid, is now generally recognized as a myth. Many estimates have been made of the cost of preventing a death at a point in time by various safety measures.[49] They vary widely. Some accidents could be avoided at a negligible cost. Overall safety could be improved through resource reallocation. In the budget-controlled British National Health Service, decisions about which medical procedures to approve are based on estimates not only of medical efficacy but also the cost of preventing (or more precisely, delaying) a death or disability. The importance of such calculations will become vital for achieving the maximum medical benefit from a given expenditure in the United States should we ever adopt health care financing arrangements that effectively constrain spending.

Necessity does not mean that the requisite information will be produced, however. The history of publicly financed agencies that try to make such estimates is not a happy one in the United States. The task that confronts economists, lawyers, and political scientists is how to create an organization that is capable of carrying out analyses on a large scale that are intellectually solid *and* that can withstand legal challenges as well as ward off political attacks.

A Greater Reliance on Market Forces and Choice or Public Regulation to Improve Resource Allocation?

Welfare economics is based on the proposition that people have well-defined and stable preferences. Psychologists flatly reject this perspective, based on hundreds of separate studies that conclusively establish the failure of basic axioms of rational choice.[50] Rather, they assert that preferences are typically manufactured only as needed in response to particular situations. The choice that emerges at that point is acutely sensitive to recent experiences, the effects of which are transitory. It also depends, often in quite bizarre ways, on how questions are framed and other considerations. Actual decisions routinely violate the standard axioms of consumer choice (such as the independence of irrelevant alternatives). Told that decision X and Y will save lives, people prefer X; told that not doing either X or Y will cost lives, people prefer Y.

The issue here is not the implications of such findings for economic analysis—it may sometimes be good research strategy to assume the validity of demonstrably false premises. Instead, the questions for health care policy are whether enabling or forcing people to make choices enhances their welfare, how much choice is best, and how choices should be structured. Increased choice at a minimum increases decision costs. In some settings, it paralyzes the consumer and prevents action.[51] But in other cases, choice matches products to wants and may legitimate the results in the eye of the consumer.[52]

Health care choices arise in many contexts. What insurance plan should a person select? Which physician should one visit? To which hospital should one go? Should one adhere to physicians' advice? Psychological and, more recently, economic research leaves little doubt that the way in which choices are presented powerfully influences what people choose. Defaults strongly influence choices, even if the default can be overridden at negligible cost in terms of money, time, mental effort, or anything else. Advance commitments result in different behavior from that associated with contemporaneous decision, particularly where sacrifices are to be made, and even if an advance commitment can be reversed at negligible cost or inconvenience. The powerful influence of defaults and the closely related phenomenon of a precommitment led Cass Sunstein and Richard Thaler to advance what they call "libertarian paternalism"—the calculated framing of decisions to boost the likelihood that people will voluntarily decide to do what expert analysis suggests is optimal in ways, but that can be undone at little or no cost.[53]

The application to health care policy is immediate and obvious. How much is choice in the type of insurance offered really worth to enrollees? I know of no attempt to study this question. Are preferences for insurance plans stable? This question is not answered by data on how often people change plans. There are two dimensions to this question. The first is whether preferences are stable even if nothing material happens to the decision maker? Thaler and Shlomo Benartzi asked savers who had voluntarily chosen a particular portfolio for their savings whether they preferred that portfolio or alternatives that had been available when the savers initially made their choices.[54] The respondents frequently ranked the portfolio they had chosen *below* one or more of the alternative portfolios. This finding raises doubt over whether people have stable preferences even on a matter—such as the allocation of a portfolio among stocks, bonds, and cash—that is considerably less complex than choices among health insurance plans.

The second dimension arises from a simple fact. Most health insurance is bought by more or less healthy people, but insurance is used by more or less sick people. The change in health status can reasonably be expected to influence not just wants but underlying preferences. In a certain sense, the person making the purchase decision is different from the person using the health care that the insurance finances. Which person—the healthy one who chose a particular insurance plan, or the sick person who consumes it—should be regarded as the authentic self whose choices should be honored? When it comes to durable powers of attorney, prior commitment is irrelevant. The law enforces only the currently competent decision. Allowing people to change the terms of their insurance as their circumstances change is clearly unacceptable. But why is a decision made under quite different circumstances regarded as best for welfare? Is either superior to expert judgment?

The conditions of choice also influence results. An employer offering employees two or more health care plans could require employees to choose among the plans. Alternatively, the employer could automatically enroll employees in a particular plan that the employer has analyzed and judged superior, but give employees a virtually costless way to switch, such as by signing a readily available form. Or the employer could make it more or less difficult for the employee to switch—for example, by mailing the form to the employee, requiring the employee to go to the personnel office, or requiring employees to listen to a ten-minute briefing before permitting changes on why the company chose the plan it did.

These questions may seem low-grade—worth the time, perhaps, of market analysts, but surely beneath the more exalted skills of economists. But we economists make a big deal out of choice. In other contexts, the conditions of choice cause huge differences in what people decide. If choice counts, so do the conditions that determine the results.

I hesitate to bring up so mundane a matter as the fact that patients go to doctors or other health care providers, but often do not listen to them. The most striking example that I know of is that six months after the first prescription for statins has been filled for patients, roughly half of these patients are reported to have stopped taking their medications. The value of reducing cholesterol is well established and widely known. The side effects are minor or nonexistent, except for a small minority of cases in which significant contraindications develop, such as abnormal liver function or muscle weakness. As a second example, diabetics are notoriously noncompliant—with dreadful consequences. Their adherence to good health habits improves if physicians or their assistants engage in behaviors that are perhaps best characterized as nagging.

Little is known about what proportion of drugs is wasted because people do not take them, how much surgery is wasted because people do not follow postoperative procedures essential for the success of that surgery (such as physical therapy after a joint replacement), or how much medical advice is wasted because people ignore it. Nor do we know how the presentation of medical advice could be modified to improve compliance. Insurers give discounts to nonsmokers. We have not explored other ways in which financial incentives might be used to promote compliance. Improving patient compliance may well be among the most powerful ways to increase the benefits of health care spending, if it can be achieved at reasonable cost. Yet economists and others have not spent much time on this subject.

Rather than promote increased reliance on consumer choice, an alternative is to promote regulation, which includes entry regulation in the form of certificate of need requirements, regulation of prices and/or budgets, and controls over use of services (for example, "utilization review"). One reason for the increased emphasis on consumer choice is that regulatory approaches adopted during the 1970s in the United States were judged to be largely ineffective. In particular, regulations to hold down spending—notably, certificate of need requirements— have been judged ineffective by economic analysis.[55] The economic studies that have discredited health care regulation have been based on U.S. data. But the United States spends dramatically more on health care than do other countries—and not just because residents are richer than those of most other nations. Rather strikingly, other nations rely on a combination of regulations and limits on supply, often buttressed by more or less fixed budgets. Their experience raises a critical question: Should we ever get really serious about using regulations to control spending, what do we need to do to make them work? The problem may not be with the general concept of regulation itself but how regulatory approaches have been implemented in health care in the United States to date.

Emerging Research and Health Policy Issues

Several decades ago, health care experts in the United States congratulated themselves for having conquered the threat of infectious disease. The experts clearly were proven wrong with the emergence of HIV/

AIDS as a major health problem in the United States and throughout the world. Even such diseases as tuberculosis, long considered overcome in high-income countries including the United States, have reemerged as health threats.

How to cope with the threat of the next pandemic is arguably the most important issue currently confronting health care policy. Natural pandemics have occurred at intervals throughout recorded history.[56] Sometimes illnesses endemic to one region are introduced into another where natural immunity is low. Sometimes a pathogen mutates.

To these threats must now be added terrorism. Recently, estimates of the economic consequences of pandemic flu have become available, but these are usually based on ad hoc assumptions about the incidence and spread of disease. Satisfactory estimates will require the cooperation of economists with epidemiologists, biologists, and as the next paragraph indicates, psychologists, sociologists, and other scientists. Such information has some bearing on how much should be spent to prepare for them and direct relevance on how limited resources to treat disease should be allocated.

The question that may bear most directly on policy is how to deploy available resources when disease appears. For example, if the U.S. supply of effective drugs is insufficient to satisfy all domestic and foreign demands, should the United States husband stocks for domestic use when and if a disease emerges here or should we ship them overseas to try to forestall spread? How much rational behavior by populations should be assumed? For example, what is the best strategy, treatment of segments of the population who refuse to be vaccinated either because they fear to go where sick people might be or because, as minorities, they fear that "we won't get the good stuff"? Should children, prime-age adults, or the elderly receive priority? What should be the policies on quarantine? Answers to such questions clearly depend on specific knowledge regarding how each disease is transmitted, how long infected people can communicate a disease to others, the duration of illness, the efficacy of treatment, and other issues. Large-scale foundation- and government-sponsored work is under way to address such problems. Contributions will be made by many disciplines, one of which is surely economics.

Conclusion

Health policy has been near or at the top of the public policy agenda in the United States for decades. The issues affect millions of lives and livelihoods. In this chapter, I have used policy issues as a starting point for identifying important questions for research by economists and other social scientists. The menu of research questions covered here differs from topics that would be addressed in a course on health economics that any of us would teach. In part, that is because a course on health economics should present positive findings about the economics of the health care system and show how economic principles illuminate these matters. In part, that is because such a course must take the field as it finds it.

But there are two other possible reasons. One is that I have missed significant areas. The other is that health economics has placed insufficient effort on topics that merit in-depth analysis.

Notes

1. Arrow (1963); Pauly (1968).

2. Acton (1975).

3. See Manning et al. (1987); Newhouse and the Insurance Experiment Group (1993).

4. Health Savings Accounts (HSAs) face negative tax rates in the sense that disposable lifetime income can be increased by borrowing to finance deposits. Interest payments on the borrowing are deductible, lowering taxes and thereby increasing disposable income. All HSA investment income is excluded from taxation if used to pay for health care, broadly defined. The principal deposited in the HSA is exempt from taxation on deposit and withdrawal, again if used for health care. Those who examine HSAs exclusively from the standpoint of health care spending miss much of their significance. HSAs are an invitation to raid the U.S. Treasury.

5. See, for example, Van De Voorde et al. (2001); Meer and Rosen (2004).

6. In recent correspondence, Joseph Newhouse wrote to me that he interprets the HIE findings as showing that cost sharing is bad for the poor and good for the rest of us.

7. See, for example, Manning and Marquis (1996), and articles references therein.

8. John Nyman (2004) argues that health insurance provides for the redistribution of income from the healthy to the sick. The additional purchasing power from insurance payments allows the sick to purchase more care than they would if they were not insured. People, Nyman contends, value a dollar of income in the sick one more than they do in the healthy one. For this reason, the transfer of income from the healthy to the sick state is efficient, and the gain from this transfer should be considered as an offset to the deadweight loss computed in the other economic studies.

9. On the income side, one would run into all of the problems associated with income-related cash transfers—determining the appropriate filing unit (which is subject to change in ways relevant to variations in cost sharing), dealing with fluctuating incomes, and factoring in assets and wealth more generally.

10. Newhouse (2006).

11. Morone (2002).

12. See, for example, Phelps (2003, 571–574).

13. Gerdtham and Jönsson (2000).

14. Ibid. (45).

15. Hall and Jones (2007).

16. The published study is Costa and Kahn (2004); the unpublished study is Hammitt et al. (2000).

17. Hsiao et al. (1988); Danzon (2000); McGuire and Pauly (1991).

18. See chapters 8 and 10 of this book.

19. Phelps (1986).

20. Aaron and Schwartz (1984); Aaron et al. (2005); Phelps (1986).

21. Wennberg and Gittleson (1973).

22. The text comments on the lack of knowledge about the trends in the variance of Wennberg variations is based on emails I exchanged with Jon Skinner.

23. Wennberg (2004).

24. Lee and Mongan (2006); Mongan et al. (2006).

25. Madrian and Shea (2001); Sunstein and Thaler (2003).

26. The following quotations from physicians practicing in Britain illustrate how resource limits condition medical ethics. All are reported in Aaron et al. (2005). While those quoted differ in their slant on how limits influence behavior, they leave little doubt about the impact of resources on medical norms.

With respect to the treatment of cholesterol and high blood pressure, some physicians observed the following:

• By and large, people in this country would not, if they were perfectly fit and well, go and have things like their cholesterol done. . . . We don't have annual physicals in this country. . . . You go to the doctor when you are ill.

• Over here, simply because of the logistics and limited resources, many times the patient will be watched. If the [coronary] pain doesn't persist and there doesn't seem to be an emergency, one will discharge the patient, do an exercise test, make sure that there are no ECG changes when the heart is stressed, and bring the patient back later.

• What I saw happening I found very disturbing. If the waiting lists are long [a coronary-artery bypass graft], you just sort of don't do as many. . . . You see people at a relatively young age . . . developing angina to the extent that their angina was severe enough that they actually got studied. . . . And often, we would find three-vessel coronary disease, and they would be referred for a coronary bypass. . . . They would go on a waiting list. And on the waiting lists, about 20 percent of them died of coronaries before they got a bypass.

With respect to diagnostic radiology, several physicians said the followig:

• I think we do everything that we can do. [W]e would tailor it [so] that we would use ultrasound wherever we possibly could, because of cost and time and patient comfort. And we would use CT where we have to.

• In the United States [CT is used for] many procedures that we would do under ultrasound because it's cheaper. . . . Now, some of those patients would have been treated more easily and more quickly under CT guidance. There's no question about that.

• I only really had to mention the ten-month waiting list, and then that's the end of numerous conversations I had. . . . Also, I spent a lot of time trying to fob people off— they wanted an MRI—trying to get the same result with an ultrasound or a plain [X-ray]. And then after some GPs rang a number of times, they didn't bother me again, really, I was giving them this absurd notion of waiting a year or two. The physician also knew that they had to come up with some other solution.

27. Danzon (2000) provides a useful overview of empirical evidence through that date.

28. Localio et al. (1991).

29. Sloan et al. (1993).

30. Kessler and McClellan (1996).

31. Kakalik and Pace (1986).

32. Mello and Brennan (2002).

33. Lowes (2003).

34. See, for example, Cutler and McClellan (2001); Murphy and Topel (2006).

35. I do not know if this problem is a general one. This six-stage approach to evaluation is based on methods applied at the U.S. Agency for Healthcare Research and Quality as described in Tatsioni et al. (2005). This paper, in turn, applies analytic methods developed in earlier papers (Fineberg et al. [1977]; McNeil and Aldestein [1976]; Thornbury et al. [1991]).

36. Aaron et al. (2005).

37. Cutler and Berndt (2001); Cutler and McClellan (2001); Cutler et al. (2006); Shapiro et al. (1999); Trajtenberg (1990).

38. For a theoretical analysis of the incentives to innovate inspired by the pharmaceutical industry, see Garber et al. (2006). The authors introduce the concept of "excessive incentives to innovate." They suggest that insurance and the resulting augmented demand encourage excessive research, and that limits on patent lives may offset this effect. But the meaning of optimality in the case of research is unclear. Research serves as the foundation of future research into subjects the benefits of which, by their nature, are not known at present. To speak of optimality, one must impose the strong assumption that the integral of expected benefits from all lines of research is the same. Given the roles of guesswork and hunch about the fruitfulness of various lines of research as well as politics in setting research budgets, I see little reason to have faith that expected welfare gains are being equalized at the margin.

39. For several reasons, the backward shifting may not be exact; see Gruber (2000).

40. Hollis (2007).

41. Such a system would resemble self-assessment under property taxation. Under this system, property tax valuations for tax purposes are set by the owner, not the assessor. Owners are obliged to sell their properties at the price they state. Potential buyers may be limited to the public or may include private parties. The idea is that the obligation to sell induces the owner to disclose the true value. The system has an obvious and, I believe, fatal shortcoming. First, selling may impose large and idiosyncratic relocation costs on the current owner that a would-be buyer may not have to incur. The result can be a large gap between the value of not having to move and any reasonable purchase

price. As a result, raiders could harass—even blackmail—the owners. The revelation characteristics of the bonus option are similar; the shortcomings are different and may not be so extreme.

42. Newhouse (1989).

43. Berndt et al. (2000), Cutler and Berndt (2001).

44. Haas-Wilson (2003).

45. Organization for Economic Cooperation and Development (2006).

46. Sandier (1989)

47. Cutler and McClellan (2001); Murphy and Topel (2006); Nordhaus (2003).

48. Viscusi and Aldy (2003).

49. Individual studies report the costs of preventing deaths from specific medical procedures (for example, implantable cardiac defibrillators), other safety measures (say, wearing bicycle helmets), personal habits (being overweight, for instance, and by inference, losing weight), preventive interventions (for example, vaccinations), and product design (such as safety caps on drug containers). See Russell (1998).

50. Kahneman et al. (1998); Ross and Nisbett (1991).

51. Marketing analysts have found, for example, that increasing the amount of alternatives in a product display beyond a small amount reduces sales.

52. Choice may be valued not only for its effects on results but also for establishing fair procedures. On this view, outcomes are legitimated by how they are achieved as well as by their results. In other words, a legitimate outcome is one that is reached by a legitimate process. This position fundamentally underlies libertarian politics; see Nozick (1977).

53. Sunstein and Thaler (2003).

54. Thaler and Benartzi (2004).

55. Salkever (2000).

56. See, for example, Philipson (2000).

3 Health Capital: Theory and Empirical Evidence

Donna Gilleskie

This chapter focuses on a particular commodity that we as individuals are likely to produce and/or consume often. It is a sustainable product that frequently requires our deliberate attention and action, and one that influences many of our daily decisions. Economists call it human capital. Like the physical capital of a firm, human capital is essentially a *stock* of an asset that an individual owns, and to which that person can allocate time and resources as inputs for its continued development. The capital good also provides a *flow* of services for the stockholder. Economists have concerned themselves with two types of human capital: knowledge capital and health capital.

What Is Health Capital?

Health capital, or health stock, is often measured by general levels of health or functioning, such as health status or the degree of difficulties with activities of daily living. Health flows describe the illness or morbidity conditions that an individual experiences over time. More specifically, an individual in excellent health (stock) may still get the flu or break leg (flow). In this chapter, I explore the economist's understanding of health capital, its formation, maintenance, and deterioration. More to the point, I examine the economist's understanding of individual health behavior since the evolution of health over one's life cycle, while partially explained by random events beyond one's control, is greatly influenced by a person's own choices regarding medical care consumption, employment, education, and lifestyle. This understanding of individual decision making with regard to health reveals the role of incentives (e.g., the interaction of governmental or market policies with individual preferences, constraints, and beliefs) that affect behavior throughout one's life.

It is reasonable to assume that many policy recommendations are supported by statistical evidence. In fact, establishing evidence of a correlation between two variables of interest in health behavior is a topic of research among many health economists, health policy researchers, and physicians. Some well-known examples include the observed positive correlation between health and income or education.[1] Statistical evidence can be found at the macroeconomic comparing aggregate measures of national income (e.g., the gross domestic product) and the health of a population (e.g., mortality or morbidity rates), and at the microeconomic with years of schooling and individual measures of health (e.g., self-reported health levels). Many other examples abound: a positive correlation between health insurance and medical care consumption, a negative correlation between exercise and heart disease, and debatable findings for the relationship between alcohol consumption and mortality. But most economists consider these observed statistical associations to be the spark that initiates further exploration into the individual behavior that generates such empirical links. That is, an economist seeks to understand the mechanisms through which such associations arise. It is only with this deeper understanding that policies—meant to provide, alter, or enhance incentives that affect individual alternatives and decision-making behavior—can be appropriately prescribed.

Modeling is a tool to help researchers understand the relationships between variables of interest. Comprehension of the causal relationships in physics may be facilitated with a model of the force at work. Computer models may be used to study and predict coastline erosion during hurricanes. Unfortunately for economists, there are no proven theories like Sir Isaac Newton's laws of motion that explain human decision-making behavior. Nonetheless, we rely on models that attempt to capture or mimic how people make decisions using the economic concepts of preferences, constraints, technology, expectations, and uncertainty.

I begin the chapter by discussing the fundamentals of the economist's model of health capital. The presentation is purposefully nontechnical, but conveys the rudiments of the theory so as to discuss the inferences about human behavior that follow from the model. Hypotheses derived from the model can be empirically tested in order to validate the theory. Extensions to the basic model are also touched on briefly. I continue the chapter by summarizing empirical research based on this theory of health capital. The empirical applications have been plentiful, and the model has been applied in several dimensions of health behavior and medical care demand. Yet there have been few attempts to estimate the formal model itself and to use it to evaluate the role of incentives. I describe the policy alternatives examined by economists who solve and estimate models of health behavior that specify the preferences, constraints, and expectations of optimizing individuals. Finally, I highlight many of the difficulties encountered in the empirical investigation of health behavior, and address the importance of an accurate and complete understanding of health behavior for policy evaluation and implementation.

Modeling the Demand for Health: The Grossman Model

The dissertation research of a young economics PhD student in the late 1960s has become the foundation on which most economists base their understanding of the individual's demand for health and medical care. Building on the premise of household production theory that was introduced less than a decade earlier, Michael Grossman developed a theoretical model to explain the health behavior he observed among individuals.[2] At the root of his model is the assumption that people do not necessarily enjoy consuming health care but rather receive happiness, or utility, from the services that health provides. An individual's health stock at a particular age determines the flow of health services or the amount of healthy time that person receives.

This stock is not fully depleted each period. Instead, like a capital good such as a refrigerator or an automobile, it stays around, yields services, and depreciates each period. Different forms of health care, both medical care as well as lifestyle choices such as exercise (and smoking), are inputs that maintain or improve (or deteriorate) one's stock of health.[3] As both a consumption and an investment good, optimal health capital accumulation requires the decision making of its owner—the individual—who is also the consumer and the producer.

Utility Maximization

In most economic models of individual behavior, a person seeks to maximize utility or happiness, which is characterized by a utility function, $U(\cdot)$. This function expresses the utility maximizer's *preferences* about things he values. In Grossman's model of health behavior, the person cares about the amount of healthy time (h_t) available to him. Healthy days are the benefits or services of that person's health capital or stock of health (H_t). The individual also cares about other "non-health" commodities (z_t) that one produces on one's own by combining market goods and time inputs, much as a factory worker produces output in a factory. Examples of one's output are a home-cooked meal, which requires the inputs of grocery items, a stove, and cooking time, or the entertainment activity of reading a book, which requires the inputs of a book, a chair, and time.[4] Yet, individual utility $U(h_t,z_t)$, which can be evaluated at each different combination of its arguments over one's lifetime, is constrained by one's available time for health production (e.g., visiting a physician), home production (e.g., preparing a meal), and income production (e.g., working for wages) as well as by one's resulting income (Y_t) used to purchase market goods (e.g., medical care, groceries, or a book). Economists label these as the time constraint and the budget constraint.

Production Technologies and the Time and Budget Constraints

The person's health stock determines the amount of time lost due to illness, and hence dictates the total amount of time available for allocation between health production, home production, and work in the marketplace.[5] Each of the production activities is governed by the *production technology* that describes the conversion of inputs into outputs.

1. Healthy time production. The health stock determines the flow of health services (i.e., healthy time) that provide utility each period:

$h_t = f(H_t)$.

2. Health stock production. Deterioration (δ_t) of the current health stock and health investment, using the inputs of medical care (m_t) and time spent in health-producing activities (T_t^H), determine future health:

$H_{t+1} = (1 - \delta_t)H_t + g(m_t,T_t^H)$.

3. Home good production. Production of the home good, like health investment, requires both market inputs (x_t) and nonmarket inputs (e.g., time) (T_t^Z):

$z_t = z(x_t,T_t^Z)$.

4. Income production. Income is a function of one's wage (w_t) and time spent working (T_t^W):

$$Y_t = w_t\, T_t^W.$$

Individuals are endowed with a fixed amount of time, Ω, each period (e.g., 365 days per year). They lose time, T_t^L, if they are ill; $T_t^L = \Omega - h_t$. Nonsick time is allocated between health-, home-, and income-producing activities. The *time constraint* is

$$\Omega = T_t^H + T_t^Z + T_t^W + T_t^L. \tag{3.1}$$

A person's initial assets (A_0) and labor income dictate which combinations of the market inputs (m_t and x_t) are feasible at prices p_{mt} and p_{xt}. All future dollars are discounted using interest rate r to reflect their present values.[6] The (lifetime) *budget constraint* is

$$\sum_{t=1}^{T} (p_{mt}m_t + p_{xt}X_t)/(1 + r)^t = \sum_{t=1}^{T} (w_tT_t^w)/(1 + r)^t + A_0. \tag{3.2}$$

An individual's choices regarding work time, time spent in health- and home- producing activities, and the purchase of medical care and other market inputs determine the end of life (T). Death occurs when the stock of health falls below a life-sustaining level. Maximizing utility with respect to the time constraint, budget constraint, and production technologies yields a set of optimality conditions that are satisfied by the optimal combination of the choice variables. These optimality conditions provide testable relationships between variables of interest.

Applications and Implications of the Grossman Model

A Real-Life Example

Type 2 diabetes is an increasingly common disease characterized by a body that is unable to produce sufficient levels of insulin or one that produces insulin that cannot adequately regulate blood sugars. High levels of glucose in the blood damages body tissues and organs. Diabetes is the leading cause of adult blindness, kidney failure, and amputations. Diabetics have a higher risk for heart disease and stroke than nondiabetics. Currently, twenty million people in the United States have diabetes and over forty million people are prediabetic.

The clinical view with regard to diabetes treatment is to follow specific practice guidelines. Diabetes care guidelines recommend frequent

measurements of blood glucose levels, periodic feet and eye examinations, and regular physician checkups. Oral medications are often recommended to control blood sugar levels, and many diabetic patients
require medications to control cholesterol and blood pressure levels.
Exactly which drugs should be taken, how often patients should
be examined, and what lifestyle changes should be made have been
clearly spelled out by physicians. The guidelines do not allow for or
specify trade-offs among these recommendations. In real life, however,
people make trade-offs. One person with diabetes may exercise
regularly, but not have eye exams at regular intervals. Another may
attend all checkups, but continue to eat an improper diet and remain
sedentary.

A policymaker may ask what the role of health insurance is in this
scenario. That is, how would the behavior of an uninsured, employed
person with diabetes change if health insurance were made available
the person unconditionally (i.e., insurance coverage that was not
dependent on employment or income and assets)? If the out-of-pocket
price of medical care were to fall, then this person would consume
more medical care. Based on economic theory, this response is accurate,
but it is not complete.

The Effect of a Reduced Price of Medical Care on Health Behaviors

To fully answer this question, I first set aside the dynamic effects
of improved future health that may be associated with an increased
consumption of medical care when the price falls. That is, medical
care may improve, maintain, or at least prevent a further decline
in health (i.e., medical care has a positive marginal impact on health).
The improvement in health may lead to different medical and
nonmedical input behaviors over time. First consider how behavior
today might change, if the price of medical care falls considering
only the effects of *anticipated* future health changes on current
behavior.

As a person with diabetes, this individual may be fully aware of
other behaviors, such as exercise and proper diet in addition to physician visits, that are important determinants of health. Depending on
the relative effectiveness of exercising versus medical care in producing
health as well as the happiness one receives from the consumption of
other (nonmedical) goods, this individual may not alter medical care
consumption behavior at all. In fact, the reduced out-of-pocket cost of
medical care may allow this person to work less and exercise more

while still enjoying the same level of medical care consumption. Alternatively, if an individual with diabetes was substituting exercise for expensive medical care to begin with, the person may find that it has become worthwhile to work rather than to exercise, earning the income to purchase the now-cheaper medical care input.

The Effect of Physician Advice on Health Behaviors

Next, consider the effect of physician advice (facilitated through a doctor's visit due to increased insurance coverage) on health behaviors. Suppose the person diagnosed with diabetes was unaware of the relevance of those nonmedical treatments, which may be complements to or substitutes for medical care itself. The individual's health knowledge may improve following a visit to a physician. The person with diabetes may be advised to increase the amount of exercise time. A change in exercise behavior, however, depends on one's relative enjoyment of exercising today versus leisure, the opportunity cost of one's time (i.e., one could be working and earning a wage with that time), and the relative effectiveness of an additional hour of exercising compared with the medical care one could buy with one more hour of wages. Similarly, one could improve one's diet by purchasing appropriate foods for diabetics. Yet these foods may be more expensive than one's previous dietary habits. But if the marginal effectiveness of a better diet in maintaining health is large enough, it might outweigh the effect of reduced consumption of other goods.

The Effect of Improved Future Health on Health Behaviors

Now consider the effect of improved future health on health behaviors. Perhaps immediately or over time, changes in (health) input behavior (e.g., a greater consumption of inputs or a more efficient allocation of inputs) may cause health to improve or, at a minimum, reduce the probability of health complications. Improvements in health may magnify the happiness the individual receives from any of the goods that are consumed (i.e., the marginal utility of exercise, consumption, or leisure may depend on health). The improved health may make one more productive at work or result in less absenteeism (e.g., fewer lost days), leading to increased income. The potential future consumption and leisure changes induced by health gains may influence current behavior today because the forward-looking individual cares not just about the present but also about happiness in the future. The weight an individual places on future happiness relative to current happiness (i.e., the person's discount rate) reflects how much the person values the future.

The Effect of Improved Health Knowledge on Health Behaviors

Additionally, this framework permits one to consider how improvements in health knowledge influence health behaviors. How informed is the individual prior to having health insurance (and increasing the number of his physician visits)? How knowledgeable is he of how his future health will evolve? Suppose he knows the technology of health production accurately; that is, suppose he knows the average marginal impact of different inputs although he may not know his particular health response exactly. In this case, expectations of one's length of life will change since, if medical care is productive, he expects his health stock to improve given changes in his current behavior induced by the acquisition of insurance. But suppose he did not know the technology and thus inaccurately predicted his future health. Information acquired through a medical care visit about the health impacts of his choices may allow him to make more accurate forecasts of his future health. A person may not have known, for example, that a change in diet was so important. This more accurate understanding of the probabilities of future adverse health events may in and of itself change behavior today.[7]

Policy Analysis

Grossman's model can be used as a tool to answer a policymaker's questions. How will people respond to changes in the health care market? How do we evaluate different public policy alternatives? It would be important to know if the increased medical care use induced by reducing the out-of-pocket cost of care leads to significant health improvement. It would be useful to know if exercise produces better results than medical treatment. Is the health knowledge that a medical care consumer gains from his provider more effective in changing behavior than a reduction in prices that induces more consumption of medical care? If so, is there a cheaper way to provide this information than extending health insurance benefits?

Next I describe how Grossman's model can help us address these questions.

Testable Implications of Grossman's Model

The Grossman model is much more elegant and comprehensive in its full mathematical presentation. Yet this simple description reveals that there are two fundamental concepts addressed by the model. First, healthy time, determined by one's health capital, provides satisfaction; to maximize one's satisfaction an individual allocates time to work, health, and home activities, and allocates income to medical care and other market inputs. Second, health capital is produced by an individual with market inputs (e.g., medical care) and nonmarket inputs (e.g., the person's time). These two aspects of the model—demand behaviors and health production—yield many testable predictions about relationships among variables in the model. Here, I summarize some of the relationships that can be addressed using the Grossman framework. Later, I will discuss attempts to empirically test or provide evidence of these relationships.

Inferences about Demand Behaviors

The theoretical framework allows economists to understand relationships among a multitude of behaviors and individual or market characteristics. The first aspect mentioned above gives rise to three demand behaviors: individuals demand health; since medical care is an input to the production of health, the demand for medical care is a derived demand for this factor of production; and individuals value healthy time, but require income to purchase market goods, and hence must optimally allocate their healthy time to income production (i.e., work), health production, and home production. The model allows us to understand how individuals satisfy these needs.

A demand curve that is downward sloping, or negatively related to price, is a basic economic concept. The solution of Grossman's optimization model yields a demand for health that is negatively related to its price. But health is not a good that can be traded in the market and thus does not have a market price. Theoretically, its price, or "shadow" price, depends on the price of medical care (which is used to augment the health stock) as well as many other things that directly or indirectly affect the cost of holding health capital, such as its depreciation rate and the opportunity cost.

Figures 3.1 and 3.2 reproduce this aspect of the mathematical model graphically. The marginal returns of health capital are represented by

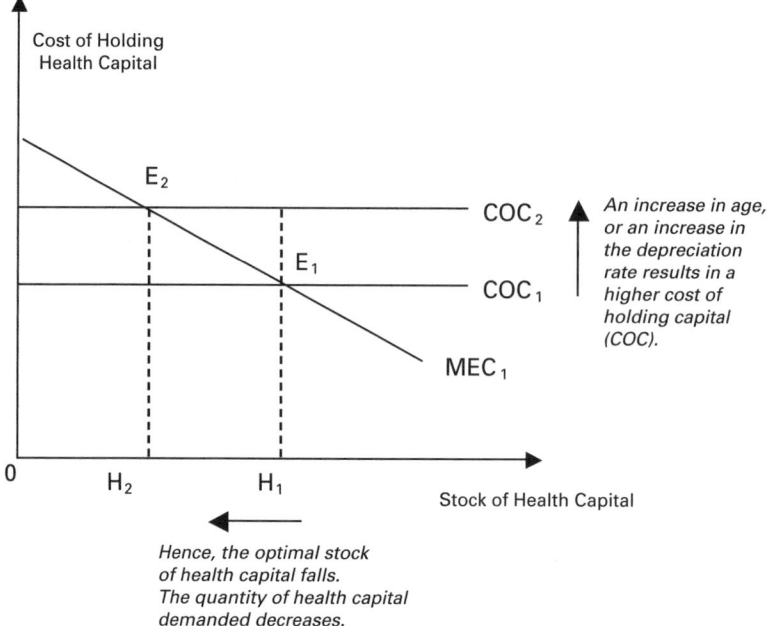

Figure 3.1
Optimal Health Capital and Changes in Age

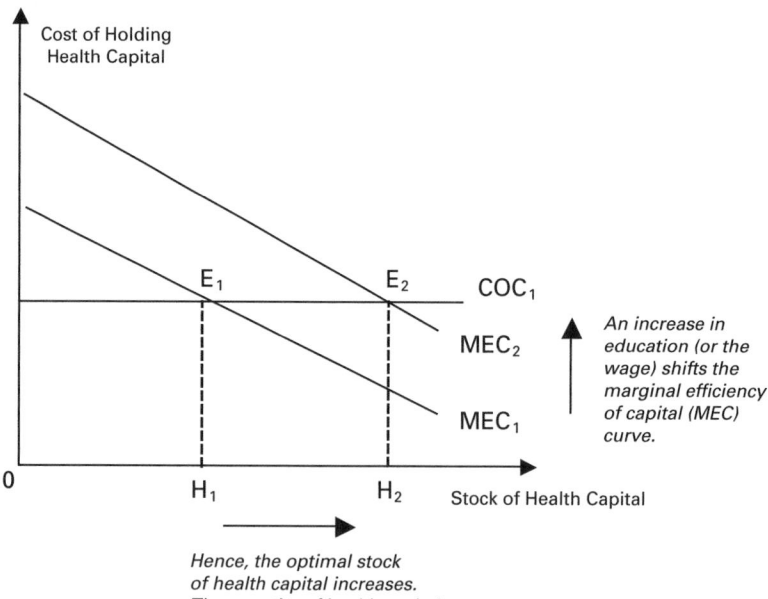

Figure 3.2
Optimal Health Capital and Changes in Education or Wages

a marginal efficiency of capital schedule (MEC). The shape and position of the curve reflects the marginal product of health capital in healthy time production, the marginal utility of health capital, and the marginal value of time (e.g., the wage rate), all expressed in monetary units. Changes in individual characteristics, or government or firm policies that alter one of these aspects of the individual's optimization problem, shift the MEC curve. The cost of capital curve (COC) represents the supply price of capital or the cost of holding an additional unit of capital. Its position is determined by the depreciation rate of the health stock, the opportunity cost of holding health capital (e.g., the interest rate), and the rate of change in the marginal cost of investment. Changes in individual characteristics or policies that affect these cost components shift the COC curve.

How does the shadow price of health change as people age? An automobile's parts typically perform worse with age. Similarly, our body's ability to function declines as we grow older; it depreciates. If the shadow price of health increases with age (an assumption consistent with an increasing depreciation rate), the solution to the model suggests that people hold less health capital (i.e., have a lower health stock) as they age. The COC curve shifts upward with increases in the depreciation rate (fig. 3.1). Put differently, the model predicts that people will demand more health capital when it is less costly.

How is health affected by education? Grossman assumes that more educated individuals are more efficient producers of health (i.e., can produce the same amount of health with fewer inputs or can produce more health with the same inputs) than those with less education. Because a given amount of investment can be generated at less cost for a more educated person, that individual experiences a higher rate of return to a given stock of health. The MEC curve will shift outward with increases in education (fig. 3.2). This relationship suggests that more educated people have a higher health stock than less educated people.

Differences in wage rates also lead to differences in the demand for health capital. But differences in wage rates operate through different channels than education, which works through the production process in Grossman's model. Higher wages increase the value of healthy time. Hence, at a higher wage, the individual wants to prevent more lost time on account of poor health. At the same time, time spent in health-producing activities (e.g., visiting a physician) is more expensive; the value of one's time is higher. One is therefore more likely to substitute market goods for time spent in health-producing activities. Still, one must recall that healthy time is also used to produce the other home good. Depending on preferences for this good relative to healthy time, and depending on the marginal effectiveness of time relative to market goods in both health and home production, individuals may reduce or increase their demand for health as wages rise.

The relationships between these variables (age, education, and wages) and the demand for medical care do not necessarily parallel that of the demand for health. Under certain conditions regarding the elasticity of demand, an increase in the cost of holding health will lead to lower levels of health demanded, but higher levels of medical care demanded. For example, consider the medical expenditures of older individuals compared to that of younger ones. Theory suggests that the higher health depreciation rate of your grandparent would lead him to have a lower health stock than your parent. (A lower wage, however, may suggest the opposite.) But your grandparent is also likely to purchase larger amounts of medical care (i.e., health investment). It takes more medical care (and time in health-producing activities) to maintain a health stock that is depreciating faster. At some accelerated rate of health depreciation, though, Grossman's model predicts that continued health investment is suboptimal and income should be used to purchase other consumption inputs that provide happiness.

Inferences about Health Production

The second area of Grossman's model that leads to testable relationships is his conception of health production. He depicts health as being determined by market and nonmarket inputs and depreciation. While his model simplifies the market input to a single scalar (such as medical care) and the nonmarket input to individual time spent in health-producing activities (such as the time it takes to travel to, wait for, and see a physician), he admits that the health inputs could be expanded. Formal medical care could be categorized into preventive, diagnostic, and curative. Each of these inputs may have different impacts on future health levels. Similarly, health investment extends beyond formal medical care. Exercise and proper nutrition are considered beneficial lifestyle practices that maintain or improve health. Housing and sanitation have been shown to improve health levels more than medical care in some developing countries. Analogously, some inputs, such as smoking, may be detrimental to health. Activities like skydiving or motorcycle riding without a helmet can also increase the risk of a sudden decrease in health stock.[8] The marginal impacts of these inputs influence the evolution of one's health stock. They also affect an individual's demand for these inputs. With multiple inputs, it may not be simply the level of each input, but the combination of inputs, that matters.

Apart from input decisions that maintain or repair our health stock, this stock deteriorates with age. But is the rate of depreciation dictated by heredity, health behaviors, or environmental factors? Does health decline at the same rate for different genders and people of different races or ethnicities? Do health behaviors simply replenish the health stock or might they also reduce the rate of health stock decline? In addition to the influence of different variables of interest on demand behaviors, health production as a technological and biological process suggests many testable relationships.

As mentioned earlier, Grossman also assumes that education increases the efficiency with which we convert input behaviors into health. Yet he admits that the relationship between education and health is not fully developed in his theoretical model. A decade after his seminal work, he issued a plea for more research that addresses the joint determination of education and health, since they are likely influenced by the same observables and unobservables.[9] But twenty years after his suggestion, an estimable model of educational attainment and health capital formulation has not materialized.[10] I will return to this issue in the discussion of empirical work based on the Grossman framework.

Inferences about Other Relationships

Although Grossman did not fully develop the relationship between health and work in his basic model, he suggested its obvious connectedness. Labor economists are increasingly finding that health plays a key role in employment participation, earnings, performance, absenteeism, job mobility, and retirement.[11] Grossman's model has implications for employment and hours of work behavior. The onset of poor health clearly results in changes in time allocation as individuals experience more ill (i.e., lost) time. As the health stock falls, the amount of lost time increases, thereby reducing the amount of available time for health, home, and income production. Depending on the relative happiness one receives from healthy time and consumption, and the marginal effectiveness of time spent producing the consumption good and investing in health, an individual whose health declines may work (for wages) more or less than he worked prior to his health decline.

The model could easily be extended to further elucidate the relationship between health and employment. One could allow preferences for income (or the marginal utility of consumption) to vary by health levels. One could also allow health levels to affect productivity or earnings. Health could influence one's ability to perform job requirements. It could affect both presenteeism (i.e., the quality of work on the job) as well as absenteeism.

While Grossman's model contains prices for medical care inputs and can be used to predict how changes in these prices influence behavior, it does not explicitly introduce health insurance as a mechanism for reducing the out-of-pocket price that a consumer faces. In the United States, nearly two-thirds of individuals with health insurance have it through employment. Herein lies another avenue through which health and employment behavior are connected.

Extensions of Grossman's Model

The sophistication of Grossman's model of individual demand for health is evidenced in its widespread use among health economists. In fact, as of late 2006, the *Web of Science* recorded that nearly four hundred articles had cited Grossman's seminal 1972 paper. Over 40 percent of those citations were from scholarly articles published between 2001 and 2006. Despite being a model that stands the test of time, there have been several extensions of Grossman's original framework.

Uncertainty

The most obvious aspect of health demand and formation that is missing from Grossman's original model is that of uncertainty. M. L. Cropper brings realism to the model by introducing different illness states that occur randomly.[12] She also allows the satisfaction one receives from consumption to depend on the illness state. As a source of illness, Cropper considers the case where employment may influence health. Some jobs that offer higher wages are associated with health hazards such as industrial pollutants or safety concerns. This aspect introduces an additional trade-off between income and health. Valentino Dardanoni and Adan Wagstaff further extend the introduction of uncertainty to the Grossman framework and the Cropper extension by allowing the effectiveness of medical care to be random.[13] The addition of uncertainty to the Grossman model permits economists to evaluate the role of risk aversion and expectations on individual behavior.

Role of Education

Jaana-Marja Muurinen also seeks to generalize Grossman's model and focuses on the role of education.[14] She considers education to be a human capital stock, much like health. Her analysis examines not only education's role in providing production efficiency but also its allocative effects. That is, education plays a role in the selection of different types of health inputs as well as the productivity of different inputs. Additionally, she allows education to directly influence the rate of depreciation of the health stock. From the outset, Grossman was deeply curious about the relationship between education and health. He proposed one causal avenue through which a positive correlation between the two would occur. Muurinen introduced two different avenues. Other economists have suggested that health knowledge, as opposed to general education, is a key determinant of the demand for health.[15] Still others suggest that the extent to which an individual is forward-looking, or the rate at which one discounts future happiness, varies across people and can determine optimal health stock.[16] Another argument claims that more educated individuals have higher-paying jobs that allow them to afford more medical care.[17] Alternatively, unobserved individual characteristics may drive a person to demand more health and more education (or less health and less education). It is this avenue of unobserved heterogeneity that requires the modeling of education and health accumulation jointly.

Mathematical Refinements

Some refinements of the mathematical assumptions of the health capital model make it more realistic. Nevertheless, as Grossman points out, many of those extensions obscure the simplicity of the model, making derivations and hence understanding more difficult.[18] For example, Isaac Ehrlich and Hiroyuki Chuma contend that the marginal cost of investment in health is not constant, as Grossman assumes.[19] Their technical extension affects the determination of the optimal investment in health. Among other technical improvements, Walter Ried suggests that the determination of an optimal length of life must be arrived at through an iterative process of resolution if the health stock level has not fallen below a life-sustaining level at the end of the optimization period.[20] Grossman discusses the merits of both considerations in detail.[21]

Child and Family Health

Many researchers, including Grossman himself, recognize that his original model applies to individual demand and production only, and adult health only. One cannot understand the health behavior of children within the original framework, since parents, who make many of the input decisions for their children, may have preferences, discount rates, or incorrect expectations that may not lead to optimal health input decisions for the child. For example, a single working parent may not have the time (or money or education) to acquire preventive care for her children. It is also interesting to understand the family dynamics of medical care consumption and the distribution of family resources to all household members. Of further interest is the effect of family members' health (and their medical care consumption) on the health of each other. Although her model assumes complete certainty, Lena Jacobson analyzes health from a family perspective.[22]

Role of the Physician

Other researchers assert that the individual is not the decision maker with regard to the use of medical care but rather the physician is.[23] Peter Zweifel and Friedrich Breyer maintain that the individual may initiate treatment, but the provider determines the amount and type.[24] They also suggest that much of the basis of Grossman's model is contradicted by empirical evidence. Zweifel and Breyer report that health and medical care are negatively rather than positively related, as Grossman's theory assumes. They propose that medical care is not a productive input to health.

Empirical Applications

With numerous citations of Grossman's original work in over a hundred different academic journals and numerous extensions to the theory of health capital by other authors, it is quite difficult to effectively summarize research that weds empirical observation and analysis with the theoretical framework in an effort to quantify or test predictions of the economic model. Additionally, in seeking to apply Grossman's unified framework of health behavior, several authors have extended it to encompass their specific areas of research. Many of these considerations have led to similar applications with different specifications of the health inputs or the included individual characteristics. But the basic model and its implications are unchanged. I sort the empirical work to date into three broad categories that describe what part of the theoretical framework the empirical findings address.

First, much health economic empirical research seeks to understand *determinants of the demand for medical and nonmedical care inputs*. The theoretical framework yields demand functions relating explanatory variables such as prices, demographic characteristics, and income to health behaviors such as medical care consumption, smoking, and exercise.

Second, the theoretical framework indicates that health is produced with various health inputs. Hence, quantifying the *role of various inputs in producing health* by estimating a health production function has been the goal of many researchers.

Finally, the economist's model of health capital seeks to fuse both elements of consumption and production in a dynamic framework with uncertainty. It is possible to specify estimable parameters of the functions in the model (i.e., utility, health production, constraint, and expectation parameters) and solve for the optimal combination of behaviors that are at the individual's discretion. The *solution and estimation of the theoretical model itself* would yield the most comprehensive empirical understanding of health behavior, and would allow for the evaluation of alternative policies that influence these individual decisions

Estimating the Demand for Medical Care and Nonmedical Inputs

The demand function for medical care is derived by solving the individual's optimization problem (not shown here). Particular assumptions about the curvature of the utility function (i.e., which indicates the degree of risk aversion) and the relationship between its arguments yield a linear demand function that depends on prices, income (i.e., wages), and individual characteristics. The estimation of this linear demand function has been a long-researched topic among health economists. They have sought to understand the marginal effects of a whole host of characteristics that influence medical care consumption; these include health insurance, age, education, race, chronic health problems, and the distance to treatment, to name a few.

This interest has led to debate about the appropriate econometric specification since the dependent variable (the quantity of medical care demanded) has a particular distribution regardless of how the variable is defined. That is, medical care expenditures, the number of physician visits, the number of hospital nights, and the length of prescription drug use tend to be characterized by a mass at zero and a remaining distribution that is skewed right (i.e., a long thin tail at higher levels of the outcome). The estimation results are available in this vast literature from an array of different models: ordinary least squares, tobit, two-part, Heckman selection, count data, and generalized linear models as well as conditional density estimation techniques.[25]

The long list of specific issues that academicians have researched regarding the demand for medical care ranges from the effects of cost-sharing insurance characteristics (published in health economics journals), to nonmonetary factors such as travel time (published in leading economic journals), to particular concerns about the effect of chronic conditions such as asthma and allergy (published in medical journals).[26] The next chapter provides a detailed summary of work assessing the effects of health insurance on the demand for medical care.

Nonmedical care inputs also influence health outcomes. Those that have received a great deal of empirical attention include behaviors such as smoking, drinking, drug use, exercise, and nutrition. Grossman's model even lends itself to understanding the effects of toilet ownership in developing countries.[27] Jonathan Gruber as well as Anthony Culyer and Joseph Newhouse summarize many of these findings.[28] From a public policy perspective, the role of prices and taxes as a means of curbing behaviors detrimental to health has evoked great interest among economists.

Understanding the role of individual demographic and socioeconomic characteristics on these health behaviors continues to interest health economists and policymakers, but other factors such as neighborhood and peer effects have also been analyzed. More recently, economists have been interested in understanding the role of expected utility maximization, uncertainty, and the future in models of individual decision-making behavior. In particular, reformulations of optimization models have been used to examine unhealthy input behaviors with habitual characteristics, such as smoking, drinking, taking drugs, engaging in risky sex, and eating excessively.[29]

Estimating Health Production Functions

Unlike the health or medical care demand functions that must be derived from solution to an individual's health optimization problem, the health production function is an explicit part of the model of health capital determination as it represents the technology an individual encounters. Medical and nonmedical inputs serve as factors of production that improve or maintain a depreciating health stock over time. Theoretically, various individual characteristics may improve the efficiency with which health is produced. Higher levels of education, for example, may increase the marginal effectiveness of medical care inputs and health behaviors. There is an abundance of research that seeks to verify these two basic assumptions posited in Grossman's work: How effective is medical care in producing health, and are more educated individuals better producers of health?

There is a voluminous literature on the role of health inputs in health production. In fact, complete summaries of this literature do not exist because the scope is so broad.[30] A snapshot of the many input and output relationships include measurement of the effects of stressful inputs—such as irregular work schedules, late-night entertainment, or the rapid crossing of several time zones—that produce insomnia; food stamp participation, to proxy for the quality of food consumption, on obesity; airborne particulate matter on bronchial health; and grab bars on elderly (bathing) functionality, each of which cites the Grossman model as the framework behind the empirical investigation.[31] One should, however, be cautious in interpreting empirical reports on the marginal effectiveness of particular health inputs. Failure to control for unobserved individual characteristics that might lead different individuals to allocate resources to different inputs will result in inaccurate measurement of the effects of those inputs.

There are several articles summarizing the evidence to date on education's role in health production.[32] Using a number of different measures of health and education, and different statistical models, the null hypothesis of no relationship between health and education is strongly refuted in this literature. A central theme in these studies, though, is that we still don't know exactly *why* education matters.

To fully understand what mechanisms are at play, researchers should model all the avenues through which educational attainment may affect health capital accumulation. The solution and estimation of a fully parameterized optimization model is necessary to quantify the interrelated effects of risk aversion, discounting, demand, production efficiency, and employment—all of which are affected by education—that leads to the positive correlation between education and health observed empirically.

Estimating the Theoretical Model of Behavior

The goals of econometric policy evaluation are often to determine the causal relevance of observed variables, consider the impact of policy interventions on the economy, compute their consequences for economic welfare, and forecast the effects of new policies. In the area of health economics and applied microeconomics in general, two approaches to accomplishing these goals stand out.

The Structural Approach

The structural approach involves specifying a formal economic model of individual optimization in which variation in preferences, constraints, technologies, and expectations of future events are defined explicitly. The stochastic and often dynamic optimization problems incorporate rational expectations and forward-looking behavior that is influenced by past and current decisions. This approach emphasizes the clarity with which identifying assumptions are postulated, and advocates an approach to estimation that tests, and consequently accepts or rejects, well-posed models. The estimated parameters of such models are the underlying primitives of decision making: the parameters that define preferences, constraints, technologies, and expectations processes.[33] One of the advantages of applying the structural estimation approach is the ability to impose and evaluate policy, and forecast the effects of new policies never previously experienced.[34]

The Natural and Social Experiment Approach

Another approach to causal analysis is the natural experiment. In an effort to measure causal parameters, researchers using this approach search for credible sources of identifying information (such as natural or social experiments), with truly random experiments being the ideal data to analyze. That is, a researcher can use information that is not correlated with individual unobservables to identify and measure the empirical effects of interest. The economic theory used to interpret data is often discussed intuitively and, in the case of health behavior, usually cites Grossman's model for a formal framework. The natural experiment approach provides estimates obtained from simple econometric methods, frequently reduced forms, whose transparency and simplicity have promoted their widespread use.[35] Much of the health literature uses this approach.

Evaluation of New Policies and Incentives

As James Heckman argues, "If a policy has previously been in place, and it is possible to adjust outcome variables for changes in external circumstances unrelated to the policy that also affect outcomes, then econometric policy evaluation is just a table look-up exercise. Structural parameters are not required to forecast the effect of a policy on outcomes although causal effects may still be desired for interpretive purposes."[36] If the policy to be evaluated is the same basic one with levels of the policy parameters that differ from what is observed in the data, then the interpolation or extrapolation of estimated relationships is all that is required. A disciplined way to do this is to impose functions forms on simple estimation equations.

Put differently, nonstructural estimation, or statistical models, can be used to evaluate new policies when the policy directly varies itself (e.g., in the case of extrapolating the effect of health insurance copayment rates on medical care consumption) or when there is policy-relevant variation (e.g., in the case of extrapolating the effect of universal health insurance that pays the full cost of medical care using existing variation in medical care prices and health insurance coverage). The case for knowing structural parameters comes in when one wants to predict the effects of a new policy that has never been implemented.[37]

Structural Estimation of Models of Health Behavior

In the thirty-five years since Grossman's formalization of health behavior, health economists have extended his model to incorporate uncertainty, health insurance, preventive care, and retirement policies, among other things. Nevertheless, few economists have attempted to parameterize and estimate the optimization behavior of individuals with regard to their health and health care consumption. Models that make explicit the dynamic behavior and the uncertainty do exist.[38] Yet few empirical studies have numerically solved these optimization problems and used iterative estimation techniques to fit the behavior generated by the solution of the model to the observed data. In fact, only five papers, to my knowledge, explain medical care and non-medical input decisions and their influence on health outcomes in a manner suggested in health economics' infancy by Grossman: Gilleskie (1998), Crawford and Shum (2005), Davis and Foster (2005), and Khwaja (2001, 2006). Rather than simply measuring correlations in linearized demand functions or stand-alone production functions, these authors estimate the preferences, constraints, technologies, and expectations of forward-looking individuals, thereby allowing for the evaluation of interesting health policy alternatives.

The estimation of a comprehensive model of health outcomes, medical care use, and time allocation over an individual's lifetime would require data that simply do not exist. Among the available data sets that detail health and health behavior of a nationally representative sample, few are longitudinal (i.e., data from surveys that track individuals and their behavior over time), and the time frame is generally short. Moreover, often the detail necessary to estimate a Grossman-like model is missing. Perhaps information is available about medical care inputs, but the data lack information about other health-related inputs such as smoking and exercise behavior. Annual measures of health may be available, but detailed measures of health that led to medical care use during the survey periods may be missing. Hence, attempts to estimate the underlying theoretical model of health demand and production have been limited to what is doable with the available data.

*Example 1: Medical Care Use and Work Absenteeism during an
Acute Illness Episode*

In a 1998 work, I model daily medical care and absence decisions
over an episode of acute infectious, parasitic, or respiratory illness.[39]
I estimate the preference parameters that determine the happiness
(i.e., utility) that an ill individual receives from work (or not
missing work) and general consumption. Also, I allow medical care
itself to affect current utility as it may be palliative today in addition
to productive for future health. A daily budget constraint reflects the
income loss associated with the consumption of medical care and
absences from work. Included in the dynamic optimization problem is
a health production function that measures the effectiveness of medical
care and recuperation (work absences) as well as time on recovery
probabilities. The model provides predictions of how health insurance and sick leave policies affect medical care consumption and
absenteeism.

My model mimics the Grossman one of health behaviors and health
production on a smaller scale. While my model is limited to behavior
during an episode of illness, it allows for the estimation of utility function parameters and parameters of the health production function.
These so-called structural parameters, or primitives, of the model are
policy invariant. That is, they reflect preferences, beliefs, or technologies that are not likely to change as policy changes. This estimation
procedure differs from nonstructural or statistical techniques that
produce quantifiable relationships between two variables, but that
often do not reflect the direction of causality. Furthermore, if the statistical model is misspecified, a seemingly significant relationship may
not really exist; the estimated parameters of interest may be biased.
Finally, the estimated marginal impact, using such statistical models,
reflects the policies that exist at the time of data collection since the
estimated parameters are actually functions of the underlying primitive parameters of the theoretical model.[40]

Alternatively, the estimation of the structural parameters of individual optimization problems (i.e., the economist's theoretical model
of human behavior) allows for the evaluation of different public policies of interest. After model parameters have been estimated (i.e., after
the values of the parameters that yield behavior similar to that observed
in the data have been found), my model can be solved under different
scenarios. My model, for example, simulates the effect of increasing

insurance coverage and eliminating sick leave policies.[41] Admittedly, extremes of insurance, and sick leave coverage exist in my data, and hence simulated effects of variation in this coverage might be similarly captured by nonstructural estimation methods. Yet I also simulate the behavior of individuals under policies that do not exist in the data. How would a person behave if medical care (for these relatively minor illnesses) were prohibited during the first three days of illness in an effort to reduce the consumption of (or reliance on) medical care inputs? That is, perhaps a day of rest, as opposed to the consumption of medical care, may be sufficient and more effective to return the individual to full health. Of course, such a policy does not exist in the United States, but it is useful for understanding the effect of waiting times or queues that might exist for medical care services.

Example 2: Prescription Drug Use during an Episode of Illness

Gregory Crawford and Matthew Shum focus on prescription drug decisions during an episode of gastrointestinal illness.[42] Tat Chan and Barton Hamilton model the use of AIDS drugs to improve immune system response among HIV-infected individuals.[43] Their models specifically address the uncertainty and learning about health production that takes place when a person consumes (or does not consume) a particular medical care input. Their models are examples of optimal behavior when the marginal product of a particular health input for a particular individual is not known with certainty in advance of using it and must be updated over time through experimentation.

Crawford and Shum's dynamic model of demand for antiulcer drugs allows for current period effects of individual decisions (i.e., the relief of symptoms or side effects) as well as productive effects that reduce the (uncertain) duration of the episode. Both of these effects, however, are uncertain prior to the use of a particular drug by the individual. Hence, the individual learns over time which drugs make one feel best while taking them, and which drugs reduce the length of one's spell (and dependence on the drug). Having solved the model and estimated the preference and belief parameters, the authors can solve the model under the case of certainty, where experimentation to discover health effects is not necessary. Despite extensive heterogeneity in drug efficacy across patients, the ability to learn which drug is best appears to minimize the welfare losses associated with initial bad decisions. Their research has implications for policy regarding information diffusion, such as direct-to-consumer advertising, in drug markets.

Chan and Hamilton's model of drug use to improve immune response focuses on the attrition that plagues many randomized experiments designed to evaluate treatment effects. The researchers find that participant failure to continue a medication can be explained by side effects and the declining efficacy of the treatment. Rather than simply calculate the treatment effect by examining the outcomes of randomly treated individuals, they model the utility of the patients as a function of both the observed health outcome (e.g., indicators of immune response) and side effects. They find that AZT—an older, traditional treatment for AIDS—yields the highest level of utility despite having the lowest impact on the immune system. This finding stems from the mild side effects associated with this treatment alone compared to being additionally treated with more recently introduced HIV drugs. The framework allows the authors to distinguish between learning, side effects, and the direct effects of treatment when explaining participant behavior over the course of the experiment.

Example 3: Mental Health Care Decisions during Childhood

Morris Davis and E. Michael Foster model semiannual mental health care decisions during childhood.[44] This research provides an example of the trade-off between completeness with regard to the types of medical care inputs considered with the duration in which health production can be modeled. The authors are able to model decisions over a long period of time (ages five to seventeen), but choose to focus specifically on mental health care services and mental health outcomes. This study provides an example of how children's demand for health may need to be modeled differently since the decision makers are parents; parents care about household consumption and the mental health of their child. While mental health care may improve mental health (i.e., through the mental health production function), the consumption of such services reduces household consumption and may cause disutility directly. Davis and Foster find a significant but small effect of mental health care services on the long-term mental health of a small subset of the children in their sample. They also find that intermediate care services could replace inpatient stay services with little differential consequences for mental health outcomes. The estimation of preference parameters indicates that the stigma associated with mental health care use is large, and is an important determinant of parental decisions regarding its use. Given these estimates, policies that attempt to promote the use of such services (i.e., parity in health insurance coverage) can be evaluated.

Example 4: Health Input Demand and Health Production during an Adult Lifetime

Finally, the work of Ahmed Khwaja models health behaviors and health production over a long period of time, most closely aligning with Grossman's model of health capital formulation.[45] Khwaja models annual smoking, exercise, drinking, and medical care decisions over an adult lifetime. Unlike Grossman, he allows for joint production where these behaviors provide current period utility while also impacting future health. Another departure from Grossman's model is that he excludes the employment decision from the complicated set of decisions that he does model. The author focuses on the role of insurance in affecting the medical and nonmedical health input behaviors both before and after eligibility for Medicare.[46] In addition to offering a model that can quantify many responses to dynamic life cycle changes over time, the research contributes to our understanding of the incentive structure of elderly health insurance and provides a vehicle for evaluating changes in the age of Medicare eligibility and coverage.

Problems Encountered in Empirical Research on Health

Despite the large empirical literature on demand for medical and nonmedical inputs and health production, a definitive understanding of behavior in these realms of health economics does not exist. The sources of the remaining questions lie largely in the difficulties associated with estimating these economic and largely biological processes. I end this chapter with a brief discussion of some of the obstacles encountered by economists doing empirical work on these subjects.

Measurement of Health

The economist's model of health behavior revolves around the central concept of health capital, or an individual's stock of health. But how does one measure health empirically? Survey questionnaires often ask respondents to self report their health as excellent, very good, good, fair, or poor. While the response provides a general measure of health, it is not objective; nor is it assessed by a physician, thereby making it difficult to compare responses across people. Alternatively, more objective measures such as the number or presence of chronic conditions, or the number of activities of daily living that are limited, provide comparability.

A related difficulty is the measurement of the flow of health from a given stock. This flow can be thought of as sickness or morbidity. In data collection, though, reports of sickness are frequently tied to work or school absences, and hence require an endogenous action (e.g., being absent or visiting a physician) in order to be recorded. Health shocks, such as the onset of a chronic condition, are sometimes used to capture health flow. Estimation of the determinants of the health stock or its flow requires a measure of health in which different inputs or input levels have the opportunity to matter. If the measure is too general, it may not vary with changes in individual behavior. If it is too specific, it might not capture changes (or stability) in other areas of health.

Health Production Is a Dynamic Process That Requires Data over Time

While the theory of health input demand and health production assumes that medical care has a positive marginal impact on health, the data do not always validate this assumption. In fact, a statistical regression of health on a medical care input, whether measured as expenditures or the number of visits, is likely to reveal a negative relationship. This result logically stems from the observation that individuals who need the most care (i.e., those in the poorest health) consume the most medical care. Yet theoretically, Grossman's model, and human behavior in general, suggests that rational individuals compare where they would be if they do not consume the medical care with where they would be consuming it (and weigh that against the monetary cost of consuming care). In many cases, health would deteriorate or not improve in the absence of care. Thus, the appropriate measurement of medical care's productivity requires observations on individuals over time. That is, health production is dynamic by nature. Many data sets are cross-sectional and do not follow individuals over time, however.[47] Econometrically teasing out the effect of unobserved individual characteristics from that of particular individually chosen inputs can only be achieved with longitudinal observations on both input behaviors and health outcomes.

Omission of Relevant Health Inputs

The evaluation of medical care as a productive input to health requires more than simply good measurement of the output and observations on individuals over time. It necessitates modeling the many inputs that might affect health. Grossman's model specifies medical care (and time spent consuming medical care) as the input. Yet other inputs affect health: preventive care, different types of medical care (e.g., hospital care, physician visits, and prescription drugs), exercise, nutrition, smoking, drinking, and risky behaviors (e.g., skydiving, motorcycle riding, etc.), to name a few. Estimation with omitted inputs that are correlated with the input of interest will lead to incorrect estimates of the marginal effect (and its variance) of included inputs. Similarly, the determination of which inputs are substitutes for or complements of one another is important for evaluating insurance policies that may provide differential reimbursement for particular services.[48]

Health Input Behaviors Are Choices

We know that the inputs that affect health are endogenous; that is, they are optimally chosen by an individual as part of attempt to achieve happiness over time. People choose whether to exercise or not. It is likely that unobserved individual characteristics affecting some input decisions will also influence the health outcomes of interest. For example, it has already been suggested that exact measures of health capital are difficult to obtain. It is quite likely that variations in unobserved health may influence health input decisions as well as the available measure of health that is being explained by the econometric model. Other examples of individual unobservables, both time varying and time invariant, include the degree of risk aversion, discounting of future happiness, self-esteem, unobserved health shocks, and unobserved determinants of both health and input behavior such as the presence of children. Proper treatment of unobserved individual heterogeneity is a must if one is to obtain reliable and useful measures of input effectiveness.

Despite these econometric concerns, modeling all the aspects of health demand and production that are captured by the economist's health capital framework is difficult empirically. For instance, we typically think that a person consumes curative care because it improves health. Such care increases the stock of health capital and hence its consumption today provides future benefits. Curative care consumption is also costly today; it reduces both the amount of money available for other consumption and the amount of time available for other activities. Only if the future benefits outweigh the current costs will an individual consume the curative care. Theory would predict, then, that a myopic individual would not seek care. Nevertheless, it is likely that curative care affects current levels of happiness also. Such care, for example, may offer immediate relief from pain. From a policy perspective, it may be important to know the extent to which demand is based on the current relief of symptoms or expectations of the future health outcome. These effects cannot be estimated without fully parameterizing and solving a model that makes these incentives (and potential policy instruments) explicit. Similarly, if one theorizes that aversion to risk or discounting of future events plays a role in health capital demand, then evaluation of the relevance of these behavioral concepts must involve an estimation procedure that explicitly accounts for or measures them.

Conclusion

A question was posed at the beginning of the chapter: How would an employed person with diabetes behave if acquired health insurance? Grossman's model and its extensions allow us to consider the different ways in which this person may respond and the variables that explain that behavior. Policymakers have a tool with which they can evaluate or interpret the effects of policies that alter the constraints faced by an individual.

For example, health behaviors and health outcomes are the focus of the Asheville Project and similar experiments being repeated in the Ten City Challenge.[49] Since 1997, the city of Asheville, North Carolina, a self-insured employer, has provided free medicine and medical devices, free counseling and education by pharmacists, and regular checkups to employees with chronic health problems such as diabetes, asthma, hypertension, and high cholesterol who take their medicine regularly and change their unhealthy lifestyles. As expected (and as indicated by my initial answer to the hypothetical scenario posed at the start of this chapter), pharmaceutical costs have gone up. But hospital costs are down. And even more surprisingly to the program administrators, absenteeism has been reduced considerably. The model of health behavior and health production presented in this chapter provides an explanation for these observed experiences.

Grossman's model of the demand for and production of health capital remains the basic framework on which most economists have based subsequent investigations of health behavior. But the nature of health itself has led to a continuous and continuing stream of research. Researchers provide policymakers with more and more information regarding the marginal impact of various incentives or mechanisms through which improved health can be achieved on an ongoing basis. There is abundant literature attempting to quantify the value of this improved health. Recent work shows that improvements in health have a substantial value and that economic theory can explain why there is value in extending life.[50]

The theoretical and empirical work to date has shed light on three important considerations for future work in this area of economics. First, empirical analyses would benefit from the use of longitudinal observations on individuals in order to provide relevant information for policy consideration. Hence, supporting the acquisition of these types of data is necessary at the data collection level. Second, researchers seeking to measure quantitative relationships must address the existence of unobserved heterogeneity that is likely to create spurious correlation or bias the measured effect unless proper steps are taken to model it. Finally, estimation of a model of individual optimization behavior that allows a researcher to recover the primitives of the model—the fundamental preference, constraint, and expectation parameters that are invariant to policy—will allow the evaluation of alternative public policies. Despite theoretical and empirical achievements, exploration of health capital behavior will continue.

Acknowledgments

I thank Frank Solan and Ahmed Khwaja for their suggestions on the organization of this chapter, and Luis Fernandez for useful comments during his discussion of this summary at the conference at Oberlin.

Notes

1. For recent surveys of this literature, see Grossman (2000); Cutler and Lleras-Muney (2006).

2. Becker (1965); Grossman (1972a, 1972b).

3. In Grossman's original model, only two inputs are considered in health production: medical care and the time spent in health-producing activities. An important component in this health production process, Grossman theorized, is education. He assumed (and tested empirically) that education improves the efficiency with which an individual converts a health input into the output health.

4. Economists refer to these goods as "home goods" or home production. Technically, health production can also be home production because there are many activities (e.g., a nutritious meal or a bike ride) that affect one's health. For expositional purposes, however, health and home production are treated here as distinct goods, as in the original Grossman model.

5. Grossman assumes no joint production. That is, an individual cannot produce a home good while also traveling to the doctor's office. Similarly, exercise cannot produce health while also producing recreational pleasure. Nor can an individual do anything productive with one's days lost due to illness.

6. Grossman's original model did not include uncertainty about future health shocks, health deterioration rates, wage rates, interest rates, or commodity prices. These rates are assumed to be known with perfect foresight.

7. It is difficult to say how behavior might change in this case without further assumptions.

8. Grossman's model assumes no joint production so exercise (smoking), for example, cannot be both a positive (negative) input to health and provide negative (positive) utility.

9. Grossman (1982).

10. Grossman (2000).

11. For a comprehensive summary of research that addresses the relationship between health and labor, see Currie and Madrian (1999).

12. Cropper (1977).

13. Dardanoni and Wagstaff (1990).

14. Muurinen (1982)

15. Kenkel (1991).

16. Fuchs (1982).

17. This argument as an explanation for the positive correlation between health and education, however, requires that medical care improve health.

18. Grossman (2004).

19. Ehrlich and Hiroyuki (1990).

20. Ried (1996).

21. Grossman (2004).

22. Jacobson (2000).

23. See the discussion of this issue in chapter 10 of this book.

24. Zweifel and Breyer (1997).

25. See, for example, Maddala (1983); Cameron and Trivedi (1998); Manning and Mullahy (2001); Gilleskie and Mroz (2004).

26. On cost sharing, see, for example, de Meza (1983); on nonmonetary factors, see, for example, Acton (1975); on chronic conditions, see, for example, Bolin and Lindgren (2002).

27. See, for example, Kirigia and Kainyu (2000).

28. Gruber (2000); Culyer and Newhouse (2000).

29. See chapter 5 of this book.

30. For summaries of work focusing on particular topics, see Culyer and Newhouse (2000).

31. Yaniv (2004); Gibson (2003); Phelan (2000); Kutty (1998).

32. See, for example, Grossman (2000, 2004); Cutler and Lleras-Muney (2006).

33. More specifically preferences are the parameters of the utility function $u(h_t, z_t)$ that define the relationship between arguments of the utility function and the level of satisfaction or happiness. Constraint and technology parameters include those that define the relationship between health stock and healthy days, $h_t = f(H_t)$; between inputs and health investment, $g(m_t, TH_t)$; and between inputs and the home good, $z(x_t, TZ_t)$. Expectations parameters include, for example, parameters that define the relationship between individual characteristics and the distribution of future wages.

34. Todd and Wolpin (2003).

35. Heckman (2000).

36. Ibid.

37. Marschak (1953). Such an evaluation, however, requires the assumption that the new policy will not alter preferences.

38. Keeler et al. (1977); Cameron et al. (1988).

39. Gilleskie (1998).

40. Lucas (1976).

41. Gilleskie (1998).

42. Crawford and Shum (2005).

43. Chan and Hamilton (2006).

44. Davis and Foster (2005).

45. Khwaja (2001).

46. Khwaja (2006).

47. Data collection surveys that follow individuals over time and inquire about health behaviors as well as outcomes are increasingly available. These include the *Health and Retirement Survey*, the *Medicare Current Beneficiary Survey*, the *National Long-Term Care Survey*, the *Longitudinal Survey of Adolescent Health*, and the *Panel Study of Income Dynamics*.

48. Yang et al. (2006).

49. Employer groups in ten different communities nationwide have established a voluntary health benefit for employees similar to that of the Asheville Project.

50. Murphy and Topel (2006); Hall and Jones (2007).

4

What We Know and Don't Know about the Effects of Cost Sharing on the Demand for Medical Care—and So What?

Joseph P. Newhouse and
Anna D. Sinaiko

Cost sharing for medical care, meaning how much the patient pays when using a medical service such as going to the doctor, has long been an important topic as well as an ideological minefield in health economics. Many, frequently on the political Left, believe that all medical care—or if it could be defined and implemented, all efficacious medical care—should be free to those seeking it.[1] In other words, proponents of this view argue that the cost sharing should be zero. Others, frequently on the political Right, believe that cost sharing should be maintained or be even higher than it is, because insured medical care leads to overuse.[2]

During the heyday of managed care in the 1990s, the debate around cost sharing for patients somewhat faded as physicians or groups of physicians began to bear more risk for the use of medical services. For example, insurers started to pay physicians a fixed amount per patient per month (a capitation) rather than a fee for each service, with the physician bearing the cost of any difference between the total cost of services delivered and this fixed amount. Such an arrangement moved the financial incentives to reduce services to the physician and away from the patient. The hope behind this strategy was that if the physician bore the financial consequences of overuse, cost sharing by patients could be kept low without triggering a great deal of overuse.[3]

Whatever the merits of this argument, the backlash against managed care and the subsequent increase in medical spending in the late 1990s and early 2000s has again brought the issue of cost sharing by patients to the fore, as employers have been raising the amount of cost sharing to keep health insurance premiums down and encourage patients to consider costs when making decisions about using health care services. Often these plans are offered under the banner of consumer-directed health care.[4] In 2005, for example, 20 percent of employers who offered health benefits offered a high-deductible health plan to some of their workers (for instance, a plan where patients pay the first $1,000 of their annual medical spending), up from 10 percent in 2004 and 5 percent in 2003.[5] We will call what consumers or patients pay "demand prices," and focus on them in this chapter. We distinguish demand prices from what medical providers such as hospitals and physicians are paid for their services, which we term "supply prices." The difference between demand and supply prices is the amount, if any, that is paid by the insurance company or companies.

Economics has much to say about both demand and supply prices in medical care. With respect to demand prices, it offers some support for both ideological views described above. In this chapter, we sketch the framework within which economists have traditionally understood cost sharing and present some empirical evidence that fleshes out that framework. We then turn to an emerging reformulation of that framework, and give some suggestions about where research should head in this domain.

The Traditional View of Cost Sharing among Health Economists

Textbook treatments of cost sharing depict it as a trade-off between moral hazard and risk avoidance.[6] On the one hand, with more complete insurance, consumers benefit because they have better protection against random losses in wealth from medical bills. On the other hand, more complete insurance induces the greater use of medical services, which is economically inefficient. As with any textbook treatment, this framework derives from several classic papers in health economics.[7] Moral hazard, a more precise term for the inefficiency that the political Right emphasizes, typically refers in this context to better-insured consumers using more services (aka demand curves slope down), though in principle it could also refer to an insurance-induced change in health habits. Risk avoidance, a more precise term for what the political Left stresses, is the classic gain from insuring the risk of a substantial loss. In addition, many on the Left are concerned that consumers do not know enough to decide when they should seek care, and that therefore any financial disincentives to seek care should be minimal or nonexistent, especially for lower-income populations. This view in effect holds that patients should face a low threshold for seeking medical advice; moreover, medical professionals should determine whether further treatment is advisable.

The traditional welfare economics view of how health insurance brings about moral hazard and the resulting inefficient use of resources is shown in figure 4.1. In this framework, the subsidy provided by health insurance is assumed to induce additional resources into the production of medical care services that would be more highly valued by consumers in the production of other goods and services. A demand curve shows the valuation placed by the consumer on each additional unit of medical care, and in a competitive economy the marginal cost curve shows the valuation placed by the consumer on those resources if used to produce other goods or services. Hence, each additional unit of medical care beyond where the marginal valuation equals the marginal cost (point *a* in figure 4.1) carries with it a deadweight loss or inefficiency equal to the vertical distance between the demand curve and the marginal cost curve. In this figure, a health insurance plan with a 20 percent coinsurance rate (i.e., a plan in which the patient pays 20 percent of the full cost of care) will result in a deadweight loss depicted by the triangle *afb*. One implication of this framework is that insurance that covers services that are more price elastic (more responsive to insurance) will induce more inefficiency than insurance-covering services that are less price elastic. To see this, if there is no response of demand to insurance coverage (i.e., when the demand curve is vertical), there is no deadweight loss from insurance. The varying response

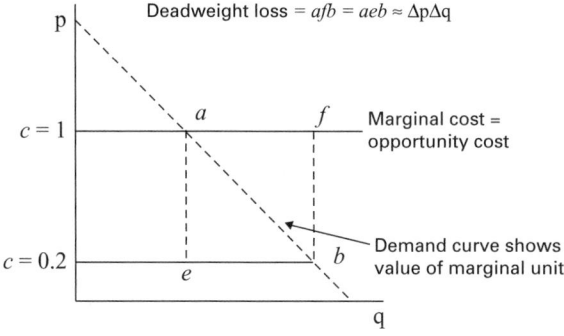

Figure 4.1
Moral Hazard
Note: Once the marginal valuation falls below marginal cost, there is a welfare loss on each unit equal to the vertical difference between the marginal cost curve and the demand curve or marginal valuation curve. At a 20 percent coinsurance rate, the loss equals the area of the triangle *afb* = the area *aeb*. This ignores any externalities, income effects, and risk aversion, and assumes the marginal cost curve shows the opportunity cost of using the resources in other ways.

of demand for different types of medical care services to insurance has been a traditional argument for better coverage (less cost sharing) of hospital services and poorer coverage (more cost sharing) of mental health services.

Although much of the health economics literature uses the traditional welfare economics framework, the normative argument requires several strong assumptions. In the medical care context, two of these assumptions in particular should be made explicit. The first and probably the more important one is that consumers or patients have well-defined preferences for medical services that have some claim to be honored. Many consumers in fact visit a physician precisely to find out what ails them and obtain the physician's advice about which treatment options are available. If that advice is influenced by factors other than what a fully informed patient would want to know—and there is certainly evidence that how the physician is paid affects how patients are treated—the usual normative claim supporting consumer sovereignty loses force.[8] In some extreme cases, consumer "preferences" may simply lack any face validity such as when a treatment decision needs to be made for an unconscious patient with no family member available, or for a delusional or demented patient. The tenuousness in the medical context of the assumption that patients have stable preferences that deserve to be honored leads many analysts not to value medical services using standard welfare economics (i.e., based on the observed demand function) but instead to directly value outcomes through such means as Quality Adjusted Life Years (QALYs) or Disability Adjusted Life Years (DALYs).[9]

Nonetheless, when patients decide to seek or not seek care for a medical problem, they presumably do so based on some calculation of whether their expected benefits will exceed their expected costs, so that patient views of benefits and costs are certainly relevant to outcomes. (Expected costs here are defined using demand prices.)

A second key assumption that is not inherent in the normative framework but often made in practice is that income effects are ignorable. In fact, a sick consumer may want additional income or purchasing power when sick in order to buy medical services. This is exactly what insurance does: the individual pays an insurance premium that only pays off if medical care is sought; thus, the person has less income when well by the amount of the premium and more income when sick. There may be a valuable lifesaving treatment in an extreme case that costs more than an uninsured person has in assets or could borrow. A person may therefore be willing to pay the premium to be insured for such a treatment, but simply not be able to purchase the treatment if not insured. If the cost of the treatment is large relative to income or wealth, the additional use of medical services by the insured patient does not entirely represent inefficiency or moral hazard.[10] Of course, if the person would not have been willing to pay for an insurance policy (or if others were not willing to pay on the person's behalf), the additional use of services would represent inefficiency. The crucial point, however, is that simply showing additional use of services by insured persons is not sufficient to show moral hazard. Yet in cases where any insurance payout is small relative to income, ignoring income effects will still be a good approximation.[11] Jeremiah Hurley provides a discussion and critique of the traditional framework.[12]

Empirical Evidence and the Traditional Framework

Much of our evidence on the effects of cost sharing on the demand for medical care—or the magnitude of moral hazard in the traditional framework—comes from the RAND Health Insurance Experiment (HIE), a large-scale project carried out in the 1970s and early 1980s.[13] The HIE randomly assigned approximately 5,800 persons in 2,000 families who lived in one of six sites around the country to one of several health insurance plans that varied the demand prices the families faced. All the persons were under sixty-five years of age, and the persons were observed for either three years (70 percent) or five years (30 percent).

At one extreme, families paid nothing for medical care ("free care"). Other families faced coinsurance rates (the family's percentage of the bill) of 25, 50, or 95 percent, but all these latter families had a stop-loss provision, or a ceiling on their out-of-pocket spending in a year. The ceiling was set at $1,000 per year, but was scaled down for low-income families.[14] If the 95 percent coinsurance figure were 100 percent, the plan would have been equivalent to a family deductible equal to the stop-loss ($1,000 for most families).[15] Finally, one plan had 95 percent coinsurance to a maximum of $150 person or $450 per family, but in this plan the cost sharing applied only to outpatient services; inpatient (hospital) services were free. The inclusion of this plan allowed estimating a cross-price elasticity between inpatient and outpatient services, and addressed the question of whether lowering demand prices for outpatient services would save money on inpatient services.

This would be the case if lower demand prices for office visits would induce patients to seek care at an earlier stage in their illness, when it could be treated more cheaply.[16] The results from the HIE showed that demand prices do matter to the use of medical services (figures 4.2 and 4.3). Relative to free care, the total expenditures on medical care, including insurance payments, were around 30 percent less when consumers faced a large deductible and about 20 percent less when consumers faced 25 percent coinsurance with a stop-loss feature. Consumers with a large deductible made one to two fewer visits per year to physicians than those with free care; this differential in the number of visits as well as fewer hospitalizations were the drivers behind lower expenditures by people on plans with higher cost sharing, not the amount of services used per visit or hospital stay. Furthermore, this response appeared to hold throughout the income distribution; it was not the case that lower-income individuals were notably more responsive to price. The use of medical care by those in the plan with the individual deductible that applied to outpatient services only (the far right column labeled IndD in the figures) was intermediate. Hence, making all services free relative to only making inpatient services free—better coverage of inpatient services was reasonably common in the insurance policies of the 1970s—added to the overall cost.[17]

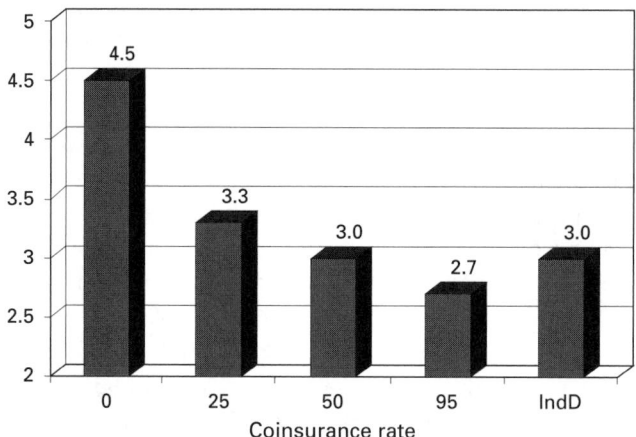

Figure 4.2
Visit Rates by Plan (per Person)
Notes: 25, 50, 95 plans have $1,000 stop-loss (late 1970s dollars).
Face-to-face visits. All s.e.'s < 0.2; chi-square (4): 69, p < 0.000001.
Source: Newhouse and the Insurance Experiment Group (1993).

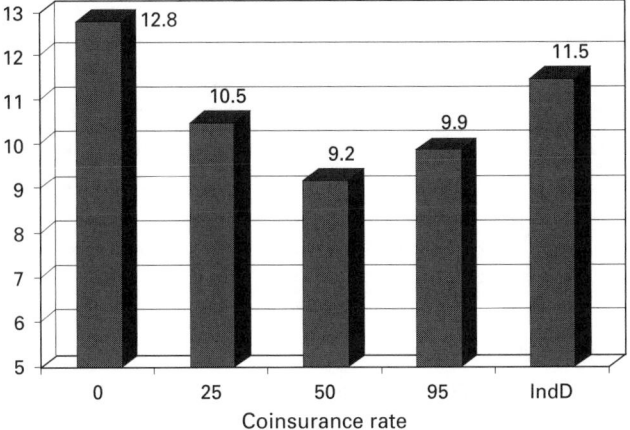

Figure 4.3
Admission Rates by Plan (/100)
Notes: 25, 50, 95 plans have $1,000 stop-loss (late 1970s dollars).
Face-to-face visits. All s.e.'s < 0.2; chi-square (4): 69, p < 0.000001.
Source: Newhouse and the Insurance Experiment Group (1993).

In the previous section, we noted several reasons why standard welfare economics may not apply in this domain and therefore why one should not necessarily consider the additional use of services induced by insurance to be per se evidence of inefficiency. In light of those arguments, the RAND group gathered a great deal of information about the health outcomes of the participants in the HIE. Although they did not calculate the number of QALYs or DALYs saved from additional care (QALYs were introduced about the time of the experiment and DALYs had not yet been introduced), the results were striking.

For the average person, the difference in the use of services across plans did not materially affect their health. This was true for both adults and children, for whom different measures were collected. To reach this conclusion, the RAND group gathered data on many different measures of health including self-assessed health, physical health, mental health, a number of physiological measures of health such as blood pressure and cholesterol, health habits such as smoking and weight, and self-assessed pain and anxiety. Almost all of these measures of health showed at most only a small difference among the plans.[18] One notable exception was blood pressure among adults, where the mean of diastolic blood pressure at the end of the HIE was 78.0 mmHg for those with free care and 78.8 mmHg for those

assigned to plans with some cost sharing. Although this 1 percent difference in blood pressure may seem inconsequential, for the poor with
high blood pressure it translated into about a 15 percent difference in
predicted future mortality rates.[19] Most of this difference in blood pressure was attributable to a physician's failure to diagnose hypertension
conditional on a visit, though some was attributable to the difference
in visit rates among the plans.

At first glance, these findings appear to fit the simple economic
paradigm described in figure 4.1 rather well; free care induced a substantially greater use of services that with the exception of the blood
pressure result, appeared to be of little or no benefit to the participant's
health or state of mind. A closer inspection of the data, however,
revealed a more complicated story. Given the physician's diagnosis,
the RAND group defined instances in which medical care should be
efficacious—for example, an antibiotic for a bacterial condition—and
instances in which it should not—say, an antibiotic for a viral condition.
When analyzed in this fashion, cost sharing appeared to reduce both
efficacious and nonefficacious care by approximately equal proportions. But this finding creates a puzzle; if cost sharing reduces efficacious care, why was there no observed effect on health status?

One possibility is that the measures of efficacious care or health
status are invalid or unreliable. Apart from the extensive tests that the
group carrying out the HIE did to show that the measures were of high
quality, there is no reason why any measurement error should differ
by the plan to which the family was assigned, especially for the many
physiological measures.[20] The more plausible explanation is that some
of the additional medical care among those with free care actually
harmed them—an effect that the medical literature terms iatrogenesis.
For example, about half of all antibiotic use on all plans was for viral
conditions. Not only is it known that such use is not efficacious, it is
also the case that in a certain fraction of patients there will be adverse
reactions.

More generally, there is now a considerable body of literature on
medical error and poor-quality care.[21] For example, Elizabeth McGlynn
and her colleagues found that only a little over half of patients seeking
care in a nationally diverse study appeared to receive care in accordance with practice guidelines.[22] Other studies suggest that states that
deliver substantially more services actually show lower-quality care
(see figure 4.4). With quality of care now a well-recognized problem,
it is plausible that the incremental care received by the generally healthy

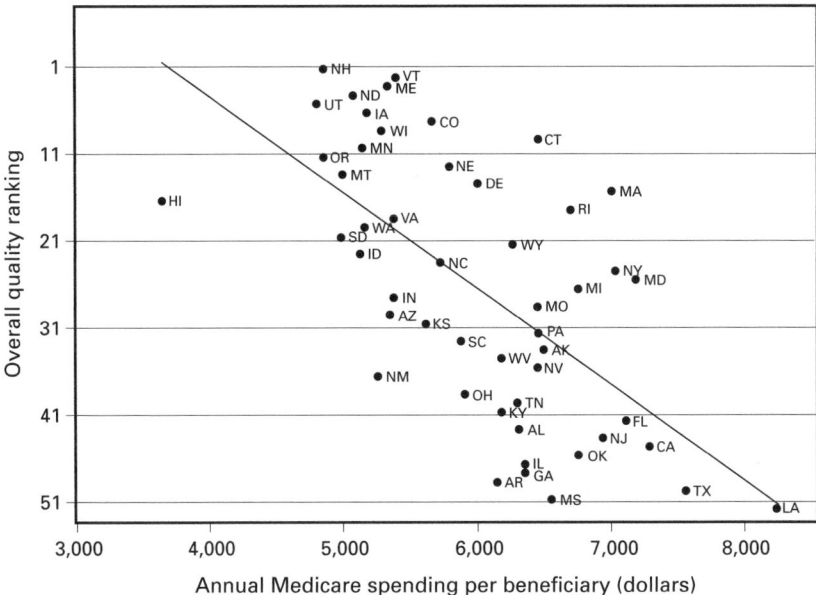

Figure 4.4
Relationship between Quality and Medicare Spending, as Expressed by Overall Quality Ranking
Source: Baicker and Chandra (2004).

people enrolled in the HIE stood as much chance of harming them as helping them. By contrast, the incremental care received by the sick poor may have had a much greater chance of being beneficial.

More Recent Evidence

The HIE was conducted more than a quarter of a century ago, and its cost-sharing provisions emulated the insurance policies of that time. Since then the nature of cost sharing has changed in two ways. First, cost sharing has become differential by provider or drug. Thus, patients now typically pay less to see a physician who is "in network" or to buy a drug that is "on the formulary."

At the time of the HIE, there were no networks of physicians outside of a few prepaid group practices and drug coverage was rare. Insurers today create networks of physicians and drug formularies in order to increase the price elasticity of demand facing physicians and drug manufacturers, thereby increasing the insurers' negotiating power in order to achieve supply prices that more closely resemble competitive prices. The incentive for the physician or the pharmaceutical company to grant a lower price or a discount to be in the network or on the formulary is to obtain a greater volume of business due to the lower patient payment for in-network physicians. Of course, the provider must assume that the profit from the difference in volume between being in and out of the network will offset the magnitude of the discount. Although early networks were heavily influenced by the provider price or the amount of the discount, some insurers are now attempting to account for a physician's quality of care in addition to price when forming their networks.

A second way that cost sharing has changed is the greater use of differential cost sharing by type of service. When the HIE was conducted, cost sharing tended to be applied uniformly to all covered services (with the exception of mental health and dental services).[23] Today, insurance policies have different levels of cost sharing across services—for example, a drug may cost a certain amount per month, a visit may cost another amount per visit, and a hospital admission may cost still a third amount. Also many plans charge patients a higher amount for emergency department visits than office visits, potentially influenced by the finding of the HIE that almost all of the additional emergency department visits in plans with less cost sharing were for minor or nonemergent problems—a finding that has been replicated elsewhere.[24]

Differential cost sharing by service implies that the theoretical framework of welfare economics described in figure 4.1 is too simple because it fails to consider cross-price elasticities. If changing the price of one medical service changes the use of another one, moral hazard may be more or less than would be indicated by only considering the change in the use of the service whose price changed. Indeed, this notion prompted the inclusion of the plan in the HIE that only applied cost sharing to outpatient services and kept inpatient services free to the patient, and the results from this part of the HIE provide some evidence about the size of cross-price elasticities. In this case, cost sharing for outpatient services decreased the use of outpatient services relative to the plan with all services free (not a surprising result), but also decreased the total expenditure; inpatient admission rates also decreased, but by an amount that was statistically insignificant at conventional levels. Thus, in this example taking account of the cross-price elasticity between the outpatient price and the inpatient services did not change the conclusion one would draw from looking at the own-price elasticity of outpatient services in isolation. More recent work on demand prices for drugs, however, suggests that accounting for cross-price elasticities could change the conclusions one would draw from own-price elasticities, especially for cross-price elasticities for certain classes of drugs or certain patients.

Overall, these more recent studies have found that increasing pharmaceutical cost sharing results in the lower utilization of prescribed drugs; that is, own-price elasticities are negative. Haiden Huskamp and her colleagues as well as and Dana Goldman and his colleagues have shown that medications known to be efficacious for certain chronic diseases—such as statins, ACE inhibitors, antihypertensives, and anti-diabetics—are sensitive to the amount of cost sharing.[25]

In the traditional framework this price sensitivity would indicate moral hazard, but other studies find that increased pharmaceutical cost sharing *increases* the use of other medical care services. Stephen Soumerai and his colleagues showed that limiting the number of pre-scriptions in a month in a Medicaid program to three saved money on drugs, but led to offsetting increases elsewhere; in the case of schizo-phrenic patients, the increase in other spending was seventeen times the savings on drugs.[26] Robyn Tamblyn and her colleagues have shown that the imposition of cost sharing for drugs in Quebec decreased the use of "essential" drugs among the elderly and welfare recipients by 15 to 22 percent, which led to an approximate doubling of serious adverse events, defined as hospitalization, nursing home admission, or death, as well as an increase in emergency department visits.[27] Although Tamblyn and her colleagues do not present cost data, the magnitude of the increase in serious adverse events seems likely to have raised the total costs.

Allison Rosen and her colleagues have simulated that it would save money and increase QALYs for Medicare to make ACE inhibitors avail-able at no charge for elderly diabetics when compared with the default cost sharing in the Medicare drug benefit; the induced increase in the use and cost of ACE inhibitors would be more than offset in averted medical costs.[28] John Hsu and his colleagues find that caps on drug benefits for those over the age of sixty-five reduce the compliance with the recommended behavior and thereby reduce drug spending, but worsen the physiological measures of health and raise spending for other medical services, even over a period as short as a year.[29] In their study the increase in nondrug medical costs, largely from in-creased emergency department visits and increased nonelective hospitalizations, is roughly the same magnitude as the induced decrease in drug costs, but could well be greater as time passes, assuming the compliance does not improve and the physiological health worsens.

These empirical findings are strongly suggestive that some individuals, especially those with certain chronic diseases, can be induced by less cost sharing to take actions today that will reduce their future use of medical services and/or improve their future health. An extreme version of this type of policy would be to pay patients to take medications—which is equivalent to imposing a negative demand price. In fact, Directly Observed Therapy programs, in which those with tuberculosis are paid to come to clinics so they can be observed swallowing their prescribed medications, use this method.

Recently, disease management programs have gained in popularity as a mechanism to induce patient compliance. Disease management programs are most commonly created by health plans for patients with chronic diseases such as diabetes. These programs use patient and physician education, patient monitoring, and case management to improve patient management of their own disease as well as achieve patient compliance with clinical guidelines for care, including compliance with prescribed drug regimens and periodic physician visits to check the progress of the disease. They may, for example, involve a nurse calling a patient to remind them to take a prescription or obtain a screening test such as a mammogram. The aims of these programs are to reduce mortality, morbidity, and overall expenditures on medical care. Disease management programs are thus a nonprice mechanism to achieve greater patient compliance; optimal cost sharing, a price mechanism, could be used with the same aims. In other words, disease management programs and demand prices are different tools with similar aims, and there will be an optimal level for each.

In sum, more recent evidence suggests that compliance with drug regimens by patients with certain chronic diseases increases with lower cost sharing and that improved compliance improves health outcomes.[30] In some cases it might save money as well, but even if it does not, the value of the improved health could be worth the cost. After all, many things that health insurance pays for, such as surgical procedures, probably do not save costs over a lifetime, but most people would pay for insurance that covered them for such services because they would want to be treated if they were sick. Lars Osterberg and Terrence Blaschke, in a review article on adherence or compliance, say that "poor adherence to medication regimens accounts for substantial worsening of disease, death, and increased health care costs in the United States," and cite high cost sharing as one reason for poor adherence.[31]

It is always good in this kind of situation to ask why, if lower cost sharing for the care of chronic conditions is a good idea because it improves compliance, it is not observed to a greater degree. The reason is likely because of adverse selection. If consumers could elect to enroll in plans that had lower cost sharing for certain drugs, only those individuals taking those drugs would choose to enroll in health plans that offered such coverage. With time, the result of this selective take-up will be that the additional cost for the coverage would equal the cost of the drugs, since only those taking the drugs would have that type of insurance. Indeed, the additional cost for coverage would likely exceed that of the drugs because the insurance company would tack on a charge for an administrative cost. Something close to that happened historically among the plans that were supplementary to Medicare and covered drugs.[32] A second reason that we do not observe lower cost sharing for the care of chronic conditions is that the majority of Americans obtain health insurance through their employer.[33] Preventing future ill health may save Medicare money, but will not reduce costs for the employer.

New Directions

Once one opens the possibility of differential cost sharing for specific services or drugs, the possibilities for new empirical work are vast.[34] What is the consequence of a lower price for statins but not other drugs? What is the consequence of a lower price for ACE inhibitors, but only for individuals with a cardiac problem? What is the consequence of making physician visits for the routine care of diabetes free?

At a theoretical level, however, one can ask why, if taking a drug or using a service is important for one's health, as it surely is for many chronic diseases, individuals do not comply with a physician's recommendations? A standard rational actor model may explain such behavior in some cases because the benefits from complying, as valued by the patient, may not be that great. Whatever ailed the patient may not have been all that annoying to the individual, or the prescribed treatment may have had little chance of success yet a high chance of side effects. But poor patient compliance is a widespread problem in medicine, and the rational actor model does not seem plausible for many chronic diseases such as diabetes, which if left untreated, can have serious and painful consequences, such as blindness and amputation.

Recent research in behavioral economics may be helpful in explaining such behavior. Much work, both theoretical and empirical, now suggests that individuals have self-control problems that interfere with compliance.[35] A new field of neuroeconomics is just becoming established with relevance to self-control problems.[36] Shane Frederick and his colleagues provide an excellent review of this and much additional literature.[37]

One class of economic models in this domain uses quasi-hyperbolic discounting, such that individuals have a higher discount rate for the present than they do for the future. In a common version of such a model, individuals are assumed to maximize a discounted lifetime utility subject to a lifetime budget constraint, and the lifetime utility is assumed to be:

$$U_t + \beta \sum_{1}^{T-t} \delta^i U_{t+i}. \tag{4.1}$$

δ and β are between zero and one, so that there is a discontinuity in the discount rate between the initial period (δ^0 is assumed to equal 1) and all subsequent periods ($\beta \delta^i$), whereas in the standard model the discount factor is simply δ^i, the special case of the expression in equation (4.1) in which $\beta = 1$.

These models have been applied to cigarette smoking by Jonathan Gruber and Botond Köszegi, with the important results that if individuals have the utility function shown in equation (4.1), welfare would be maximized with much higher cigarette taxes than at present.[38] The welfare gains occur because health benefits accrue to individuals who would otherwise begin to smoke. In effect, the tax is inducing individuals to comply with a no-smoking regime. Further, because smoking is concentrated among low-income individuals, the benefits of not beginning to smoke accrue disproportionately to them. Cigarette excise taxes are thus much less regressive than usually assumed and may even be progressive.

This class of economic models can apply straightforwardly in the context of lowering cost sharing to induce greater compliance.[39] In particular, there may well be cases in which subsidizing certain medical goods or services increases the total medical cost, but also increases health sufficiently such that the benefits outweigh the cost increase.

From a social perspective, the optimum in this case would decrease cost sharing until the marginal health benefit equaled the marginal increase in induced cost.

Discovering opportunities where more extensive coverage of specific services for specific persons results in overall cost savings and/or benefits to health that outweigh any additional costs is an exciting future research agenda.

What We Know and Don't Know about Cost Sharing—and So What?

A great deal of empirical research over the years has established that individuals respond to demand prices in the form of cost sharing for medical services. In other words, insurance policies specify how much a person must pay when using medical services, and the amount the policies specify affects the average person's use of medical services. This effect on use, moreover, appears to hold throughout the income distribution; it is not just the poor who are affected.

Our understanding of the effects of cost sharing is best for cost sharing that changes proportionately for all medical services, or when the patient pays a certain percentage of the cost of any medical service regardless of the type. For that kind of insurance, higher cost-sharing requirements induce less use of services—some of which would have been medically efficacious ones.

For many reasons it is problematic to infer welfare consequences from observed behavior in medical care, and therefore many health economists find direct measures of the process of care or health outcomes more credible for inferring the welfare effects of alternative cost-sharing arrangements. When examined in this light, the available evidence suggests that for most people, the reduced use induced by greater cost sharing does not much affect their health for either good or ill. Because greater cost sharing induces less use of efficacious services, one can infer that it also reduces the use of some harmful services and that for most people these two effects seem to roughly cancel each other out. For those who are sick and poor, however, it appears that the reduced use of services leads to worse health. And although this chapter has focused on the amount of initial cost sharing, if any, a lack of any insurance is the extreme form of cost sharing (being uninsured is equivalent to 100 percent cost sharing), and there is evidence that no insurance adversely affects health.[40]

Much insurance, though, no longer has the type of cost sharing that varies demand prices proportionately for all services. Instead, it has various amounts of copayment (fixed dollar amounts) for different types of services such as physician visits or drugs. Evidence on this type of cost sharing has shown that the size of these dollar amounts affects use; the greater the dollar amount that patients are required to pay, the less the use of the service. For example, the more persons have to pay for pharmaceuticals, the fewer drugs they use.

We know much less about the effects of changes in use of medical services due to differential cost sharing on the total cost of medical services and health. In the case of drugs for certain chronic diseases, it appears that health can be adversely affected by higher copayments and that the use of other medical services may rise as a result. We also do not know what the optimal amount of cost sharing should be in an insurance policy. It seems likely that the optimal amount will vary across persons and specific medical goods and services, but work is just beginning on what cost sharing would be found in a more nearly optimal insurance contract. Further research on this topic will likely be important to informing how to structure appropriate incentives to encourage demand for high-quality, effective medical care.

Notes

1. Physicians' Working Group for Single-Payer National Health Insurance (2003).

2. Cogan et al. (2005); Friedman (1991).

3. Ellis and McGuire (1986).

4. Blumenthal (2006). A deductible is the amount the patient must pay before the insurance policy pays any benefits—for example, $250 per year. A copayment is a fixed amount per service—for example, $15 for a physician visit or a month's supply of a drug. Coinsurance is a percentage of the bill that a patient must pay—instance, 20 percent.

5. Kaiser Family Foundation and Health Research Education Trust (2005).

6. See, for example, Phelps (2003, chapter 10); Feldstein (1999, chapter 6); Zweifel and Breyer (1997, chapter 6).

7. Arrow (1963); Pauly (1968); Zeckhauser (1970).

8. For evidence that physician payment affects physicians' actions, see McGuire (2000, this volume); Newhouse (2002). In addition, the wide variation across areas in how illness is treated suggests that treatment is affected by a good deal more than what an informed patient's preferences would dictate. See figure 4.4; Phelps (2000).

9. See Sloan (1995).

10. de Meza (1983); Nyman (1999b).

11. More technically, the usual analysis presumes either the approximately constant marginal utility of income or an income-compensated demand function. In practice, however, income-compensated demand curves are rarely used, though the RAND Health Insurance Experiment effectively did use income-compensated demand curves.

12. Hurley (2000).

13. Newhouse and the Insurance Experiment Group (1993).

14. More precisely, the ceiling was the minimum of $1,000, or 5, 10, or 15 percent of the family income; families were randomly assigned to the percentage of income. Medical spending per person today is about six times medical spending in the late 1970s, but it would not be correct to say that the $1,000 limit in the experiment would be equivalent to a $6,000 limit now because the nature of medical services has changed considerably. See Berndt et al. (2000).

15. The coinsurance rate was set at 95 rather than 100 percent to give the families a financial incentive to file a claim.

16. See, for example, Roemer et al. (1975).

17. Physician office visits were not covered at all in many insurance policies at that time.

18. The precision was sufficient to rule out clinically significant differences among almost all measures. In addition to the blood pressure result described in the text, there were a few other differences of note among the plans. Corrected vision was slightly better among the free plan participants, and free care participants were more likely to have decayed teeth filled. The prevalence of serious symptoms was less in the free plan, although it is hard to know what to make of that because medical care cannot prevent many serious symptoms. Cutting in the other direction, the frequency of disability days was less on the cost-sharing plans.

19. More specifically, the vulnerable groups with increased mortality are those who, at the beginning of the experiment, were in both the lowest 20 percent of the income distribution and the top 25 percent of diastolic blood pressure readings.

20. For a discussion of the validity of the measures, see Newhouse and the Insurance Experiment Group (1993) and the literature cited there.

21. On medical error, see Institute of Medicine (1999). On poor-quality care, see Institute of Medicine (2001); McGlynn et al. (2003).

22. McGlynn et al. (2003).

23. Dental services then (and now) were generally covered by a separate insurance policy.

24. Hsu et al. (2006a); Selby et al. (1996).

25. Huskamp et al. (2003); Goldman et al. (2004). Consistent with patient sensitivity to price, Huskamp et al. (2005) find that implementing a three-tier formulary, which creates price differentials between pharmaceuticals within a therapeutic class such as antidepressants to give patients a financial incentive to select certain brand drugs over others, results in patients switching to the lower-tier (cheaper) drug within a therapeutic class along with increased out-of-pocket spending by patients on pharmaceuticals.

26. Soumerai et al. (1994); Soumerai et al. (1991).

27. Tamblyn et al. (2001).

28. Rosen et al. (2005).

29. Hsu et al. (2006b).

30. Fendrick et al. (2001).

31. Osterberg and Blaschke (2005).

32. McCormack et al. (1996).

33. Agency for Health Care Research and Quality (2003).

34. This section draws on Newhouse (2006).

35. Phelps (1968); Thaler and Shefrin (1981); Ainslie (1991); Akerlof (1991); Laibson (1997); O'Donoghue and Rabin (1999a, 1999b).

36. Work in neuroeconomics indicates that time-inconsistent behavior may have a biological basis, in that different parts of the brain process behavior dealing with immediate gratification or avoidance of harm than behavior consistent with the rational calculation of future consequences; see Bernheim and Rangel (2004).

37. Frederick, Loewenstein, and O'Donoghue (2002). Pricing to achieve improved compliance is somewhat analogous to those cases considered by della Vigna and Malmendier (2004), who show that if the consumption of a good today raises the future demand, a profit-maximizing firm will price the good today below the marginal cost, and conversely.

38. Gruber and Köszegi (2001, 2004).

39. The use of models such as those in equation (4.1) is but one use of behavioral economics in health economics; other applications of behavioral economics to health care are discussed in an insightful work by Richard Frank (2006).

40. Institute of Medicine (2004); Levy and Meltzer (2004).

5

Adverse Selection and Moral Hazard: Implications for Health Insurance Markets

Mark V. Pauly

Research shows that people who do not have any health insurance or who have less generous health insurance use less and lower-quality medical care than those who have more generous insurance. This reduction occurs not just for low-income and low socioeconomic status people; it also occurs, to a similar extent, for upper-middle-income, well-educated people.[1] Much of this chapter is about aspects of health insurance and consumer behavior that we do not know, but we do know this: people do not just use medical care based on how sick they are, and what doctors order is not just based on their medical training; in both cases, insurance matters.

While the fact of a positive relationship, other things equal, between insurance and medical spending is beyond doubt, what is less well-known is what it all means. Specifically, why has this relationship materialized, and is it a good or bad thing? How people behave when it comes to insurance, and whether that relationship is efficient or equitable, is my topic for this chapter.

By "efficient," here I mean economically efficient: not just the minimum cost for whatever is done but also the close matching of both care and insurance coverage with consumers' true demands (given the income they have). With risk present (and without it, there would be no reason to have insurance), what consumers ultimately should obtain is assumed to be based on what would maximize their expected or average utility over the possible health states that might occur. Equity as usual cannot be crisply defined, since it depends on value judgments that are not universal. The main equity criteria I will use are: horizontal equity—people who are the same should be treated the same; vertical equity—transfers if made will be from the better off to the less well off; and fair distribution of income—the distribution of well-being in society will be in accord with social preferences as expressed through a society's chosen institutions.

There are two apparently obvious (but actually quite complex) alternative explanations for the observed positive relationship between coverage and cost. One explanation supposes that the decision to buy insurance, and how much to buy, is independent of the person's expense risk level. If so, then larger spending or a larger quantity of care obtained by people with more insurance (compared to those with less or none) represents a response to the lower user price associated with more generous coverage; this phenomenon is usually termed moral hazard.[2] The other possibility is that each person consumes the same amount of care whether insured or not, but people who expect to get more benefit from insurance buy more generous coverage. If they do so in a setting in which the premium they would be charged for a given nominal policy is the same regardless of the risk, this behavior would be called adverse selection. In reality, of course, both behaviors could occur simultaneously.[3]

Compared to a theoretically ideal insurance market (whether feasible or not), both behaviors are undesirable and therefore represent a prima facie case for inefficiency. But the possible inefficiency takes different forms and has different degrees of salience in terms of practical public policy, rather than the abstract theory of welfare economics, depending on the cause. So it will be useful to both spell out what might be happening as well as discuss how theory and evidence ought correctly to be interpreted.

I will take a particular viewpoint on the relative importance in the United States of each potential source of inefficiency and inequity. I conclude that competitive insurance markets, undistorted and (for people who are not poor) unsubsidized, can deal relatively well with potential inefficiency from either moral hazard or adverse selection, with the case being somewhat clearer for moral hazard. Adverse selection will remain when governments choose for (sometimes good) equity reasons to alter the market. Competitive insurance markets will not be perfect, but their flaws will be both small and hard to correct.

Ideal Insurance

Both moral hazard and adverse selection arise from imperfect information. Somewhat surprisingly for those of us programmed to distrust insurers, it is perfect information for insurers that will make markets work efficiently. Specifically, in an ideal world, insurers need to know both an insured's risk level and the state of health that actually occurs. By "risk," I mean everything that would help to predict the person's future expected or average claims for a given insurance policy, not only for the illnesses they are likely to have, but also whether the person is a hypochondriac or a stoic, tends to use expensive or cheap doctors, or goes for generic or brand-name products. By "state of health," I mean how sick the person actually becomes: whether the upper respiratory infection is a cold or bacterial pneumonia, whether the knee pain is mild or incapacitating, and/or whether the need to urinate is really frequent or occasional.

Then ideal insurance has two characteristics. For a given level of coverage, its premium is tailored to the person's risk level: high if the person has a health condition or is predisposed to seek costly care no matter what; and low if the person is healthy and a frugal consumer of medical care. Then, when illness strikes, the insurance benefit is a fixed dollar amount, a so-called indemnity, conditional on the person's state of health. That is, given prior determination of the average indemnity, the insurer sends a check, which is smaller than average if the illness is less serious and larger if it is more serious. The "extent of coverage" can then be defined by the average size of this payment. Given the person's risk level and the state of health, the premium increases the higher the level of the average indemnity.

Buyers of insurance choose the size of the indemnity by comparing the costs and benefits of additional medical care in each health situation. Basically the consumer decides how much medical care will be worth the cost (in terms of a higher premium) should a particular illness occur, determines the total cost of treating that illness, and sets the indemnity payment to cover much of that cost.

If buyers could obtain insurance at premiums that contain no administrative costs (actuarially fair insurance), they would set the indemnity payment for each illness at different levels, equal to the total cost of care that they would choose if that illness strikes. If the amount is set correctly, the coverage would be complete because the buyer would not want to buy more care than the indemnity would pay for and would not incur costs that the indemnity payment did not cover. Put slightly differently, the buyer would be willing to incur higher premiums for more generous indemnity benefits as long as those benefits covered their costs.

In reality, insurance does have positive administrative costs, and thus even a risk-averse person might be willing to bear some out-of-pocket costs by agreeing to deductibles, reckoning that the savings from reducing the administrative costs of paying claims that the deductible avoids would offset increasing the risk of having to cover the deductible if illness should strike. The higher the administrative cost (or the difference between premiums and expected benefits), the higher the deductible one would choose.

What is so great about this arrangement? First, at least in theory, if people are risk averse, they will generally want to pay for the insurance rather than remain uninsured, because they will all prefer to pay a premium in advance rather than experience the risk of paying out of pocket for costly care in the unlucky event that illness strikes. This willingness to buy insurance will be true even for high risks: their premiums will be higher even at the same indemnity levels because their illnesses are more frequent. Since they would have been willing to pay for the care that the insurance will now cover, they must be able to afford the insurance premium that would just pay for that care. Second, assuming that consumers know what they are doing, the amount of care and the level of expense represent an appropriate balance between the value of medical care and its cost: the indemnity level is set based on a trade-off between coverage that will pay for more or better care and the higher premium, but will only pay for care that is worth what it costs. And once the illness happens, if the indemnity is set correctly in the first place, there will be no desire to spend more than intended because any benefit from additional or more costly care, which offers fewer side effects or is more likely to present future illness, will not be worth the full additional cost that the person would have to pay out of pocket.

When the dust clears, everyone will have insurance, expenses will be almost fully covered, and spending will be at the efficient level where the marginal benefit equal the marginal cost; things will be efficient. And every dollar spent on health care will be consumer directed.

Could alternative insurance systems be better than this perfect indemnity? Sometimes the claim is made that managed care insurance is superior in theory to fee-for-service insurance. But compared to this ideally insured fee-for-service system, this claim must be wrong. Perfect indemnities are perfect. More to the point, one can either describe the perfect indemnity insurance as a fee for service with a benefit equal to the indemnity or as managed care insurance where the managed care guideline is the amount of care that the perfect indemnity would pay for. With perfect knowledge, the two types of insurance are equivalent in all but name.

Some Impostors

Moral hazard and adverse selection arise when the insurer does not have the kind of information just discussed. Before I get into the details on inefficiency and the evaluation associated with this, it is worth noting that moral hazard and adverse selection each have a mimic— one that is surely different from the genuine article in terms of a value judgment. These mimics can arise even if the information is perfect, and in contrast to real moral hazard, they do not imply that the increase in use is inefficient. One possibility is that higher use, given risk, may not be a response to the lower price of care but rather only a response to the receipt of insurance benefits. The notion here is that compared to the absence of insurance, a person with insurance ends up with more wealth or income when sick (because one gets an insurance check or payment) and less wealth when well (because one pays premiums but gets nothing in return).[4] It is plausible, but by no means assured, that the mere receipt of a transfer in the sick state, even one perfectly attuned to the person's valuation of the benefits from care, will increase the amount of care that the person would seek; in jargon, there could be an "income effect" that will boost use in the sick state (and by mirror image, depress use in the well state). It is also surely possible, but by no means assured, that the former will outweigh the latter, and then on balance, people with more insurance will use more care. In effect, because insurance makes me richer when I am sicker, that extra wealth may cause me to increase the value I place on more or better care, so I will choose to use more than I would without insurance. And if I do not get serious illnesses but only mild ones, being impoverished by today's health insurance premiums may cause me to cut back a little on my care for the illnesses I do get. If the positive income effect in the sick state more than offsets the negative effect in the not-so-sick one, the net effect will be an increase in the net use of care associated with having insurance compared to no insurance.

John Nyman at the University of Minnesota (following on earlier work by David de Meza and me) has explored this case in detail.[5] Nyman discusses the theoretical point that this insurance-related increase in use from income effects is not inefficient because it comes only from the effects of shifts in levels of wealth, not from incentives to consume care worth less than its cost.

The other mimicking case arises if insurance premiums are based on risk, which is perfectly measured, but the people who happen to be higher risk also happen to be more intrinsically risk averse. There is some theoretical basis for expecting this kind of correlation. Then, given a level of insurer administrative costs, the less risk-averse buyer might choose less comprehensive coverage. Of course, it is also possible that the reverse is true—that the lower risks happen to be more risk averse. There is evidence for the "favorable risk selection" hypothesis.[6] I will not treat this case in more detail, and instead usually assume the more traditional adverse selection model, where risk aversion is independent of risk, as what will generate any important selection effects at all. But the reverse possibility should also be kept in mind.

Moral Hazard and Little White Lies

What if insurers cannot precisely and accurately determine how sick I am? Then I would worry, under a pure indemnity policy that paid a given dollar amount based on the observation of apparently different health states, that I could be really sick, attach high value to care, and yet be harmed by being mistakenly classified into a state that generates a low indemnity payment because it appears to be one of mild illness and cheap treatment. I would worry about underprotection when I am sicker in reality than I look to the insurer, and also worry about paying the cost of overprotection when I am healthier than I appear. In order to avoid the chance of high out-of-pocket expenses or insufficient care in such cases of mistakes, I might instead prefer insurance that makes the payment based on what I and my doctor agree to do in terms of spending on treatment, viewing this as a reasonably close proxy for how sick I am.

But while such "service benefits" insurance—insurance that defines its benefits in terms of the payment of the cost of medical services—at little or no out-of-pocket expense to the insured at the time services are received provides better risk protection than indemnity insurance, it opens up a possible issue of inefficiency. Specifically, suppose that I can get higher benefits, which surely are worth something, by pretending to be sicker than I really am and in need of more or better care than I really do. If I can get away with this, good for me. But if everyone behaves as I do, we will all find that the premiums we are being charged rise. In effect, I now face out-of-pocket prices that are zero or low for additional mildly beneficial yet more costly care, and I may rationally seek such care (with my doctor as a willing coconspirator), even though I am not really that sick and do not "need" it in the economic sense of valuing an additional dollar's worth of care at a dollar or more. This is moral hazard, and it will lead to a positive correlation between the generosity of coverage and the use and total expense for medical care.

A way to diminish this inefficiency is to pull insurance coverage away from comprehensive levels, and to do so even if the administrative cost is zero. Putting more consumer "skin in the game" (financial, not dermatologic) is then a sensible thing for a person to want in an insurance policy, reckoning that compared to the higher insurance premiums and high total medical care costs of complete coverage, the loss of some modest protection against risk is worth the lower premium and lower average total spending from a less comprehensive policy. The key point to be made here, however, is that high cost sharing in insurance is not intrinsically desirable; quite to the contrary, it interferes with the risk protection goal that was the main reason for having insurance in the first place. We should therefore not be eager to have high cost sharing in health insurance; rather we should only use it, kicking and screaming, if other less painful methods to limit benefits to care that is worth its cost (and no more) have failed. Cost sharing may well end up being the best game in town, but it is not a happy game.

There is a sharp edge to the pro-cost-sharing argument, which policymakers, physicians, and even some insurers, who should know better, try energetically to avoid mentioning. For someone with a typical illness, it is often possible to render a great deal of care that will do the person some good, but will cost a lot; there will be care that is unequivocally beneficial, but that is not worth the cost. If the person gets utility from the health produced by medical care yet also from other consumption, there will often be a close trade-off. Not always, there may only be one useful treatment for a fractured femur, and people may always want broken bones to be treated (though not necessarily hairline fractures). The need to deal with such care of low but definitely positive benefit surely is possible, and is certain to materialize at some point.

The classic example is the more intensive use of a harmless diagnostic test, which will yield more useful information on average and do no harm, cost a lot per piece of new information, and thus be undesirable from an economic, but not a medical, viewpoint. This is needed care, but care that is not needed enough. It is this kind of mildly beneficial though costly care that is efficiently sacrificed because of the ideal treatment of moral hazard in health insurance. So efficient cost sharing must harm health, just not "that much" relative to cost savings.

Yet this is a hard case to make. Who wants to market insurance that will make people sicker (though richer)? So even advocates of high cost-sharing consumer-directed health plans gloss over true moral hazard and its optimal control.

How should moral hazard be controlled? I begin by assuming, in this day and age, that consumers have the final say on what care they get; physicians advise, but they cannot order. Let us take the most extreme case of total consumer ignorance. Suppose that consumers, even when advised by wise and kindly physicians, simply cannot tell which care yields higher marginal health benefits and which yields lower ones. But let us assume that the world is not perverse: if they cannot eliminate low-value care, at least they do not by mistake consistently cut out high-value care either. Rather, the mix of care between high and low true clinical value, and the amount of those values, remains constant as people choose different amounts of spending. In economic jargon, the marginal health product of a dollar of spending remains constant. If the best that can be done therefore is to decide how much health I want to buy, I will not want to spend an unlimited amount. I will reckon instead that beyond some point, the constant additional amount of health I get from spending another dollar on health care through health insurance is worth less to me than the other good and useful items of consumption I will have to sacrifice to get it.

That is, I am certain to experience the diminishing marginal *value* of health spending, even if I do not experience the diminishing marginal health *benefit*. I can have too much of a good thing with zero cost sharing, even if the marginal health product of medical care does not diminish. To prevent that from happening, I will rationally and nobly choose insurance with positive cost sharing. In this world of rational behavior in the face of indiscriminate ignorance, I can at least keep my insurance simple: my ideal cost sharing will be positive, and it will be uniform across the board, the same for all types of care whose marginal benefit I cannot distinguish.

More specifically, I will increase my cost sharing if the sum of what I lose, the value of health expected to be foregone because of my reduction in the use of medical care plus the value of the increased financial risk, exceeds what I gain: the sum of the lower premiums and the lower average out-of-pocket payments. The more price responsive or price elastic my demand for health, the higher the level of uniform cost sharing I will choose.[7]

In this simple case, is cost sharing a good thing? The short answer of course is yes—up to a point, and especially up to the optimal point at which greater exposure to risk just offsets the additional waste associated with care worth less than its cost.

Part of this conclusion contains an implication that only an economist could love or at least accept: compared to free care, positive cost sharing is desirable even though it worsens health. This follows because the value of worse health is more than offset by the value of increased wealth, or at least disposable income. So to a true believer in economics, the thought that high cost sharing might harm health is what is to be expected; if raising cost sharing to its current level from zero did not do at least some harm, it should have been raised even further until we hit the zone where trade-offs are occurring. That higher cost sharing would cut care that is somewhat effective for health is by no means a fatal flaw. If the care meant life or death with a probability of close to one, it would be a different story, but as seen below, moral hazard effects on the use of care in such critical settings have never been a part of any advocated policy.

What Do We Know and What Do We Think We Can Know about Cost Sharing?

All of this is theory thus far; what do we know about what higher levels of cost sharing actually do to health, and is there information that might allow us to go beyond the perfect ignorance assumption of the constant and positive marginal health product of all medical care spending?

The mother lode of information on the effect of cost sharing on spending and health, as mentioned in previous chapters, remains the RAND Health Insurance Experiment (HIE) reported in the early 1980s.[8] The HIE assigned people to different levels of cost sharing, ranging from zero (free care) to 95 percent of all medical expenses up to 15 percent of a household's income.[9] Drugs were insured in all plans.

There is considerable controversy (and discomfort) about what this experiment really said about cost sharing and health outcomes. One partisan and incomplete summary as part of a negative review of the politically charged Health Savings Account program is this:

The landmark RAND Health Insurance Experiment . . . , which examined the effects of cost sharing, confirmed the observation that when consumers face cost sharing they consume fewer services. Studies of the RAND experiment found that cost sharing also reduced the likelihood of receiving effective medical care, particularly by low-income children and adults. Even higher-income children and adults had a lower probability of receiving effective medical services than those in the "free care" plan.[10]

While true, this summary only conveys part of the story as represented by the consensus summary of those who actually managed the HIE:

Our results show that the 40 percent increase in services in the free care plan had little or no measurable effect on health status for the average adult. . . . Restricted activity days fell with cost sharing [but] only the sick poor [6 percent of the population] were adversely affected. . . . It is highly improbable that there were beneficial effects [of free care on rare conditions] that we failed to detect. We can rule out any important effects on the General Health Index, our best summary measure. . . . A one-time blood pressure screening exam [for poor high risks] achieved most of the gains in blood pressure that free care achieved.[11]

The HIE seems strongly to say that serious negative effects on health from cost sharing are unlikely for the great bulk of the population. Cost sharing is not for everyone (in contrast to the view of those who favor Health Savings Accounts), but some of it is for almost everyone.[12]

Why such confusion about the conclusion (beyond the obvious temptation for political spin)? The HIE tried to assess the relationship between medical spending and the effectiveness of care for health in two ways: by measuring the differences in health outcomes for people with different health insurance plans, and by examining differences in the process, as measured by the clinical appropriateness of care used by different groups. The main problem is that the messages from the two different ways are not consistent.

The message on actual observed overall health outcomes is that except for the approximately 6 percent of the sample who were low-income people in poor initial health, there was little impact on any of the dozens of health indicators that could be linked to variations in cost sharing. Only vision correction and oral health were different; everything else was indistinguishable statistically. A further look at whether the use that was reduced by cost sharing was less strongly related to health based on a priori clinical judgment yielded more mixed results. Cost sharing did cause people to cut emergency room use by a larger proportion when the condition that prompted use was less urgent. But for the use of antibiotics, the use of hospitals as an inpatient, and episodes of ambulatory care, cost sharing had the same proportional effect whether clinical opinion suggested relatively high or low average medical effectiveness. That is, cost sharing caused people to forego care that clinicians judged to be effective as well as care that clinicians judged not to be effective, and to about the same extent for both. The inconsistency is clear: if the clinical judgments were valid, how do we explain why people who used much less effective care were still as healthy?

The only explanation of which I am aware that has been offered by some is that the care that was not regarded as effective was worse than that: it was so positively harmful that it just offset the good effects of the other care.[13] This tortured logic either implies enormous iatrogenic injury or that the effectiveness of the effective care was not all that great. Perhaps the bad health effects would have occurred outside the five-year window of the HIE, but the HIE was designed to measure health outcomes and explore clinical judgments that should show results in the short term.

My own conclusion is that although there is still much that is puzzling, I think it plausible that foregone care, whether labeled effective or ineffective, did have positive but small benefits—too small to measure and perhaps not in the form of health benefits as they are usually conceived. It is, after all, hard to prove a positive effect of anything on all-cause population health. Even the positive health effects of miracle drugs that lower cholesterol or blood pressure tend to disappear in the face of competing health risks at the population level.

Moreover, we need to have limited expectations. It is not true that "economic theory suggests that there should have been a greater reduction in ineffective care" from cost sharing.[14] Economic theory would not have suggested that there should be any positive amount of care used that was known in advance to be really and truly ineffective (and inconvenient) or harmful. One possibility is that the marginal benefit curves for two types of care were as shown in Figure 5.1. Note that in the care type A case, the marginal benefit is always greater at any

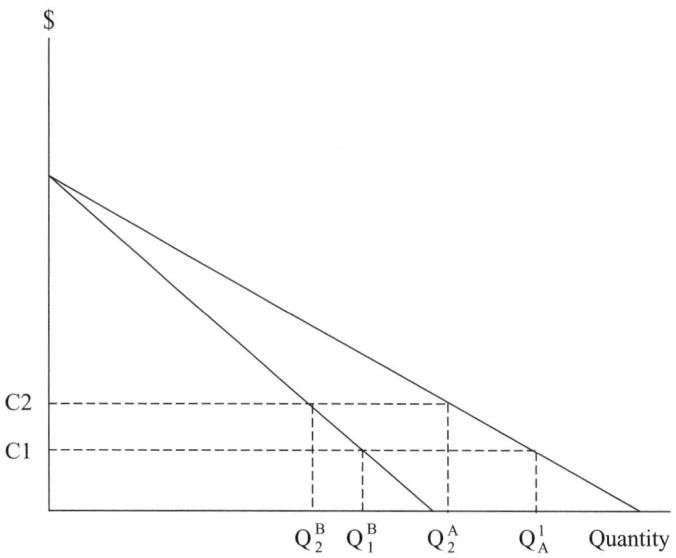

Figure 5.1
Effects of a Change in Cost Sharing for Services with Different Marginal Benefits

quantity (or expenditure) than in the care type B case. But if the cost sharing were raised from C1 to C2, both care types experience the same proportional reduction.

The interpretation of these mixed and confusing data in the policy discussion has been interesting. Opponents of high-deductible insurance, as noted above, have frequently quoted the RAND result on a cost-sharing-induced reduction on the use of some types of supposedly effective care. What is surprising is not that opponents ignored the absence of any negative effect on health in spite of the lower use but that even advocates of high-deductible insurance have been quiet about the negative health effects on low-income high risks. Perhaps that is because advocates wish to argue, and some do, that high-deductible plans can actually lead to improved health as care becomes more consumer directed. That hypothesis is also not supported by the evidence from the HIE. The care whose use is encouraged or deterred by cost sharing in the usual range just does not materially affect the health of the typical middle-class household one way or the other.

A more general "zero-measured health effects" hypothesis is not without its own exceptions. There is some good evidence that especially for the poor and elderly but even for the lower-middle class, being wholly without any insurance is harmful to health. Taking Medicaid away from the poor makes them sick, and going on Medicare by a lower-middle-class person who formerly was uninsured does improve health. But no one has ever used moral hazard as an assertion for advocating that people be totally uninsured; moral hazard is an assertion for limited coverage, not zero coverage. The primary policy assertion was that the coverage of the upper-middle class who were induced by tax distortions to choose more generous coverage with lower cost sharing should be reduced, with potentially beneficial effects on medical care spending and modest harm to the health outcomes for a population already quite healthy.[15]

The other empirical issue that the HIE illuminated was the actual value of the demand elasticity for medical care. For most services, the elasticity seems similar (at about 0.2 in absolute value). It appears to be somewhat lower than that level for inpatient care especially for children, and somewhat higher for dental care and outpatient mental health care. The variation in responsiveness is important because in an argument analogous to the one already discussed, it is possible to show that optimal insurance to control moral hazard should involve coinsurance percentages that vary directly with demand responsiveness or elasticity for a given configuration of risk.[16] Absent regulation, actual insurance seems to follow the pattern of the lowest out-of-pocket payment for hospital inpatient care, and higher cost sharing for dental care and outpatient mental health care—a rough positive correlation with elasticity. The market appears to have yielded a generally rational pattern of coverage. That is, private insurance markets seem to deal reasonably well with the trade-off between risk spreading and incentives for the efficient choice of care; no intervention to encourage or discourage cost sharing among the middle class seems necessary.

But demand responsiveness is not the only thing that matters. The easiest exception to understand is a type of care that has substantial "cost offsets": that whatever its own cost, it lowers the use and cost of other insured care. Highly effective preventive care would be a good example. In this case, we may want insurance to cause moral hazard, especially if the care producing cost offsets is itself uncomfortable or unattractive.[17] Obviously, cost sharing should be lower for care with larger cost offsets, and less obviously, cost sharing should be lower for preventive care with a higher own-price responsiveness of demand, because (in effect) lower cost sharing is more effective in producing cost offsets in such cases.

There is also some more recent evidence for particular medical conditions and particular kinds of treatments—for example, drug therapy for asymptomatic chronic conditions and especially high blood pressure—that moderate cost sharing does cause people who are not poor to fail to obtain or fill prescriptions for which there is strong clinical evidence of a health benefit.[18] The most common conditions are ones like high blood pressure and high cholesterol where most of the effect on health will be in the distant future, so the evidence from the HIE is not necessarily contradicted; it found that effects for high blood pressure and effective treatments for high cholesterol were not available for most of the period it covered.

But some of the data do suggest (though not prove) larger impacts on health in these selected cases, which raises a new puzzle: If these treatments are indeed highly beneficial at the margin, why do patients forego them at cost-sharing levels below the real cost of the treatment even when there are no major cost offsets? From a cost-effectiveness standpoint, to say that the treatment is sufficiently effective to justify its cost is to say that the value of the health benefits to those for whom it is being prescribed should, from a fully informed perspective, be greater than the full cost, and therefore definitely greater than any fraction of that cost. So nonpoor patients should always seek the treatment even without insurance, and surely should do so if insurance covers any part of the cost.

The all-purpose answer, of course, is patient ignorance. Some patients do not realize or appreciate how beneficial these treatments are, and hence (apparently) value them less than the $50 copay (for instance) to which they might be subjected, even when their incomes are high enough that they could make such payments and not be pushed into financial misery.

The most obvious solution to ignorance is information. Perfectly informed physicians should persuade their patients of the benefits of these highly effective treatments to such an extent that they would not forego them for a small cost. The underuse of high-benefit treatments by patients already under care means that physicians are not acting as effective patient agents.

But there is another option. If reducing the copay from $50 to $5 would get the patient to stay on the drug, and if it would cost more than $45 per month to get physicians to be sufficiently persuasive, such "benefits-based cost sharing" might make sense.[19] Rather than impose uniform copayment or coinsurance, it might make sense to reduce copays for those types of treatments that patients undervalue, and raise them for those treatments that patients overvalue, all relative to the true measures of benefit and cost.

Undervaluation alone is not enough to lead to a low copay.[20] Demand responsiveness will still be important. Given two services of equal but equally undervalued marginal benefit at a uniform copay, it will still make the most sense to set a lower copay for the one with a less responsive demand. Yet compared to an otherwise-similar situation in which patients do not underconsume, with poor information coinsurance should be lower at each level of demand responsiveness. That is, ignorance of this type suggests lower copays than with good information, but the optimal copay for a high-elasticity service might still be high. There surely also are examples where ignorance causes patients to overuse some types of care; the symmetrical contention here is that copays should be higher but should still vary directly with the responsiveness. Since patient ignorance might actually push use that would have been excessive because of moral hazard back closer to more cost-effective levels, it would be desirable to increase coverage because such an increase would improve financial protection without causing so large an increase in care with small benefits relative to the cost. That is, the economic reason to lower cost sharing for the care of low misperceived benefit but high actual benefit—benefits-based cost sharing—is not so much to encourage more use of care to improve health but rather because greater financial protection is now possible with less waste. And there is no reason to lower cost sharing for high-benefit care that is fully appreciated, relative to that for other care of positive but lower benefit.

An evenhanded treatment of moral hazard regards it as neither good nor evil, but rather as a phenomenon to be managed with potentially varying levels of cost sharing. To do so well from a clinical perspective has heavy requirements in terms of research knowledge. One needs to know how care affects health outcomes and what its cost is—the evidence-based medicine and cost-effectiveness information. But one also needs to know how insurance affects the use of care and how people feel about financial protection. This means that medical information alone is not sufficient to make a judgment about cost sharing. For many types of care, even medical information on effectiveness (the benefit from of the evidence-based medicine that all seek yet few have found) is not enough; the information on differential moral hazard and the value of risk protection that is also needed is even scarcer.

Given the imperfect current state of knowledge about differences in both effectiveness and responsiveness, plans with fairly simple cost-sharing rules therefore may be efficient today, but the door should always be kept open for modifications. Someone who advocates imposing or encouraging generally lower cost sharing than people now choose, based on medical benefits grounds, does not presently have a strong knowledge base for an actual empirical determination of ideal levels of cost sharing. Not that the advocate is necessarily wrong, but no one can prove things one way or the other. For the middle class and persons more affluent than this, public policy should be aggressively neutral, favoring through regulation or taxation neither high nor low cost sharing, neither uniformity in coverage nor heterogeneity, and neither requiring nor forbidding the coverage of specific services. Competitive insurers, however, should be encouraged to vary cost sharing when they think there is adequate evidence to do so; the market can then sort out whether such experiments have good payoffs in terms of improved risk protection and more cost-effective care.

Lower-income people, especially those at high risk, reluctantly prefer high cost sharing if they must pay for insurance with no assistance. But community concern about the underuse of highly beneficial care suggests most obviously that individual actions may need to be altered by the use of targeted subsidies paid by taxpayers, and that taxpayer preferences about health and financial risk ought to matter to some extent at the margin. In principle, the subsidies could be limited to plans with specific kinds of cost sharing that most encourage effective care, but our current poor state of knowledge indicates that using public policy to foster highly specific designs cannot lead to good design, though it can lead to endless arguments and aggressive lobbying.

These thoughts suggest that the current tax treatment of medical savings accounts linked to high-deductible health plans is not ideal. While there is some flexibility, the laws limit tax breaks for savings accounts to plans with deductibles above specified minimum levels, without evidence that the deductible levels specified in the law correspond to efficient levels for many people. While current tax policy favoring high-deductible plans probably has little chance of harm to higher-income families, high cost sharing may be significantly harmful to the health of lower-income people, especially those at high risk. A logical though politically charged implication of this view is that such low-income persons should perhaps not be eligible for the tax advantages that encourage such plans because of the potential for harm; lower-income people should get different kinds of tax breaks.[21] Of course, since tax deductibility means much less to lower-income people than to higher-income ones, the current Health Savings Account policy should have little effect on them in any case; few of the RAND HIE 6 percent should select such plans. Still, offering low-income people tax credits that are limited to high-deductible plans seems unlikely to produce an efficient outcome (though it might improve equity).

Adverse Selection

While moral hazard arises because insurers do not have good information on what illnesses have already happened to a person, adverse selection occurs when insurers do not have good information about that person's risk of future illness, and about any other factors that might affect the person's future claims under a given insurance policy.

The adverse selection story is simple. Suppose that individuals know their risk levels, but insurers do not. Facing necessarily identical premiums per unit of coverage, lower-risk individuals will initially choose less generous coverage than higher-risk individuals. If the premium for each policy is then linked by competition to the risk of the people who choose it, the premium for more generous policies will rise above one that would have been based on the average risk, potentially provoking departures from this policy by somewhat lower risks. More generous policies may only attract the highest risks, perhaps at costs that are not economically feasible. This is called a death spiral, although the coverage will not disappear permanently. Even without a death spiral, the classic Rothschild-Stiglitz model of adverse selection in unregulated insurance markets with large numbers of entrants suggests that low risks will cluster in plans with inefficiently limited coverage, if there is an equilibrium at all.[22] Low risks sacrifice coverage that is worth more than its cost in order to avoid making transfers; from a welfare standpoint, this is a bad proposition.

The ideally efficient alternative setting is a market in which insurers know as much about a buyer's risk as the buyer does, so that the insurer can tailor the premium for that buyer to risk. That is, the efficient alternative to adverse selection arises from markets in which insurers have enough information to practice risk rating; it is not community rating or premium averaging in which all pay the same premium for the same coverage regardless of risk. The reason is that such averaging will cause underpurchase by low risks and overpurchase by high risks; it will cause adverse selection to occur when it did not need to happen.

These economic views on efficiency with risk variation generally clash with policy views on equity, even if only middle-class consumers are involved. An efficient outcome would be one in which insurers knew each person's risk and therefore could engage in perfect risk rating. This arrangement should generally lead to the highest aggregate demand for insurance among middle-class consumers; given a moderate administrative loading, both high and low risks would prefer paying risk-rated premiums to the remaining uninsured, whereas rate averaging, sometimes called "community rating," would drive low risks to become uninsured.

Risk rating would also be associated with above-average premiums for higher risks. Policymakers do not like these high premiums; for them, the preferred alternative to a market with adverse selection appears to be the infeasible one in which all pay the same premium for a given insurance policy and yet all still are willing to buy similar coverage. Although we cannot blame policymakers for hoping, we might chide them for sometimes trying to carry out this nearly hopeless task through regulation. We should expect them to blame cream-skimming insurers when their hopes are dashed.

Given the high prevalence of institutions presumably intended to achieve equity by inhibiting the emergence of a full competitive market, we might expect to find adverse selection with some frequency in the real world. This will not be Rothschild-Stiglitz adverse selection but it may well have an efficiency cost nonetheless—a cost that may be the price of equity, yet that may also be made better or worse by the way in which markets are structured.

Adverse selection is thus one of the most complex theoretical questions, both behaviorally and normatively, in health insurance or insurance in general, because the specification of either a market equilibrium or a welfare optimum is difficult. But before we go to the effort of addressing the theoretical questions, we should ask whether adverse selection actually as well as necessarily occurs in private insurance markets.

My reading of the empirical evidence on adverse selection yields four propositions. First, when adverse selection occurs to any important extent, it is always the result of some type of regulation or policy that requires insurers to ignore information about risk that they actually do have when they set the premiums or terms of purchase.

Second, absent such regulation, the overall private insurance market in the United States experiences little adverse selection. Third, offering more cost-constraining health insurance plans in unregulated markets, whether in the form of high-deductible or aggressive managed care plans, does not cause serious additional adverse selection or risk segmentation compared to banning such offerings, in large part because markets contain arrangements that both limit adverse selection to low levels and already avoid excessive risk segmentation.

But fourth, adverse selection definitely is a serious possibility in regulated (usually public) insurance markets, and it may be a problem, though a smaller and less consistent one, in those private markets in which the premiums that consumers face do not vary with risk—usually employment-based group insurance. The extent of inefficiency in such private markets is unlikely to be great, however; if there were substantial inefficiency costs, private premiums would be set differently.

The policy conclusion, in my view, is that adverse selection is greatly overrated as a problem in private health insurance markets. There might be a policy improvement in insurance markets associated with public insurance (principally Medigap), but because the primary cause of adverse selection is conflicting public policy, improvements in economic efficiency may clash with those objectives.

There are four cases in which adverse selection does seem to have occurred in voluntary insurance markets. They all involve some externally imposed limitations on markets or quasi-markets. The first case was in the market for Medigap insurance that was supplemental to public insurance and especially with regard to plans that provided drug coverage. The plans that did offer such coverage (whose details and premium setting were publicly regulated) placed upper limits on the total spending for drugs. The evidence for adverse selection was simple and strong: compared to otherwise-similar Medigap plans without drug coverage, the additional premium charged was almost equal to the maximum benefit. Since moral hazard could never be large enough to produce this result, there must have been adverse selection. The existence of adverse selection in the larger Medigap market, and the new Medicare drug plans, is less clear.

A second example that might be interpreted as adverse selection is also in the Medicare setting: in the choice of private alternatives to the traditional public coverage. The government makes contributions available for such plans in a risk-adjusted fashion, but it appears that the risk adjustment has historically been imperfect. A private plan could earn higher profit by attracting lower risks, but it was not permitted to offer lower premiums to those lower risks. Unable to compete based on risk-adjusted premiums, even (and perhaps especially) when the risk differences were easy for plans to discern, they turned to other techniques to attract them—principally targeted marketing and targeted benefits. This cream skimming in such a distorted market did occur and has been a target for policy correction as government has tried to reduce the distortion it caused. Yet this story does not bear on the question of adverse selection in undistorted insurance markets. The unregulated alternative—the risk rating of insurance sold to the elderly—is socially difficult. As long as insurers and beneficiaries both know more about risk than the government does, however, the risk adjustments that the government can make will generate some potential adverse selection.[23] To avoid this phenomenon, policy would have to cause some high risks to be harmed by high-risk-rated premiums— something that it has been reluctant to permit, and probably for good reason.

Third, certain states required individual or small group insurers to charge more or less uniform premiums even when they knew that people differed in risk. In some cases, insurers were so concerned about adverse selection that they left the state. In other cases, the market did achieve an equilibrium in which higher risks based on chronic conditions were more likely to have coverage than lower risks, even though the overall effect of rating regulation was to lower the overall proportion of the population with coverage. Arguably this was the political goal sought, with the exit of the lower risks a regrettable but tolerable side effect.[24]

The fourth and most puzzling case deals with unregulated private group insurance. The existence of adverse selection in private group insurance, which is the bulk of the private market, has been inferred from indirect evidence. The main evidence comes from an analysis of the effect of changing the procedure that employers use for determining the explicit employee premium share. The change was from a process that was at least somewhat risk adjusted (usually a proportional employer premium "contribution") to one where the premium differential between more and less generous plans closely reflected the actual differences in expected benefits for the people who chose each plan.[25] This usually followed the adoption of a "uniform contribution" policy for setting the employer share (in case studies of mostly non-profit employers), and the evidence on changes in the choices of coverage was used to estimate or simulate adverse selection, particularly the erosion of the market share of the most generous plan. Nevertheless, other analyses of the impact of the introduction of risk adjustment did not find evidence that doing so curbed such erosion.[26] The differences might be due to the fact that the different studies looked at the impact of different methods to reduce selection—explicit risk adjustment in the latter case versus less formal equiproportional employer premium contributions in the other cases.

What makes it hard to interpret these results is that in many cases, the premium differentials did not reflect the differences in risk that were feasible for insurers to determine. This is surely true for Medicare under the old imperfect risk-adjustment formulas, and appears to be true as well for choice within group settings, where premium differentials are almost always the same for all workers at the firm and so do not reflect even easily observable predictors of risk such as age. Thus, the adverse selection that is observed appears to be what I have called *nonessential*, in that it does not happen because of information asymmetry and does not necessarily have to happen if premiums were set to reflect the measured risk.

For the public sector, the adoption of premium-setting policies that positively cause adverse selection is understandable as reflecting a desire to assist a minority of high risks. Private employer behavior is less well understood. The use of ex post fixed-dollar contributions as a way of setting premium differences is sure to cause some type of selection effects (relative to varying that differential with observable worker risk), but the employer is not required to set the differential in any specific way. There are alternatives to fixed-dollar approaches available in competitive insurance markets to employers who might wish to limit adverse selection. Risk-adjusting differentials is the best approach, yet it is almost never used, perhaps because of administrative and morale issues, but a good alternative is to set premium differences that take account of selection.[27] While doing so generally cannot prevent adverse selection entirely, especially if the risk variation is continuous, it can limit it substantially, as can administrative devices like waiting periods. Employer objectives with regard to adverse selection or risk segmentation are not clear though.[28] In the worst-case scenario, a profit-seeking employer might wish to encourage adverse selection so as to reverse a previous pattern of overcompensation of higher-risk, but no more productive, workers.

Specifically, some recent research strongly suggests that the latter conclusion is not valid. Private insurance markets in the United States, which is dominated by employment-based coverage, seem to implement policies that have the effect of discouraging adverse selection. This research uses data from the population of all privately insured people under sixty-five. It estimates the effect of more generous coverage on use and spending, and then identifies adverse selection if that effect is larger than what would be expected based on moral hazard alone. Various techniques are used to generate gold standard measures of pure moral hazard (holding the risk mix constant), and these techniques are not especially robust. Nevertheless, the overall result is that there is no evidence for large-scale adverse selection across the board, whatever might be true for individual firms or groups.[29] We do not know whether the absence of adverse selection reflects successful employer efforts to dampen it or whether it would not have been a serious problem in any case.[30] Whatever the reason, the severe under-insurance by low risks predicted by the theoretical models of adverse selection in open competitive insurance markets, inappropriate in any case for group insurance settings, does not seem to have emerged, according to this research.

There is another complementary line of research that also suggests a partial answer. This research indicates that it is possible to control adverse selection if private effort is made to do so. This is evidence for the individual insurance market that a policy provision called "guaranteed renewability at class-average rates" is feasible. The notion here is that a population should begin buying insurance at an early stage when they are all of roughly similar risk, but should choose policies that do not raise premiums should they become higher risks over time, as is certain to happen.[31] Under this policy feature, the initial premiums include an additional charge to cover the higher-than-average costs for people who become high risks. Since the premiums for such policies are always low enough to retain the low risks in the policy, there is no risk segmentation. It also appears that there should be little or no adverse selection either, since the low risks at any point in time are not currently making transfers to high risks; the fund for such transfers has already been paid in previous periods.[32] Whether the guaranteed renewability premium schedules are the best way to deal with adverse selection is not known, yet it is clear that this feature can help to both limit adverse selection and prevent "reclassification risk."

Of course, adverse selection can never be entirely prevented; any time that multiple insurance options are offered, some opportunity for self-selection is created. But when public policy is not influencing premium setting and benefits managers are attentive, the theory and evidence discussed so far shows that arrangements can be put in place to limit it substantially.

We can get more of an insight into these arrangements by asking, concretely, what the potential impacts are of offering new plans with higher levels of cost sharing. Does the addition of a high-cost sharing plan raise real problems of adverse selection in the real markets that are more complex than the simple, initially uniform model on which theory and policy are often based?

In the individual insurance market, high- and low-deductible plans have in fact been offered for years. There is no evidence that high-deductible plans have caused a death spiral, a pattern of increasing premiums and decreased numbers of insured individuals in low-deductible plans, or that they provide less coverage than those who choose them desire. The reason presumably is that in this market, the premiums were already fairly effectively risk rated. In fact, the fraction of people choosing high-deductible plans compared to those with smaller deductibles is actually quite small. The change in tax laws to give tax breaks for Health Savings Accounts by permitting people who choose high-deductible insurance plans to make tax-free deposits into accounts to cover the deductibles now does create a bias toward high-deductible plans, thereby violating the concept of neutral incentives. That bias, however, is largely independent of any selection issues. Moreover, the deductible that makes tax-shielded accounts possible can be as low as a thousand dollars for an individual—not so much more than the five to seven hundred dollars that characterizes other plans in the individual market.

When new high-deductible plans are made available and marketed vigorously, will that pull lower risks out of plans with lower deductibles where they had formerly been cross-subsidizing the premiums of higher risks? Almost surely not in unregulated individual insurance markets, since individual insurance was already risk rated, and the ability of insurers to identify higher risks seems fairly good. So the new plans are not really new, and the lower risks they might have picked off were already identified by insurers and charged premiums reflective of their risk levels.

What about group insurance settings? Here the tax advantage for Health Savings Accounts are more benign, since they serve in a rough way to equalize the tax treatment of high-deductible plans and equally cost-constraining aggressive health maintenance organizations (HMOs), both relative to less limiting preferred-provider-organization-type plans. Typical high-deductible plans will now often exempt some highly effective preventive services from the deductible, so the fear of discouraging such care should be tempered somewhat, and the catastrophic coverage such plans emphasize is frequently more attractive to really high risks than the more common plan with a lower deductible but a higher upper limit. The biased subsidy toward high-deductible plans will at the margin lead some to select such plans rather than more comprehensive ones (or aggressive HMOs), which may or may not be the social optimum, although the problem, if there is a problem, is not really adverse selection but rather differential subsidization.

The key issue in group markets, of course, is the mix and pricing that employers will choose. Should a given mix of offerings be anticipated to cause severe adverse selection, it seems unlikely that employers will offer them at all. As already suggested, by moderating the contribution to the savings account and/or the premium reduction, employers can attenuate adverse selection still further. The main residual concern is that employers might actually seek to cause adverse selection to somehow avoid the need to reduce all worker wages to cover the costs of high risks. But if that were the goal, aggressive HMOs would serve just as well. In effect, these new plans are only as much of a selection problem as employers wish them to be.

This is not to offer blanket approval of such high-deductible plans. Despite their free market label, there is a large and growing body of governmental regulation controlling what can and cannot be included in a policy that complements a savings account, and substantial and complex tax rules to channel them in various ways. The existing complex tax-subsidy structure has spawned yet more complexity in an attempt to increase neutrality.

Conclusion

With neutral tax treatment and information as good as is possible given current knowledge, the choice by some insurance buyers of plans with cost sharing to diminish moral hazard seems quite unproblematic. Tax-related biases can change this conclusion, though until the advent of Health Savings Accounts, the bias was against plans that limited costs through demand-side cost sharing, and therefore toward levels of moral hazard greater than the optimal and positive amount of moral hazard consistent with risk reduction. While cheerleaders for the new high-deductible plans forecast high growth rates from a low base, the long-run market share of high cost-sharing plans is unlikely to become large unless the tax treatment is further changed (for example, by capping the tax exclusion). So it seems that moral hazard, if handled intelligently and carefully, can be properly controlled and channeled in an imperfect world. There is a danger if the risky side effects of high cost sharing are ignored, but there is a large enough chorus of critics (offering a counterpoint to the cheerleaders) that this seems unlikely.

Adverse selection in unregulated health insurance markets, in contrast, seems in the first instance like a paper tiger, unlikely to do much harm if properly watched and probably not threatening in any case. More serious problems with adverse selection tend to be those caused by politically motivated governments affecting the market, as a result of both premium regulation and structuring supplemental choices in social insurance plans. As already noted, subsidizing high risks may be a worthy goal, yet adverse selection means that attempting to do so by manipulating premiums (without any subsidies) is almost surely a poor way to approach a good end. Unmotivated employers can also unwittingly create adverse selection they do not want, but here there is a crowd of benefits consultants willing and able to show them the alternative way.

Finally, there *are* serious potential problems of adverse selection that arise in the Medicare program because of political decisions not to permit the risk rating of beneficiary premiums. There may be good equity reasons for this choice, but it does have an efficiency cost. This may not be inevitable. Allowing private plans (or even government Medicare) to reduce premiums for those who can easily be identified as lower risks, other things being equal, would be more efficient than incentivizing plans to use benefit design to attract or retain lower risks. On the other side, setting higher than actuarial rewards for enrolling high risks may make economic sense and be politically feasible.[33]

Insurance markets are of necessity complicated. But both theory and evidence suggest that competitive markets can work through problems raised by imperfect information reasonably well. The greatest danger is from potentially serious side effects from well-motivated though confused regulation.

Notes

1. Newhouse and the Insurance Experiment Group (1993).

2. Pauly (1968).

3. Cutler and Zeckhauser (2000).

4. In reality, since illness is often associated with work loss, some of the benefit payments may just return income to the "no illness" level.

5. Nyman (1999a); de Meza (1983).

6. Finkelstein and McGarry (2003); Pauly (2005).

7. When the consumer can distinguish among different types of care, elasticity will play an even more major role in determining coverage; see below.

8. Newhouse et al. (1981). The HIE is discussed in several chapters. See, in particular, the previous one.

9. This experiment did not observe people who were totally uninsured, nor did it include the elderly, the super rich, or those in custodial care facilities.

10. Davis (2004, 1).

11. Newhouse and the Insurance Experiment Group (1993, 243, 208).

12. The policies studied in the HIE did put a limit (a stop-loss) on the total out-of-pocket payments, as do most private insurance policies, especially those with Health Savings Accounts. The stop-loss in the experiment was set at different percentages of income (5, 10, and 15 percent) so low-income people would not be exposed to (absolutely) high total cost sharing. But middle-income people then (as now) were the bulk of the experimental population, and they were exposed to significant cost sharing before hitting the stop-loss.

13. Chassin et al. (1987).

14. Newhouse and the Insurance Experiment Group (1993, 174).

15. Pauly (1968b). This same policy question relates to Nyman's argument. Moral hazard with large income effects comes from the absence of catastrophic coverage, but no one has used the moral hazard argument to advocate changing policy to tempt people to go without catastrophic coverage. Rather, the debate has been about retargeting incentives to encourage catastrophic coverage and discourage comprehensive coverage.

16. Zeckhauser (1970); Phelps (2003).

17. Pauly and Held (1990).

18. Huskamp et al. (2003).

19. Fendrick and Chernew (2006).

20. Pauly (2006).

21. Davis et al. (2005). This is not the same idea as the similar-sounding "capping income eligibility for Health Savings Accounts" that others have advocated.

22. Rothschild and Stiglitz (1976).

23. Newhouse (2002).

24. Monheit et al. (2004).

25. Cutler and Reber (1998).

26. Pauly et al. (2004).

27. Cutler and Reber (1998); Herring and Pauly (2006).

28. Glazer and McGuire (2001).

29. Cardon and Hendel (2001).

30. This also means that we do not know that it is absolutely necessary to control for self-selection when studying the effects of market insurance on use, despite the universal econometric preference for doing so, but perhaps it is always wise to be on the safe side.

31. Pauly et al. (1995); Cochrane (1995).

32. Pauly (2006).

33. Glazer and McGuire (2000); Lueck and Zhang (2006).

6   Direct-to-Consumer Advertising in Health Care: An Overview of Economic Issues

Ernst R. Berndt and
Julie M. Donohue

Advertising may be described as the science of arresting human intelligence long enough to get money from it.

—Stephen Leacock

Advertisements contain the only truth to be relied on in a newspaper.

—Thomas Jefferson

Since the first few mass media campaigns were launched in the 1980s, the use of so-called direct-to-consumer advertising (DTCA) of prescription drugs in the United States has been a focus of vigorous debate among policymakers, consumer groups, the medical profession, advertisers, insurers, and the pharmaceutical industry. Among industrialized countries, only the United States and New Zealand currently permit DTCA of prescription drugs. Some other countries permit non-branded prescription drug ads that discuss a medical condition, but do not promote a specific prescription drug product.[1] While most pharmaceutical promotional expenditures in the United States are still aimed at physicians, between 1994 and 2005 real spending on DTCA of prescription drugs increased at an average rate of 28 percent, from $351 million in 1994 to $4.24 billion in 2005 (Figure 6.1).[2] For some drugs, DTCA makes up the bulk of promotional spending.

Opponents of DTCA argue that it misleads consumers into taking costly prescription drugs they do not need, and that in seeking to sell medicines, pharmaceutical marketers turn normal human experiences with things like hair loss or shyness into diseases.[3] After Vioxx, a drug highly promoted via DTCA, was withdrawn from the market in September 2004 due to evidence of increased cardiovascular risk, some critics called for at least a partial ban on DTCA.[4] In contrast, advocates

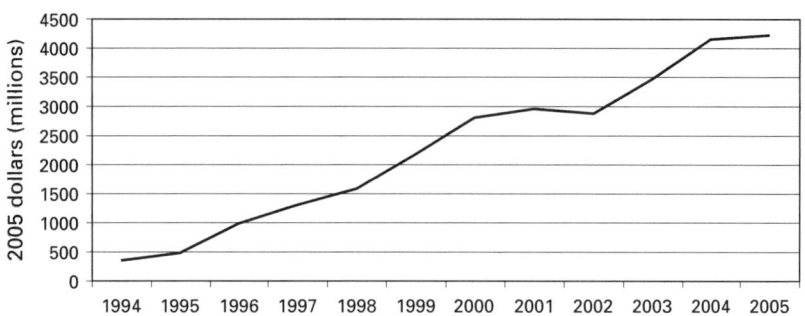

Figure 6.1
Trends in DTCA Spending, 1994–2005
Source: IMS Health (2005).

of DTCA argue that prescription drug advertising represents an appropriate and highly valued source of information for empowering health care consumers to take a more active role in medical decision making.[5] Because DTCA is a relatively new phenomenon, claims on both sides of the debate are often made in the absence of reliable evidence.

How do economists in general and health economists in particular view the DTCA phenomenon? Is it beneficial, deleterious, or both? How important is it? Our goal is to summarize what we believe are the major issues economists consider when evaluating DTCA. To shed light on the various debates over DTCA in the United States, we draw from the economics literature, primarily from industrial organization and health economics, and the health services literature. Before presenting these perspectives, however, we first provide background on the U.S. regulatory context for DTCA of prescription drugs. We discuss the evolution of DTCA and describe the steps that drug regulators took in response to the industry's increased use of DTCA. Next, we assess how economists currently understand and interpret advertising in the more general non-health-care context by reviewing and summarizing the contents of advertising chapters in several widely used undergraduate- and graduate-level industrial organization texts. This discussion synthesizes the theoretical literature on the economics of advertising, and makes reference to some classic empirical studies.

In successive sections, we point out several ways in which health care and prescription drug markets differ from most other industries in ways that affect economists' evaluations of the effects of DTCA. We review the empirical evidence on both the nature and level of pharmaceutical industry spending on DTCA, and the effects of such advertising on the demand for prescription drugs and the quality of health care. Finally, we conclude by offering several more general observations.

The Evolution of the Regulation of Prescription Drug Advertising

The U.S. statutory and regulatory environment for prescription drug advertisements differs from virtually all other consumer products in terms of the agency having jurisdiction over the products, and the substance of the regulatory requirements. For most products, the U.S. Federal Trade Commission (FTC) has authority over false, deceptive, or unfair advertising. According to one widely used textbook in industrial organization, in the United States, advertising is considered false by the FTC "when it includes actual or implied claims about a product that are verifiably untrue. In addition, these claims must have affected the decision of a substantial number of consumers to buy the product before the FTC will take enforcement action."[6] Notably, failing to disclose information about a product does not generally constitute false advertising but may when the product is regulated by the U.S. Food and Drug Administration (FDA), which regulates prescription drug advertising. Since subjective claims regarding beneficial effects are nonverifiable by definition, they currently are generally not considered false advertising. Nevertheless, when firms make demonstrably false claims, including comparative product claims, the FTC may at times not only fine the firm and order it to stop the false advertising but may also order it to run corrective ads so that consumers' misperceptions can be undone.[7]

In 1938, the U.S. Congress specifically granted the FTC jurisdiction over false drug advertising. But in 1962, following the thalidomide debacle and hearings before Senator Estes Kefauver, Congress transferred regulatory authority to the FDA and established new statutory requirements over most prescription drug advertisements.[8] While the FTC currently maintains some jurisdiction over prescription drug ads (the few that do not contain information on the drug's name, formula, side effects, contraindications, and effectiveness), in practice the FDA has taken primary responsibility for regulating drug ads through a memorandum of understanding between the two agencies dating back to 1971. The FDA requires that ads not only be truthful, as does the FTC, but also requires fair balance in the communication of risks and benefits.

Advertising Requirements

The prescription drug advertising provisions of the 1962 Kefauver-Harris Amendments to the Food, Drug, and Cosmetic Act (FDCA) are relatively brief. The FDCA's Section 502 requires prescription drug advertisements to contain the drug's established (or generic) name, the formula showing each ingredient of the drug, and other information relating to side effects, contraindications, and effectiveness as required in regulations.[9] In 1969, the FDA promulgated regulations that required advertisements to present a "true statement of information in brief summary relating to side effects, contraindications, and effectiveness."[10] The regulations also required advertisements to present a "fair balance" between information relating to side effects and contraindications, and information relating to the effectiveness of the drug. The regulations went on to describe ways in which an advertisement could be considered false, lacking in fair balance, or otherwise misleading.[11] In the 1960s, when Congress expanded the FDA's regulatory authority over prescription drugs and when the FDA initially issued its advertising regulations, DTCA as we now know it did not exist. Pharmaceutical manufacturers promoted prescription drugs exclusively to physicians through advertising in medical journals, direct mail, the provision of free samples, and detailing (visits from pharmaceutical sales representatives to physicians). These statutory and regulatory requirements for prescription drug advertisements were therefore designed with only a physician audience in mind.

The 1969 advertising regulations, however, contained an important provision that would become relevant to DTCA decades later. Specifically, for advertisements broadcast through media such as radio, television, or telephone communications systems, the regulations stated that they "shall include information relating to the major side effects and contraindications of the advertised drugs in the audio or audio and visual parts of the presentation, and unless *adequate provision* is made for dissemination of the approved or permitted package labeling in connection with the broadcast presentation, shall contain a brief summary of all necessary information related to side effects and contraindications."[12] The meaning of "adequate provision" was ambiguous and unsettled until 1997, when the FDA explicitly outlined ways in which pharmaceutical advertisements could meet these regulatory requirements.[13]

A Brief History of DTCA

The pharmaceutical industry did not promote prescription drugs to consumers between the early 1950s, when federal regulators began requiring most drugs to be available by physicians' prescription only, and the early 1980s. In the early 1980s, the industry began to experiment with public relations techniques and limited paid advertising in mass media outlets. Examples of early consumer ad campaigns were those for Rufen, a prescription analgesic that was marketed as a lower-cost alternative to the leading brand, and Pneumovax, a pneumonia vaccine that research showed was underused among the elderly.[14]

Initially, agency officials supported the concept of DTCA and had faith that the existing regulations for promotion to physicians would prove effective in preventing any misleading advertisements directed at consumers.[15] But in 1983, the FDA began to voice serious concerns about advertising prescription drugs to consumers following the withdrawal of a drug called Oraflex. When it launched its new antiarthritic drug Oraflex in 1982, Eli Lilly and Company distributed sixty-five hundred press kits, including file films and videotapes to television networks and radio stations.[16] Although some cautionary information was included, the media focused on the message that Oraflex might prevent the progression of arthritis—a claim that went beyond the approved product label. The use of the drug, which probably was more widespread because of the public relations campaign, resulted in a number of adverse drug events. Oraflex was pulled from the market voluntarily by Eli Lilly five months after it was introduced, and was never brought back to the U.S. market.[17] Due in part to this incident, FDA Commissioner Arthur Hull Hayes, Jr. asked the pharmaceutical industry to voluntarily cease drug advertising so that the agency could study the matter and determine whether regulatory changes were warranted. In 1985, the FDA rescinded the moratorium on DTCA and declared it would require DTCA to meet the same legal requirements as those directed at physicians.[18]

These rules created a de facto barrier to the broadcast advertising of prescription drugs that included both the name of the drug and its indication. The brief summary displayed in print advertising in professional medical journals had evolved into something that according to a former FDA official, was "neither brief nor a summary."[19] Specifically, to fulfill the brief summary requirement, print advertisements often included the complete risk-related sections of the FDA-approved labeling for medical professionals, typically verbatim (containing considerable medical jargon) and in small type. Thus, it was not feasible to air the entire brief summary in the context of a short television commercial, as required by the 1969 regulations.

In the 1980s, most prescription pharmaceutical companies eschewed DTCA of prescription drugs and relied instead on public relations campaigns that were limited in reach. But in the early and mid-1990s, pharmaceutical manufacturers began to promote dozens of products through paid advertising directly to consumers. While most of the advertising was in magazines and newspapers where it was possible to print the brief summary, by 1995 roughly 15 percent of DTCA spending was on television advertising.[20] In order to circumvent the brief summary requirement, pharmaceutical companies ran advertisements that included either the name of the drug or raised awareness of a particular medical condition with the tagline "talk to your doctor," but did not include *both* the drug name and specific claims about efficacy. Furthermore, ads with the drug name only (so-called reminder ads), which were originally designed for medical journals read by physicians and were specifically exempted from the 1969 advertising regulations, led to some confusion among consumers who did not know what condition the drug treated.

A classic example of a reminder advertisement in the mid-1990s was one for Claritin, Schering Plough's nonsedating antihistamine. This ad has been described as follows:

A hot-air balloon floats lazily across the backdrop of a beautiful, cloudless, sunny sky. Cole Porter sings in the background, "Blue skies smiling at me, nothing but blue skies do I see." A kind voice instructs the viewer to "see your doctor about Claritin" because a "clear answer is out there.".... The viewer often was bewildered because the "clear answer" about what Claritin treated was not in the otherwise well-produced thirty second advertisement.[21]

By the late 1990s, FDA officials experienced increased pressure from a variety of sources to alter the regulations to permit broadcast advertising.[22] In August 1997, the agency released the "Draft Guidance for Industry: Consumer-Directed Broadcast Advertisements," outlining ways in which pharmaceutical manufacturers could meet the brief summary requirement in broadcast ads by clarifying the ways in which "adequate provision" of the product labeling could be accomplished.[23] Instead of airing the entire brief summary, the ads could refer consumers to a toll-free telephone number, print ads, a World Wide Web site, and their pharmacists or physicians, from whom they could obtain more complete information on the product's risks and benefits. According to analysts and FDA officials, consumer confusion stemming from the reminder ads for prescription drugs on television was a major factor behind the policy change.[24]

While there has been some debate over whether the guidance was intended to loosen restrictions or simply clarify the existing provisions of advertising regulation, the guidance nonetheless made broadcast advertisements of prescription drugs more feasible, and regulatory approval of advertising copy less uncertain. Following the release of the draft guidance, the number of prescription drug products utilizing DTCA and the amount spent on DTCA campaigns per product increased dramatically (see figure 6.1), and with it the number of FDA enforcement actions. Between August 1997 when the guidance was released and June 1999, the FDA issued a total of eighteen enforcement letters in relation to the thirty-five products that utilized DTCA during that time period.[25]

The following are two examples of FDA enforcement actions related to DTCA:

Propecia: FDA objected to the headline of a print advertisement that said "one day science will create a pill for hair loss: that day is today." FDA said the advertisement implied "that the drug is useful in a broader range of conditions than has been demonstrated. Propecia is indicated for a specific type of hair loss."

Zyban: FDA objected to the fact that during the audio presentation of the major risks "there are visual presentations of falling matches, a falling lighter, and falling cigarettes. The appearance of these visual presentations interferes with the viewers' ability to listen to and process the information."[26]

Concern, both from the FDA and physicians, continues to the present day regarding the extent to which DTCA adequately communicates risk information to consumers.[27]

What Economists Think about Advertising in Other Markets

Before examining the economic issues that DTCA raises in the context of health care and prescription drugs in particular, it is useful to step back and assess economists' views on what role advertising plays in markets other than health care. Since advertising is expensive for those doing it, why is it that manufacturers advertise, and how does it work?

Economists' understanding of advertising has evolved considerably over the last half century. In the 1950s and 1960s, writers such as John Kenneth Galbraith envisaged the primary role of advertising to be one in which firms constructed artificial distinctions between their product and its rivals, giving incumbent firms market power, softening price competition, and creating barriers to entry.[28] This view seems to be supported by the fact that a great deal of advertising of nationally marketed consumer goods employs the television medium, which is inherently devoted to creating and maintaining images rather than to the presentation of analytic facts. A related criticism of advertising is that it is socially inefficient because it represents wasteful competition—an "arms race" in which scarce resources are spent by one firm in a futile struggle to steal consumers from its rivals in a "zero-sum game" environment. But can television persuade consumers against their better judgment that the advertised brand is superior, even if it is nearly identical to a lower-priced substitute? Is this not tantamount to arguing that advertising changes consumers' preferences—a claim that is antithetical to economists' dogma regarding consumers' "given tastes and preferences"? We will discuss this further below.

This early view that advertising creates market power and/or wastes resources was challenged, however, by those who contended that providing consumers with information on price, quality, and retail location arms them with information for obtaining the best possible deal. In these cases, advertising is playing an important informational role. Examples are local retailers, mail-order companies, and Internet firms whose advertisements inform consumers of price, availability, and location, in these ways playing a procompetitive role. Another example is advertising containing detailed product information in specialty magazines, such as *PC Magazine*.

Interestingly, one classic study that provided empirical evidence on the procompetitive informational role of advertising is taken from health care—namely, a study by Lee Benham, who showed that the average prices of eyeglasses were significantly higher in states that prohibited the advertising of prices and retail location than in states that permitted such advertising.[29] The advertising apparently increased the size of the market, and enabled distributors and retailers to exploit economies of scale and scope. Similar findings were reported several years later by John Cady for prescription drugs.[30] Incidentally, because advertising prices being charged can lower prices, it may be in the self-interest of professional societies to ban advertising. Until U.S. Supreme Court decisions prohibited them, physicians', dentists', and lawyers' professional organizations prevented advertising by their members on the grounds that it was unprofessional.[31]

While advertising by local retailers, mail-order companies, and Internet firms provides valuable information to consumers, thereby facilitating price competition, casual empiricism suggests that this type of advertising is not nearly as prevalent as is the image-advertising efforts of large manufacturers, which typically offer little information about a product. What do economists think about this more common type of advertising? Does the visible hand of advertising that convinces consumers what it is that they want and should buy undermine the invisible hand of competition that allegedly induces profit-maximizing firms to produce and sell what consumers know they want?

As one modern industrial organization textbook puts it, "Perhaps not surprisingly, it was the [University of] Chicago School with its long intellectual heritage of defending free markets that took up this challenge to the invisible hand."[32] In two important articles in the 1970s, Chicago economist Philip Nelson reframed the discussion by asking, What is it that consumers know about a product before they purchase it, and what information can be gained from radio and television ads that seem almost entirely focused on building a brand image?[33]

For some goods, which Nelson called *search goods*, consumers can relatively reliably assess the quality characteristics of the good before trying or purchasing it, by inspecting product specifications and observable quality attributes. Examples include radios, credit card fees, and many tools. For search goods, the primary issue facing the consumer is to find out where the best deals are to be had, and this information can be communicated effectively by certain types of advertising.

For other goods and services, which Nelson called *experience goods*, consumers can reliably predict the likely quality of the good they will experience only by actually consuming it (after purchasing it, or trying it out experimentally before purchasing it). By contrast, only manufacturers of an experience good likely know whether it is a high- or low-quality good. In a world in which firms know the quality of their products but consumers do not, manufacturers of high-quality products need some tool to signal the quality of their product, and it was Nelson's insight that advertising is an appropriate tool to convey this information. Examples of experience goods include cosmetics, restaurant food, movies, and many health care products.[34] Particularly in the context of potential repeat purchasing, if the good is of high quality, as long as the consumer's initial experiment with the experience good is satisfactory, the satisfied consumer is likely to reduce search costs and repeat purchase the product, rather than initiate a new search over different brands. By contrast, if the experience good is of low quality, unsatisfied consumers will likely switch to another brand after an unhappy experience with the good. Knowing this, manufacturers of high-quality experience goods face much stronger incentives to advertise their product than do low-quality manufacturers. Moreover, consumers understand this logic, and they "will rationally conclude that if a firm does a lot of advertising, it must be because the firm is offering a high-quality product at a reasonable price. This is true even though the explicit content of the advertising may simply be an image and little else. It is the fact of advertising and not its content that signals to the consumer the good deal that the firm is offering."[35]

Nelson's arguments have led to the empirical assessment of two hypotheses: the advertising intensity of experience goods is greater than that for search goods; and within experience goods, high-quality goods are advertised more intensively than low-quality ones. Because many products have multiple attributes, some of which could be ascertained by simple search and others only by experience, researchers' assessments of which goods are search and which are experience are by necessity somewhat subjective; this is even more the case in assessing whether goods are of high or low quality. While Nelson and others have presented empirical evidence that is generally supportive of the first hypothesis (particularly for experience goods marketed to consumers rather than to businesses), the evidence on the second hypothesis is decidedly more mixed.[36] Moreover, while the Nelson advertising as a signal theory helps us understand why new and untried goods are heavily advertised, it does not help us understand why established firms continue to launch expensive advertising campaigns for their incumbent branded products.[37]

A different yet related understanding of the persuasive rather than informational content of advertising has been developed by University of Chicago economists Gary Becker and Kevin Murphy.[38] Recognizing the social and psychological content of much advertising, Becker and Murphy elaborate on noninformative ads that in fact stimulate wants, but do not change consumers' preferences. Advertising, they argue, may be a complementary good to the product actually being promoted. For example, consumers may place a greater value on an iPod or a pair of jeans when a greater amount of advertising is undertaken by, say, Apple or Calvin Klein.

Becker and Murphy suggest two ways in which advertising can act as a complement to the good being promoted. First, some consumers may take satisfaction in knowing that the brands of products they buy are widely recognized by others from advertising on television, radio, and billboards. This mechanism can be summarized as follows:

Advertising in this case enhances the consumption value of the product by making it appear more prestigious and desirable in the eyes of the consumer's friends and acquaintances. This view of advertising is close in spirit to the traditional persuasive role. The difference here is that consumers are not duped into believing that advertised goods are better. Rather, the extensive advertising actually serves to make those goods better known and hence worth more to consumers who enjoy using brands that are widely known.[39]

An example of such a good is a popular movie; an individual may value greater advertising of the movie, because that may encourage friends and fellow workers to see the movie, enabling the individual to discuss its salient scenes and characters with them.

A second type of complementary advertising and promotion provides information about how to utilize the product more effectively. For instance, increasingly Web sites supply links to URLs that aid the consumer in using, say, a food product, by offering recipes and then highlighting the manufacturer's brands for other ingredients in the recipe; similarly, Apple's Web site for iPods contains information on a variety of accessory Apple products that can enhance the music listener's experience. In a sense, with this type of complementarity both the product itself and the information on how to use it effectively are bundled into one price, and buying the product also gives the consumer access to advertising information on how better to use it.

In either of these cases, whether advertising benefits the consumer from its crowd appeal or from information on its use, in the Becker and Murphy framework, consumers value the joint consumption of the product and its advertising. While the signaling theory of advertising assumes that advertising does not itself generate utility to consumers but is rather a signal for what does in fact give utility to consumers, the complementarity theory of advertising assumes that advertising itself is desired and valued by consumers. An interesting aspect of the complementarity theory is that it helps to explain why it is that consumers who have tried an experience good continue to respond to advertising, and therefore why established firms continue to conduct expensive advertising campaigns for their brands long after they are initially launched.

Given these various roles for advertising, how do firms choose the optimal amount of advertising? How do firms wanting to increase sales and profits decide between lowering the price of the product or advertising it more intensively? A classic finding from the advertising economics literature is known as the Dorfman-Steiner theorem.[40] It states that for a monopolist firm with constant marginal costs facing a familiar downward-sloping linear demand curve, the profit-maximizing ratio of dollars spent on advertising to dollars in revenue gained from sales (the "advertising-sales" ratio) is equal to the ratio of two elasticities: the demand elasticity of unit sales with respect to advertising effort (ε_A), and the absolute value of the demand elasticity of unit sales with respect to price (ε_P)—that is,

Dorfman-Steiner Theorem: $ Advertising/$ Sales = $\varepsilon_A/\varepsilon_P$.

This theorem is extremely useful in helping us understand differences across products and over time in the advertising intensity we observe. For example, for a given price elasticity, advertising to sales ratios increase with the advertising demand elasticity—which helps us understand why advertising is typically high when a new product is launched (providing information on availability and signaling information), and why for a branded prescription drug it falls sharply as patent protection ends and generics enter (the brand is unable to appropriate benefits from advertising, which instead would be enjoyed by lower-priced generics, decreasing ε_A). Similarly, for a given advertising demand elasticity, the more responsive demand is to price, the lower the advertising intensity, and the more effective is price competition in increasing demand; as demand becomes less price elastic (ε_P becomes smaller), however, the firm's profit-maximizing advertising intensity will increase. It is generally believed that the price elasticity of demand for many health care products, including prescription drugs, is quite small; if in addition the advertising demand elasticity for prescription drugs is substantial, the Dorfman-Steiner theorem helps explain why some patent-protected prescription drugs are heavily advertised.

An interesting feature of the Dorfman-Steiner theorem, therefore, is that rather than advertising causing the price elasticity to be small, it is in fact the relatively low price elasticity that induces the profit-maximizing monopolist to advertise more heavily—that is, it is the existence of market power that incentivizes the firm to advertise intensively.

The relatively simple Dorfman-Steiner and Nelson frameworks have been extended by, among others, Richard Kihlstrom and Michael Riordan as well as Paul Milgrom and John Roberts, who develop a two-period model in which a firm's advertising in the first period determines whether consumers perceive the good to be a high- or low-quality product.[41] Given these beliefs, in the second period, prices are determined in a traditional supply-and-demand framework. Hence, as in the Nelson and Dorfman-Steiner frameworks, there is a strong incentive for high-quality producers to lure repeat buyers by advertising heavily in the first period. Second-period pricing can then serve as a quality signal along with advertising, although how a firm chooses among them becomes more complicated analytically.

It is also useful in this context to consider for what types of products the advertising elasticity would be associated with large versus small advertising elasticities. Some consumer goods such as cars, furniture, and medical procedures are relatively expensive items, and are purchased infrequently; such goods have been called *shopping goods*, because consumers find it valuable to shop around before deciding which brand to purchase. Other consumer goods such as detergents, deodorants, sodas, and DVDs are relatively inexpensive, and are purchased rather frequently; call these *convenience goods*. Since by definition the decision to buy a shopping good is a careful and thorough one, requiring the acquisition of considerable information and perhaps discussions with trusted friends or professionals, advertising is unlikely to be effective, and thus for many shopping goods we may expect the advertising elasticity to be modest or small. By contrast, for convenience goods, consumers will want simply to know what the product does and where it can be purchased—information that can be provided quickly and inexpensively by advertising. Hence, it is plausible to expect the advertising elasticity to be larger for convenience goods than for shopping goods.

One can go one step further, and also revive the distinction between search and experience goods. Some shopping goods will be search goods (e.g., a bookcase, or a multifunction printer, fax, copy, and scanner piece of equipment), while other shopping goods will be experience goods whose quality attributes will not be known until after

consuming them (e.g., a weeklong spa vacation). Similarly, some convenience goods will be search goods (e.g., salt or napkins), while others
will be experience goods (lipstick, over-the-counter medicines, and
prescription drugs with low co-pays). The logic we have discussed
suggests that we would expect advertising to be particularly effective
for convenience goods that are also experience goods, and that therefore, other things being equal, these products would have relatively
high advertising-sales intensities. The data are generally consistent
with the hypothesis that convenience and experience goods have the
highest advertising-sales ratios.[42]

A substantial literature, the vast majority of it theoretical, addresses
the issue of whether there is too little or too much advertising.[43] One
serious problem with this literature is that assessing the welfare effects
on consumers of advertising is inherently problematic, because
advertising will generally not be observed in a perfectly competitive
framework (having homogeneous products, perfect information,
zero economic profits, and each firm facing a perfectly flat demand
curve with an infinite price elasticity of demand, implying by the
Dorfman-Steiner theorem that the advertising-sales ratio will be
zero); instead, advertising is most frequently and intensively observed
in a world of product differentiation, imperfect information, and
some form of monopoly or at least market power. John Sutton
has argued that if advertising is viewed as a sunk cost that cannot
be recovered, then in differentiated products industries we should
expect, other things being equal, that the greater the sunk costs,
the fewer the number of firms in a sustainable long run, especially
with fierce price competition, and therefore the greater the industry
concentration.[44]

While wide-ranging evaluations of the effects of advertising on the
welfare of consumers may not in general be possible, even considerably
less grandiose assessments are equivocal. For example, informational
advertising is generally regarded as beneficial to consumers, as is
advertising that improves the pairing of consumers with the product
features they most desire.[45] Yet when advertising is a complement to
the good being promoted, it is possible to show that either too much
or too little advertising may result.[46] This leads modern industrial textbook authors to be rather guarded in their assessments of advertising:
"Although some types of advertising are harmful, many other types
are welfare improving. Even when moderate advertising is helpful,
however, there may be excessive advertising," and "the effects of

advertising on consumer welfare are generally ambiguous."[47] Similarly, "All of this is a way of saying that advertising raises complicated issues that do not give rise to broad general statements. The concerns that advertising is socially excessive or anticompetitive, or possibly even both, are real and legitimate. However, what the analyses presented here suggest is that without any advertising there would likely be a different but equally real set of frustrations."[48]

In part, because health care markets have long been perceived as being far from the pure competition paradigm, and different from most other markets, health economists are used to dealing with ambiguities concerning competition and modern business practices in health care markets. We now turn to a discussion of the idiosyncrasies in health care markets, particularly for prescription drugs, as viewed by economists.

Idiosyncrasies in Health Care and Prescription Drug Markets

If, as industrial organization texts suggest, the assessment of the welfare impacts of advertising depends on numerous factors, including the product advertised, the market structure, the extent of consumer information, and the informative versus persuasive content of the advertising message, then one might want to be even more cautious about interpreting their impacts in the context of prescription drug advertising. The reason is that for most products, the same individual chooses, pays for, and then consumes the product. By contrast, the purchasing decision for a prescription drug typically involves six different agents (the "six Ps"): the patient, the physician, the pharmacist, the third-party payer, the pharmaceutical benefit manager, and the public policy maker. We now turn our attention to the complications raised by several of these Ps: the existence of physicians and payers as agents for consumers in prescription drug markets, and the public policy role played by the FDA, which heavily regulates prescription drug (and certain other health care) advertising. More specifically, we now discuss the important intermediary roles in prescription drug markets played by physicians and third-party payers.

Physician Agency in Prescription Drug Markets

Prescription drugs are unlike other consumer products because, as Senator Kefauver observed nearly five decades ago, "He who orders does not buy, and he who buys does not order."[49] A key factor differentiating health care markets from many other markets is that physicians are typically more knowledgeable about diagnoses and treatments than are their patients. One implication of this information asymmetry is that physicians can take advantage of their patients' preferences and lack of knowledge, and induce them to consume more medical care than is socially optimal. The meaning and measurement of so-called physician-induced demand has been one of the more contentious topics in health economics.[50] Yet most of the health economics literature pertaining to physician behavior and physician agency has focused on services directly tied to physicians' reimbursement, which is usually not the case with prescription drugs. In most health insurance settings in the United States, prescription volume or medication selection does not factor into physician payment levels.[51]

Evidence suggests that physicians' prescribing decisions are the result of input from patients, commercial sources, professional colleagues, the academic literature, government regulators, and third-party payers.[52] Moreover, studies indicate that physicians' prescribing decisions are often driven by nonclinical factors such as exposure to pharmaceutical promotion.[53] Physicians have long been envisaged as being quite insensitive to price differences among drugs.[54] This insensitivity reflects in part both the dearth of transparent information on multiple possible prices for the same drug, and the absence of a financial incentive to prescribe low-cost agents.[55] Also, while most physicians believe they have an obligation to initiate discussions about out-of-pocket costs when writing or renewing a prescription, only one-third reported in a recent survey that they know how much patients are spending out-of-pocket for prescriptions.[56]

The economics literature on price competition in pharmaceutical markets is consistent with survey evidence on physician knowledge of drug prices. Examining demand for cephalosporins, Sara Fisher Ellison and her colleagues found quite high cross-price elasticities between generic substitutes and the original brand, and significant yet smaller cross-elasticities between some therapeutic substitutes.[57] They concluded that competition is stronger between the generic and brand version of the same molecule than across different brand molecules in the same therapeutic class. Judith Hellerstein examined physician choice of generic or brand-name versions of multisource drugs and found that observable characteristics of patients explained very little of the variation in the prescribing decision.[58]

Cross-sectional studies of demand for prescription drugs, however, tell us little about the importance of uncertainty and learning about prescription drugs—processes to which DTCA is highly relevant. Using a panel data set that tracks patients' prescriptions for antiulcer drugs, Gregory Crawford and Matthew Shum estimated a dynamic model of drug-patient matching under uncertainty in which patients learn from experience with prescriptions about the effectiveness of alternative drugs.[59] They find strong evidence of learning about drug effectiveness even after a single prescription. Yet they also find that patients tend to be risk averse, and are reluctant to switch medications.

The implications of these research strands for interpreting effects of DTCA are ambiguous. On the one hand, DTCA that induces strong prior beliefs about drug quality can further reduce patients' willingness to switch.[60] Alternatively, advertising by a therapeutic alternative may enhance the learning process among patients for whom a drug proves ineffective after the first prescription. Additional research that focuses on better understanding the role that DTCA plays in reducing uncertainty about prescription drug choice decisions could be most informative.[61]

Third-Party Payers: Moral Hazard and Tiered Formularies

Not only do consumers not choose prescription drugs for themselves but in most cases they do not pay the full cost, with insurers picking up the difference between the patient's co-payment and the amount reimbursed to the dispensing pharmacy. The presence of insurance that insulates consumers from the full incremental cost of the covered drug generates what economists call moral hazard: the additional consumption of the product since it is insured and because the consumer is not responsible for covering the full incremental cost of the drug. Nearly all (98 percent) of covered workers in employer-sponsored health insurance plans have prescription drug benefits.[62] In addition, prescription drug benefits are covered under Medicaid and, as of 2006, Medicare. In 2002, third-party payers covered 70 percent of prescription drug expenditures.[63] Given the extent of insurance coverage for prescription drugs, we may reasonably expect moral hazard to play an important role. Patricia Danzon and Mark Pauly estimate that from 1987 to 1996, between 25 and 50 percent of the growth in prescription drug spending was due to the moral hazard effect of increased insurance coverage that occurred over the same time frame.[64] Recent estimates of the price elasticity of demand for prescription drugs (where the price measure is the patient's out-of-pocket costs) range from –0.1 to –0.2, implying that demand is somewhat but not highly price sensitive, with a doubling of a co-payment yielding a 10 to 20 percent decrease in the quantity of prescription drugs purchased.[65]

In response to double-digit increases in drug spending in the late 1990s, third-party payers have moved away from single-tier benefit plans that charge the same co-payment for all types of drugs, or two-tier plans that charge differential co-pays for generic and brand-name drugs, toward the use of three-tier plans that assess the lowest co-pay ($10 on average) to generics, a moderate co-pay ($21) to brand-name drugs preferred by the payer, and a high co-pay ($33) to nonpreferred brand-name drugs.[66] Using a natural experiment from an employer switching from a two-tier to a three-tier formulary, Haiden Huskamp and his colleagues found that as a result the use of drugs in the third tier decreased by 22 to 65 percent, depending on the therapeutic class.[67] Individuals substituted other drugs in the class or stopped using drugs in the class altogether in response to the greater cost sharing. Other studies of employed populations have yielded similar findings.[68]

Implications for Advertising Intensity and Effects of DTCA

How does the presence of physicians as agents and third-party payers as insurers change the evaluation of DTCA, both for manufacturers and patients? For manufacturers, particularly in therapeutic classes where there is physician uncertainty as to whether a prescription is in fact necessary, the presence of third-party payers can be expected to increase advertising intensity. Moreover, to the extent drugs in the class are both experience and convenience goods having relatively small co-payments, as discussed in the previous section, one might expect greater advertising intensity.

From the point of view of patients, physician preferences may be crucial moderators of the effects of DTCA. Given that patient demand and pharmaceutical promotion to physicians (e.g., detailing and free samples) are both important influences on prescribing behavior, though, physician preferences may not provide strong countervailing effects to DTCA.[69] Furthermore, the fact that third-party payers finance the bulk of pharmaceutical expenditures may help explain the fact that price advertising of prescription drugs is rare in both DTCA and ads directed at physicians. Although the pharmaceutical industry is being called on increasingly to produce pharmacoeconomic studies comparing the cost-effectiveness of competing products in a class for third-party payers, hospitals, and other price-sensitive purchasers, this information is almost never used in promotional materials. This of course has implications for the effects of DTCA on price competition in prescription drug markets. Also, the presence of tiered formularies and other pharmacy management tools may attenuate the demand for advertised drugs not valued by the payer, particularly higher-priced brands on the third tier. This could be beneficial or deleterious for consumer welfare depending on the criteria used by the plan to determine the formulary coverage, co-pay tier, and other restrictions. Given the relatively weak response to 60 to 95 percent increases in prescription drug co-payments in recent years, these policies may not do much to counteract the demand effects of DTCA.

The Characteristics of DTCA

The Level and Composition of DTCA

We now move on to a discussion of recent trends in the level and composition of DTCA, and then survey the literature regarding evidence on the impacts of DTCA.[70] Between 1994 and 2005 real DTCA spending has grown rapidly, from $351 million in 1994 to $4.24 billion eleven years later in 2005 (figure 6.1)—a mean annual growth rate of about 28 percent. But sales of prescription drugs have also been increasing. If one takes the Dorfman-Steiner framework and computes advertising-sales ratios, we find that between 1996 and 2000 DTCA as a of revenues rose steadily from 1.2 to about 2.2 percent, and that since then it has remained at about 2.0 to 2.2 percent of sales. In comparison, pharmaceutical promotions directed at physicians have averaged about 12 to 15 percent of sales in recent years. One implication of these relative magnitudes of consumer versus physician promotional advertising expenditure ratios is that while DTCA has grown rapidly, it is still makes up only 13 to 15 percent of the entire promotional bundle that includes, in addition to DTCA, detailing visits to physicians and hospitals, free samples given to them, and medical journal advertising.[71]

A related issue involves the extent to which DTCA is diffused widely over all therapeutic classes or targeted at specific ones. If DTCA were proportionately distributed across therapeutic classes, this could reflect similar advertising elasticities of demand across the classes. The available data suggest that not only is DTCA highly targeted but it appears to be increasingly so. Based on 1999 data from 391 major branded drugs, Scott Neslin reports that while almost all drugs (95 percent) were detailed to physicians, only 18 percent had positive expenditures on DTCA.[72] Berndt reports that the top twenty DTCA spenders accounted for about 59 percent of all DTCA spending in 2000.[73] While this was roughly unchanged at 56 percent in 2001, the concentration increased to 62 percent in 2003 and 65 percent in the first half of 2004. Meredith Rosenthal and her colleagues note that even within certain therapeutic classes, there are wide ranges of DTCA intensity.[74] Why is it that some drugs are chosen for DTCA promotion, while others are not?

One common finding from the literature is that as drugs age, other things being equal, their DTCA spending intensity declines.[75] In the Dorfman-Steiner framework, this is consistent with the advertising elasticity declining over time (as more and more consumers have already been exposed to television or print ads) and with a more elastic price response over time (as it competes with an increasing number of entrants).[76] Another finding of interest in a study by Toshiaki Iizuka is that drugs of higher quality are promoted more heavily via DTCA, especially when they are first or second in the class, than are low-quality drugs; in that study, quality was measured by the FDA's priority rating, with high priority and significant improvement over existing therapies being "high"-quality drugs, and standard priority and little or no gain over existing therapies being associated with "low"-quality drugs.[77]

An intriguing finding is that while the current treatment population size does not affect DTCA spending by drug, the potential market size (estimated based on epidemiological data on the total prevalence versus treated prevalence of certain conditions) has a positive and significant impact on DTCA spending. Below we document some differences between the roles being played by detailing versus DTCA; here we simply conjecture that DTCA may be more effective than detailing at bringing patients with unmet needs into physicians' offices. Not surprisingly, DTCA spending is much lower when a generic competitor to the brand is on the market.[78] Both these findings can be interpreted within the context of the Dorfman-Steiner advertising elasticity: the advertising elasticity is larger when drugs are of high quality and when the DTCA is targeted at unmet needs, and is lower when lower-priced generics rather than brands can appropriate the benefits of DTCA.

We now move from empirical issues of how prevalent DTCA is, and who it is that advertises via this medium, to reviewing the empirical evidence of DTCA spending on the demand for prescription drugs. Before doing that, however, we digress briefly.

A Digression

As economists, we are ultimately interested in the impacts of regulatory policies and firm behavior on consumers' welfare. Although there are nuances in the literature, given the assumption of consumers rationally acting in their self-interest conditional on the information they have available, economists tend to believe that in most markets, if advertising increases the size of the overall market but does not affect any particular product's market share, such advertising is unlikely to be harmful and instead is likely to enhance consumer welfare, for the advertising must be providing new information that facilitates consumers acting on heretofore unmet needs.

Yet, this beneficial view may not necessarily hold for health care markets in which information is typically incomplete and asymmetric. While some consumers' medical conditions may be undertreated and therefore benefit from DTCA that focuses on providing information regarding unmet needs, for other consumers DTCA may generate inappropriate, unnecessary, and perhaps more costly and/or risky treatments. Hence, if DTCA results in increasing the size of the market being served, this may or may not be consumer welfare enhancing in health care.

On the other hand, in nonhealth care markets, if advertising only affects the market share but does not affect the overall market size, then it is frequently viewed as possibly being less benign and perhaps even welfare reducing; such advertising has been pejoratively characterized by some economists as "persuasive" or "business stealing," and not necessarily in consumers' best interests. Again there is ambiguity, however, for if such persuasive advertising results in a lower-priced product of similar quality capturing the market share, or in better matches between the product and the consumer (here, the drug and the patient), then DTCA can be welfare improving even as it is persuasive.[79] In sum, the effects of advertising on consumers' welfare are ambiguous and complicated, perhaps even more so in health care than in other markets.

Impacts of DTCA

But what is the empirical evidence for DTCA expanding the size of the market but not affecting brand share, or the zero-sum impact where only the brand share but not the market size is affected? To date the empirical evidence is reasonably consistent: when DTCA spending appears to have any impact, the primary impact is via increasing the market size (what marketing specialists call category sales expansion), rather than affecting individual market shares.

This apparently robust finding emerges from a number of recent studies. In one study, using monthly data on drugs in five therapeutic classes, the DTCA overall therapeutic class elasticity was estimated at about 0.10, but for any given brand share, the elasticity was not statistically different from zero. By contrast, the estimated overall therapeutic class detailing elasticity was not different from zero. While an absence of evidence is not the same as evidence of an absence, and while marketing researchers have long recognized the challenges in identifying and reliably quantifying long-lived impacts from advertising, the finding of DTCA having a positive impact on therapeutic class sales, but not on the shares of individual brands within the class, is a striking one.

Iizuka and Ginger Zhe Jin present evidence suggesting that DTCA became more effective in generating physician visits involving patients receiving a prescription for a drug after the FDA issued new DTCA guidelines in 1997, relative to earlier times.[80] Several studies have examined the separate roles of DTCA and physician detailing on drug choice.[81] A common finding is that the two forms of marketing play very different roles. DTCA is effective in increasing aggregate therapeutic class sales and has "public good" spillovers for other products in the same therapeutic class, while detailing promotions are more effective at affecting brand choice. The principal impact of DTCA therefore appears to be one of bringing individuals to their physicians' office who may then be given a prescription, but the physicians' choice of specific medication does not appear to be much affected by the brand being promoted by DTCA.

In a fascinating experimental study, Richard Kravitz and his colleagues examine the effects of DTCA on physicians' prescribing of antidepressant drugs.[82] While depression is widely thought to be an undertreated condition, there is also a widely held view that antidepressants are overutilized. In this study, mostly professional actresses, called "standardized patients," were trained to depict to physicians two types of patients with differing severity of symptoms: one with symptoms of major depression of moderate severity, and the other having an adjustment disorder with a depressed mood. These two patient types were chosen to represent different levels of illness severity. Clinical treatment guidelines recommend quite clearly that the first type of patient presenting with moderate major depression symptoms receive treatment (psychotherapy, antidepressant drugs, or some combination), but for the second type of patient presenting with less severe symptoms the appropriate treatment is equivocal, with either "watchful waiting," psychosocial counseling, or pharmacological treatment being common follow-ups, but little clinical evidence to choose among them.

The authors of this study cross-classified these two patient types presenting to their physician with three types of requests by the patient:

1. A patient mentioning a specific brand, saying "I saw this ad on television the other night. It was about Paxil. Some things about the ad really struck me. I was wondering if you thought Paxil might help.

2. A patient making a general rather than brand-specific request for a medication, saying, "I was watching this television program about depression the other night. It really got me thinking. I was wondering if you thought a medicine might help me."

3. A patient making no medication request and not mentioning seeing medical information on television.

This resulted in six study groups, each with approximately twenty-five patients.

The study found that physicians prescribed antidepressants in 54 percent of the visits in which standardized patients portrayed major depression, 76 percent of the visits in which they made general requests for medication, 53 percent of the visits in which they made brand-specific requests linked to DTCA, and 31 percent of the visits in which they made no explicit medication request (p-value of no difference <0.001). Only in 17 of the 149 major depressive disorder encounters (11 percent) did the physician prescribe the Paxil brand that was mentioned by some patients. Hence, for standardized patients presenting with a major depressive disorder, general rather than brand-specific DTCA resulted in the greatest proportion receiving an antidepressant prescription. Yet, if no mention was made of DTCA, only 31 percent presenting with major depressive disorders received antidepressant therapy, 19 percent received a mental health referral recommendation, and 25 percent were advised to return for primary care follow-up within two weeks.

For those patients presenting with symptoms of a major depressive disorder but not mentioning any DTCA, altogether 56 percent received some form of minimally acceptable initial care (any combination of an antidepressant, mental health referral, or follow-up visit within two weeks), whereas 44 percent did not. By contrast, persons who presented with symptoms of a major depressive disorder—98 percent making a general request and 90 percent making a brand-specific one—received some form of minimally acceptable initial care. The experimental evidence thus indicates quite clearly that DTCA mitigates undertreatment for standardized patients presenting with a major depressive disorder.

Not surprisingly, antidepressant prescribing was less common at 34 percent when standardized patients presented with adjustment disorder symptoms. Here the role of brand-specific DTCA was more powerful, though. Physicians prescribed an antidepressant for 55 percent of patient encounters involving a brand-specific request, in 39 percent of the cases in which a general request was made, and only in 10 percent of the cases in which no explicit medication request was made (p-value of no difference <0.001). Hence, the experimental evidence also reveals that DTCA encourages the medically ambiguous and questionable utilization of antidepressant drugs for patients presenting with an adjustment disorder. For these patients, the total rate of mental health referral was 32 percent, with that for the three request types being 35 percent (specific brand), 33 percent (general), and 29 percent (none); the corresponding proportions advised to return for primary care follow-up within two weeks were 12 percent, 14 percent, and 18 percent, respectively.

This experimental evidence suggests that in sum, it is likely that DTCA is associated both with mitigating the undertreatment of depression (in the case of those presenting with a major depressive disorder) and encouraging overtreatment with an antidepressants (for those presenting with an adjustment disorder, where, as the study authors argue, the prescription of antidepressants "is at the margin of clinical appropriateness").[83]

The final study described here is by Joel Weissman and his colleagues, who randomly sampled 632 physicians regarding what they call "DTCA visits"—recent office visits during which patients initiated discussion about a prescription drug they had seen advertised on broadcast media.[84] The study found that most DTCA visits (61 percent) did not result in a prescription for the advertised drug, with the three most common reasons being that a different drug was more appropriate (29 percent of the visits), a less costly equally effective drug was available (25 percent), or another course of nondrug treatment was more appropriate (24 percent). Physicians, however, reported that 25 percent of DTCA visits resulted in a new diagnosis. Of these new diagnosis DTCA visits, the ten most common are listed in figure 6.2. This list includes both some conditions that are likely to be identified and treated effectively due-to DTCA advertising, thereby mitigating under-

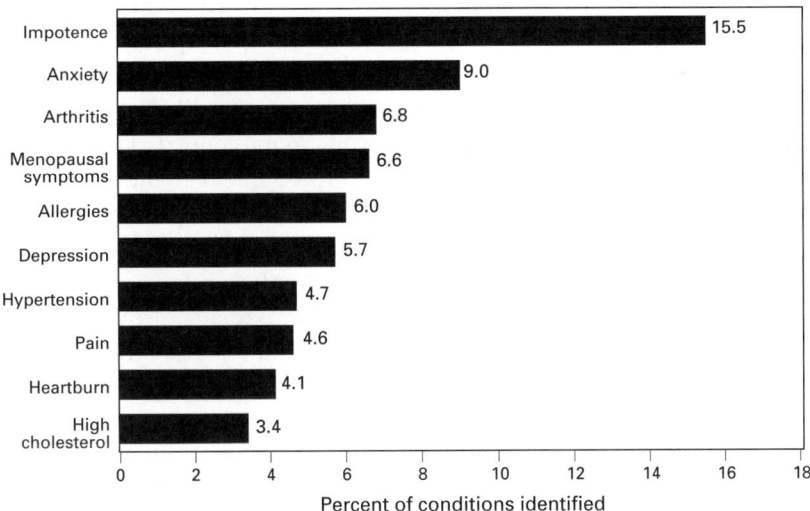

Figure 6.2
Ten Most Common New Diagnoses Identified from DTCA Visits
Note: DTCA visits were defined as physician visits in which the patient initiated discussion about a prescription drug that had been advertised on the broadcast media.
Sources: Reproduced from Berndt (2005); taken from Weissman et al. (2004).

treatment (e.g., depression, anxiety, hypertension, and hyperlipidemia) as well as some conditions that have allegedly been targeted for persuasive advertising of certain prescription drugs, even though less expensive alternative treatments are available (e.g., heartburn, allergies, and arthritis).[85]

Summary and Concluding Remarks

Advertising has long been controversial, and for decades economists have struggled with understanding and interpreting the impacts of advertising on consumers. Of particular concern to economists is how one can conceptualize the effects of advertising without envisaging advertising as changing consumers' preferences—a bedrock assumption within economists' traditional conceptual paradigm. Developments in the theory of industrial organization over the last fifty years have involved building on the insight that advertising constitutes a response by firms to consumers' lack of complete information regarding the availability and quality attributes of the products being sold. Moreover, consumers can obtain information about products in various ways, depending in part on the nature of the product (search versus experience goods, or shopping versus convenience goods); in some cases, the mere fact of advertising and not its content signals useful information to consumers.

While the effects of advertising on consumers are likely ambiguous in many industries, commercial advertising in the context of health care goods and services is particularly contentious, and even more so when it is directed at consumers rather than at health care professionals or payers. Information asymmetry is a most prevalent and powerful phenomenon in health care, and worse yet, not only is information asymmetric, currently it is typically still meager for patients, providers, and payers. This information scarcity and asymmetry is at the heart of many current health care policy controversies regarding competition, quality assessment, pay for performance, and pricing transparency.

DTCA of prescription drugs can be envisaged as an attempt by manufacturers to provide increasingly empowered consumers with information about the availability and quality attributes of drugs. Much of the content communicated via DTCA, however, conveys relatively little medically relevant information, and instead contains images suggesting substantial benefits but downplaying the risks.[86] Although our literature review suggests that persuasive advertising is not necessarily "bad" (the mere fact of advertising might signal a message concerning product quality, especially to repeat buyers), undoubtedly some DTCA advertising is socially wasteful, resulting in "arms races" among various brands to treat the same condition.

On a priori grounds, therefore, like students of other industries, health economists are likely to conclude that DTCA is ambiguous in its effects on consumer welfare. The empirical evidence we have reviewed regarding the effects of DTCA on physician prescribing behavior also indicates ambiguity. As seen in one experimental study, for example, for a chronic condition such as depression, DTCA mitigates undertreatment and addresses unmet needs, but it also results in greater questionable and perhaps even inappropriate treatment.

The economics profession has for the most part been deeply ambivalent about advertising and its impacts, recognizing both its potential beneficial and deleterious features. A fundamental problem economists face is how to place advertising, product quality, learning, and prices into the consumers' decision-making framework that has to date been one of consumers maximizing utility subject to budget constraints. In recent years, behavioral economics has begun to flourish, and potentially it offers to help us better understand consumer decision making beyond that based on the classic paradigm of utility maximization.

Richard Frank touches on how long-standing research impasses involving physician-patient interactions, insurance and moral hazard, and cognitive errors by decision makers in health care might be illuminated by developments in behavioral economics.[87] Unfortunately, that survey does not devote much attention to the role of advertising in health care. Neoclassical economists may have much to learn from behavioral economists, and likely also from other social scientists and brain researchers who have alternative perspectives on how decisions are made, and the factors affecting them, including both information and persuasion.

As with other forms of advertising, DTCA both informs and persuades. Its effects on consumers' welfare are complex, heterogeneous, and ambiguous. While consumers, payers, and health care providers are understandably frustrated with expensive ads containing much more imagery than detailed medical information, it is likely that in a world without advertising frustrations of a different nature would emerge. Moreover, legal precedent in the United States has interpreted the First Amendment of the Constitution as generally protecting commercial free speech, and thus it is unlikely that bans on DTCA or other forms of health care advertising would survive legal challenges.[88] Given this, the FDA, with guidance from Congress, the executive branch, and the courts, will likely continue to have the mandate to regulate the content of DTCA. Regulating the communications content of advertisements and other promotions that attempt to balance information on risks and benefits is inherently difficult and challenging. Undoubtedly, DTCA and its regulation will continue to be controversial, even as we continue to learn more about its impacts.

Acknowledgments

Berndt acknowledges general funding support from the MIT Center for Biomedical Innovation, while Donohue acknowledges support a grant from the National Center for Research Resources, a component of the National Institutes of Health; Roadmap for medical Research. Comments from Emmett B. Keeler, Mark V. Pauly, and Frank A. Sloan are gratefully acknowledged, as are those from several anonymous reviewers. Any opinions and views expressed in this chapter are those of the authors, and not necessarily those of the institutions with which they are affiliated or the research sponsors. The authors can be reached at <eberndt@mit.edu> and <jdonohue@pitt.edu>, respectively.

Notes

1. Berndt (2006).

2. IMS Health (2005).

3. Angell (2004); Mintzes (2002).

4. Saul (2005).

5. Bonaccorso and Sturchio (2002); Holmer (1999, 2002).

6. Pepall et al. (2005, 520).

7. For an example in which the FTC ordered the manufacturer of Doan's Pills, an analgesic, to run corrective ads that undid the claim that the analgesic was specifically made for back pain, and that it was superior in that regard to other pain relief medications, see Pepall et al. (2002, 535).

8. The pharmaceutical industry was under intense scrutiny in the late 1950s and early 1960s. The industry's pricing and promotional practices were the subject of congressional hearings led by Senator Kefauver in 1959. In addition, after the use of the drug thalidomide resulted in serious birth defects in children in Europe, the effectiveness of the FDA's drug approval process at identifying unsafe drugs was called into question.

9. FDCA, § 502(n), U.S.Code 21, § 352(n).

10. U.S. Food and Drug Administration (1969, 74).

11. Ibid.

12. Ibid. (74) (emphasis added).

13. U.S. Food and Drug Administration (1997).

14. Pines (1999).

15. Altman (1982).

16. Kolata (1983).

17. Basara (1992).

18. U.S. Food and Drug Administration (1985).

19. Feather (1997).

20. Kreling et al. (2001).

21. Reeves (1998, 661).

22. Feather (1997).

23. U.S. Food and Drug Administration (1997).

24. Pines (1999); Woodcock (2003).

25. Pines (1999).

26. Ibid. (503).

27. Berndt (2005); Kallen et al. 2007.

28. Galbraith (1958).

29. Benham (1972).

30. Cady (1976).

31. Carlton and Perloff (2005, 481).

32. Pepall et al. (2005, 516).

33. Nelson (1970, 1974). These articles built on work by Stigler (1968).

34. Some marketing economists also identify a third category, in which the quality of some good cannot be determined even after consumption. Called *credence goods*, examples include roof repairs, predeath purchases of embalming and funeral services, and certain types of medical care. In each of these cases, the consumer must rely on the provider's assurances that the work was or will be done properly.

35. Pepall et al. (2005, 517).

36. Nelson (1974); Carlton and Perloff (2005); Pepall et al. (2005); Bagwell (2007) and Nelson (1974, 738–740) reported that advertising-sales ratios were three times as large for the goods he classified as experience goods than for products classified as search goods.

37. One caveat to the Nelson repeat purchase rationale behind the advertising of experience goods has been made by Richard Schmalensee (1978), who noted that if the

price-cost margin of the low-quality good were sufficiently large, there would be strong incentives for fly-by-night firms to dishonestly advertise their product even if there would be no repeat purchases. This is, however, an example of fraudulent advertising.

38. Becker and Murphy (1993).

39. Pepall et al. (2005, 540).

40. Dorfman and Steiner (1954).

41. Kihlstrom and Riordan (1984); Milgrom and Roberts (1986).

42. Pepall et al. (2005, table 20.2).

43. Tirole (1988); Church and Ware (1999); Sutton (1991); Carlton and Perloff (2005).

44. Sutton (1991).

45. In some instances, however, lowering search costs and making information more accessible can lead to a reduction in consumers' welfare, provided that the search costs are still positive. For a discussion, see Carlton and Perloff (2005, 452–467).

46. Tirole (1988); Pepall et al. (2005).

47. Carlton and Perloff (2005, 474, 494).

48. Pepall et al. (2005, 555).

49. Harris (1964, 90).

50. See McGuire (2003), see also other chapters in this book, especially chapter 10.

51. Physician capitation payments typically do not include prescription drug costs. For the services included in capitation payments, see Landon et al. (2005). Rather, pharmacy utilization is carved out and managed separately by pharmaceutical benefit managers, who develop a formulary and structure consumer cost sharing in such a way as to contain costs.

52. Soumerai et al. (1989); Huskamp et al. (2003).

53. Hellerstein (1998); Kravitz et al. (2005); Avorn et al. (1982)

54. Temin (1980); Reichert et al. (2000); Shrank et al. (2005).

55. Frank (2001).

56. Alexander et al. (2005).

57. Ellison et al. (1997).

58. Hellerstein (1998).

59. Crawford and Shum (2005).

60. Ibid.

61. For further discussion of the role of uncertainty in the demand for medical care, see Chapter 3 in this book.

62. Kaiser Family Foundation (2005).

63. Smith (2004).

64. Danzon and Pauly (2002).

65. Fendrick et al. (2001).

66. Gibson et al. (2005).

67. Huskamp et al. (2003).

68. Goldman et al. (2004).

69. Relman (2003).

70. For a more detailed review of the literature, see Berndt (2006).

71. Because the free samples given to physicians are by convention evaluated at their average wholesale price (approximately what cash-paying customers pay for a retail prescription) rather than the marginal production costs, and because these free sample costs comprise roughly half of physician promotion expenditures, the physician promotion to sales ratio considerably overstates pharmaceutical firms' physician promotion costs to sales ratios; moreover, this implies that DTCA as a proportion of the entire promotion bundle is likely considerably higher than 13 to 15 percent. For further discussion, see Berndt (2006).

72. Neslin (2001); see similar findings from Iizuka (2004).

73. Berndt (2006).

74. Rosenthal et al. (2002).

75. Rosenthal et al. (2003).

76. Julie Donohue and her colleagues find that manufacturers typically begin DTCA campaigns within a year of FDA approval. See Donohue et al. (2007).

77. Iizuka (2004).

78. Ibid.

79. Berndt et al. (2002).

80. Iizuka and Jin (2005b).

81. Iizuka and Jin (2005a); Donohue and Berndt (2004).

82. Kravitz et al. (2005).

83. One caveat is that this study dealt only with a onetime visit to a physician, and that compliance and long-term treatment impacts were not examined. For a review of the modest empirical evidence available regarding the effects of DTCA on patient quality of care, see Berndt (2006).

84. Weissman et al. (2004).

85. Ibid.; Berndt (2005).

86. Bell et al. (2000); Woloshin et al.(2004).

87. Frank (2004); see other chapters in this book, especially chapter 7.

88. An influential legal precedent in the United States is the case *Central Hudson Gas and Electric v. Public Service Commission*, which was considered by the U.S. Supreme Court in 1997. The Supreme Court justices ruled that the First Amendment protects consumers' "right to receive information," but that regulations affecting commercial free speech do not violate the First Amendment if: the regulated speech concerns an illegal activity; the speech is misleading; or the government's interest in restricting the speech is substantial, the regulation in question directly advances the government's interest, and the regulation is no more extensive than necessary to serve the government's interest. Additional Supreme Court rulings invalidated state laws prohibiting price advertising of prescription drugs and alcohol, and laws banning news racks for primarily commercial publications, such as real estate guides. For further information, see "Government Regulation of Commercial Speech. The Issue: How Far May Government Go in Regulating Speech That Proposes an Economic Transaction?," available at http://www.law.umkc.edu/faculty/projects/ftrials/conlaw/commercial.htm> (accessed May 2, 2005).

7
Reefer Madness, **Frank the Tank, or** *Pretty Woman:* **To What Extent Do Addictive Behaviors Respond to Incentives?**

John Cawley

Unhealthy behaviors such as drinking alcohol, smoking, taking drugs, engaging in risky sex, and eating and physical activity patterns that lead to obesity are of considerable policy concern for a variety of reasons. First, they have been linked to external costs imposed on taxpayers through private group health insurance and public health insurance programs.[1] Second, some (noneconomists) make the normative argument that these behaviors are morally wrong, and the government should intervene to tax or otherwise regulate these activities.[2] Both of these arguments lead proponents to recommend taxes: Pigovian taxes that internalize externalities in the first case; and sin taxes to reduce consumption in the second case.

This raises the broader question of whether health behaviors respond to incentives such as taxes. This chapter discusses three economic models of addictive behavior that posit differing extents to which health behaviors respond to incentives. It also synthesizes evidence from economic research on which of these stylized models is most accurate.

This chapter focuses on the following habitual or addictive activities: drinking alcohol, smoking, drug use, sex,[3] and obesity-related behaviors such as diet and physical activity. This is a subset of the known addictive activities; researchers have also found evidence of addiction for other behaviors, including gambling, romantic relationships, masturbation, physical self-mutilation, television watching, video games, surfing the Internet, caffeine consumption, sugar consumption, work, shoplifting, spending money, religiosity, and risk taking.[4]

In economics, a good or activity is considered addictive if it has three characteristics. The first is *tolerance*—the amount of past consumption directly affects utility. For example, someone who has consumed a lot of drugs in the past is unhappier (all else equal) than someone who has abstained. Drugs are an example of a harmful addiction, but beneficial addictions are also possible. For example, exercise can be habitual, and the amount of past exercise that one has engaged in can raise one's utility by improving health. The second characteristic of addiction is *withdrawal*—consuming the good raises the person's instantaneous utility. In other words, the good has a positive marginal utility of consumption. The third characteristic of addiction is *reinforcement*—the good has a higher marginal utility of consumption when the person has engaged in a lot of consumption in the recent past. In other words, consumption of any addictive good in two consecutive time periods are complements; the marginal utility of today's consumption is raised by consumption yesterday, just as the marginal utility of peanut butter is raised when it is consumed with jelly.[5] The fact that consumption in neighboring (or adjacent) time periods are complements has led economists to refer to reinforcement as *"adjacent complementarity."* To illustrate adjacent complementarity in the opposite way, quitting an addictive good or activity is harder the more often you've engaged in it in the recent past, and continuing to abstain gets easier over time.

In economics, the terms habit and addiction are used interchangeably, as they both refer to adjacent complementarity.[6] I will follow this convention, though most noneconomists would probably consider the term addictive most appropriate for describing alcohol, drugs, and cigarettes, and the term habit most appropriate for describing sex, eating patterns, and physical activity.

Models of Addictive Behavior

Research on addictive behaviors is challenging for several reasons. First, addiction is a dilemma because it involves people choosing to participate in activities with severe consequences in the long term and sometimes in the short term as well. This raises the question of whether people are acting irrationally, lack important information about the consequences, or simply ignore the future; Jon Elster and Ole-Jorgen Skog refer to this as "the paradox of voluntary self-destructive behavior."[7] Second, addiction is an issue that transcends traditional academic disciplines, and no single researcher has the ideal training to study all aspects of the problem. Neurobiology, for instance, has documented how addictive substances produce sensations of pleasure or reward by manipulating the brain's chemistry in various ways: some drugs stimulate the release of neurotransmitters such as dopamine (which creates feelings of pleasure), others block the brain's reabsorption of neurotransmitters, and still others bind with the receptors for such neurotransmitters.[8] Clearly, understanding the chemistry of addiction is critical, but most of those findings are based on animal studies, and a full understanding of human addiction requires the insights of various social science disciplines. Economics is informative on the role of price and income. Sociology is useful for understanding the possible role of peers, neighborhood, and culture. Few, if any, researchers have expertise in all of the relevant fields.

Before turning to a synthesis of research on findings regarding the extent to which addictive behaviors respond to incentives, I first discuss models of addictive behavior that underlie research, policy discussions, and treatment decisions. The following sections describe three competing social science models of addictive behavior: the irrational actor model, the perfectly rational actor model, and the imperfectly rational actor model.

The Irrational Actor

Economists define rationality as the ability to solve constrained maximization problems—for example, the ability to make yourself as well-off as possible given the constraints on your budget and time.[9] Since we do not observe each other's utility functions or constraints, strong evidence is necessary to prove that someone is unable to act in their own best interest. To illustrate how difficult it can be to determine whether or not self-destructive behavior is evidence of irrationality, keep in mind that even suicide can be a rational decision.[10]

The irrational actor model posits that people behave irrationally when engaging in addictive behaviors like drinking alcohol, taking drugs, and having sex. The following anecdote about alcoholism, which is almost two hundred years old, provides a vivid example of the irrational actor model: "When strongly urged, by one of his friends, to leave off drinking, he [the alcoholic] said, 'Were a keg of rum in one corner of a room, and were a cannon constantly discharging balls between me and it, I could not refrain from passing before that cannon, in order to get at the rum.'"[11]

Another version of the irrational actor model is that people have split personalities: a person could be completely normal when not consuming alcohol or drugs, but wild and utterly irrational when consuming.

The irrational actor model of addictive behavior was arguably the dominant early view in social science and medicine. Elster, a social scientist who has made a career studying addiction, writes:

A common pretheoretical view of human addiction does in fact suggest that the behavior of the addict is based on an irresistible craving: compulsive, mechanical, and insensitive to all other rewards and punishments. At least this is supposed to be true for the most strongly addictive drugs, such as crack cocaine. In their use of these drugs, human beings allegedly do not differ from rats in their tendency to ignore all other considerations for the sake of the euphoria of consumption or relief from the dysphoria of abstinence.[12]

George Lowenstein offers a modern variant of the irrational actor model. He interprets addiction as the result of visceral urges that are provoked by external cues. The urges make people impulsive and do things that they later regret, and when the urges are particularly strong they "overwhelm decisionmaking altogether, superceding volitional control of behavior."[13]

The irrational addict model is presented most starkly (and perhaps most comically) in the film *Reefer Madness*. In this movie, previously normal people change dramatically after smoking marijuana (i.e., they seem to have split personalities), becoming sexually promiscuous and even murderous. They are manic consumers, unwilling or unable to moderate their consumption. Toward the end of the film, one of the main characters, recalling how under the influence of marijuana she and her friends did awful things, and apparently knowing that she can never restrain her consumption, throws herself from a window to commit suicide. Her suicide is actually the most rational action taken by a marijuana user in the movie, since it presumably reflected farsightedness and a cost-benefit analysis about the attractiveness of death relative to continued addiction.

The Rational Actor

A landmark paper that modeled rational behavior concerning addictive goods is "A Theory of Rational Addiction" by Gary Becker and Kevin Murphy. Becker and Murphy use the term "rational" to refer to farsightedness by the individual; that is, one's ability to anticipate the future consequences of one's actions and take those consequences into account when deciding how much of an addictive good to consume. In the Becker and Murphy model, a person for whom a good is highly addictive (i.e., has high adjacent complementarity) might voluntarily become an addict, even though he perfectly forecasts the consequences of his actions, because he calculates that he enjoys greater utility by being an addict than by abstaining. The Becker and Murphy model spells out carefully how decisions about unhealthy behaviors respond to prices, the marginal utility of consumption, and the future consequences of unhealthy behaviors.[14]

Rational decision making concerning habitual activities is portrayed in the movie *Pretty Woman*. In that film, Richard Gere makes an offer (that he describes as a business proposition) to a prostitute played by Julia Roberts (who he calls an employee). Gere describes the services he wants and the two engage in an unemotional, logical negotiation over price. A bonus for the economist viewer is that at the end of their negotiation, when the price has been agreed on, the two parties reveal their reservation prices. A transcript of the relevant dialogue appears below:

Edward [Richard Gere]: Vivian, I have a business proposition for you.

Vivian [Julia Roberts]: What do you want?

Edward: I'm going to be in town until Sunday. I'd like you to spend the week with me.

Vivian: Really?

Edward: Yes. Yes, I'd like to hire you as an employee. Would you consider spending the week with me? I will pay you to be at my beck and call.

Vivian: Look, I'd love to be your "beck-and-call girl," but you're a rich, good-lookin' guy. You could get a million girls free.

Edward: I want a professional. I don't need any romantic hassles this week.

Vivian: If you're talkin' twenty-four hours a day, it's gonna cost you.

Edward: Oh, yes, of course! All right, here we go. Give me a ballpark figure. How much?

Vivian: Six full nights, days too. Four thousand.

Edward: Six nights at $300 is $1,800.

Vivian: You want days too.

Edward: Two thousand.

Vivian: Three thousand.

Edward: Done.

Vivian: Holy shit! [Laughs]

Edward: Vivian. Vivian, is that a yes?

Vivian: Yes. [Laughing] Yes!

[Splice]

Vivian: I would have stayed for two thousand.

Edward: I would have paid four.[15]

The calm, dispassionate way in which both parties to future sexual acts negotiate the price of those activities suggests that their sex drives are not (in words of Elster) "compulsive, mechanical, and insensitive to all other rewards and punishments."[16] Instead, their sexual activities are sensitive to price; Edward has a maximum willingness to pay, and Vivian has a minimum willingness to accept.

The Imperfectly Rational Actor

The third model of addictive behavior is that of the imperfectly rational actor. In this model, the strong assumptions of the theory of rational addiction are relaxed. In particular, this model allows for rationality to be imperfect or bounded.[17] Actors may have only limited ability to solve constrained maximization problems or process information. Alternately, there may be nontrivial deliberation costs so that rather than evaluate the present discounted value of utility associated with every possible option, one simply adheres to rules of thumb or heuristics that guide behavior in complicated situations. These heuristics may result in the individual failing to maximize utility.

The field of behavioral economics studies the ways in which the decision making of economic agents deviates from rationality. Ted O'Donoghue and Matthew Rabin describe the difference between traditional economics and behavioral economics in the following way.[18] In traditional economics, actors can make incorrect predictions about the future, but these errors cannot be systematic. Actors are assumed to learn and adjust their expectations, and therefore not continue to make the same mistake again and again. Behavioral economics, in contrast, allows for *systematic* incorrect predictions; for example, a person might consistently underestimate his self-control, never adjust his expectations, and therefore keep making the same mistakes over and over.

One explanation for such systematic error is time-inconsistent preferences. This is the tendency to discount tomorrow relative to today more than one discounts the day after tomorrow relative to tomorrow. This results in an inconsistency: when considering strategies such as quitting smoking or dieting that would increase long-term utility at the expense of utility today, a person with time-inconsistent preferences would rather start sooner than later, with the exception that they do not want to start today. Time-inconsistent preferences are useful for understanding what otherwise looks like irrational behavior, such as a person frequently saying that he wants to quit smoking tomorrow, but when tomorrow comes, he always puts it off quitting for another day. In essence, people with time-inconsistent preferences have a principal-agent problem with their future selves, and must find ways to precommit their future selves to the course of action that will require short-run sacrifices in order to maximize long-run utility. Richard Thaler and Hersh Shefrin describe this as a struggle between a "farsighted planner" who wants to maximize long-run utility and a "myopic doer" who wants to enjoy today and ignore future consequences.[19] Someone trying to quit an addiction is trying to empower the farsighted planner side of their personality to control the myopic doer side.

The movie *Old School* provides an example of imperfectly rational behavior with respect to addictive goods. Will Ferrell plays Frank, who is aware that when he drinks he has a different personality, known as Frank the Tank. This portrayal includes elements of the split personality view of addiction described under the irrational actor model, but what differentiates Frank from an irrational addict is his awareness of his situation and ability to use that knowledge to at least partly control his behavior. He knows that he becomes Frank the Tank when he drinks, and knows he does not want to become Frank the Tank, so he chooses not to drink.

Nevertheless, Frank appears to have time-inconsistent preferences. As he walks through a keg party carrying soda pop, some college students encourage him to funnel some beer. He is at first able to resist the temptation, explaining that he cannot drink because he has a big day with his wife tomorrow—they're going shopping at Home Depot and Bed Bath & Beyond. As he tells the students this, however, he sees the scorn on their faces and suddenly succumbs to the desire for peer acceptance. (Frank's demand for beer is partly a derived demand—derived from the demand for peer acceptance.) Frank promised his wife he would not drink, and he starts out insisting that he will have just one funnel of beer, but after the first one he is completely unable to control his consumption. A transcript of the relevant dialogue appears below.

Marissa Ricard: You've come a long way since Frank the Tank and we don't want him coming back now, do we?

Frank Ricard [Will Ferrell]:   Honey, Frank the Tank is not coming back. OK? That part of me is over, it's water under the bridge. I promise.

[Splice]

Frank: [Squeezing through a crowded party holding cans of soda pop] Excuse me. Pardon me. I just want to get through there, this door over here, if you don't mind. Thank you.

Kid 1:   This is the guy I was talking about. This is his house.

Kid 2:   What's up, man?

Frank: No, that's my friend, Mitch. You're mistaking me. That's my friend Mitch, he owns the house.

Kid 1:   Anyway, come hit this right here. [Indicates a funnel and tube filled with beer] You need to hit this.

Frank: No, I appreciate it, but I told my wife I wouldn't drink tonight. Besides, I've got a big day tomorrow. But you guys have a great time.

Kid 2:   A big day? Doing what?

Frank: Well, um, actually a pretty nice little Saturday. We're gonna go to Home Depot, yeah, buy some wallpaper, maybe get some flooring, stuff like that. Maybe Bed Bath & Beyond, I don't know. I don't know if we'll have enough time. [Kids look disgusted] You know what? Give me that thing. I'll do one. I'll do one.

Kid 1:   He's gonna do one! He's gonna do one!

[Frank chugs the entire amount]

Kid 2:   That's a talented man right there.

Kid 1:   That's what I'm talking about.

Frank: Fill it up again! God, that's good. It's so good! Once it hits your lips, it's so good!

[Splice]

[Frank is chugging yet another funnel of beer]

Group of kids: Frank the Tank! Frank the Tank! Frank the Tank!

[Frank exults in their cheers, and then grabs a female student and drunkenly licks her face][20]

Overall, Frank is an accurate illustration of the imperfectly rational actor. He is farsighted and can see the consequences of his actions, and is usually able to abstain. Yet he overestimates his ability to resist temptation, and as a result he is sometimes unable to stick to the strategy that maximizes his long-term utility and succumbs to his short-term interest.

Derived Demand and Peer Effects

It is likely that the demand for addictive goods or activities is a derived one—derived from the demand for peer acceptance (as illustrated by Frank's behavior at the keg party in *Old School*). In other words, what people may truly demand is the approval of their peers, and one way to achieve that is to engage in addictive behaviors. A teenager might start smoking, for example, not because he finds the cigarettes inherently enjoyable at first but in order to look cool.

Harvey Leibenstein formalizes how peer effects can affect demand.[21] He notes that there may be a "bandwagon" effect, which is consistent with peer pressure; that is consumers want to consume what others are consuming. The existence of a bandwagon effect makes the market demand curve more elastic; when price falls, the total demand increases not only because of the price effect but also because of the bandwagon effect. For example, a lower price increases the quantity demanded, which makes the good more popular and therefore more attractive via the bandwagon effect, which increases the demand even more. Thus, the bandwagon effect multiplies the price effect.

Leibenstein also notes an opposite effect: a "snob" effect. Once something becomes common, people may not want to consume it anymore. Since the snob effect is the opposite of the bandwagon effect, it is not surprising that it has the opposite impact on the demand curve. Whereas a bandwagon effect makes the market demand curve more elastic, the snob effect makes the market demand curve less elastic. If price falls, the price effect is for the quantity demanded to increase, but the snob effect attenuates that because when use of the good becomes more common, it is less appealing. Both the bandwagon and snob effects imply that the market demand curve is not simply the horizontal summation of all individual demand curves in the market (which is the basic model taught in intermediate microeconomics). Leibenstein also observes a "Veblen" effect: people may want to consume goods that are expensive, presumably to impress others with their conspicuous consumption.[22]

If only strong bandwagon effects are present than either everyone would end up consuming the good "because as it increased in popularity it would become increasingly attractive to the people still not consuming" or no one would consume the good. If only strong snob effects are present, in the end only one person (at most) would consume. Thus, it is likely that bandwagon and snob effects operate simultaneously. When teenagers rebel against the majority of their peers, for example, they tend not to rebel in a purely individual way, wearing things no one else is wearing and doing things no one else is doing. Instead, they often rebel by joining a group in which all rebel in the same way—say, by dressing in Goth clothing and smoking. The members of such a group would derive utility from snob effects by rebelling against the majority of their peers, but simultaneously derive utility from the bandwagon effect by conforming with a select minority. For most addictive goods, people may strike a balance between bandwagon and snob effects.

Economics mostly takes preferences as given (though the field of behavioral economics is changing that), so economic theory has little to say about why certain goods have strong bandwagon or snob effects. While economics may not focus much on the formation of preferences, marketers do.[23] Producers recognize that the demand for cigarettes and alcohol may be a derived demand for peer acceptance, and they pay for advertisements so consumers can produce more coolness with their product than with that of a rival manufacturer. In other words, they seek to increase the marginal product of their brand in the consumer's production function for coolness or peer acceptance.[24] Sometimes marketers are successful in doing this, as with Joe Camel (which appears to have worked to increase the coolness of Camel brand cigarettes, given that the Master Settlement Agreement between the tobacco companies and the state attorneys general specifically bans that cartoon).

Sometimes marketers fail in their attempts, as with the alcoholic beverage Zima, which became a laughingstock among consumers. I cannot explain why the Joe Camel ads succeeded and the Zima ads backfired in their attempts to increase the amount of coolness and peer acceptance that could be produced using the brands. The definition of coolness is elusive, and consumers appear to react severely to awkward or heavy-handed marketing attempts to alter their preferences.

For youths, one might add yet another effect to those discussed by Leibenstein: a "rebellious" effect. Teenagers enjoy doing things of which authority figures disapprove. This differs from the snob effect because the goal is not to do things that none of your peers are doing but to do things that authority figures do not want you to do. It differs from the bandwagon effect because utility is derived from rebelling against authority distinct from doing what all other teenagers are doing. The rebellious effect does not affect the price elasticity of market demand because this effect does not describe a dependence between the demand curves of individual teenagers (in contrast to the bandwagon and snob effects) but does affect the intercept of the demand curve—more disapproval by authority shifts the demand curve to the right (as teenagers demand more at any given price).

Models of Addictive Behavior Have Different Implications for Policy

Which model of addictive behavior is true has implications for policy. For instance, if one believes the irrational addict (e.g., *Reefer Madness*) model of addictive behavior, then prohibition may be the only effective policy to decrease consumption. Since addicts are presumed to be completely irrational when consuming, demand is likely to be completely price inelastic. Taxing the substance would have little or no impact on the quantity demanded. Likewise, providing additional information about the consequences is unlikely to have any impact on the consumption of an irrational addict. If even the smallest amount of consumption is predicted to lead irresistibly to destructive behavior, one might infer that any and all consumption should be banned.

If one believes the perfectly rational model of addictive behavior (e.g., *Pretty Woman*) then a much wider range of public policy levers is appealing. For example, raising taxes on alcohol and cigarettes (perhaps motivated by a desire to internalize external costs) would be predicted to lower consumption. Raising the legal penalties for drug use would likewise be expected to decrease consumption. If one believed that consumers simply lack information about the consequences of their actions, they could be informed using surgeon general's reports, such as the 1964 report on smoking, or straightforward public service announcements such as Nancy Reagan's "Just Say No" campaign, which simply stated that drugs were bad and asked people not to consume; its entire message consisted of the following: "Nancy Reagan: Hello, this is Nancy Reagan. If you just say 'no' to drugs, you'll be saying 'yes' to a whole lot more." One would only expect this simple statement to decrease drug use if one implicitly had the rational actor model of addictive behavior in mind: perhaps potential users lack information that drugs have negative consequences, but once told this they will be able to abstain (i.e., they have no problem with time-inconsistent preferences).

In addition, if consumers are at least somewhat rational, then there may exist bandwagon, snob, or other nonprice effects. (These effects are not relevant for an irrational addict because such a person is oblivious to what others are doing.) These peer effects are policy relevant because they can generate incentives to which the consumption of addictive goods might respond. A public health campaign that made smoking, drinking, drug use, or unprotected sex uncool could, in the reverse of the bandwagon effect, cause a stampede away from that activity. This is an example of what Leibenstein calls the "social taboo" effect, which is the bandwagon effect in reverse; consumption is more stigmatizing when fewer are consuming. Recently, public service announcements have emphasized that cigarette companies try to manipulate teenagers, in an effort to make teenagers resent tobacco companies as authority figures and rebel against their advertising.[25] The goal, in effect, is to divert youth away from rebelling against their parents by smoking and towards rebelling against corporate America by refusing to smoke. Interestingly, public health campaigns need not actually make such activities uncool; if there exist social taboo effects, then such campaigns can decrease consumption simply by making the activities seem uncommon.

If the imperfectly rational model of addictive behavior (as illustrated by *Old School*'s Frank the Tank) is most accurate, then the ideal policies lie somewhere between those implied by the irrational addict model and the perfectly rational model. Imperfectly rational addicts might be somewhat price sensitive, but perhaps less sensitive than if they were perfectly rational. If they have time-inconsistent preferences, they may seek ways to precommit to abstention. Jonathan Gruber and Sendhil Mullainathan argue that if preferences are time inconsistent, then the optimal sin tax should reflect not only all of the external costs to society but also some of the internal costs to the consumer.[26] The logic is that time-inconsistent individuals may be grateful for the tax, because it helps them to do what they want like, but are unable to do unassisted: reduce their consumption.

If addicts are imperfectly rather than perfectly rational, relative to the perfectly rational case, then public finance strategies may be less effective because prices have less influence on the behavior of a less rational person. Likewise, simply providing information may be less effective because consumers may ignore it or heavily discount the future consequences of consumption.

The Research Evidence on Whether Addictive Behavior Responds to Incentives

This section evaluates which model of addictive behavior is most consistent with the findings of empirical economics research.[27] In the following discussion, the evidence is organized not by activity (e.g., smoking) but by the type of incentive (e.g., price) and where research has looked for a response to incentives (at the extensive margin—whether one participates in the activity at all—or the intensive margin—how much one consumes conditional on participating). This organization reflects the belief that research on each addictive behavior can be informed by the findings regarding other addictive behaviors.

In the subsequent sections, I review the evidence concerning the following three research questions:

1. Do abstainers respond to incentives when deciding whether to start consuming? In other words, do unhealthy behaviors respond to incentives at the extensive margin?

2. Do users respond to incentives when deciding how much to consume? In other words, do unhealthy behaviors respond to incentives at the intensive margin?

3. How can this information be used to better set health policy?

An empirical model commonly used to study the consumption of addictive goods is John Cragg's two-part model, in which participation (any use) and frequency (quantity consumed conditional on any use) are estimated separately.[28] Since the consumption of addictive goods may be differentially elastic to the incentives at the extensive margin (participation) and the intensive margin (frequency), I examine the evidence on each separately.

To what different incentives might people respond? I take it for granted that consumers respond to the marginal utility of consumption. For example, if two drugs were of equal cost and had equal side effects, but one was twice as enjoyable as the other, I take it for granted that people would consume the more enjoyable drug. Another more general example of people responding to in cultures is addiction itself: if it has been greater, past consumption creates an incentive to consume more today (specifically, past consumption raises the marginal utility of consumption today)—an incentive to which addicts frequently respond. Since it is obvious that people respond to the incentive of feeling good (i.e., to the marginal utility of consumption), I do not consider it further in this chapter.

Price is another incentive to which people may respond. In the subsequent sections, I review the evidence on the price elasticity of demand for addictive goods at both the extensive and intensive margins.

A third class of incentives includes the nonprice components of the total cost; instance, the search and time costs of acquiring the substance. The nonprice components of the total cost also include health impacts and legal ramifications such as the chance of apprehension and jail time for substances that are illegal. If the information about the consequences is imperfect, it is possible that the consumption would respond to information about the consequences. Peer effects represent another incentive, and they may take the form of bandwagon/social taboo, snob, or rebellion effects.

In the sections that follow, I briefly summarize literatures that are large and that use a variety of methods, data, and assumptions. Reconciling different results in light of the variation in methods and data is beyond the scope of this review, since my interest is not in stating with the greatest precision the consensus estimates but simply providing a sense of whether addictive behaviors generally respond to specific incentives.

Incentive Response at the Extensive Margin

Does Participation Respond to Price?

A large body of economic research consistently finds that smoking is negatively correlated with the price of cigarettes; the price elasticity of smoking participation is around –0.48.[29] The price elasticity of smoking participation varies by age, gender, and other factors. There is general agreement that adults and youths are differentially responsive to price, but there is debate over whether youths are more or less price sensitive than adults. Early studies suggested that youths were more price elastic than adults in their smoking participation, but more recent studies using richer data suggest that price has less impact on the smoking initiation of youths than that of adults.[30]

When deciding whether to start smoking, boys but not girls appear to be sensitive to price.[31] Price sensitivity also varies with smoking history; specifically, higher cigarette prices decrease the probability of current use by those who have not smoked in the past, but have no impact on the probability of current use by previous smokers.[32]

Cigarette taxes have been shown to affect how many years pass before smokers quit; a 5 percent increase in the cigarette tax would reduce by 2 to 3.5 percent the number of years spent smoking.[33] Pregnant women are sensitive to price when deciding to quit smoking; a 10 percent increase in cigarette prices would increase by 10 percent the probability that pregnant women quit smoking.[34] Quits by young adults are also sensitive to price.[35]

The Master Settlement Agreement between major tobacco companies and the state attorneys general in November 1998 resulted in an immediate increase in cigarette prices of 43.5 cents per pack, or nearly 20 percent of the presettlement price, and the price continued to rise for the next two years.[36] This price rise reduced smoking rates by 13 percent among youths and by 5 percent among adults.[37] Smoking by pregnant women, however, fell by less than 3 percent in response to the price hike.[38]

Almost every study that estimates the price elasticity of demand for alcohol finds that the use of alcohol decreases when its price rises.[39] A 10 percent increase in the price of alcohol decreases by 5.5 percent the probability that an individual is a current drinker.[40] A dollar increase in the beer excise tax reduces the prevalence of drinking by 2 percentage points among youths.[41]

Marijuana use is also sensitive to price; a 10 percent increase in the price of marijuana decreases its use at the extensive margin among high school seniors by 3 percent.[42] Even the use of hard drugs is price sensitive. A 10 percent increase in price is estimated to reduce the probability of cocaine use by approximately 10 percent.[43] And the price elasticity of cocaine use is similar across race, gender, and age groups.[44] The price elasticity of heroin participation is −0.89, and is similar across race, gender, and age groups.[45]

The responsiveness of drug use to incentives is the basis for an innovative substance abuse treatment known as *contingency management* or *voucher-based reinforcement therapy*.[46] This therapy offers incentives for addicts to remain abstinent by providing them with vouchers in exchange for negative results on drug tests; the vouchers can then be exchanged for market goods.[47] (Vouchers are awarded instead of cash because recovering addicts might be tempted to spend cash on drugs.) In essence, this program raises the total price of engaging in the addictive behavior. This program was devised for cocaine addicts but has since been applied to the treatment of addiction to alcohol, marijuana, nicotine, and opiates.[48] A meta-analysis of studies evaluating the impact of voucher-based reinforcement therapy found overwhelming evidence that the incentive of vouchers increased abstinence; they estimate that the vouchers raised compliance by an average of 30 percent.[49] Larger effect sizes were found for programs that offered more valuable vouchers and those that delivered vouchers immediately.[50] A striking feature of these programs is the modest amount of the youcher; for example, as little as $2.50 for a single negative test result for cocaine[51] or as little as $137 paid on average over a three-month period.[52]

Sexual activity also responds to price. Paul Gertler, Manisha Shah, and Stefano Bertozzi surveyed over a thousand female prostitutes in two Mexican states and collected data on the details of the last three or four transactions, including customer characteristics, services rendered, and price.[53] The prices are the result of a negotiation between the prostitute and the client, so their data allow them to test whether prices respond to the services requested by the customer. (In contrast, prices for cigarettes and alcohol are set at the market level, and are not the result of a negotiation between agents.) They find that prostitutes charge 23 percent more if the client requests unprotected sex. If the client requests oral sex in addition to vaginal sex, the client pays an average of 18 percent more. If stripping is requested in addition to sex, the premium is 27 percent. Clients are also willing to pay an 11 percent premium for prostitutes with a secondary education and a 29 percent premium for those who are very physically attractive (in the opinion of the interviewer). The price a prostitute earns falls by 2 percent for each additional year of her age above the mean of 27.8.

There is also evidence that participation in addictive activities responds to the prices of other goods. Higher gas prices are associated with a lower probability that teenagers drink alcohol, which is consistent with several hypotheses: teens drive to acquire alcohol; teens drive to hide their consumption of alcohol; or that drinking and driving are complements.[54]

An important caveat is that many studies that measure the price responsiveness of health behaviors treat variation across states in taxes on cigarettes or alcohol as a quasinatural experiment—they implicitly assume that variation in such taxes across states is random, uncorrelated with factors unobserved by economists that might affect health behaviors. However, a limitation of this strategy is that state taxes are not set randomly but are chosen by state legislatures based in part on the sentiment of their constituents regarding health behaviors. For example, the tobacco-producing states of Kentucky and North Carolina have historically had the lowest cigarette tax rates in the nation, while Utah (a relatively religious state) and California (a relatively health-conscious state) have among the highest cigarette tax rates. A naive comparison of smoking prevalence with state tax rates would conclude that the higher taxes in California and Utah are responsible for the lower prevalence of smoking, but in fact both the prevalence and the tax rates might truly be due to anti-smoking sentiment. In other words, the omission of anti-smoking sentiment from regressions of cigarette consumption on state cigarette tax rate results in omitted variable bias and overestimates of the true impact of price on behavior.[55]

Even with this caveat, there is overwhelming evidence that participation in habitual or addictive activities responds to price. Table 7.1 summarizes the typical estimates of elasticities of demand at the extensive margin for several addictive goods.

Table 7.1
Estimates of Price Elasticity of Demand at the Extensive Margin (Any Use) for Various Addictive Goods

Addictive good	Estimate of price elasticity of participation	Source
Cigarettes	−0.48	Gilleskie and Strumpf (2005)
Alcohol	−0.55	Manning et al. (1995)
Marijuana	−0.3	Pacula et al. (2001)
Cocaine	−1.0	Chaloupka et al. (1999)
Heroin	−0.89	Saffer and Chaloupka (1999)

Does Participation Respond to Nonprice Costs?

The nonprice costs of addictive behavior include the time cost of acquiring addictive substances, the health risks associated with consumption, and the risk of legal penalty. Laws barring youth possession, use, and/or purchase of tobacco appear to deter smoking participation by teens.[56] Presumably this is because such laws increase the time cost for teens to acquire cigarettes. A large body of research suggests that restrictions on smoking in public places (e.g., clean indoor air laws) and private workplaces reduces the prevalence of smoking.[57]

Smoking also appears to be sensitive to information about health consequences. The most dramatic example of an information revelation about the harmful effects of an addictive commodity is the release of the first surgeon general's report on smoking and health in 1964. This report led to an immediate 5 percent reduction in smoking; other research literature indicates that both warning labels on cigarette packs and paid antismoking advertisements also significantly reduce smoking.[58] The better educated tend reduce their smoking more than the less educated in response to such information.[59]

State laws regarding the minimum age to purchase alcohol raise the time cost for teens to acquire alcohol. As a result, youths who are younger than the minimum purchase age for alcohol in their state are 5.5 percentage points less likely to drink in the past thirty days.[60] Yet minimum purchase age laws may have unintended consequences because they may lead youth to switch from alcohol to drugs. (In other words, youths may regard alcohol and drugs as substitutes.) For example, raising a states minimum legal drinking age from eighteen to twenty-one has been estimated to increase the prevalence of youth marijuana consumption by 2.4 percentage points.[61]

Legal penalties deter drug use. Fines for marijuana possession and an increased probability of arrest are associated with a lower probability that young adults will use marijuana.[62] It has been estimated that a doubling of fines for marijuana possession would reduce the probability of youth marijuana use by less than 1 percent, and that marijuana decriminalization would raise the probability of marijuana use by 4 to 5 percent.[63] It is estimated that a doubling of the fines for cocaine possession would reduce the probability of youth cocaine use by roughly 4 percent.[64]

Research on the responsiveness of substance use to legal penalties faces the same problem that confronts research on the responsiveness of smoking to cigarette taxes: the policies studied are often treated as quasi-natural experiments when in fact they may be determined by the sentiment of state residents (which may directly affect health behaviors). Specifically, states that tend to enact harsher penalties for underage drinking, selling cigarettes to minors, smoking in public places or worksites, drunk driving, or drug use may be those with citizens most opposed to the behaviors, and thus a correlation between tougher penalties and lower use may reflect the sentiment rather than the true effect of the law. The same problem applies to variation across states in enforcement of such laws.

Providing information about adverse health consequences can deter use. Teenagers' perceived risk of harm from the regular use of marijuana is associated with a lower probability of using marijuana in the past year.[65] The Nutrition Labeling and Education Act (NLEA), which required the fat content of foods to be listed on a nutrition label, resulted in a larger fraction of consumers choosing low-fat options.[66] In unregulated food markets, not every brand reveals health information that consumers may consider relevant to their choice, and as a result mandatory labeling may improve population health.[67]

Sexually transmitted disease is one potential cost of sex, and sexual activity appears to respond to variations in that risk.[68] For example, teenage girls are more likely to be virgins when they live in states with a higher prevalence of AIDS, but no such pattern exists for boys, perhaps because boys are less likely to contract a sexually transmitted disease through heterosexual vaginal intercourse.[69] The use of condoms is positively correlated with the local prevalence of AIDS in the state, and this behavioral response is greatest among those thought to face the greatest risk of infection: black rather than white men, and unmarried rather than married men.[70] Moreover, before the AIDS epidemic the use of condoms did not vary regionally across the United States, but after the AIDS epidemic took off the use of condoms rose faster in the regions with the greatest prevalence of AIDS.[71] An experiment was conducted in Kenya in which teenagers in randomly selected schools were provided information about HIV in particular; they were informed that the prevalence of HIV is higher among adult men than among teenage boys. The result was that the incidence of teenage girls impregnated by an adult male fell by 65 percent as teenage girls substituted away from unprotected sex with adult men and toward condom-utilizing sex with teenage boys.[72] Better-educated individuals appear more responsive to information campaigns to prevent HIV and AIDS in Africa.[73] In general, an area for future research is to identify the mediators (e.g., education) that may affect the responsiveness of risky behaviors to incentives.

Does Participation Respond to Peers?

Behaviors generally tend to be correlated within peer groups. For example, drug and alcohol use are correlated among teens living in the same neighborhoods.[74] High school seniors are more likely to have smoked marijuana in the past year if a high percentage of their peers have also smoked it.[75] Obviously, since people choose their peer groups, these correlations cannot be interpreted as causal effects; the correlation could simply reflect the fact that youth who intend to smoke, drink, and use drugs want to socialize with others with the same preferences.

Several papers have addressed the endogeneity of peer influences using variation in peers that is not chosen by youths. For example, Daniel Eisenberg exploits as a natural experiment the fact that in some school districts, eighth graders attend middle school while in other districts they attend high school; students who by chance live in the latter districts are exposed to an older set of peers.[76] Petter Lundborg exploits the random assignment of a student to a classroom in a given grade of a given school.[77] And Laura Argys and Daniel Rees exploit as a natural experiment the fact that some children are born just before the cutoff data for attending kindergarten; these children are likely to be younger than their eventual classmates and therefore more susceptible to peer influence.[78] In general, this literature finds substantial peer effects on the probability that a youth smokes, drinks alcohol, and uses drugs.[79]

The importance of peers in determining alcohol use, drug use, and overeating is implicit in the strategy followed by Alcoholics Anonymous, Narcotics Anonymous, and Overeaters Anonymous: regular group meetings and assigned sponsors to establish a community of peers for affirmation and support for abstention. An interesting research question is how much of any effectiveness of these organizations is due simply to a new set of peers.

Incentive Response at the Intensive Margin

While the evidence provided above is overwhelming that the decision to initiate consumption or continue to abstain responds to a variety of incentives, one might be concerned that use on the intensive margin may not respond to incentives. Perhaps when one is abstaining one is capable of conducting a cost-benefit analysis and responding to incentives, but once one is under the influence of addictive habits, use becomes uncontrollable. This section summarizes the evidence from economics research on whether use at the intensive margin responds to incentives.

Does the Intensity of Use Respond to Price?

Among smokers, price is a greater deterrent to heavy smoking (eleven-plus cigarettes per day) than lighter smoking (six to ten cigarettes per day), and demand is relatively price-elastic at both amounts.[80] Evidence also indicates that smokers respond in strategic ways to increases in cigarette taxes. For example, smokers living in states with high cigarette taxes are more likely to buy longer cigarettes or ones with a higher nicotine content. For most age groups, this compensating behavior of smokers is so large that the average daily tar intake is unaffected by cigarette taxes. Among those aged eighteen to twenty-four, cigarette tax hikes actually result in an increase in tar and nicotine consumption.[81] This compensating behavior in response to cigarette taxes has also been detected using measurements of the concentration of cotinine (metabolized nicotine) in saliva.[82]

The number of alcoholic drinks consumed in the past two weeks is negatively correlated with the price of alcohol.[83] The price elasticity of demand for alcohol differs for light, moderate, and heavy drinkers. Specifically, it has a U shape across drinking intensity; the demand is relatively inelastic ($\varepsilon = -0.55$) at the fifth percentile of drinkers (ranked by the amount typically consumed), the median drinker is price elastic ($\varepsilon = -1.19$), and at the ninety-fifth percentile the elasticity is not significantly different from zero and the point estimate is positive.[84] The lack of price sensitivity by the lightest users is probably due to consuming on a whim; such rare and low-cost purchases may not be very responsive to price.

Increases in the beer excise tax have no detectable impact on binge drinking by youths.[85] In models estimated separately by gender, heavy drinking is elastic to the price of beer for.[86]

Table 7.2
Estimates of Price Elasticity of Demand at the Intensive Margin (Amount Used by Users)
for Various Addictive Goods

Addictive good	Estimate of price elasticity of demand conditional on use	Source
Cigarettes	–1.96 for probability of being a heavy smoker (11+ cigarettes per day) versus a lighter smoker	Gilleskie and Strumpf (2005)
Alcohol	–0.55 for light drinkers, –1.19 for median drinker, and essentially zero for heavy drinkers	Manning et al. (1995)
Cocaine	–0.3 to –0.4	Grossman and Chaloupka (1998); Chaloupka et al. (1999)

A 10 percent increase in the price of either fast food or full-service restaurant food is associated with a decline of 0.7 percentage points in the probability of obesity and the association of the price of food at home on the probability of obesity is slightly less.[87]

For all of the behaviors discussed in this chapter, the evidence for a rational response to incentives should be hardest to find among users of hard drugs. Yet even among users of cocaine, price has been found to decrease consumption. A permanent 10 percent increase in the price of cocaine is associated with a 3 to 4 percent decrease in the number of times cocaine users take the drug.[88]

In sum, there is overwhelming evidence that the consumption by users of addictive goods responds to price. Table 7.2 summarizes the typical estimates of the short- and long-run elasticities of demand at the intensive margin for several addictive goods.

Does the Intensity of Use Respond to Nonprice Costs?

There is little evidence that laws barring youth possession, use, and/or purchase of tobacco decrease the number of cigarettes smoked by adolescent and young adult smokers.[89] Nevertheless, bans on smoking in public places may have the unintended consequence of decreasing consumption of alcohol by women but not by men, which is consistent with smoking and drinking being complements for women but not for men.[90]

Clearly one of the most dramatic policies to limit the consumption of an addictive substance is Prohibition, which outlawed the sale and purchase of alcohol (but interestingly, not its consumption) in the United States from 1919 to 1933. Individual-level data on alcohol consumption from this era do not exist, but the impact of Prohibition on heavy alcohol consumption has been estimated using deaths from cirrhosis of the liver or alcoholism, and from police records regarding arrests for drunkenness.[91] These different proxy measures for alcohol consumption give similar results: alcohol consumption fell sharply at the beginning of Prohibition before rebounding over the next several years to 60 to 70 percent of the pre-Prohibition level. After the repeal of Prohibition, the level of consumption remained unchanged at first and then slowly over the next decade returned to the pre-Prohibition level.

Some less-restrictive alcohol control policies also deter heavy use. Youths who are younger than the minimum purchase age for alcohol in their state are 2.5 percentage points less likely to binge drink.[92] Mandatory minimum fines for first offense drunk driving and minimum drinking age laws decrease alcohol consumption, but mandatory license revocation and minimum mandatory jail terms have little, if any, effect.[93]

The provision of nutritional information appears to affect diets in ways that prevent obesity. The Nutrition Labeling and Education Act, which required significant changes in the information that manufacturers of packaged foods must provide to consumers, lowered the prevalence of obesity among white females by 2.36 percentage points relative to what it would have been without the new labels.[94] Public health campaigns, and even simply allowing food manufacturers to make health claims about their products in advertising, may lead to consumers choosing healthier diets. Between 1975 and 1985, when the government was engaged in public health campaigns to encourage a lower consumption of fats, U.S. women's consumption of fat decreased. It fell even faster after 1985, when the government began to allow food companies to make health claims about their products.[95]

Lower time costs of acquiring food may lead to increased consumption and risk of obesity. For example, the per capita number of restaurants in an area is strongly correlated with the probability of individual obesity.[96] However, the reason for this correlation is not known. It could be due to: people consuming more food when there are more restaurants in their neighborhoods because the time cost of acquiring it is lower, restaurants choosing to locate where they are likely to be most profitable (i.e., where demand for the food is greatest, all else equal), or some combination of the two.

A variety of public health initiatives have sought to prevent obesity by making sedentary people more active—in particular by encouraging walking. A large number of studies document a correlation between walking and neighborhood characteristics that either decrease the costs or increase the benefits of walking (e.g., the presence of sidewalks and stores), but most of these studies are observational and suffer from selection bias.[97] That is, people who wish to walk are likely to choose to live in neighborhoods that have sidewalks and places to walk. The few studies that have attempted to address this selection by either exploiting natural experiments or using structural modeling have found much weaker evidence of an association between physical activity and these neighborhood characteristics.[98]

Evidence of Time-Inconsistent Preferences

There is evidence that people struggle with time-inconsistent preferences when making decisions about addictive behaviors. For instance, an increasingly common treatment for morbid obesity is bariatric surgery, which restricts the size of the stomach and may also involve bypassing part of the intestines. Bariatric surgery does not repair any medical problem; it is nothing more than a precommitment device for those who wish to lose weight but are unable to stick to a diet. Bariatric surgery is an effective precommitment device for two reasons: first, the restriction of the stomach limits one to small meals; and second, bypass creates negative feedback—vomiting and other gastrointestinal distress (colorfully named dumping syndrome) can result when nutrient-rich food passes quickly into the lower intestines. As a result of morbid (or extreme) obesity quadrupling between 1986 and 2000, and a lack of other effective treatments, the number of bariatric surgeries performed in the United States rose from 13,365 in 1998 to an estimated 102,794 in 2003.[99]

A precommitment device also exists for alcoholism in the form of the prescription drug Antabuse. Addicts who want to abstain from drinking but doubt their willpower to resist temptation can take Antabuse in the morning; if later that day they drink alcohol it will make them ill, providing negative reinforcement. Randomized trials indicate that Antabuse is not particularly effective, though; the illness it produces in combination with alcohol may not be sufficient to deter alcoholics from drinking.[100]

Twelve-step programs seem designed in part to address imperfections in rationality, and time-inconsistent preferences in particular. For example, programs like Alcoholics Anonymous teach that the essence of relapse prevention is H.A.L.T.: never get too Hungry, Angry, Lonely, or Tired. This is consistent with imperfect rationality because addicts may need to be reminded that if they put themselves in certain situations, they may not be able to resist temptation, so they need to plan ahead to avoid being exposed to temptation. If addictive behaviors were completely rational, there would be no need for concern about hunger, anger, loneliness, or tiredness. If addictive behaviors were completely irrational, then it would be impossible to predict relapse, and there would be no point in warning people anyway because they would be unable to resist temptation.

This raises the question: How important are these departures from perfect rationality, and what do they imply about the usefulness of traditional economics models? In general, traditional economic models and behavioral economic models generate the same qualitative predictions (e.g., that demand falls when price rises), but behavioral economics may predict more accurately the magnitude of such behavior (e.g., the amount that demand falls when price rises).[101] In other words, behavioral economics models are a refinement, not a complete rejection, of traditional economic models.

Summary of Results: *Reefer Madness*, Frank the Tank, or *Pretty Woman*?

The evidence reviewed in this chapter overwhelmingly supports the hypothesis that addictive behaviors respond to incentives at both the extensive margin (whether to use) and the intensive margin (how much to use conditional on using). There is also evidence of time-inconsistent preferences. Overall, the evidence is most consistent with the model of the imperfectly rational actor illustrated by the character Frank the Tank in the movie *Old School*.

This is not to say that the imperfectly rational actor is the best description of everyone at every time. There may be heterogeneity across the population (i.e., some people may be more or less rational than others) and there may be heterogeneity within people over time (i.e., the same person may be perfectly rational at certain times but less so at others). For example, the alcohol demand of light drinkers is elastic to price, but that of heavy drinkers is not.[102] In addition, more educated individuals may be more responsive to information about the health consequences of behaviors.[103] All of these results are consistent with heterogeneity across people in their responsiveness to incentives. People also could be differentially responsive to incentives for different behaviors (e.g., responsive to health information when it comes to smoking but not to cocaine use).

With those caveats in mind, overall the evidence supports the model of the imperfectly rational actor: addictive behaviors respond to incentives at both the extensive and intensive margins, and people may struggle with time-inconsistent preferences when engaged in these activities. This has the following implications for health policy.

Expect Consumers to Respond Shrewdly to Policy

Smokers engage in compensating behavior after a tax hike such as buying cigarettes with higher tar and nicotine. If the goal of cigarettes taxes is to reduce the health harms of smoking, policymakers may want to deter such shifts by basing the amount of the tax on the tar and nicotine content of the cigarette.

Raising the minimum purchase age for alcohol was found to have the unintended consequence of increasing the use of marijuana by youths. An implication of this finding is that if the government wishes to decrease the use of addictive goods, taxes or penalties for use should be strengthened for all addictive goods simultaneously; otherwise, consumers may simply substitute toward those that become relatively less costly.

Time-Inconsistent Preferences Imply Higher Optimal Taxes

Jonathan Gruber and Botand Köszegi argue that if consumers have time-inconsistent preferences, then optimal sin taxes should incorporate not just the amount of the externality but an additional amount to help the consumer avoid consumption.[104] Because the internal costs of smoking (such as the health consequences to the smoker) are far higher than the external costs (such as the health consequences of secondhand smoke), the needed tax increase could be large. For example, Frank Sloan and his colleagues estimate that the internal costs of smoking are $32.78 per pack, compared to the external costs of $5.44 per pack imposed on the smoker's spouse and children as well as the external costs of $1.44 per pack imposed on nonfamily-members.[105]

The Heaviest Users May Respond Least to Taxes

Heavy drinking appears to be unresponsive to price, but these may be the consumers of greatest policy concern. If one wishes to reduce heavy drinking, policy levers other than taxes should be considered.

The Provision of Health Information Can Reduce the Consumption of Addictive Goods

Consumers have been found to decrease smoking after discovering the full health impacts of the habit, and to be more likely to abstain from sex or use condoms when the local prevalence of AIDS rises. The consumption of specific foods and cigarette smoking are responsive to labels that provide health information. This suggests that the provision of information through the surgeon general's reports or labels can be a promising initiative to reduce the consumption of harmfully addictive substances.

Public Health Campaigns to Increase the "Social Taboo" of Use May Backfire

Some public health campaigns try to create or increase a social taboo effect through the use of public service announcements designed to stigmatize users and prevent initiation among those still abstaining. Such announcements may backfire, however, if they instead generate "rebellious" effects, from which consumers derive additional utility by rebelling against authority. Advertisers and policymakers may not know how to design public service announcements to increase the social taboo of substance use without triggering teenagers to begin consuming the substance in order to defy authority.

Acknowledgments

I thank my coauthors on past research on health behaviors who have informed my thinking on these topics: Richard Burkhauser, Sheldon Danziger, Don Kenkel, Sara Markowitz, Chad Meyerhoefer, John Moran, David Newhouse, Kosali Simon, John Tauras, and Jay Variyam. For helpful comments, I thank Frank Sloan, Harsha Thirumurthy, Jim Rebitzer, Mark Smith, and the participants at the conference

Incentives and Choices in Health Care: Contributions and Limitations of Economics, held at Oberlin College, September 8–10, 2006.

Notes

1. Manning et al. (1991).

2. Kersh and Morone (2002).

3. Readers of the draft version of this chapter expressed surprise to see *sex* listed as a potentially addictive activity. The scientific and clinical evidence for sex addiction is discussed in Carnes (2001) and Irons and Schneider (1996).

4. Ainslie (1992); Elster and Skog (1999).

5. Two goods are complements if a rise in the price of one results in a decrease in the demand for the other; that is, the cross-price elasticity of demand is negative.

6. Becker and Murphy (1988).

7. Elster and Skog (1999, 1).

8. Gardner and David (1999).

9. Becker (1962).

10. Hamermesh and Soss (1974).

11. Russ (1812, 266). This anecdote is also quoted in Elster (1999).

12. Elster (1999, x).

13. Lowenstein (1999, 235).

14. Becker and Murphy (1988).

15. On the *Pretty Woman* DVD, this dialogue appears in chapter 6, 35:58–37:19, spliced with 37:42 to the end of chapter 6.

16. Elster (1999, x).

17. Simon (1982).

18. O'Donoghue and Rabin (2001).

19. Thater and Shefrin (1981).

20. On the *Old School* DVD, this dialogue appears in chapter 3, 16:19–16:31, spliced with chapter 4, 17:26–18:35, spliced with chapter 4: 19:41–20:08.

21. Leibenstein (1950).

22. Veblen (1899).

23. For more on the advertising of health inputs, see chapter 6 in this book.

24. Advertising may be cooperative, raising the demand for an entire class of products irrespective of brand. Alternately, advertising may be competitive, with advertisers mocking the other brand as uncool, seeking to simultaneously increase the marginal

product of their brand and lower the marginal product of rival brands in the production of coolness.

25. Maryland Department of Health and Mental Hygiene (2004).

26. Gruber and Mullainathan (2005).

27. Reprints of many of the papers described in this chapter are available in Cawley and Kenkel (2007).

28. Cragg (1971).

29. Chaloupka and Warner (2000); Gilleskie and Strumpf (2005).

30. DeCicca et al. (2002, 2005).

31. Cawley et al. (2004).

32. Gilleskie and Strumpf (2005).

33. Forster and Jones (2001).

34. Colman et al. (2003); Gruber and Koszegi (2001).

35. Tauras and Chaloupka (2001).

36. Levy and Meara (2006).

37. Sloan et al. (2004).

38. Levy and Meara (2004).

39. Cook and Moore (2000).

40. Manning et al. (1995).

41. Cook and Moore (2001).

42. Pacula et al. (2001).

43. Grossman and Chaloupka (1998); Chaloupka et al. (1999).

44. Saffer and Chaloupka (1999).

45. Ibid.

46. I thank Mark Smith of the VA Palo Alto Health Care System for bringing this literature to my attention.

47. Higgins et al. (2002).

48. Higgins et al. (2002).

49. Lussier et al. (2006).

50. Lussier et al. (2006).

51. Higgins et al. (2002).

52. Petry and Martin (2002).

53. Gertler, Shah, and Bertozzi (2005).

54. Markowitz and Tauras (2006).

55. DeCicca et al. (2006).

56. Tauras et al. (2005).

57. Chaloupka and Warner (2000).

58. Ibid.

59. Grossman (2001).

60. Cook and Moore (2001).

61. DiNardo and Lemieux (2001).

62. Farrelly et al. (2001).

63. Chaloupka et al. (1999); Saffer and Chaloupka (1999).

64. Chaloupka et al. (1999).

65. Pacula et al. (2001).

66. Mathios (2000).

67. Ibid.

68. For a comprehensive review of the literature on how sexual activity responds to nonprice costs such as search time and social stigma, see Posner (1994).

69. Levine (2001).

70. Ahituv et al. (1996).

71. Ibid.

72. Dupas (2006).

73. DeWalque (2005).

74. Case and Katz (1991).

75. Pacula et al. (2001).

76. Eisenberg (2004).

77. Lundborg (2006).

78. Argys and Rees (2006).

79. Lundborg (2006); Argys and Rees (2006); Gaviria and Raphael (2001); Norton et al. (1998).

80. Gilleskie and Strumpf (2005).

81. Evans and Farrelly (1998).

82. Ibid.

83. Waters and Sloan (1995).

84. Manning et al. (1995).

85. Cook and Moore (2001).

86. Markowitz and Grossman (2000).

87. Chou et al. (2004).

88. Grossman and Chaloupka (1998); Chaloupka et al. (1999).

89. Tauras et al. (2005).

90. Picone et al. (2004).

91. Miron and Zwiebel (1991); Dills et al. (2005).

92. Cook and Moore (2001).

93. Waters and Sloan (1995).

94. Variyam and Cawley (2006).

95. Ippolito and Mathios (1995).

96. Chou et al. (2004).

97. Transportation Research Board (2005).

98. Ibid.

99. Sturm (2003); Santry et al. (2005).

100. Suh et al. (2006).

101. See O'Donoghue and Rabin (2001).

102. Manning et al. (1995).

103. DeWalque (2005).

104. Gruber and Köszegi (2001).

105. Sloan et al. (2004).

8   Medical Career Choices and Rates of Return

Sean Nicholson

Physicians play a central role in the U.S. health care system by influencing the amount and type of medical services that consumers receive. The U.S. government has taken an active role in determining the number and specialty mix of physicians. In fact, one could make a case that the government exerts a stronger influence on the physician workforce than any other profession. Between World War II and the early 1970s, the government's main concern was a perceived shortage of physicians. Large federal subsidies encouraged forty-two universities to open new medical schools between 1960 and 1982, and existing medical schools to accept more students. As a result, enrollment in U.S. medical schools doubled between 1960 and 1982.

The number of physicians practicing in the United States has increased substantially as a consequence, growing from 280,000 in 1965 to 744,000 in 2004.[1] Consistently over this time period, one-third of physicians practice in one of the primary care specialties of family practice, pediatrics, and general internal medicine, with the remaining two-thirds in nonprimary care specialties such as obstetrics-gynecology, psychiatry, and general surgery. In the mid-1970s, the government became concerned that its policies were too successful. In 1976, the Graduate Medical Education National Advisory Committee (GMENAC) was formed and tasked with determining the number of physicians required to meet the health care needs of the United States, the most appropriate specialty distribution of these physicians, ways to achieve a more favorable geographic distribution of physicians, and how to finance graduate medical education.[2] GMENAC published a report in 1981 predicting a physician surplus of approximately 20 percent in most specialties by 1990.

As managed care grew throughout the 1980s and 1990s, policymakers became worried that the United States was producing too few primary care physicians. Primary care physicians were believed to be instrumental to the success of managed care by determining which patients would and would not benefit from expensive, high-tech specialized (nonprimary care) medicine. In 1993, the Health Security Act proposed by the Clinton administration would have restricted the number of first-year residency positions to 110 percent of the graduating medical school class, thereby restricting the growth of the physician workforce. Moreover, a federal authority would ensure that one-half of all residency positions would be in primary care specialties, thereby increasing the primary care mix over time. If one waits long enough, health care policy sentiment often comes full circle. A recent study predicted that the United States will soon have a shortage of physicians, especially in medical specialties.[3]

Some readers may wonder why the government is involved in physician workforce planning at all. A well-functioning market should produce the "correct" number and specialty mix of physicians. Surpluses and shortages are self-correcting. If physicians supply more services than consumers are willing to buy at the prevailing price, physician fees will fall. This will make medicine a less attractive career, thus reducing the number of college graduates entering the profession. The reduced flow of newly trained physicians will increase physician fees until the financial return to medical training is once again on par with the return in other professions. Similarly, if patients must wait months to schedule a visit with a pediatrician, they will bid up the fee, thereby encouraging more medical students to enter pediatrics until the long-run supply again equals the demand.

Proponents of physician workforce policy, such as Fitzhugh Mullan, would counter with several arguments.[4] First, there is a considerable lag between when students apply to medical school and when they begin practicing medicine in a particular specialty. Although this is true, it is not clear that government regulators forecast future demand and supply conditions any better than do prospective physicians, who clearly have substantial private incentives to acquire good information. Mullan's second argument is that because patients rely heavily on physician recommendations, physicians are able to induce demand for their own services. Therefore, if "too many" physicians are trained, physicians will shift out demand for their services such that the fee for physician services will not fall as it does in markets where consumers are well-informed. Third, prices for physician services are not established by the interaction of supply and demand but are negotiated by public and private health insurers. If health insurers are not perfect agents for their enrollees, they may pay physicians (and/or physicians in a certain specialty) more or less than a well-informed patient who is paying the bill on their own.

In this chapter, I will not attempt to resolve the debate regarding whether the government should or should not actively manage the number and mix of physicians in the United States. Instead, I take the more pragmatic approach of acknowledging that the government already exerts a strong influence on the physician workforce and is unlikely to cease doing so in the near future. The government allows private medical organizations to essentially determine the number of medical students who are trained each year and the number of residents that may be trained in each specialty; pays teaching hospitals in excess of $50,000 per year for every resident trained; and affects physician earnings by managing approximately one-half of all health care spending through Medicare, Medicaid, the Veterans Administration, and other public programs.[5]

One way the government may try to alter the number and/or specialty mix of physicians is by changing the financial return to becoming a physician or specializing within medicine. This could be accomplished by changing Medicare and Medicaid physician fees, or relieving physicians of medical school debt if they practice in a particular specialty. This chapter focuses on the importance of money in medical career decisions. To what extent do college graduates enter medicine because it pays well, and to what degree do they pick a specialty based on expected lifetime earnings?

The next section reviews the key features of the market for training new physicians in the United States. I then present a simple conceptual model of how students decide whether to enter medicine and which specialty to choose on completion of medical school, which is followed by a description of the two common methods of evaluating the rate of return to medical training and specialization within medicine, and then review empirical studies on the rates of return. Next, I review studies that examine how medical students choose specialties, focusing on the significance of monetary and nonmonetary attributes of specialties, and offer some concluding thoughts in the final section.

The Market for Training New Physicians

Most physicians who practice in the United States attend a U.S. medical school. The Liaison Committee on Medical Education, which is formed by the Association of American Medical Colleges and the American Medical Association, accredits U.S. medical schools. Because it is difficult for a student who attends a nonaccredited medical school to practice medicine in the United States, the number of U.S. medical schools is essentially determined by physician organizations, with the implicit agreement of the federal government. In 1960, there were eighty-one U.S. medical schools.[6] When the federal government launched Medicare and Medicaid, it wanted to increase the supply of physicians to ensure that the beneficiaries of these programs would have access to physician care. As a result of financial incentives offered to universities, forty-two new medical schools opened between 1960 and 1982, and existing medical schools increased their enrollment, as noted earlier.[7] The number of students entering medical school per year doubled from 8,100 in 1960 to 16,600 in 1982. There have been few changes since 1982 in either the number of medical schools or the aggregate size of the entering medical school class.

Medical school graduates must receive at least one year of residency training at a program accredited by the Accreditation Council of Graduate Medical Education before they can be licensed to practice medicine in the United States.[8] Residency positions are available in twenty-six different specialties at twelve hundred teaching hospitals.[9] Primary care specialties (pediatrics, family practice, and general internal medicine) require three years of residency training, while non-primary care specialties require four (e.g., OB/GYN, radiology, and anesthesiology) or five years (e.g., general surgery and orthopedics). The Accreditation Council establishes general policies for residency programs such as the number of hours residents can work per week, and allows a Residence Review Committee in each specialty to set specialty-specific policies. These committees decide whether or not to accredit each residency program and determine the number of residents each program can hire.

Most medical students are assigned to residency positions in the National Resident Matching Program. After interviewing with residency programs in their fourth year of school, medical students rank programs in descending order of their preferences. Likewise, each residency program ranks applicants in terms of their desirability. In a span of minutes, students are allocated to programs using an algorithm that makes Pareto-optimal matches. Students who receive an assignment are obligated to attend, and those who do not may seek a position in the postmatch "scramble."

The size and specialty mix of the U.S. physician workforce changes slowly over time. In most specialties, the flow of newly trained physicians from residency training is about 3 to 5 percent of the stock of physicians. Few physicians switch specialties once they start practicing because the opportunity costs of additional training are large. Therefore, a shock to earnings in a specialty will affect the physician workforce with a long lag. U.S. immigration policy can affect the size and specialty mix of the workforce by determining how many international medical graduates are allowed to enter U.S. residency training programs.

Conceptual Framework

In this section I review a general economic model that describes how people choose occupations, discuss how economists measure the importance of money on occupational choice, and highlight some of the unique characteristics of the choice of medicine as a career. The following model is adapted from Sherwin Rosen's chapter in the *Handbook of Labor Economics* on equalizing differences.[10]

Assume, for simplicity, that there are only two occupations available to college graduates—medicine and law—and the same amount of graduate education is required for each occupation. (The same model is relevant for whether a graduating medical student decides to enter a primary care versus a nonprimary care specialty.) People derive utility from consumer goods and the nonmonetary attributes of a specialty, W. Examples of nonmonetary attributes that people may care about include prestige, the intellectual content of an occupation, the types of customers and colleagues one interacts with, and the flexibility of the work schedule. The expected difference in earnings between medicine (M) and law (L) is defined as $\Delta Y = (Y_M - Y_L)$, and the equalizing difference is defined as Z. Z, which could be positive or negative, is the additional earnings an individual must receive in medicine in order to be exactly indifferent between entering the two occupations.

Consider two different students, each of whom expects to earn $100,000 more over their lifetimes if they become physicians versus if they become lawyers (i.e., $\Delta Y = \$100,000$). Marcus loves medicine and would become a physician even if medicine yields $150,000 less over his lifetime than law (i.e., Z is −$150,000 for Marcus). Marcus will clearly choose to enter medicine because he can earn more in that occupation, *and* he reaps the nonmonetary benefits as well. Perry, on the other hand, loves law and cannot stand medicine. Perry's equalizing difference is $150,000; he will only enter medicine if he expects to earn at least $150,000 more over the course of his career in that occupation relative to law. Although Perry can earn more in medicine than in law, he will choose to become a lawyer because the expected earnings difference in medicine is less than his equalizing difference. In general, if the earnings difference between medicine and law (ΔY) exceeds a person's equalizing difference (Z), he/she will select medicine; otherwise he/she will select law.

This simple model highlights that students need to estimate the monetary and nonmonetary benefits of an occupation far into the future before making a choice. Furthermore, students' preferences for the nonmonetary attributes of an occupation will affect the earnings we actually observe. If all students are willing to take a substantial pay cut to be lawyers, like Perry, then the expected earnings in medicine will have to be $150,000 greater than in law before any student will enter medicine.

How many more students will choose to become physicians if the expected lifetime earnings in medicine increase due, say, to an increase in the demand for physicians' services? In theory, this will depend on how many students have an equalizing difference that is close to ΔY. If there are many students who would enter medicine only if they earn between $100,000 and $110,000 more over their lifetime relative to law, then a relatively small increase of $10,000 in expected lifetime earnings would trigger a large increase in the supply of students to medical school. If, on the other hand, there is a lot of variation among students in how much they value the nonmonetary attributes of an occupation, then relatively few students will choose medicine over law when the expected earnings in the former occupation increase.[11] In the latter case, money matters, but not as much as the nonmonetary attributes of a profession.

From a policy perspective, the easiest way for the government to alter the specialty mix of physicians would be to change the fees that Medicare and Medicaid pays to various specialties or pay off a medical student's debt if he/she enter a particular specialty. To evaluate the likely effect of policies that increase the expected earnings associated with entering a particular specialty (or policies that increase the expected earnings of medicine generally), one needs to know the income elasticity of supply: the percent increase in the number of medical students who choose a specialty associated with a 1 percent increase in the expected earnings of entering that specialty.

To estimate an income elasticity of supply to an occupation, economists need to find a situation where there are differences in expected earnings between students who are contemplating entering an occupation, but no differences in their preferences for the nonmonetary attributes of that occupation. The most common method is to take advantage of changes in the earnings of physicians in various specialties that occur from year to year. If graduating medical students expect the current mean physician income in a specialty to remain unchanged in the future, then one can estimate an income elasticity by examining what proportion of students choose each specialty among successive cohorts of graduating medical students as the "menu" of expected earnings changes.

The key assumption for identifying the income elasticity of supply is that shocks in the market for physician services create different expected earnings for each successive cohort, and any changes in nonmonetary attributes are assumed to be uncorrelated with changes in specialty-specific earnings.[12] That is, if expected earnings in surgery rise, for example, there is assumed to be no change in the attractiveness of surgery other than through earnings. If surgeons' earnings rise but the risk of being sued for malpractice also rises, there should be two offsetting effects on the number of medical students who choose surgery, and one could not measure a pure earnings elasticity.

One simplistic assumption in the paragraph above is that medical students expect to receive the current mean earnings in a specialty for every year of their career if they enter that specialty now. Rather than using annual earnings, most economists assume students calculate the expected net present value of lifetime earnings over their entire career when choosing an occupation or specialty. This takes into account that most physicians' earnings increase as they build their practice and attract patients, peak at some point when they are working a relatively long number of hours, and then decrease as retirement approaches.

Consider college graduates who are trying to determine how much they can expect to receive over their lifetime if they enroll in medical school in a particular year. Most studies of occupational choice assume that people expect to earn the same amount over their career as physicians currently do, perhaps adjusted for expected inflation. For example, in their first year after completing residency training, they expect to earn what physicians with zero years of postresidency experience currently earn, and so forth. Earnings (Y) will be negative for the first four years when this person pays tuition, will be small and positive while a resident, and larger thereafter when practicing medicine. Years are indexed by t, so that $t = 1$ in the first year of medical school, and $t = T$ when the person expects to retire (e.g., if a twenty-two-year-old college graduate expects to retire at age sixty-two, T would be forty):

$$\text{NPV} = \sum_{t=1}^{T} \frac{Y_t}{(1+r)^t} \qquad\qquad (8.1)$$

A dollar received today is worth more than a dollar received tomorrow because a person can receive interest on any money invested. Therefore, one should discount future earnings using the interest rate (r) that a person can receive on investments. The net present value (NPV) of lifetime earnings is a summary measure of the financial attractiveness of an occupation. "Net" indicates that the cost of education and training has been accounted for, and "present value" indicates that the dollars are expressed in the year when the student enrolls in medical school. The income elasticity of supply can thus be measured by examining whether students are more likely to enter medicine in years when their expected NPV of medicine relative to an alternative occupation is particularly large.

Although the decisions whether to enter medicine and which specialty to choose after medical school share a number of features with the simple model described above, there are some important distinctive features. A college graduate must receive between five and nine years of medical education and residency training before she can practice medicine, whereas law requires only three extra years, and many other occupations require none. This means that the earnings advantage in medicine will have to be larger, relative to a situation where both occupations require the same amount of education, in order to make it worthwhile for students to postpone their high-earning years. Second, the number of college graduates applying to medical school far exceeds the number of available slots, and in order to be competitive, college graduates must take a series of premed courses before knowing for sure that they will be accepted to medical school. Students will only be willing to incur these additional costs and expose themselves to the risk of not being accepted if the reward to becoming a physician is sufficiently high. The same is true of many specialties, where the number of medical students seeking to enter the specialty exceeds the number of available residency positions. Thus, physician earnings need to be even higher than other occupations in order to reward students for the additional costs and risk.

There are many reasons, then, why one would expect physicians to earn more once they have completed their education and are practicing relative to equally qualified individuals who chose occupations requiring less education and have higher entry probabilities. Nevertheless, many economists are interested in comparing physician earnings to other occupations for several reasons. First, there is a pragmatic reason. The earnings a student can expect to receive over a lifetime in medicine and in other similar occupations are the building blocks for estimating the income elasticity of supply, so if one has calculated lifetime earnings it requires little extra work to compare these earnings across occupations. Another reason is that these comparisons may help inform policymakers whether the monetary returns to medicine are "reasonable" and will produce an adequate supply of physicians. Ideally the market would determine the correct number and specialty mix of physicians, but if consumers are poorly informed about the value of physician services, policymakers may need to adjust the financial incentives. A final reason for comparing physician earnings to other occupations is to examine whether there are barriers to entering medicine. If the number of medical school or residency slots in certain specialties is purposefully held down, then the physicians who are able to enter will earn rents and fewer physician services will be provided than would be optimal. The problem with this logic, as elaborated on below, is that it is difficult to determine how much more physicians would earn than other occupations if there were no barriers to entry due to differences in nonmonetary attributes, the length of training required, and the cost incurred to become a qualified applicant.

The most common way to evaluate whether medicine is financially attractive is to calculate the discount rate (the internal rate of return, or IRR) that equates the NPV of lifetime earnings in medicine with a profession requiring fewer years of education and training.

$$\sum_{t=1}^{T} \frac{\left(Y_{jt} - Y_{kt}\right)}{(1+\text{IRR})^t} = 0 \tag{8.2}$$

The numerator in the expression above is the difference in earnings between medicine (profession j) and the alternative profession (profession k) in year t. The earnings in medicine are after all practice expenses, including the malpractice insurance and administrative costs associated with billing and collecting payments from patients and insurers, but before income taxes. Consider a college graduate who is deciding whether to enter medical school or seek a full-time job. If that person enrolls in medical school rather than entering the workforce, the numerator will be negative for the first four years (and probably longer because residents are generally paid less than college graduates). The opportunity cost of medical education is the sum of the tuition and the foregone salary in those early years. Once a physician begins practicing medicine, his or her earnings will likely be larger than those of college graduates, so that the numerator in equation (8.2) will be positive in the later years. The IRR is the discount rate that makes the expression above zero, or equivalently, it is the discount rate that equates the NPV of medical earnings with the NPV of earnings in the alternative profession. If the IRR exceeds the interest rate a person can receive in the financial markets, then the investment of a person's time to become trained in medicine is a good one in a financial sense. If the IRR is lower than the interest rate, the alternative profession is more lucrative than medicine.

Once students complete medical school, they choose a specialty, which in turn affects how many years they will spend as a resident. One can calculate the IRR to a particular specialty using a method similar to that in equation (8.2). The IRR to the incremental training in specialty j relative to specialty k is the discount rate that equates the expected NPVs in the two specialties. Mechanically, the alternative specialty must require fewer years of training than specialty j so that the expected earnings difference will be negative at least once over the course of a person's career. For example, a general surgeon will earn less as a resident in the fourth and fifth years of training than would a family practitioner, who would already be practicing at that point.

There are two crucial assumptions that economists make when estimating IRRs. Ideally the alternative profession is the one that most medical students would choose if they decided not to become a physician, or at least the earnings in the alternative profession should be similar to the earnings that medical students could have earned if they decided not to become a physician. Medical students are smarter than the average college graduate, as measured by grade point average and SAT scores, so using the earnings of college graduates as the opportunity cost of attending medical school would likely overstate the true IRR of medicine.

A second assumption is how prospective medical students form earnings expectations. Almost all published studies on the return to medicine use cross-sectional data to estimate what a person can expect to earn over a lifetime. These data sets contain the earnings of physicians with different experience levels at a point in time. The key assumption is that if a person enters medical school today, in the first year of practicing medicine, s/he will earn the same amount as physicians who just completed residency training and are in their first year of practicing, and so forth over the rest of a person's working career. This is equivalent to assuming that students expect the contemporaneous experience-earnings profile of practicing physicians to remain constant in real terms in the future. In the next section, I will review studies that examine the reasonableness of this assumption.

Some authors have used the high IRRs to conclude that medical organizations must be restricting the number of medical school and residency positions, thereby restricting the supply of physicians and creating rents for those who are able to enter the medical profession.[13] According to this reasoning, if there were no entry barriers, the supply of physicians would increase until the IRR of medical training would be equal to the market interest rate. As Frank Sloan points out, however, "positive or negative net returns (to medicine) are consistent with equilibrium in a labor market without entry barriers and are really just as plausible as zero net returns."[14] Sloan's argument is that people choose occupations based on both monetary and nonmonetary attributes, such as working conditions and intellectual content. If being a physician is less satisfying than being a dentist, a PhD biologist, or a college graduate in general, holding income fixed, then the IRR of medicine would need to exceed the interest rate in order to compensate physicians for putting up with the unpleasant features of the profession.

Empirical Studies on the IRR to Medical Training

How Do Medical Students Form Earnings Expectations?

As mentioned above, most economic studies of the IRR to medicine and the income elasticity of supply to medicine assume that students form earnings expectations based on the contemporaneous earnings of physicians, or in the case of specialty choice, the contemporaneous earnings of physicians in the specialty they are considering. Economists are implicitly making two separate assumptions: that medical students can accurately assess what physicians currently earn, and that medical students believe the experience-earnings profile in the future will be identical to the current experience-earnings profile. Are these reasonable characterizations of how medical students behave?

Over the last twenty years, Jefferson Medical College, a large medical school in Philadelphia, asked its first- and fourth-year medical students to estimate how much physicians in six different specialties earn. I examined the accuracy of the students' estimates, whether the earnings estimates are biased upward or downward, and how much students learn about earnings during medical school.[15] The median student underestimated physician earnings by 15 percent between 1974 and 1998, and the median absolute value of the estimation errors was 26 percent of actual earnings. Thus, students' assessments are relatively inaccurate and are biased downward. Yet their accuracy improved by 35 percent between the first and fourth years of school, so students learn a considerable amount before formally choosing a specialty.

Jefferson Medical College also asks its fourth-year medical students to report how much they expect to earn over the course of their career. With my Colleague Nicholas Souleles, I found that medical students base their earnings expectations on personal characteristics such as gender and ability.[16] Women, for example, expect to earn considerably less than men, controlling for ability and the specialty they plan to enter. Expectations are also forward-looking; when students report relatively high earnings expectations for a given specialty (i.e., they expect to earn more than physicians in that specialty currently do), physicians practicing in that specialty subsequently tend to experience high earnings growth relative to physicians in other specialties. This means that medical students do not necessarily expect the current experience-earnings profile to persist indefinitely into the future but rather able to forecast *some* of the changes in the earnings that actually occur.

The results above do not invalidate studies that assume medical students can accurately forecast current earnings and assume those earnings will remain constant. It is likely that students underestimate the earnings in alternative occupations as much as they do in medicine, which would imply that rate of return calculations will not be affected by these consistent inaccuracies. Furthermore, although students are able to forecast some of the actual growth in earnings, it is probably more accurate to assume that they expect current earnings to persist than to assume students can perfectly forecast the actual earnings they will receive.

The IRRs to Medicine

Table 8.1 summarizes the results of eight different studies that examine the IRRs to medicine. The studies are presented in chronological order to focus on the trend in the IRR to medical training. Milton Friedman and Simon Kuznets define dentists to be the alternative occupation.[17] They find that between 1929 and 1934, physicians earned 32.5 percent more per year, on average, than do dentists. Based on physicians' additional training time, a 17 percent difference in income would be required to equate the NPV of lifetime earnings between the two professions.[18] The authors conclude that the remaining 16.5 percent difference was likely due to the greater difficulty of entering medicine relative to dentistry. That is, physicians on average have higher ability than dentists, and therefore the earnings of dentists is an underestimate of what physicians could have earned if they in fact decided not to enter medicine.

Sloan compares the earnings of general practitioners in 1955, 1959, and 1965 with those of white male college graduates in the same years.[19] He finds that general practitioners had an IRR of 29, 24, and 24 percent in those three years, respectively. Rashi Fein and Gerald Weber compare physician earnings in 1966 with those of biology PhDs, and conclude that the IRR to medical training ranges from 15 to 34 percent depending on the specification.[20]

Taken together, these three studies indicate that medicine was a lucrative career in the 1930 to 1966 period. One must be careful, however, in interpreting these high IRRs. Many features of the health care market have changed since the mid-1960s, including the launch of Medicare, Medicaid, and the development of managed care. Furthermore, medical schools receive two to three times as many applicants as there are positions available, so they are able to select accomplished college graduates. Students accepted to medical schools in 1992, for example, had a high grade point average of 3.24.[21] Using the average earnings of all college graduates or even of dentists probably underestimates what medical students could earn if they decided not to become physicians, and therefore may overstate the IRR to medical training.

Matt Lindsay also criticizes the three studies mentioned above for ignoring differences in the hours worked between physicians, dentists, biology PhDs, and college graduates.[22] He argues that specialized training raises a physician's wage, which in turn induces physicians to work more hours and enjoy fewer leisure hours than people in alternative

Table 8.1
Rates of Return to Medicine

Study	Period examined	Counterfactual profession	Adjust for hours worked?	Results
Friedman and Kuznets (1945)	1929–1934	Dentists	No	Physicians earn 16.5% more than dentists after adjusting for differences in investment costs
Sloan (1970)	1955, 1959, 1965	White male college graduates	No	General practitioners (GPs) had an IRR of 29.1%, 23.7%, and 24.1% in the three years
Fein and Weber (1971)	1966	Biology PhDs	No	Physicians had an IRR between 15% and 34%
Lindsay (1973)	1929–1934, 1955, 1959, 1966	Recalculated Friedman and Kuznets (1945), Sloan (1970), and Fein and Weber (1971) results	Yes	Medicine Less attractive than dentistry between 1929 and 1934; IRR for GPs less than 5% in 1955 and about 15% in 1959; physicians had an IRR of about 10% in 1966
Leffler (1978)	1947–1973	Male college graduates	Yes	IRR for GPs grew over this time period, from less than 8% in the late 1940s, to 10% in 1953, to 12% in 1964, and over 12% thereafter
Mennemeyer (1978)	1969	Dentists, pharmacists, veterinarians, lawyers, science PhDs, engineers, and college teachers	Yes	Physicians had an IRR of about 4% relative to dentists, and greater than 10% relative to all other professions
Burstein and Cromwell (1985)	1967–1980	Lawyers, dentists, and college graduates	Yes	GPs had an IRR between 12% and 15% relative to college graduates over this time period, between 14% and 16% relative to dentists, and between 5% and 8% relative to lawyers
Weeks et al. (1994)	1990	High school graduates; compare physicians' IRR with dentists', lawyers', and MBAs'	Yes	IRRs relative to high school graduates: primary care MDs (16%), dentists (21%), procedure-based MDs (21%), lawyers (25%), and MBAs (29%)

professions. The failure to standardize the number of hours worked in the two professions will overstate the IRR in medicine because physicians enjoy less leisure time than the alternative profession. There are two ways to adjust for differences in the hours worked. A Laspeyres-type adjustment calculates annual earnings in each profession by multiplying the hourly wage rate in the profession by the annual hours actually worked in the benchmark profession (not medicine).[23] A Paasche-type adjustment calculates annual earnings by assuming that people in both professions work as much as physicians.

Lindsay recalculates the returns to medical training in the three studies mentioned above after adjusting for differences in the hours worked. He concludes that the IRR to medical training between 1929 and 1934 was actually less than the market interest rate, so that medicine was not a lucrative profession. Likewise, Lindsay concludes that the IRR for general practitioners in 1955 and 1959 was about 10 to 20 percent lower than Sloan's estimate, and also substantially lower in 1966 than Fein and Weber's report.[24]

The rest of the studies summarized in table 8.1 all follow Lindsay's advice to adjust earnings for differences in the hours worked. Using male college graduates as the counterfactual profession, Keith Leffler estimates IRRs for general practitioners from 1947 to 1973.[25] He finds that the IRR to medical training was fairly consistent over this time period, increasing from about 8 percent in the late 1940s to 12 percent or more in the early 1970s. Stephen Mennemeyer estimates the IRR to medical training in 1969 relative to seven different occupations.[26] He finds that physicians had an IRR of only 4 percent relative to dentists, but an IRR of greater than 10 percent relative to the other six occupations. Philip Burstein and Jerry Cromwell conclude that between 1967 and 1980, general practitioners had an IRR of 14 to 16 percent relative to dentists, and between 5 and 8 percent relative to lawyers.[27]

Finally, William Weeks and his colleagues estimate the IRR for physicians in different specialties and three other occupations relative to high school graduates for 1990.[28] They find that primary care physicians (16 percent), dentists (21 percent), procedure-based physicians (21 percent), lawyers (25 percent), and MBA graduates (29 percent) all had large IRRs relative to high school graduates. The earnings of high school graduates are clearly underestimates of what members of these four professions could earn if they had decided on alternate careers, which means the IRR values themselves should not be taken too seriously. What is of greater interest in the Weeks and colleagues study, however, is the comparison of the IRRs between these four occupations that all attract talented college graduates. Although medicine pays well relative to the jobs of high school graduates, it is on par with occupations that attract talented college graduates.

Taken as a whole, the eight studies summarized in table 8.1 indicate that the financial returns from entering medicine are generally in line with those from similar occupations. Although no IRR studies have been conducted with data more recent than 1990, the medical IRR would likely be lower now than in the Weeks and colleagues study. Based on American Medical Association surveys, the mean physician income fell by 7 percent in real terms between 1993 and 2000 (figure 8.1).[29] A recent report by the Center for Studying Health System Change notes that between 1995 and 2003, mean physician income fell by 7 percent in real terms while the mean income of professional and technical workers, a plausible alternative profession, increased by 7 percent.[30]

The Rates of Return to Specialization within Medicine

The results of four studies that estimate the returns to medical specialization are summarized in table 8.2. Taken together, these studies clearly show that the returns to specializing in a particular area within

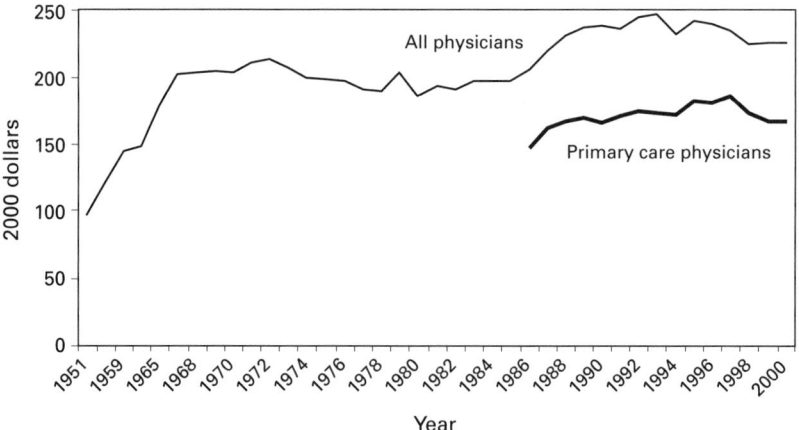

Figure 8.1
Mean Physician Income, in 2000 Dollars
Note: Primary care physicians include pediatricians, family practitioners, and general internists.
Source: American Medical Association (2003).

Table 8.2
Rates of Return to Medical Specialization

Study	Period examined	Counterfactual specialty	Results
Sloan (1970)	1955, 1959, 1965	General practice (one year of residency training)	**1955**: pediatrics and internal medicine had negative IRRs; general surgery, OB/GYN, and psych had IRRs between 6% and 7% **1959**: similar results as 1955 **1965**: IRR positive for seven specialties and negative for pediatrics; anesthesiology, ophthalmology, general surgery, and radiology had IRRs of 10% or more
Burstein and Cromwell (1985)	1951–1980	General practice (one year of residency training)	**General surgery**: positive IRRs throughout 1951–1980, increasing from 4% in 1951 to 14% in 1980 **Obstetrics/gynecology**: positive IRRs throughout 1951–1980, increasing from 5% in 1951 to 15% in 1980 **Pediatrics**: small positive IRRs in 1950s; negative IRRs between 1977 and 1980
Marder and Willke (1991)	1987	Practicing primary care physicians with one to two years of residency training	Small positive IRRs in **primary care**: pediatrics (2%), family practice (4%), and general internal medicine (13%) **Nonprimary care**: large IRRs, ranging from 19% in medical subspecialties and 22% in general surgery, to 47% in radiology and 50% in pathology
Nicholson (2003)	1986–1998	Family practice (three years of residency training)	Consistently large IRRs in nonprimary care specialties: ranging in 1986 from 41% in psychiatry and 44% in general surgery to 105% in anesthesiology and 107% in radiology; and ranging in 1998 from 17% in psychiatry and 25% in general surgery to 50% in OB/GYN and 83% in radiology

medicine (e.g., surgery, radiology, or obstetrics) have increased sharply over time. Sloan estimates the IRR of nine different specialties relative to physicians who received one year of residency training and became general practitioners.[31] Surprisingly, the IRR to pediatrics and internal medicine were negative in 1955 and 1959, implying that the cost of investing in these specifically exceeds the return from such investments, even at a zero discount rate. The IRR for pediatrics was still negative in 1965, although it was slightly positive (1.5 percent) for internal medicine. One explanation for this finding is that pediatrics and internal medicine have desirable nonmonetary attributes relative to general practitioners.

Sloan also finds that the IRR to specialization increased between 1955 and 1965. In 1955, the IRR in general surgery, obstetrics/gynecology, and psychiatry were between 6 and 7 percent, which is about double the real interest rate. In 1965, four specialties had an IRR of 10 percent or more (anesthesiology, ophthalmology, orthopedic surgery, and radiology), and three specialties had an IRR between 2 and 5 percent (internal medicine, psychiatry, and general surgery).

Burstein and Cromwell also use general practitioners as the benchmark or counterfactual specialty to estimate the IRR to four specialties between 1951 and 1980.[32] The IRR for general internists was between 5 and 13 percent, with larger values in the late 1970s. Two specialties requiring four and five years of residency training—obstetrics/gynecology and surgery, respectively—enjoyed larger returns. Between 1975 and 1980, the IRR in these two specialties were consistently above 10 percent.

William Marder and Richard Willke estimate even higher IRRs to training in the nonprimary care specialties using data from 1987: pathology (50 percent), radiology (47 percent), anesthesiology (40 percent), ophthalmology (30 percent), surgical subspecialties (29 percent), obstetrics/gynecology (26 percent), psychiatry (24 percent), general surgery (22 percent), and medical subspecialties (19 percent).[33] They define the counterfactual specialty to be all primary care physicians with fewer than three years of residency training, which consists mostly of general practitioners. The IRRs in primary care specialties were much smaller: pediatrics (2 percent), family practice (4 percent), and general internal medicine (13 percent).

The most recent study that calculates returns to specialization is one I did in 2003. I use family practice as the benchmark specialty because graduate medical education in this field involves a relatively short residency period, is chosen by a large number of medical students, and entails general clinical training.[34] I find strikingly large IRRs in the nonprimary care specialties, especially between 1986 and 1992.[35] In 1986, the IRR in anesthesiology and radiology, specialties that require only one additional year of training relative to family practice, exceeded 100 percent. Returns in the other four specialties studies were between 41 percent (psychiatry) and 72 percent (orthopedic surgery). Cross-sectional IRRs fell in all specialties between 1992 and 1998, but still remained high in the most recent year studied: psychiatry (17 percent), general surgery (25 percent), orthopedic surgery (39 percent), anesthesiology (47 percent), obstetrics/gynecology (50 percent), and radiology (83 percent).

I mentioned earlier that one should be careful about concluding that an occupation or specialty with a high IRR is necessarily earning rents due to entry restrictions into the profession or specialty. The IRRs can be higher or lower than the market interest rate when nonmonetary attributes are important. One possibility is that nonprimary care specialties pay well, but have highly undesirable nonmonetary attributes, such as inconvenient work hours or a higher risk of malpractice lawsuits. Unless nonprimary care specialties have become less attractive along these dimensions over time, though, this seems an unlikely explanation.

But the most convincing evidence that nonprimary physicians are earning economic rents is the sheer magnitude of the IRRs described above. Consider the 105 percent IRR experienced by anesthesiologists in 1986. A family practitioner who began residency training in 1986 and earned the same amount in real terms over the course of their career as family practitioners already in practice in 1986 would earn $2.6 million. A radiologist, on the other hand, would earn $5.2 million. Four years into their post–medical school career, the anesthesiologist would be making $22,000 as a fourth-year resident while the family practitioner would be earning $66,000 in their first postresidency year. If the family practitioner invested this $44,000 earnings difference ($66,000 to $22,000) and was able to double the investment year after year for thirty-five consecutive years, then they would accumulate as much money over their lifetime as the radiologist. Anyone who can invest that skillfully, even for two years, should quit their day job and go to Wall Street.

Given the rising returns to specialization, it should not be surprising that a smaller percentage of U.S. medical students are entering primary care over time. Forty-four percent of the graduating medical students who entered the 2006 National Resident Matching Program ranked a primary care residency program as their first choice—a decrease from 56 percent in 1998.[36] Furthermore, the returns to specialization have probably increased since 1998. Between 1995 and 2003, the mean income of primary care physicians fell by 10 percent in real terms, while the income for all physicians fell by a smaller amount (7 percent).[37] The high IRRs have persisted for such a long time period. It is therefore unlikely that the explanation is that nonprimary care physicians experienced a positive income shock, and that there is a lag between the shock and the eventual increase in the supply of physicians in that specialty.

There are other explanations for high IRRs to specialization, such as the inability of medical students to borrow enough money to undergo the long residency periods required of nonprimary care, or the possibility that medical students' income expectations are biased such that they overestimate what they can earn in primary care relative to nonprimary care.[38] If the explanations pertain only to the desirability of the various specialties in the medical students' eyes, however, then we should expect the supply of medical students to each specialty to be roughly equal to the demand for residents in each specialty. But this is not what one observes.

Figure 8.2 shows the ratio of the number of medical students who rank each specialty first in the match to the number of first-year residency positions that are available in that specialty. In 1991, there were 30, 50, and 70 percent more medical students who wanted to become radiologists, obstetricians, and orthopedic surgeons, respectively, than there were residency positions available. These specialties had IRRs between 74 and 134 percent in 1990, so the interest among medical students was understandable.

In a well-functioning labor market, we would expect this excess supply of medical students to reduce the wage for nonprimary care residents, drive up the number of first-year residency positions, increase the number of trained nonprimary care physicians entering the market, and eventually create lower and more equal (but not necessarily equivalent) IRRs across specialties. Although the supply-to-demand ratios in figure 8.3 have trended down a bit since 1991, they are still substantially greater than one in many high-paying specialties, including a ratio of two to one in dermatology. Thus, there appear to be barriers restricting entry to certain nonprimary care specialties.

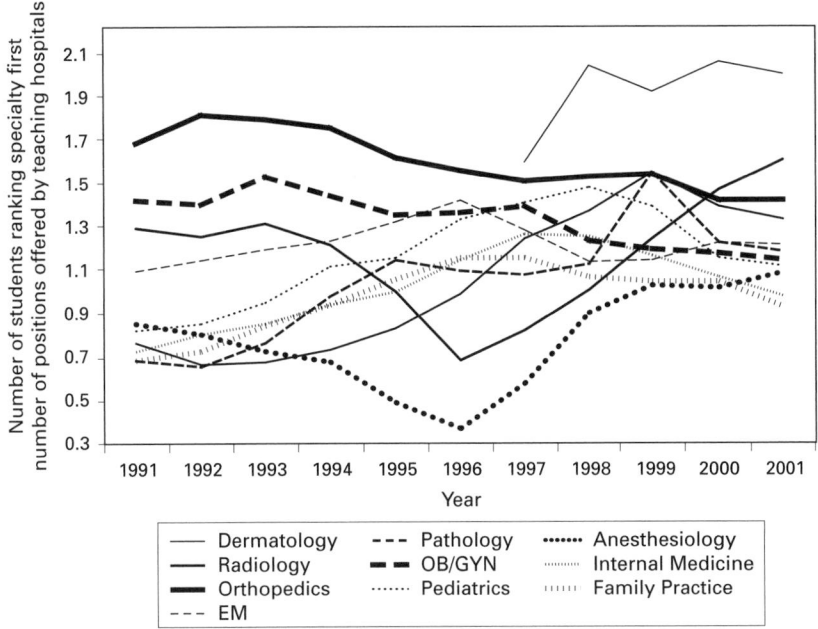

Figure 8.2
Ratio of Supply to Demand of Residents by Specialty, 1991–2001
Notes: "EM": emergency medicine. Foreign medical graduates are included in the ratios presented above.
Source: National Resident Matching Program (2006).

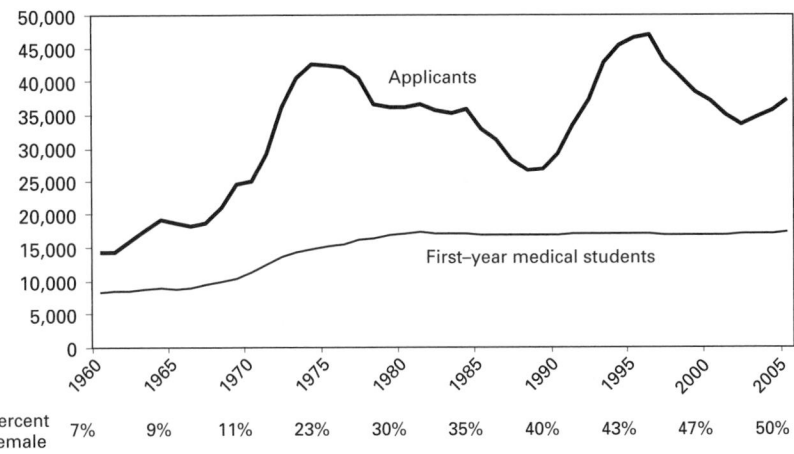

Figure 8.3
Number of Applicants to U.S. Medical Schools and Number of First-Year Medical Students, 1960–2005
Source: Association of American Medical Colleges (2006).

Jayanta Bhattacharya finds that one-half of the income difference between primary and nonprimary care physicians can be explained by differences in the hours worked, ability, and the required length of residency training. He concludes that "the most likely explanation for the remaining income differences is differential entry barriers across specialties."[39] In one study, I evaluate three possible reasons why the market for residents does not clear in the manner described above, thereby creating entry barriers.[40] One possibility is that residents require a minimum number of procedures in order to become proficient, but there are not enough patients in certain specialties to train the number of medical students who would like to enter. A second explanation is that by requiring that all residents receive an "adequate" stipend, the Accreditation Council of Graduate Medical Education has prevented hospitals from driving down the residents' wages in certain nonprimary specialties. A final explanation is that the residency review committees that have the authority to determine the number of residents that each hospital may train have consciously restricted entry in order to maintain high earnings in nonprimary care specialties. In fact, a group of physicians filed an antitrust suit in 2002 against the Accreditation Council and other organizations that run the matching program, but the suit was dismissed in 2004 after Congress created an antitrust exemption for the residency match.[41]

The Effect of IRRs on Medical Career Choices

The Influence of Expected Earnings on Entering Medicine

Now I turn to the question of whether expected earnings have a strong influence on medical career decisions. To the best of my knowledge, there have been no formal studies of the importance of money on the number of physicians trained. This is not surprising because money should not have a strong influence on the number of accepted medical students. Figure 8.3 depicts the number of students applying to U.S. medical schools and the number of first-year positions available over the 1960 to 2005 time period. Although the number of applications has fluctuated substantially over time, there have always been at least 50 percent more applicants than positions, and in some years the ratio was four to one. As long as the marginal applicant is of sufficiently high ability, the number of entering medical school students will be determined by the number of first-year positions available, not by the number of applicants. When the expected earnings of prospective medical students rise or fall, the number of applicants may rise or fall, but the number of students entering medical school should be unaffected, at least in the short run.

There is one study that examines whether the number of applicants to medical school depends on the earnings that college students expect to receive as physicians, the earnings they expect to receive in alternative professions, and the direct cost of medical school. If expected earnings increase the number of medical school applicants, medical schools may subsequently decide to expand their class size because they are likely to attract a higher-quality applicant than before. Thus, changes in expected earnings can indirectly increase the number of trained physicians. Sloan finds that increases in expected earnings do attract more applicants, but earnings are not as important as changes in the direct cost of medical school.[42] He also finds that more college students apply when they believe their chances of being accepted are particularly good, which is what one would expect. Increasing the number of medical school positions, and thereby increasing the probability that a student will be accepted, reduces the risk to the applicant.

The Influence of Expected Earnings on Medical Specialization Decisions

As mentioned above, to estimate the significance of money on specialty choices, economists need to find a situation where there are differences in the expected earnings between medical students who are contemplating entering a set of specialties. In this section, I review five studies, organized according to the reason why there are differences in the expected earnings, and whether the studies address the barriers to entering specialties. Two studies take advantage of the differences in expected earnings that exist between medical students who graduate in different years. The key assumption in these studies, which is quite plausible, is that changes in specialty-specific nonmonetary attributes are uncorrelated with changes in specialty-specific earnings.

In one study, Sloan uses aggregate data from 1955, 1959, and 1965.[43] Rather than observing the specialty that each individual chooses, his dependent variable is the total number of residents in each of nine specialties who are graduates of a U.S. or Canadian medical school. His key independent variable is the expected NPV of lifetime earnings, which is constructed using the experience-earnings profile of contemporaneous physicians. Sloan concludes that an increase in the expected earnings of a specialty would attract more medical students to that specialty, but this effect is small. He reports specialty-specific elasticity estimates (the percentage change in residents associated with a 1 percent increase in the NPV of expected earnings in that specialty) that range from 0 to 0.28. Large changes in earnings prospects would be required to substantially change the distribution of residents across specialties.

Gloria Bazzoli estimates a model of specialty choice to focus on the issue of whether a policy that reduces medical students' debt (and therefore increases expected lifetime earnings) would encourage more people to enter primary care specialties, which require fewer years of training but offer lower lifetime earnings than nonprimary care specialties.[44] Her data set consists of about four thousand medical residents who were surveyed in 1983 when they were in their first, second, or third year of training. Bazzoli's key independent variable is the difference in the NPV of primary versus nonprimary care expected earnings. She finds that medical students are more likely to choose primary care when the expected earnings are relatively large, but this effect is small. Specifically, a $10,000 increase in the expected earnings of primary versus nonprimary care (about a 20 percent increase in the mean value, which is a large change) is associated with a 1.4 percent increase in the probability of choosing primary care. Thus, both Sloan and Bazzoli find that money matters, yet it does not matter very much. Medical students appear to place great importance on nonmonetary attributes when selecting a specialty.

Jeremiah Hurley estimates a specialty choice model using data from a longitudinal survey of students who entered a U.S. medical school in 1960.[45] Because all the students in Hurley's data set make their specialty choice in the same year, he needs a way to create differences in the expected earnings. In his model, the expected earnings differ between students due only to differences in their age at the time of entering medical school; older students will practice fewer years before they retire, and hence will have relatively high expected (discounted) lifetime earnings in specialties that require few years of training. Although mathematically correct (as long as students expect to retire at the same age), this method does not create a great deal of variation in the expected earnings between students, and therefore the estimates are less persuasive than the two above. Hurley finds that students are fairly responsive to differences in expected earnings. He reports an earnings elasticity of 1.05; a 1 percent increase in the expected earnings of a specialty is associated with a 1.05 percent increase in the proportion of students choosing that alternative.

Joel Hay addresses the possibility that high-ability medical students will have higher expected earnings in specialties that place a premium on ability.[46] He uses data on two thousand physicians who were practicing in 1970 and had different amounts of experience. Unlike the studies reviewed above that use the average income of all physicians at the time of the specialty decision, Hay uses the income actually reported by each physician in his data set. He groups the chosen specialties into three categories: general practice and family practice, internal medicine, and all other specialties.

Hay's main contribution is to estimate a physician's income and specialty choice simultaneously, thereby allowing the error terms in the two equations to be correlated. This modification of a Heckman selection model will be crucial if physicians have characteristics that are difficult to observe (e.g., surgical skill, problem-solving skills, motivation, or bedside manner), and these characteristics influence how much they can earn in each specialty. In Hay's model, a physician who enters family practice, for example, might expect to earn more or less in internal medicine than the physicians who actually chose internal medicine. If family practitioners have an absolute advantage relative to internists in both specialties, they would expect to make more than internists in both specialties.

Hay finds that a medical student is more likely to choose a specialty when the expected earnings in that specialty are large relative to the expected earnings in the other two specialties, and when the expected earnings in a specialty are large relative to students who made the specialty choice decision in different years. It is difficult to tell from this study how responsive students are to expected earnings in Hay's model. Hay does report that if one assigns each student to the specialty with the highest predicted income for that person, 57 percent of the students would be assigned to the specialty they actually chose. This success rate is clearly better than randomly assigning a physician to one of these three specialty groupings, although this is a pretty low hurdle. Again, these results are consistent with money playing a role but not being decisive in determining a person's specialty.

The studies reviewed above assume that medical students can enter whatever specialty they like. That is, these studies do not account for the possibility that some medical students who want to enter a specialty are unsuccessful. In fact, residency positions in high-income specialties are rationed and many medical students fail to enter their preferred specialty. For instance, about 40 percent of the students who ranked an orthopedic surgery program as their first choice in the matching program during the 1990s did not receive an assignment in that specialty, which is evident from the ratios of supply to demand in figure 8.2 that are well above one.

In my 2002 study, my main contribution was to examine how changes in expected earnings in a market with barriers to entry affect the supply of medical students to various specialties.[47] I present a model where medical students decide which specialty to rank first in the National Resident Matching Program by considering the probability that they will be accepted in each specialty, based on their ability. Using a data set that contains the specialty that each U.S. medical student who graduated in 1992 ranked first in the matching program, I define the dependent variable to be one if a student ranks a specialty first in the match, and zero otherwise. The expected earnings in a specialty differ across students according to the probability of receiving a position in that specialty, which in turn depends on a student's ability (measured in this study by a student's MCAT score). Students with relatively low entry probabilities will have low expected earnings because there is a relatively high probability they will have to spend an extra year receiving general training before reentering the matching program.

I find that medical students' specialty choices are responsive to differences in expected earnings between specialties. Specifically, the average income elasticity across the seven specialties is 1.42. This implies that policies that change the demand for physician services or the fee per service can substantially increase the number of students who would like to enter that specialty.

As noted above, Sloan's income elasticity of supply estimate is close to zero, Bazzoli's is also small, and mine is 1.42. How can we reconcile such seemingly disparate estimates of the importance of money? Sloan and Bazzoli measure the impact of money on the number of students who *enter* a specialty, whereas I measure the impact of money on the number *desiring* to enter a specialty. I show that medical students are willing to incur the risk of not receiving any residency position in order to secure the extremely large returns in certain nonprimary care specialties. If residency programs do not respond to this increased interest among medical students by increasing capacity, however, there will be no change in the number of students who successfully enter the over-subscribed specialties. If medical students do not always choose the specialty that maximizes their expected earnings, what else matters? The studies reviewed above clearly indicate that two other factors are as important, if not more so, than money: personal characteristics and the nonmonetary attributes of specialties.

My study finds that men are much more likely than women to choose a nonprimary care specialty, once I account for the expected earnings differences across specialties. Common explanations for this finding are that women prefer specialties with relatively short training periods, specialties that are more conducive to raising a family, and those that allow them to interact frequently with patients. Men, on the other hand, may enjoy technology-oriented specialties. My study also finds that nonwhite medical students are more likely than whites to choose a nonprimary care specialty.

In Bazzoli's study, medical students whose parents are relatively well educated are more likely to choose nonprimary care. This may occur if these families are wealthier and can help finance the relatively long nonprimary care training programs, or if the students from these families have low discount rates and are willing to wait longer before they generate substantial practice earnings. Alternatively, students of relatively high ability may prefer intellectual depth (i.e., becoming an expert in a narrow clinical domain, such as in a nonprimary care specialty) over intellectual breadth (i.e., knowing a little bit about all health conditions, such as in primary care). My study finds that married medical students are more likely to choose a primary care specialty, which is consistent with the first two explanations offered above. A married medical student may prefer specialties with short training periods because that student has greater consumption needs in the short run, and may not be able to borrow sufficiently to finance those needs.

There are two reasons why it is difficult empirically to estimate the significance of specific nonmonetary specialty attributes such as the hours worked, the malpractice risk, the length of the required training, or the percentage of time spent interacting with patients. In many cases the specialty attributes do not vary over time, which makes it impossible to identify the impact of that attribute on specialty choice. For example, since the 1960s and 1970s, primary care specialties have required three years of training; obstetrics/gynecology, radiology, and anesthesiology have required four; and general surgery and orthopedic surgery have required five—so every cohort faced the same choice set. In other cases, a nonmonetary attribute may change over time due to the decisions of physicians already practicing in those specialties. This makes it difficult to determine the true source of the change.

My study controls for the importance of nonmonetary attributes in regression analysis by including a constant term for each of seven specialties. The coefficients on these constant terms are large in magnitude and statistically significant. For example, large positive coefficients on family practice, pediatrics, and general internal medicine indicate that many students choose primary care specialties even though their earnings would be greater in other specialties. If money was the only thing that matters, students would always choose the specialty with the highest expected earnings. The most likely explanation is that most students choose a specialty based on factors other than money; the equalizing differences are large.

Conclusions

This chapter has examined the importance of money in medical career decisions. To what extent do college graduates enter medicine because it pays well, and to what degree do they pick a specialty based on expected lifetime earnings? The early literature in this area focused on measuring the IRR to medical training and, more recently, specialization within medicine. Although the results differ slightly from study to study, on average college students who choose medicine earn amounts similar to what they could have earned in professions that attract similarly intelligent and highly motivated students. The returns to specialization within medicine, on the other hand, have increased substantially over time. The fact that these large returns are persistent and, more important, that many medical students are trying unsuccessfully to enter specialties with large returns, indicates that there are barriers to entering certain specialties.

One critical research area in the future will be to determine why these barriers exist, and how to eliminate them or reduce their influence. A market-based personnel policy will only succeed if the market functions well: the earnings of current physicians send signals to college and medical students, who are able to respond to these signals.

Studies estimating the income elasticity of supply to medical school and supply to specific specialties show that money is an important consideration in medical career decisions, but that it is not as important as the nonmonetary attributes of specialties. This seemingly noneconomic decision making is easier to comprehend when one considers that even the lowest-paying specialty currently has a mean income ($140,000) that is about three times greater than the median household income in the United States. Students are not necessarily ignoring money; rather, the income effect of being able to earn substantial amounts in medicine allows them to "spend" some of that income on other things that are important to them. Surveys of medical students support this interpretation. When asked why they selected a particular specialty, fourth-year medical students listed in descending order of significance the following: intellectual content, challenging diagnostic problems, emphasis on people skills, predictable working hours, prestige, and finally relative income.[48]

Acknowledgment

Artem Gulish provided exceptional research assistance.

Notes

1. American Medical Association (2006).

2. Robertson (1981).

3. Cooper et al. (2002).

4. Mullan (2003).

5. About 60 percent of medical schools are public schools supported by the state. Therefore, state governments are likely to influence the size and specialty distribution of the physician workforce.

6. Association of American Medical Colleges (2006, 5, 9).

7. Ibid. (5).

8. Since the mid-1970s, most medical students receive at least three years of residency training.

9. National Resident Matching Program (2006).

10. Rosen (1986).

11. For example, some students think medicine is much more intellectually stimulating than law and place a large value on this attribute, others feel just as strongly that medicine is more intellectually appealing than law, and all other students are evenly dispersed between these extremes.

12. Examples of such shocks are an increase in patients' demand for a particular service or a reduction in physician fees.

13. See, for example, Lindsay (1973).

14. Sloan (1976, 118).

15. Nicholson (2005).

16. Nicholson and Souleles (2001).

17. Friedman and Kuznets (1945).

18. They used a 4 percent discount rate when deriving the NPV of lifetime earnings.

19. Sloan (1970). Until the 1970s, many physicians received one or two years of residency training before entering general practice. Since the 1970s, few physicians receive fewer than three years of residency training, with family practice replacing general practice as a specialty.

20. Fein and Weber (1971).

21. Association of American Medical Colleges (2006).

22. Lindsay (1973).

23. Lindsay (1973) demonstrates that a Laspeyres-type adjustment may over- or understate the rate of return to medicine. Nevertheless, if an investment in medical training is worthwhile with a Laspeyres-type adjustment, it will always be worthwhile.

24. Lindsay (1973); Sloan (1970); Fein and Weber (1971).

25. Leffler (1978).

26. Mennemeyer (1978).

27. Burstein and Cromwell (1985).

28. Weeks et al. (1994).

29. American Medical Association (2003, 193).

30. Tu and Ginsburg (2006).

31. Sloan (1970).

32. Burstein and Cromwell (1985).

33. Marder and Willke (1991).

34. Nicholson (2003). Eleven percent of U.S. medical students who entered the 2001 National Residency Matching Program received a position in family practice. Although internal medicine was a more popular specialty (25 percent of U.S. medical students), many of these individuals will eventually practice in an internal medicine subspecialty such as cardiology or gastroenterology.

35. Because my study (2003) uses a specialty that requires three years of residency training as the benchmark, I cannot calculate IRRs to pediatrics and general internal medicine, other specialties with three years of training.

36. National Resident Matching Program (2006).

37. Tu and Ginsburg (2006).

38. Jayanta Bhattacharya (2005) examines whether differential observed and unobserved ability might explain income differences between primary and nonprimary care specialties. That is, if the highest-ability medical students are attracted to nonprimary care specialties, and these students have an absolute earnings advantage relative to lower-ability students in both primary and nonprimary care, then the IRRs to specialization would be biased upward; the earnings of those who actually enter primary care would understate what nonprimary care physicians could earn if they chose to enter primary care. Bhattacharya concludes that the differences in ability between physicians in different specialties explains a relatively small percentage of the observed income differences.

39. Ibid. (15).

40. Nicholson (2003).

41. Madison (2005).

42. Sloan (1971).

43. Sloan (1970).

44. Bazzoli (1985).

45. Hurley (1991).

46. Hay (1991); see also Nicholson (2003).

47. Nicholson (2002).

48. Ibid.

9

The Effects of Incentives on Pharmaceutical Innovation

Frank A. Sloan and
Chee-Ruey Hsieh

By increasing total factor productivity, thereby allowing more output to be produced for a given set of inputs, technological change is a major source of economic growth. According to one view, the mere accumulation of capital, even when extended to include human capital, cannot sustain growth without end since at some point the continued accumulation of capital must inevitably encounter a substantial decline in its rate of return. For this reason, to ensure sustained economic growth, technological process is needed to avoid diminishing returns in the long run.[1] Further, although much new knowledge is a global public good, the amount of knowledge production within a country can boost a country's national income.[2]

In health care, there is a plausible link between technological change, in particular the rate of product innovation, and the increased total factor productivity of health care inputs. Without technological know-how, physicians and other healers working in the nineteenth century and earlier had a low marginal product at best. The story of President James Garfield's treatment and, in today's terms, unnecessary death in 1881 is just one of many poignant illustrations.[3] The gains in health are indeed dramatic, and a large part of the gains plausibly reflect technological change.[4]

In industrialized countries, the life expectancy of females at birth over a 160-year period up to the end of the twentieth century increased by three months per year or forty years in total.[5] There have also been substantial reductions in the rates of disability in the last hundred years, although the improvements are not as well documented, especially before about 1980.[6] Reductions in mortality have been attributed to such factors as improvements in nutrition, public health, vaccination, and new medical and surgical therapies with different factors receiving varying degrees of emphasis depending on the study.[7]

Certainly by every indication, the marginal product of personal health care services is substantially higher at the beginning of the twenty-first century than it was in the nineteenth century.[8] The mechanisms through which technological change has affected gains in health are complex. The introduction of new health care products, such as vaccines and antibiotics, have had major and direct effects on health.

But technological change has plausibly had indirect effects as well. For example, improvements in sanitation in part reflect a growing awareness of how infectious disease spreads.[9] Nutritional gains reflect increased productivity in agriculture, which is largely the result of technological change.[10] One pharmaceutical innovation, aspirin, is unique in that it took decades after the innovation for the full scope of applications in which it could be of benefit to be recognized.

Pharmaceutical innovations, including new vaccines, are among the more important new health care products. Vaccines for polio and smallpox have nearly eradicated these diseases. With the advent of antibiotics, in both developed and developing countries, millions who would have otherwise died of infectious diseases became easily treatable. Antibiotics have nearly eliminated some diseases as major public health problems in high-income countries, and have dramatically lowered the incidence in low-income countries. The availability of new vaccines has not only improved population health but has marked a technological advance in that they can be administered by persons with relatively little training or without expensive equipment. Nevertheless, in spite of the great gains that have been realized, no vaccines exist for major diseases causing both the loss of life and productivity in low-income countries, such as for malaria, schistosomiasis, and HIV. There is also ample room for new pharmaceuticals, including vaccines, for the prevention and treatment of heart disease, cancer, and other major chronic diseases, making it particularly important to understand the effects of various incentives on pharmaceutical innovation.

Clearly, many technological changes in health care provision in general and pharmaceutical innovation are worth having. Given their significance, the main focus of this chapter is to analyze the determinants of research and development (R & D) investment behavior in the pharmaceutical industry, and review the empirical evidence on the impacts of various incentives on product innovation in this industry. Specifically, we analyze how various factors exogenous to individual firms—such as the market size as well as government health and industrial policies—affect firms' incentives for pharmaceutical innovation under the patent system. In addition, we investigate how other incentive mechanisms can be designed to promote pharmaceutical innovation when the patent system fails.

Overall, the empirical studies provide consistent evidence that incentives affect firms' investments in pharmaceutical R & D. This may seem like an obvious finding to economists, but a widespread view is that such firms earn substantial economic rents and that product innovation can be realized by offering pharmaceutical companies appreciably lower returns than they enjoy currently.

Given market size and various government policies, the patent system provides strong incentives for pharmaceutical innovation in high-income countries. Yet there is market failure for some types of products, such as for R & D for diseases that are highly prevalent in low-income countries and some vaccines. Given the low ability to pay, the market power derived from owning a patent is insufficient to generate a sufficiently high anticipated product price to elicit the required return on R & D for products that primarily prevent and treat diseases that are mainly prevalent in low-income countries.

In the next section, we provide a synthesis of the literature on the benefits of pharmaceutical innovation, which is followed by a discussion of the factors that influence a firm's optimal investment decision on pharmaceutical R & D. The next two sections describe the institutional features of pharmaceutical R & D and the existing evidence on the effects of incentives on pharmaceutical innovation, respectively. We then analyze incentive mechanism design when the patent system is insufficient to elicit appropriate amounts of pharmaceutical R & D. Finally, we summarize our results and discuss the public policy implications based on these findings.

The Benefits of Pharmaceutical Innovation

There is little disagreement across the political spectrum with broad statements about the social value of new pharmaceutical products. Nevertheless, the subject of pharmaceutical innovation is controversial. New drugs tend to be much more costly than older ones, and whether or not the additional benefit exceeds the additional cost is widely debated, especially when much of the extra cost is covered by private or public health insurance. The debate about the value of new drugs primarily occurs in high-income countries. In low- and middle-income countries, many new drugs are considered to be unaffordable.

Economists have quantified the benefits of innovation in health care.[11] Although this research deals with health improvements in general, it does not isolate the health benefits of pharmaceutical innovation in particular.[12] Paul Heidenreich and Mark McClellan summarize findings from randomized controlled trials (RCTs), which show the benefits of administering certain drugs introduced in the late twentieth century (such as beta-blockers, ACE inhibitors, and thrombolytics) for treating patients admitted to hospitals with heart attacks.[13] The advantage of using information from RCTs is that other confounding factors are not likely to have affected the health outcome so that the measured effect is truly that of the drugs.

But although they have important advantages, data from trials also have deficiencies. The outcomes measured tend to be short, such as mortality within thirty days of admission to the hospital, and results from a trial in which drugs are administered according to protocol may not generalize to the community where drugs tend to be used much differently.

The other approach is to use observational data to assess benefits. Observational data have several advantages. Sample sizes tend to be larger. The patterns observed are those for the technology as applied in practice, not, as in trials, for the technologies as applied under ideal circumstances. Further, it is possible to study longer-term effects and often for a larger number of outcome types than with data from trials.

Researchers have used observational data to quantify the benefits of pharmaceutical innovations in three different ways. First, many studies use cost-effectiveness analysis to investigate the effects of a specific new drug on certain health outcomes. These studies provide useful information for insurance coverage and reimbursement decisions for individual drugs.[14] The results of individual studies, however, cannot be generalized to evaluate the benefits of pharmaceutical innovation as a whole.

Second, several other studies have empirically estimated the relationship between the pharmaceutical spending level and health outcomes using variation across countries and over time within individual countries. This group of studies has generally found that higher pharmaceutical spending is associated with better health outcomes, as measured by such health indicators as increased life expectancy or lower infant mortality rates.[15] These findings suggest that spending more on pharmaceutical products, such as introducing new drugs into the formulary, is good for population health.

A third type of study focuses on the role of pharmaceutical innovation as a whole on population health. This approach uses the cumulative number of new molecular entities available in the market or the average vintage of a drug to measure pharmaceutical innovation, and empirically estimates the impact on population health. These studies have found a significantly positive relationship between pharmaceutical innovation and life expectancy.[16] The results imply that pharmaceutical innovation as a whole is worth the increased spending, but they do not imply that the marginal benefit of each new pharmaceutical technology exceeds its marginal cost.

In a number of papers, Frank Lichtenberg has assessed the benefits of new drugs.[17] His research examines the effects of a broad range of drugs, including older and new drugs, finding that the introduction of new drugs does have benefits in terms of decreased mortality. An econometric issue with observational data, but not with data from RCTs, is that other factors, such as health behaviors not observable by researchers, may not be held constant. Lichtenberg argues that such other factors should not be correlated with the fraction of total drugs that are new—his measure of innovation.[18] Also, he reports that his results are not sensitive to the inclusion of two other variables. Based on his findings, he concludes that new drugs have important effects on longevity across a broad range of therapeutic categories, with the implication being that pharmaceutical innovation is socially valuable and worthy of public support.

There is another school of thought that new drugs are often not productive, certainly not relative to their added cost. This body of research starts with the finding that there are appreciable differences in spending on personal health care services among countries and within regions of countries—in particular, the United States—but the differences in health status are not associated with the spending differences.[19] In economic terminology, the marginal product of such spending is low, very low, or even zero. In health jargon, this is called "flat of the curve medicine."

Proponents of the view that much new technology is not productive make the argument for medical care in general, not only for new drugs; this category of spending is treated with the same brush as other medical services. The implication for public policy makers is to hold

on to your wallets—that is, implement various cost-containment strategies, including price controls and restricted drug lists ("formularies").

Jonathan Skinner and his colleagues attempt to reconcile the two
views with a graph shown as figure 9.1, which depicts the relationship
between a health outcome, such as survival, and expenditures on
medical care.[20] Each curve is a health production function (PF) showing
the effects of expenditures on survival. The PFs shift for one of two
reasons: technological change or a policy change resulting in more
efficiency in the care provision. Between one period (e.g., 1986) and
another (e.g., 2006), some suppliers of health care services move from
point A on the 1986 PF to point C on the inefficient 2006 PF. Other
providers who have become more efficient move from point A to point
B on the efficient 2006 PF. Technological change is productive; the
slopes of the arrows in figure 9.1 are fairly steep, suggesting that technological change boosts efficiency for both inefficient and efficient providers—but more so for the latter. Yet for a given technology, added
spending can have a low marginal product. Cross-sectional comparisons are between points such as B and C, or between B' and B and C'
and C.

The implication is that innovation in general and pharmaceutical
innovation in particular is productive and should be promoted. There

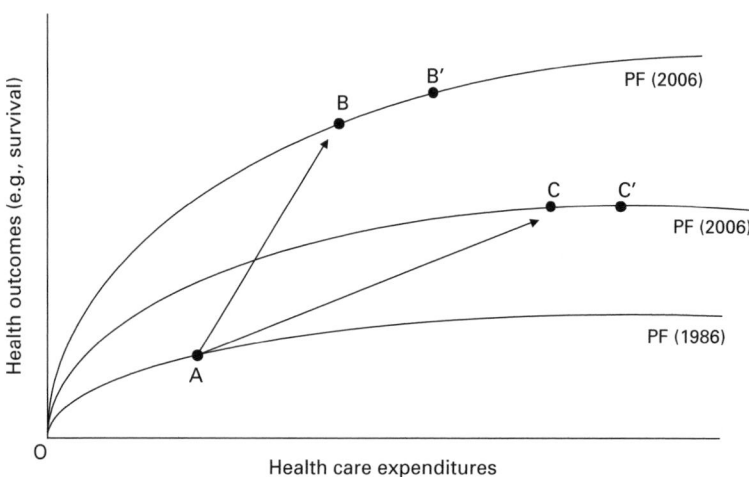

Figure 9.1
Health PF and Technological Change in Health Care

is plausibly considerable heterogeneity in effects, though. Thus, mean effects are not likely to be equal in effect among drugs in a therapeutic category. Moreover, health care inputs, including drugs, can be applied at a margin at which they are not productive, and incentives should be implemented to prevent such overuse.

In sum, pharmaceutical innovation is productive on the whole, but this does not imply that every new drug technology is always productive at the margin at which it is used. This rather straightforward point is often confused by lobbies for the pharmaceutical companies and other groups charged with advocating for manufacturers of pharmaceuticals and other medical products.

Middle- and low-income countries are likely to be much further to the left on the expenditure axis than are high-income countries. In middle-and low-income countries, spending is likely way to the left on the expenditure axis, particularly for the latter. Given the lack of availability of health inputs, particularly the lack of highly skilled personnel and equipment, which is complementary with many innovations emanating from high-income countries, new methods of preventing disease may be given a relatively higher priority than are new methods of diagnosing and treating disease. Developments of new vaccines, which require less skilled personnel than other health interventions to administer, are relatively attractive to lower-income countries for this reason.

The Determinants of Pharmaceutical R & D Investment Behavior

For private firms, the goal of investing in R & D is to increase profit. The R & D investment decision-making process of pharmaceutical firms is thus similar to that of firms in other industries. Optimal investment decisions are made by investing up to the point at which the marginal returns from investment equal the marginal cost of capital to the firm.

Marginal returns can be represented by a marginal efficiency of investment schedule (MEI). The MEI shows investment projects ranked by their anticipated rates of return. As the firm invests more in a given period, the MEI declines (figure 9.2). The shape and position of the MEI partly reflects the demand curves for the final product.

The marginal cost of capital (COC) schedule shows the marginal COC as investment activity expands in any period. The COC can have a zero or positive slope. A positive slope indicates that the firm must

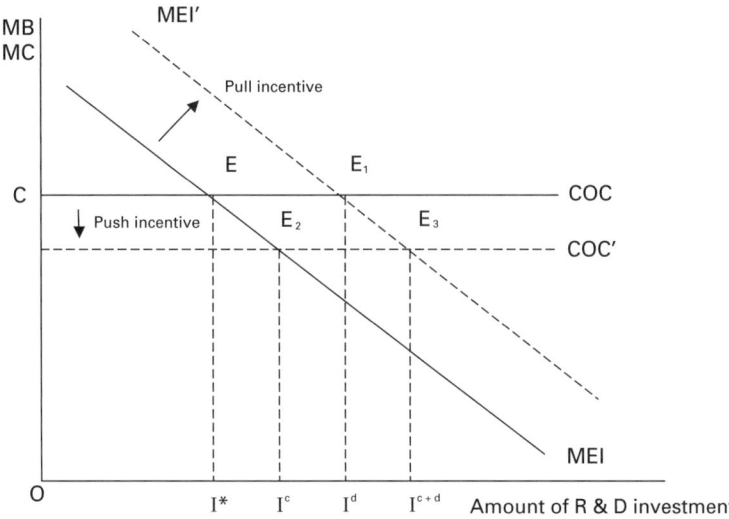

Figure 9.2
Optimal R & D Investment and Induced Innovation by Pull and Push Incentives

pay a higher price for capital if it invests more per period of time. For simplicity, the COC is shown with a zero slope in figure 9.2. The position of the COC depends in part on the creditors' assessment of a firm's bankruptcy risk.

Optimal investment by a pharmaceutical company is shown where the MEI and COC curves intersect, point E, and the amount of investment chosen by the firm is I*. Here, the anticipated marginal returns from investment in R & D and the marginal cost of funds for such investment are equal; at this level of investment, the firm achieves the maximum expected profit from its R & D investment.

More formally, such firms face a two-step decision process. In the first step, they decide whether to devote resources to a specific R & D project. Firms expend the resources if the marginal return is greater than or equal to the marginal cost of funds, and reject the project otherwise. In the second step, such firms decide on the optimal price at which to sell the newly invented good. This price determines the profit flow at each date and hence the rate of return on the investment.

The problem is solved by backward induction. First, the optimal price is derived under the assumption that the R & D investment has already taken place. Optimal pricing reflects government patent policy since patents confer market power on firms contemplating an R & D investment. Second, the results from the first stage are used in calculating whether or not the investment should be undertaken—based on a comparison of the *anticipated* marginal returns and the marginal cost of the capital.

Governments are interested in the amount of private investment undertaken for several reasons, including the effect of such investment on aggregate economic activity, employment effects, and the effects of the output of such investments on the welfare of their citizens.

To assess the effects of specific government policies affecting incentives for firms to undertake R & D investment, specifically investments in pharmaceutical R & D, economists have classified incentives to stimulate R & D into two categories: pull and push incentives.[21]

Pull incentives affect the demand for the final product resulting from the R & D and hence shift the MEI curve outward. Such shifts occur, for example, in response to an exogenous increase in market size, reflecting in part countries' decisions to cover the new product under their public insurance systems, new product coverage decisions by private insurers, and an increase in the willingness of such insurers to pay a higher price for the new product. The MEI shifts for nonpolicy reasons as well, such as from exogenous increases in population size, increases in the number of types of persons especially likely to use the new product, and growth in income that affects individuals' willingness (and ability) to pay for the new product.

Referring to figure 9.2, the MEI curve shifts outward to MEI' if there is an exogenous change that leads to an increase in the expected revenue from new products. Other things being equal, the new MEI curve (MEI') intersects the COC curve at point E_1; the firm's optimal R & D investment now becomes I^d. The increase in R & D investment, as measured by the difference between I^d and I^*, represents the new R & D investment induced by an exogenous change, such as a pull incentive.

Push incentives affect the marginal cost of funds to the firm for investments in R & D. For example, by affecting the cash flow associated with the investment, a government grant, a more generous depreciation policy, or an investment tax credit affects the supply of funds. Likewise, granting the firm access to funds from the sale of securities, the income from which is not subject to personal income taxation, increases the supply of funds—that is, shifts the COC downward (and if positively, sloped to the right). Macroeconomic policies affecting the market rates of interest also affect the COC.

The COC curve shifts downward to COC' if there is an exogenous change that leads to a decrease in the user cost of capital. Other things being equal, the new COC curve (COC') intersects the MEI curve at point E_2, with I^c being the firms new optimal R & D investment. The increase in R & D investment, as measured by the difference between I^c and I^*, represents the new R & D investment induced by push incentives.

The effectiveness of push incentives depends on the elasticity of the MEI—that is, the percent rate of change (decline) in the MEI for a given percent change in investment. The elasticity of the MEI reflects the anticipated product demand conditions—for example, the new product's price elasticity of demand. A given push policy will be more effective, other factors being equal, if the MEI is more elastic.

Conversely, there are push disincentives. For instance, as mentioned above, the position of the COC is affected by the anticipated credit risk of the firm. If the firm's assets are subject to expropriation by the government, or if its assets were subject to the risk of a terrorist attack, this would raise the firm's COC, thereby discouraging private investment.

Negative pull incentives arise, for example, when countries' drug coverage and payment policies become more uncertain. Or the national agency responsible for approving new drug products for sale in a country may lengthen or add complexity to its approval process. This in turn delays the time at which positive cash flow from the new product can be anticipated and lowers the expected rate of return. In general, the probability that a new drug will ever appear on the market is reflected in the MEI. If government regulatory agencies become more stringent in approving drugs, this too affects private investment in R & D.

Theoretically, the relative effectiveness of pull versus push incentives cannot be deduced. This is instead an empirical question. It has been argued on the basis of institutional factors, however, that pull incentives tend to be more promising.[22] With pull incentives, the reward is for results; with push incentives, by contrast, rewards can be made on the basis of promises. For example, an applicant for a government grant, a push incentive, can make various claims about the uniqueness of an approach, but once awarded the grant, there is no direct incentive to deliver on the promise except the threat that nonperformance will result in fewer grants in the future. Unfortunately, conclusive empirical evidence from comparisons of pull versus push incentives is lacking.

A combination of pull and push incentives may induce more invest-ment than when only one type of incentive is implemented (figure 9.2). For this reason, rather than choose between the two, a government may include a mix of pull and push policies in its R & D stimulus package.[23] A mix of policies can shift the MEI up and the COC curve down simul-taneously, leading to a new equilibrium point for optimal investment at points such as E_3 and I^{c+d}. In this example, the new R & D investment induced by adopting both pull and push incentives simultaneously ($I^{c+d}-I^*$) is greater than any new investment induced by pull incentive (I^d-I^*) or push incentive (I^c-I^*) alone.

Of course, governments may not develop strategies to maximize the value of investments in R & D. Public policy decisions often reflect other motives. Also, there may be important implementation barriers specific to particular investment stimulus policies.

This reservation notwithstanding, the above analysis provides a general conceptual framework for understanding the effect of various incentives on the firm's R & D investment decision. Below, we review the empirical evidence on these incentive effects, focusing specifically on the pharmaceutical industry. As background, we first describe crucial characteristics of pharmaceutical R & D.

Institutional Features of Pharmaceutical R & D

Four features of pharmaceutical R & D are rather unique to this sector. First, pharmaceutical companies typically allocate a relatively larger share of their resources to investments in R & D than do their counter-parts in most other industries. In the United States, for example, R & D expenditures as a percentage of sales ranged from 3 (motor vehicles) to 8 percent (communication equipment) in 1995. By contrast, pharma-ceutical manufacturers allocated over 10 percent of their sales revenue to R & D in the same year.[24] Furthermore, there is a positive secular trend in the share of R & D expenditures as a percentage of sales revenue. Among the top ten pharmaceutical firms in the United States, the share of sales revenue allocated to R & D increased from 10.9 percent in 1990 to 13.7 percent in 2000.[25]

Second, the mean of R & D cost per new chemical entity (NCE) is substantial, which can be attributed to three factors.[26] Because of gov-ernment protocols, for one, drug discovery and development is expen-sive. DiMasi and colleagues estimated that the mean out-of-pocket R & D cost for NCE approval in the 1990s exceeded $400 million (in 2000 dollars).[27] About three-quarters of these R & D expenditures are spent on the preclinical and human testing required by the regulatory agency in the United States, the Food and Drug Administration (FDA), to establish proof of safety and efficacy.[28] Also, pharmaceutical R & D is a time-consuming process. It takes twelve to fifteen years to successfully develop a new drug. By applying a real discount rate of 11 percent to capitalize the out-of-pocket cash flows over these lengthy periods, the estimated average R & D cost per NCE increased to $802 million (in 2000 dollars).[29] There are also higher failure rates in the drug discovery and development process than in many other sectors.

Third, the long R & D process in the pharmaceutical industry can be decomposed into two distinct stages: discovery and development.[30] The discovery stage includes basic science research and the application of "upstream" basic research to search for new compounds for developing new drugs. The development stage refers to "downstream" market-oriented R & D, including preclinical testing as well as three phases of clinical tests to demonstrate the safety and efficacy of the specific compound. A characteristic of the upstream basic research is its public good nature. For this reason, private firms lack incentives to invest in basic research. Rather, as with the financing of other public goods, such as national defense, the financing of basic scientific research is highly dependent on public funding.[31] As a result, compared to other industries, public investment accounts for a relatively large portion of the total R & D investment in the pharmaceutical industry. In 2003, for example, the public sector invested about $28 billion on basic biomedical research, which accounted for about 47 percent of the total health-related R & D investment (including basic and applied health research) in the United States.[32] Over two-thirds of the public investment on health R & D in the United States is through the National Institutes of Health in the form of grants to research universities.[33] By contrast, public investment only accounts for about one-third of the total R & D investment in other nonhealth industries.[34]

Finally, the fourth rather unique characteristic of pharmaceutical R & D is that it is highly dependent on patent protection to recoup the R & D investment. Pharmaceutical companies are more dependent on patent protection than are many other research-intensive industries.[35] The difference between the marginal cost of bringing the first unit of a product to market (the first-copy cost) and the marginal costs of units beyond the first is extremely large. Compared to the high R & D cost per new NCE, the estimated cost of applying for an abbreviated new drug approval required for bringing the imitative products (generic drugs) into the market was approximately $603,000 in the early 1990s, which only accounted for 0.15 percent of the out-of-pocket R & D cost per new NCE.[36] Therefore, the research base of the pharmaceutical industry could not long survive without patent protection.[37]

The conceptual basis rationale for patent protection is readily explained. Once a new product has been developed, the marginal cost of manufacturing and distributing a new drug is quite low. If new drugs were priced at their marginal cost, there would be no way for the firm to recoup the high fixed cost of R & D. The fixed cost of R & D must be covered somehow, and the method used to date has been to allow pharmaceutical companies to have a monopoly on their new products for a stated period of time so as to recoup their investments from the monopoly profit. This is not unambiguously a good approach in that there is a welfare loss from monopoly pricing.

Incentives under the Patent System

On the one hand, the market power created by patents provides a mechanism for the pharmaceutical research firm to recoup its R & D cost and hence creates incentives for innovation. But on the other hand, such market power allows firms to set higher prices, which in turn restricts the use of the drug below the socially optimal rate of use. At the monopoly price, that is, there are consumers with a willingness to pay for the drug far in excess of the marginal cost of producing the good.

Furthermore, rather than charge a single monopoly price, pharmaceutical firms often engage in price discrimination to sell identical products to different sets of consumers at different prices. Price discrimination allows firms to extract even more money from consumers (more consumer surplus) than under simple monopoly pricing, but it has the positive feature of leading to output levels that are closer to the socially optimal rates of output than occurs under monopoly pricing. One often hears complaints in public forums about the high price of new pharmaceutical products, which imposes substantial cost burdens on public and private payers as well as individuals who pay for new prescriptions out of pocket. Economic efficiency often plays a secondary role to the distribution effects in public policy decision making.

The marginal cost of new drugs is low once these products are developed, receive government approval, and are marketed. But the required rate of return for firms to engage in R & D investment activity is high (given where the MEI intersects the COC curve) before new drugs are developed, approved, and marketed, thereby creating a time-inconsistency problem.

At a given point in time, the amount of pharmaceutical innovation is fixed. The optimal allocation of resources in the short run is therefore guided by setting the social marginal benefit equal to the marginal social cost of producing and distributing the good. In the absence of externalities, *static* efficiency could be achieved by market competition driving the prices of new drugs down to the marginal cost. Given the high R & D cost in the pharmaceutical industry, however, competitive prices do not allow firms to recoup their expenditures on R & D investment. Consequently, *dynamic* efficiency considers the optimal resource allocation over time, which requires pricing a new drug at a high level sufficient to preserve incentives for R & D investment (assuming reliance on the patent system).

It is tempting for public decision makers, especially in small countries, to emphasize static efficiency since they perceive that their policies will not adversely affect the development of new products. Public policy makers with short time horizons in larger countries may be similarly tempted. The key policy challenge is how to achieve an appropriate balance between static efficiency that considers the short-term benefits from greater price competition and dynamic efficiency that considers the long-term benefits from appropriate incentives for innovation.[38]

Effective Patent Life

Effective patent life (EPL) is defined as follows: it equals the nominal patent life minus the time lost prior to regulatory approval. The current patent system, which operates globally, gives the protection of intellectual property rights—this nominal patent life often begins before human clinical trials. As mentioned above, the new drug development process takes about twelve to fifteen years on average. Thus, much of the nominal patent life is lost before the product is approved by the regulatory agency. The EPL for a representative new drug compound, according to one estimate, was less than ten years in the United States. during the early 1980s, which implies that a policy of increasing the EPL can provide an important incentive for pharmaceutical R & D investment.[39]

Since the nominal patent life is now fixed at twenty years, a government can increase the EPL by reducing or restoring the patent time lost during the clinical and regulatory periods. In the United States, the FDA classifies the review process for new drug application into two categories: "priority" and "standard." Drugs offering "significant improvement compared to marketed products in the treatment, diagnosis, or prevention of a disease" are assigned to priority review. Drugs that "appear to have therapeutic qualities similar to those of one or more already marketed drugs" use the standard review process.[40]

The standard review takes approximately 18.4 months in the United States while priority review only takes 6.4 months on average.[41] This suggests that a priority review process could increase the EPL by one year. Based on sales data from the top ten U.S. pharmaceuticals, the market value of increasing the EPL by one year is approximately $300 million (in 2004 dollars).[42] This policy would provide a major incentive to encourage firms to invest in new drugs with significant therapeutic gains over the existing drugs.

In 1984, the United States enacted the Drug Price Competition and Patent Term Restoration Act, also known as the Hatch-Waxman Act. This law increased the EPL through a partial restoration of the patent time lost during the clinical and regulatory periods.[43] The passage of the Hatch-Waxman law increased the EPL by 2.3 years.[44]

Market Size

A second pull incentive for increasing pharmaceutical innovation is through expanding of market size, which depends on several factors, such as the demographic structure of the population, health policies, and income levels. Several studies have documented the empirical relationship between market size and pharmaceutical innovation from various settings.

Daron Acemoglu and Joshua Linn measure changes in market size from demographic trends in the United States.[45] During a recent thirty-year period, demographic trends have led to a decline in the market for drugs mostly consumed by the young (newborn to thirty). By contrast, the markets for drugs mostly consumed by middle-aged persons have increased. More specifically, Acemoglu and Linn's measure of the potential market size for each drug category reflects a combination of the number of consumers and their incomes. They find that the change in the potential market size has a significantly positive impact on pharmaceutical innovation, as measured by the number of new drugs entering the U.S. market. A 1 percent increase in the potential market size leads to about a 4 percent increase in the entry of new drugs, either in the form of new nongeneric drugs or new molecular entities.

Amy Finkelstein investigates how changes in health policies affect R & D investment behavior in the U.S. vaccine industry.[46] She considers the following recent health policy changes. In 1986, the U.S. government introduced a no-fault compensation system for injuries attributable to the use of certain childhood vaccines. This system reduced the expected liability costs for vaccine manufacturers since compensation for injuries under no-fault was much lower than under the tort system previously applicable to such injuries. In 1991, the U.S. Centers for Disease Control recommended that all infants be vaccinated against hepatitis B. And in 1993, Medicare extended coverage for influenza vaccinations administered to its beneficiaries. These latter two policies increased the potential market size for vaccines, which in turn, in combination with the adoption of the no-fault system in 1986, substantially increased the expected return from developing new vaccines for infectious diseases.

Comparing changes in the number of new vaccine clinical trials between treatment (affected by the policies) and control diseases (not affected by the policies), Finkelstein finds evidence linking the policy changes to rates of innovation in vaccine markets. She estimates that a one dollar increase in the annual expected market revenue from a vaccine leads to a six cent increase in vaccine R & D investment.

Acemoglu and a group of colleagues further investigate whether the introduction of Medicare in 1965 increased pharmaceutical innovation.[47] Before 2006, Medicare did not cover outpatient prescription drugs but did provide coverage for other types of medical care. To the extent that physicians' services and outpatient drugs are complements, decreasing the price of physicians' services to the U.S. elderly by extending public insurance coverage to this group would be expected to increase the demand for pharmaceutical products as well. By comparing the drug expenditure between "treatment" (persons age sixty-five to seventy-four) and "control" groups (persons age fifty-five to sixty-four), the authors find no evidence of increased pharmaceutical innovation attributable to the introduction of Medicare. It is much too early to tell whether or not the Medicare prescription drug benefit introduced in 2006 will increase drug innovation.

Frank Lichtenberg investigates the effect of market size, as measured by the burden of disease, on pharmaceutical innovation.[48] He measures the burden of disease by the number of disability-adjusted life years attributable to the disease in 2001, as calculated by the World Health Organization. Disease burden potentially represents a more accurate measure of the potential use than broad demographic characteristics such as age. Lichtenberg finds that the amount of pharmaceutical innovation, as measured by the number of new chemical entities launched since 1982, is positively related to the burden of disease in developed countries, but there is no statistically significant relationship between disease burden and innovation in developing countries. For diseases more commonly found in developing countries, the burden of disease is not identical to the market size of pharmaceuticals because per capita incomes are lower, there is weak patent protection, and government regulation places binding constraints on drug pricing.

The evidence of a positive effect of market size on pharmaceutical innovation suggests that pharmaceutical firms may lack adequate financial incentives to discover and develop new drugs with small market sizes. Although developing countries account for 78 percent of the world's population and 85 percent of the global burden of disease, new molecular entities for treating tropical diseases in humans in an important subset of developing countries accounted for less than 1 percent of all new molecular entities licensed worldwide during 1975–1997.[49] Given the evidence that the larger burden of disease does not provide adequate profit incentives to induce pharmaceutical innovation in low-income countries, it is critical to investigate how alternative incentive mechanisms could promote pharmaceutical innovation for the prevention and treatment of diseases that are mainly prevalent in low-income countries. We return to this issue below.

Price Regulation

Many developed countries provide insurance coverage for prescription drugs. Consequently, most pharmaceutical expenditures in these countries are made by third-party payers.[50] As a by-product of pharmaceutical innovation, new prescription drugs are introduced into markets in these countries annually. Added expenditures from these new drugs, however beneficial they may be in terms of their health-enhancing effects, increase pressure on public budgets. Therefore, these countries have implemented regulatory mechanisms to control the growth of spending on pharmaceuticals.[51]

The most commonly used form of regulation aimed at controlling increases in public expenditures on pharmaceuticals involves the direct control of product prices. In contrast to the expansion of effective patent life and the market size, price regulation of pharmaceutical products *decreases* incentives for R & D investment. This is a negative pull policy.

Several studies have documented the empirical relationship between price regulation and disincentives for innovation in the pharmaceutical industry. In conceptual terms, price regulation directly reduces R & D investment through the following two channels.[52] First, price regulation reduces the price of regulated products, and hence it decreases the expected returns of R & D output. Second, the decrease in the expected returns of R & D output in turn decreases the profit margins, thereby negatively affecting the availability of internal funds for investment— an effect reflected in the COC curve. The cost of capital from internal funds may be lower than that of external funds, such as for debt and equity.[53] Showing this in the supply and demand for capital funds framework of figure 9.2 would require that we draw the COC with a positive slope. Price regulation would then shift the COC curve upward to the left, leading firms to invest less in R & D than they did before the price constraints were imposed.

Using panel data from fourteen large pharmaceutical firms in the world for the period 1994 to 1997, John Vernon estimates the effects of expected profitability and cash flow on R & D investment intensity, as measured by the ratio of R & D expenditures to total sales.[54] He uses the firm's current period pretax pharmaceutical profit margin as a proxy to measure the expected future profitability. Also, he uses the percentage of pharmaceutical sales from non-U.S. markets to measure the firm's exposure to price regulation and simulate the effects of price regulation.

His empirical analysis yields three important findings. First, both pharmaceutical profit expectations and lagged cash flows have significantly positive impacts on the firm's R & D investment intensity. Second, the mean pretax pharmaceutical profit margins in the non-regulated (U.S.) market are approximately four to five times as large as those in the regulated (non-U.S.) markets. Third, Vernon's simulations reveal that R & D investment intensity would decline by 23 to 33 percent if the United States also adopted a price regulation. The cash flow effect would account for about half of this decline in R & D, and the rest of the decline would come from the expected profit effect.

Carmelo Giaccotto and colleagues use U.S. industry-level data for the years 1952 to 2001 to estimate the relationship between real drug prices and R & D investment intensity.[55] They measure the real price of drugs by dividing the pharmaceutical consumer price index (CPI) by the all-items CPI, and find that real drug prices have a significantly positive impact on R & D investment. The elasticity estimate of about 0.6 suggests that a 10 percent increase in real drug prices leads to a 6 percent increase in R & D investment. Based on this result, they simulate the effect of price regulation by assuming that the federal government limited the rate of growth in drug price increases to the rate of growth in the general CPI from 1980 to 2001. They find that the capitalized pharmaceutical R & D expenditure during this period would have declined about 30 percent as a consequence of implementing such price regulation.

In addition to the direct effect on the firm's R & D investment behavior, price regulation also affects incentives for pharmaceutical innovation indirectly through its impact on market competition. Several studies have shown consistent evidence that price regulation leads to decreasing product prices with product age and undermines market competition.[56] Both effects create disincentives for pharmaceutical innovation.

Z. John Lu and William Comanor as well as Mats Ekelund and Bjorn Persson provide interesting comparisons of the pricing of new pharmaceuticals in an unregulated (U.S.) market versus a regulated one (Sweden).[57] Lu and Comanor find that in a market not subject to price regulation, pharmaceutical companies adopt a penetration strategy in pricing their new products that offer little or no therapeutic advantages over existing products by setting launch prices at or below those of existing products. The mean real price, however, increased substantially with time since the drug introduction.[58] By contrast, Ekelund and Persson report that real prices for NCEs fall substantially over time in their study for all classes of therapeutic innovations, new products that represent real breakthroughs, and those that represent at most minor advances over existing products in the regulated Swedish market. This result is consistent with empirical results obtained by Patricia Danzon and Li-Wei Chao for Japan, Italy, and France.[59]

Regulatory pressure on prices over their product life cycles is expected to provide a disincentive for the pharmaceutical firm to develop a new product with important therapeutic gains.[60] Pharmaceutical firms in regulated countries tend to introduce line extensions by introducing a stream of minor new products (such as new dosage forms) in order to obtain a higher price.

Henry Grabowski and R. Richard Wang use global NCEs and first-in-class NCEs to measure the importance of pharmaceutical innovation across countries.[61] They define global NCEs as those introduced in at least four of the G7 countries (Canada, France, Germany, Italy, Japan, the United Kingdom, and the United States), which represent the world's largest pharmaceutical markets. Grabowski and Wang define first-in-class NCEs as the first NCE in a therapeutic class. They find that global NCEs accounted for over half of all NCEs launched in the United States during the period 1982 to 2003, and first-in-class NCEs accounted for about one-fifth of all NCEs launched in the United States during the same period. By contrast, the shares of global and first-in-class NCEs were only about 10 and 3 percent, respectively, in Italy and Japan, which provides strong empirical support for the view that price regulation reduces both the quantity and quality of pharmaceutical innovation.

Ekelund and Persson, moreover, find no correlation between the number of branded substitutes and the launch prices in the Swedish market, which stands in contrast to Lu and Comanor's result that the number of branded substitutes has a substantial negative effect on launch prices in the U.S. market.[62] Danzon and Chao argue that price regulation undermines generic competition in countries such as France, Italy, and Japan.[63] Generic competition often leads to a large decline in the sales of branded drugs within a short period.[64] The threat of generic competition consequently forces firms manufacturing branded products (those still under patent) to implement various strategic responses. One such response available to the producer of the branded product is to invest in new products and maintain a healthy pipeline of products under development.

Market pressures arising from generic competition are clearly one of the key incentives for pharmaceutical innovation. The decline in generic competition resulting from price regulation therefore weakens incentives for innovation signaled by market pressure emanating from generic competition.

Furthermore, price regulation reduces incentives for innovation through its impact on the launch delay of new drugs. Danzon, Wang, and Wang point out that the price regulation imposes two negative external effects on the firm's expected revenue.[65] First, it induces parallel trade. The arbitrageur purchases prescription drugs in low-price countries for resale in high-price countries. Second, price regulation creates an external reference price based on which countries set the regulated price. In such cases, accepting a lower price in one country may undermine the price that the firm can obtain in another country. The pharmaceutical firm may thus postpone the launch of new drugs or choose to have no launch at all if the regulator sets the price of the new product too low.

Based on a sample of eighty-five NCE launches between 1994 and 1998 in twenty-five major markets, Danzon, Wang, and Wang report that the expected price of a new product, measured by a lagged average price of other drugs in the same or related therapeutic class, significantly affects the timing and occurrence of a launch.[66] Countries with lower expected prices tend to have fewer launches and longer launch delays. Clearly, delays in the launch of new drugs or no launch at all reduce the expected revenues that the firm can recoup for R & D investment, thereby decreasing pharmaceutical innovation.

In sum, price regulation affects innovation incentives in the pharmaceutical industry through the following four channels. First, it lowers the firm's R & D incentives by reducing the expected profit from innovation and increasing the cost of capital for R & D investment by decreasing the internal funds for investment. The empirical evidence reviewed above supports the theoretical prediction shown in figure 9.2 that price regulation leads to a reduction in the *size* of optimal R & D investment. Second, price regulation reduces the drug's effective price over its product life, which in turn creates incentives for pharmaceutical firms to focus on quick but minor innovations in order to secure higher prices on new products. Overall, pharmaceutical innovation in countries subject to a strictly regulated system lags behind that in countries with less regulated or unregulated systems. Third, price regulation reduces competition in pharmaceutical markets, in turn further diminishing competitive pressures to develop new products. Fourth, it negatively affects the timing and occurrence of new product launches, which in turn reduces the expected revenues from countries globally.

Our review of the empirical evidence is based on the reality that some countries impose regulation on pharmaceutical prices while other countries do not regulate prices. Nevertheless, our conclusion that price regulation reduces incentives for R & D investment (almost) as if buyers around the world were to form a single monopsony and impose price regulation on pharmaceutical products. One might argue that under this hypothetical situation, a pharmaceutical firm would still invest in finding new drugs as long as the pharmaceutical industry remains the most profitable industry, and hence price regulation may not affect R & D investment at all. Yet we reject this argument, given the evidence that price regulation significantly affects the profit expectation and cash flow of the pharmaceutical firms. As shown in figure 9.2, the reduction in expected profit and the increase in cost of capital both lead to reduced investment. Thus, our analysis suggests that price regulation *always* leads to a reduction of the *optimal size* of R & D investment (from the firm's standpoint), although the firm may still find it is profitable to undertake R & D investment provided the marginal return from investment exceeds the marginal cost of capital.

Industrial Policy

Industrial policies refer to government policies designed to promote the growth of a specific industry in a country. Such growth may be viewed as desirable for several reasons, including its effects on employment, synergies with other industries, and in the case of pharmaceuticals, the potential impact on population health. Industrial policies may be of either the pull or push variety. In the context of pharmaceuticals, industrial policies have mainly been of the push type, targeting the availability of funds for investments in R & D. One specific example of a push policy is a tax credit for R & D expenditures. This policy reduces the cost of capital for R & D investment and hence increases the firm's incentive to undertake such investment.

The 1983 Orphan Drug Act in the United States is an example of a government using tax credits to promote pharmaceutical innovation. The rationale for the act was to stimulate R & D investment in orphan drugs, which are defined as drugs designed to treat conditions affecting less than two hundred thousand persons in the United States, or affecting more than that number but having limited commercial value so that innovative firms have no reasonable expectation of recouping the R & D costs. The act provides a tax credit for up to 50 percent of certain clinical testing expenses by pharmaceutical firms to generate required data for marketing approval. In addition, the act offers grant support for the investigation of rare disease treatments through the establishment of the Office of Orphan Product Development. The act also provides seven years of marketing exclusivity, which is a pull incentive that increases the expected market revenue from developing the drug for treating rare diseases.[67]

Following the implementation of the Orphan Drug Act, the mean annual number of new drugs brought to market for treating rare diseases increased appreciably. During the decade prior to the act's enactment, there was only one orphan product developed by the pharmaceutical industry per year. Between 1983 and 1994, the FDA had designated about 600 pharmaceuticals as orphan products, allowing firms to obtain tax credits for clinical testing expenses. During the same period, the FDA also approved 111 orphan drugs for marketing, allowing firms to obtain the protection of marketing exclusivity for seven years.[68]

In 1993, Japan also enacted similar legislation, which contains several provisions that reduce the cost and increase the expected revenue for R & D investment in rare diseases, including a direct government subsidy for R & D investment, tax credits, exclusive marketing rights, and priority review for new drug applications. As in the United States, the enactment of this law in Japan has provided a meaningful incentive for drug innovation in the treatment of rare diseases. Between 1993 and 1996, the Japanese Ministry of Health designated seventy-eight drugs as orphan drugs and approved twelve orphan products for marketing.[69]

Since this legislation in both the United States and Japan involved a mix of pull and push incentives to stimulate R & D investment for rare diseases, it is difficult to assess the separate effects of the tax credit (push incentive) and marketing exclusivity (pull incentive) provisions on pharmaceutical innovation. Nevertheless, the success of these laws in both countries implies that industrial policy of either the pull or push variety is effective in stimulating pharmaceutical innovation.

Public Investment on Basic Research

In spite of its public good nature, upstream basic research is not free from the firm's standpoint.[70] The dissemination of scientific knowledge from the public to private sectors can be costly and time-consuming. Firms must invest in knowledge capital so that they can access and absorb upstream basic research findings.[71] The form of investment in knowledge capital includes some in-house basic research, and maintaining an extensive connection between pharmaceutical company scientists and publicly funded researchers by collaborative efforts in publishing scientific papers. Iain Cockburn and Rebecca Henderson report that the number of coauthorships of scientific papers is positively related to the firm's private research productivity, as measured by the number of important patents.[72]

Since private research mainly focuses on downstream market-oriented R & D for developing new drugs, Cockburn and Henderson's work suggests that upstream basic research and downstream market-oriented R & D are complements rather than substitutes in the pharmaceutical R & D process. Based on detailed case histories for the development of twenty-one key drugs introduced between 1965 and 1992, Cockburn and Henderson find that fourteen drugs were developed with at least some input from the public sector. This evidence indicates that the investment in basic research by the public sector plays a significant role in the rate of drug discovery and development.

Public investment in upstream basic research provides the input for downstream market-oriented R & D in three ways. It supplies: the fundamental biological and chemical knowledge for the discovery of new drugs; the clinical knowledge for the design of human clinical trials required by regulatory agencies as proof of drug safety and efficacy; and the insights for potential new indications for drugs once they have been approved.[73] Increases in public investment in upstream basic research decrease the cost of acquiring knowledge capital for pharmaceutical innovation. Furthermore, public investment in basic research expands the stock of scientific knowledge used by applied researchers, which in turn increases R & D productivity and helps an innovative product to reach the market sooner.[74] These two effects together suggest that public investment in basic research creates an incentive for increasing spending on downstream R & D investment by private firms.

Other Incentive Mechanisms When Patents Fail

Under the patent system, pharmaceutical firms receive rewards for their R & D investment through market valuations—that is, the monopoly profit they can earn due to the entry barrier that patents erect. The firm's decision rule for R & D investment is to maximize profit, not to maximize health gains. This implies that the allocation of R & D resources by private firms is guided by market demand (or the ability to pay) rather than on the basis of health needs. In high-income countries, people are able and willing to pay for good health. Thus, there is no significant deviation between the ability to pay and health needs. The patent system appears to function fairly well in providing incentives for pharmaceutical innovation.

By contrast, there is a substantial disparity between the ability to pay and health needs in low-income countries. Judging from data on the global burden of disease, there is a great health need in low-income countries.[75] In these countries, income is low, and the effective demand for disease prevention and therapy is correspondingly low. R & D investment spending on the search for the prevention and cure of some diseases that are highly prevalent in low-income countries is consequently low or even negligible (hereafter referred to as neglected diseases), indicating there is indeed a mismatch or market failure in allocating R & D resources according to health needs.

There is another type of market failure in vaccine R & D investment that arises from external benefits in consumption. The social benefits of vaccines not only include the internal benefits from disease prevention for specific individuals who are vaccinated but also the external benefits from preventing the spread of disease to others. Individuals' willingness to pay for vaccines is not likely to reflect the external benefits from being vaccinated. Vaccines for major communicable diseases may have much larger social benefits than many drugs. But firms tend to earn lower profits from vaccines than from drugs.[76] Thus, private firms have less incentive to discover and develop new vaccines because of the low profit, although the vaccines' potential value to population health is high.

In these two cases, the patent system may not generate a sufficient incentive for pharmaceutical innovation. Economists have therefore investigated other mechanisms to stimulate pharmaceutical innovation when the patent system fails.

One alternative is a system of rewards paid by the government or private foundations (hereafter referred to as sponsors) to pharmaceutical firms. A well-known example involves the Bill and Melinda Gates Foundation.[77] Other organizations engaged in sponsoring or undertaking R & D on drugs for neglected diseases include the Institute for OneWorld Health, a U.S.-based nonprofit pharmaceutical company, and the Drugs for Neglected Diseases Initiative, an independent, not-for-profit drug development initiative.

Under the reward system, the property rights of an innovation are purchased by the sponsors in the form of rewards; sponsors in turn place the innovation into the public domain, making it available freely to competing manufacturers. An advantage of the reward system is that the sponsor can provide incentives for pharmaceutical R & D investment without granting the firms monopoly power over the price and removing the legal barrier for other firms to enter into the market. As a result, the new drugs can be sold at the price equal to the marginal cost, which in turn reduces the welfare loss from the patent, increases the accessibility of new drugs, and reduces the cost burden on payers.

One of the practical issues that this system faces is how to determine the size of rewards. Theoretically, the problem is rather straightforward. One could compute the consumer surplus, assuming pricing at the marginal cost and the output at which the demand curve intersects the marginal cost curve. As shown in figure 9.3, the consumer surplus is represented by the triangle area AP_cE. The size of this area (in dollars) divided by the quantity Q_c is equal to the size of rectangle P_rP_cEC. This suggests that sponsors can set the rewards equal to $P_r - P_c$ per unit of output up to the quantity of Q_c. Under this reward system, the innovative firm receives the subsidy in the amount of a consumer surplus from the sponsors as a reward to recoup its spending on R & D investment. The new pharmaceutical product in turn can be produced and sold in a competitive market by the innovative firm or other firms at price P_c.

The analytic framework of figure 9.3 implies that the reward system provides two advantages over the patent one. First, the reward system avoids the social welfare loss created by the patent system. Under the patent system, the monopoly price of a new pharmaceutical product is P_m, which is higher than the competitive price (P_c) and hence reduces the quantity of consumption to Q_m. This in turn leads to a social welfare loss in the amount of the decrease in consumer surplus minus the monopoly rent. Second, sponsors can select the magnitude of research incentives by adjusting the level of rewards. When there are consumption externalities, for example, one would need to adjust for this since the consumer surplus as revealed by the market would be an underestimate. The maximum price would be the area of the adjusted (for externalities) consumer surplus divided by the socially optimal output (again accounting for externalities). Citing these two advantages, Steven Shavell and Tanguy-van Ypersele conclude that an optional

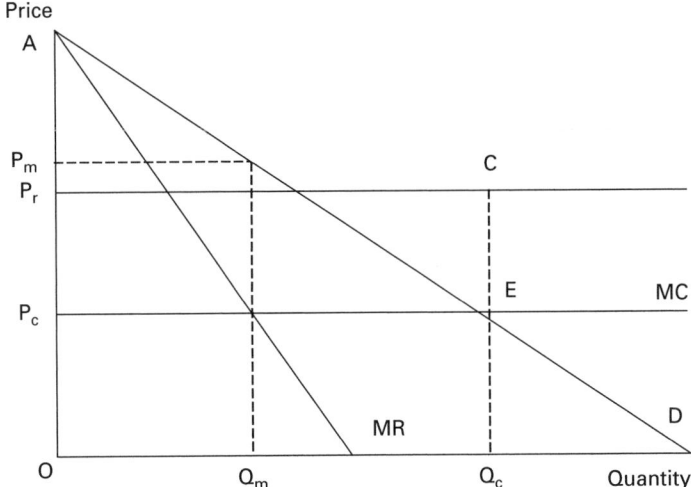

Figure 9.3
The Determination of Rewards

reward system, in which the firm can freely choose between rewards and patents, is superior to patents.[78]

In practice, computing the maximum price or reward is of course complex. For one, Alan Garber and his colleagues caution that with insurance and moral hazard, monopoly profit may exceed the relevant consumer surplus.[79] It is thus conceivable that rewards to firms under the patent system are too high—not too low, as in the presence of externalities.

The calculations also involve new, not existing products. Hence, many assumptions are required to obtain estimates of the maximum prices or rewards. If the rewards are set too low, the incentives for innovation will be insufficient. Yet there is also a risk if the rewards are set too high. In particular, there will be too much investment in R & D.[80] The following subsections analyze three proposals that use the reward system to provide incentives to develop new drugs and vaccines for developing countries.

Advance-Purchase Commitments

Michael Kremer and Rachel Glennerster propose using an advance-purchase commitment as an incentive mechanism to induce innovation for a malaria vaccine.[81] This approach offers the innovator a subsidy of a fixed value per unit for a given number of units if the innovators develop a new vaccine that has certain technical characteristics.

The rationale for this approach is to use the subsidy offered by the sponsors to close the gap between high R & D costs for new vaccines and the low ability to pay in low-income countries. In figure 9.4, the ability to pay for a certain amount of vaccines is represented by the market demand curve D. The market price would be equal to P if a country needs to consume OQ amount of vaccine in order to effectively prevent the outbreak of a certain disease. The average cost of a vaccine at this quantity is C, however. The pharmaceutical firm does not have an incentive to invest for vaccine R & D because the sustainable market price (P) is insufficiently high to allow it to recoup the R & D cost (C). If the sponsor offers a subsidy in the amount of C − P per unit up to quantity OQ, then the total revenue received by the innovator equals the market revenue (as represented by OPEQ) plus the sponsor's subsidy (as represented by PCBE), which is large enough to cover the R & D cost. In sum, an advance-purchase commitment increases the expected revenues from investments in R & D without constraining the extent of the patent system.

A principal difficulty with advance-purchase commitments, though, concerns the sponsor's need to identify the desired, feasible technical

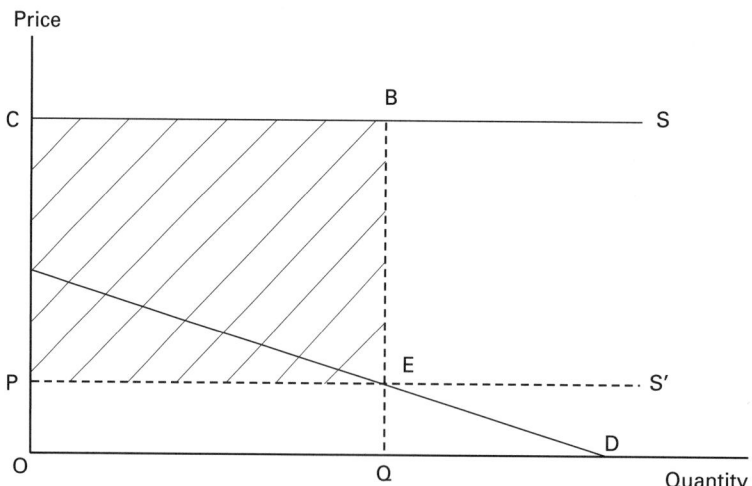

Figure 9.4
The Innovation Incentive Created by Advanced Purchase Commitments

characteristics of a vaccine that has not yet been developed. This difficulty in turn creates two distortions in incentives for R & D investment.[82] First, firms lack incentives to develop a new product that exceeds the technical standard set by the sponsors. The commitments therefore provide no incentive for firms to conduct incremental innovation that could improve the quality of a new product over time. Second, the sponsors run a risk of exhausting the funds available for subsidy if the technical standard is set too low. The firm, by contrast, would have no incentive to develop the new product if the technical standard is set too high. If the sponsor allows some flexibility in identifying the technical standard, the system would leave a great deal of discretion in the hands of the members of the technical committee. This discretion in turn makes the subsidy program committee driven rather than market driven. The funds for the subsidy may not be used in a socially optimal way as a consequence.

Optional Rewards Based on the Therapeutic Effect

Aidan Hollis proposes an optional reward under which the pharmaceutical firm can choose between the reward and patent systems, and the firm is paid for pharmaceutical innovation directly by the sponsors based on the therapeutic effectiveness of drugs if it opts for the reward system.[83] This system explicitly links the profitability of drug innovations to their therapeutic impacts rather than to the consumer's ability to pay. Thus, this payment scheme closes the gap between pursuing profit or health, and provides an incentive to guide R & D resources into drugs that have large health impacts rather than products demanded by relatively affluent persons.

Compared to the advance-purchase commitment, the advantage of the optional reward system is that the sponsors do not need to set the technical specifications in advance. Rather, the sponsors only need to evaluate the therapeutic effectiveness after the new drugs have received regulatory approval. The success of the optional reward system lies in the details of its implementation, such as whether or not there are valid and reliable measures of treatment effects, and whether or not the commitment of payment for innovative drugs is regarded as credible by the firms that do the investing.[84]

Several countries have adopted various methodologies of comparing the costs of new drugs with their effects on health outcomes, termed "economic evaluation."[85] Although the methodologies have shortcomings and many practical issues remain, the international experience suggests that measuring the therapeutic effect is workable, and to date, no country formally adopting economic evaluation has abandoned it. Although low-income countries may have greater difficulty in collecting data for measuring the therapeutic effect than do higher-income countries, there will inevitably be learning by doing. Some mistakes must be made for progress against some major diseases to be realized. Making rewards a function of both the therapeutic impact and the number of persons affected seems feasible, and represents an efficient approach for inducing pharmaceutical innovation for preventing and treating diseases concentrated in low-income countries.

Priority Review Vouchers

David Ridley and colleagues propose a reward system under which firms receive a "priority review voucher" if they successfully develop new drugs for treating diseases concentrated in low-income countries.[86] The voucher is transferable and gives a privilege to the bearer to use the priority review process in the new drug application for another drug. It has been estimated that the market value of one-year EPL for a blockbuster drug is approximately US$300 million.[87] Thus, the voucher would generate significant rewards to innovators if there is a market for the priority review voucher, so that the innovators can sell this voucher to other pharmaceutical firms that have a potential to develop blockbuster drugs.

The rationale for this incentive scheme is to use a market mechanism in high-income countries to solve market failures in middle- and low-income countries. By linking incentives in two different markets, this system provides benefits not only for developing countries but also for developed ones. The drug that consumers and payers in developed countries value more would reach the market sooner if the voucher market functions well. Furthermore, the advantage of the priority review voucher is that effective incentives for induced innovation are not limited by the size of the funds available to the sponsors. Rather, the sponsor relies on a market mechanism in developed countries to create an incentive for pharmaceutical innovation in developing countries. The size of the rewards is determined by the market, instead of relying on the judgment of committee members or cost-effective analysis conducted by an outside advisory group. As a result, both the administration and reward costs to the sponsor (and the taxpayer) are low, and so this incentive scheme could be applied to a wider class of diseases than those of the above two incentive systems.

Conclusion

This chapter's focus has been on the positive and normative aspects of setting incentives for pharmaceutical innovation. Overall, our review reveals that profit incentives do affect pharmaceutical innovation. In this context, incentives *do* matter. Given the evidence that the profits received by the innovative pharmaceutical firms are generated from the protection of the patent system that imposes a cost of welfare loss to the society, our analysis suggests that there is a trade-off between preserving incentives for innovation and reducing the welfare loss arising from monopoly power.

The empirical evidence we have reviewed shows a consistent pattern that R & D investment decisions by pharmaceutical firms are significantly and substantially affected by changes in profit incentives exogenous to individual firms. Increases in the effective patent life, market size, and public investment in upstream basic research provide important incentives for pharmaceutical innovation. By contrast, price regulation of pharmaceutical products discourages such innovation. Although price regulation does not necessarily rule out all R & D investment for finding new drugs, the existing literature shows strong evidence that price regulation reduces the size of R & D investment, which in turn leads to a reduction in both the quantity and quality of pharmaceutical innovation.

This analysis offers several implications for public policy. First, economic growth provides the engine for stimulating pharmaceutical innovation. Economic growth not only leads to an increase in the ability to pay but also is associated with demographic change and population aging. Both factors increase the market size for drugs treating chronic diseases. As a result, global economic growth would boost the global demand for pharmaceuticals, which in turn creates strong incentives for pharmaceutical firms to invest in drug discovery and development.

Second, health policy has crucial consequences for pharmaceutical innovation. The expansion of insurance coverage for prescription drugs and/or vaccines, on the one hand, increases the market size of these products and hence creates incentives for innovation. Innovation in pharmaceuticals is in this case consistent with public goals in both the economic and health sectors. On the other hand, no matter how attractive it is as a short-run fix to rising public expenditures on pharmaceuticals, price regulation of prescription drugs or vaccines reduces incentives for R & D investment. This creates a conflict in policy goals between the economic sector, which aims to promote innovation and technical change, and the health sector, which seeks to contain health care costs.

Third, our conclusion that incentives matter implies that there is a market failure in allocating R & D resources for essential drugs in low-income countries due to the lack of sufficient profit incentive there. The patent system fails to provide effective incentives to develop therapies for diseases concentrated in low-income countries. Several papers have focused on the design of alternative incentive mechanisms to induce innovation for essential drugs and vaccines in developing countries.

This chapter has reviewed three proposals for alternatives to patents. Conceptually, these proposals substitute rewards for patents and provide pull incentives to promote innovation. Specifically, the advance-purchase commitment uses subsidy to close the gap between the lower ability to pay and the higher R & D cost. The optional reward system closes the gap between pursuing profit or health by paying the rewards to innovators on the basis of the therapeutic effectiveness. The system of priority review vouchers corrects market failure by linking incentives for developing essential drugs in developing world with those for pursuing profit resulting from blockbuster drugs in the developed countries. These are theoretical concepts, however, rather than implemented payment schemes that have been subject to empirical evaluation. Patents will continue to do the heavy lifting in promoting investment in R & D in the pharmaceutical sector for some time to come.

Notes

1. Barro and Sala-i-Martin (2004, 285).

2. Temple (1999). Somewhat surprising to we outsiders who do not study the subject, the empirical evidence on the role of growth in total factor productivity as a determinant of economic growth is conflicting. See, for example, Temple (1999), Bosworth et al. (2003); Baker et al. (2005). One reason for the lack of conclusive findings is that technological change in the aggregate is measured as a residual—that is, it is not directly measurable. A further complication is that technological change is endogenous to various factors, reflecting ex ante returns on investment in research and development, which in

turn reflects such factors as population and income (see, for instance, Kremer [1993]). Government policies affecting such returns are plausibly related to such factors as income as well. Although both important and interesting, a full discussion of this topic is well beyond the scope of this chapter.

3. Garfield was shot twice. One of the bullets lodged in his back. Physicians could not find the bullet; they used unsterilized instruments and bare hands to search and dislodge the bullet. Alexander Graham Bell used a metal detector to search for the bullet, but this effort failed as well. Garfield died after eighty days. It is estimated that today, he would have been released from the hospital after a two- or three-day stay. Joseph Lister had developed sterile techniques in Great Britain in the 1860s, but these techniques had not diffused to the United States by the 1880s, although they were becoming common in Europe. See Schaffer (2006).

4. It is estimated that 70 percent of the 6.97-year increase in life expectancy between 1960 and 2000 in the United States is attributable to reductions in mortality from cardiovascular disease (Cutler et al. [2006]). Reductions in the rate of death in infancy accounted for another 19 percent of the increase in life expectancy during the same period. Although causes of mortality reductions from cardiovascular disease and infant death are multifactorial, several prior studies have documented that at least half of the reductions in mortality resulted from medical advances (ibid.).

5. Oeppen and Vaupel (2002).

6. Crimmins et al. (1997); Freedman and Martin (1998); Costa (2000); Manton and Gu (2001).

7. Cutler and Lleras-Muney (2006).

8. For example, Lee (2005, 354) notes that in the mid-nineteenth century, there were few effective medical or health care services to be purchased. Markel (2006) depicts a lecture at the newly opened Johns Hopkins School of Medicine in which the course of fever was described at a time before the microbiological etiology of particular infectious entities were identified. Some medical care arguably had a negative marginal product, such as bloodletting, which continued throughout the nineteenth century.

9. For an analysis of lead water mains in U.S. cities, see, for example, Troseken and Beeson (2003).

10. Nutritional improvements are described in Fogel (1997).

11. See, for example, Cutler et al. (1998); Murphy and Topel (2003); Sloan et al. (2006).

12. David Cutler and his colleagues (1998) classified heart attack patients into several categories. One was "medical management." This allowed them to assess the outcomes from a combination of medical therapies, including various drugs.

13. Heidenreich and McClellan (2000).

14. Drummond (2007).

15. Cremieux et al. (2007).

16. Hsieh et al. (2007).

17. See, for example, Lichtenberg (2003).

18. Ibid.

19. Much of this research has been conducted by Jack Wennberg and his colleagues at Dartmouth College. See, for instance, Fisher et al. (2003a, 2003b).

20. Skinner et al. (2006).

21. See, for example, Kremer and Glennerster (2004).

22. See ibid.

23. As we will discuss below, the 1982 U.S. Orphan Drug Act incorporates both pull and push incentives to promote pharmaceutical innovation for rare diseases.

24. Murphy and Topel (2003, 66).

25. Reinhardt (2007).

26. Danzon et al. (2005).

27. DiMasi et al. (2003).

28. Maurer (2007).

29. DiMasi et al. (2003).

30. Cockburn and Henderson (2001).

31. For example, the U.S. government spent $8.8 billion for health-related research in 1995, which accounted for 36 percent of the nondefense federal research budget (ibid.).

32. Murphy and Topel (2006).

33. Murphy and Topel (2003, 66, table 2.6).

34. Ibid. (table 2.5).

35. Mansfield (1986); Levin et al. (1987); Cohen et al. (2002).

36. Reiffen and Ward (2005).

37. Reinhardt (2007).

38. Grabowski (2007).

39. Grabowski and Vernon (2000).

40. U.S. Food and Drug Administration (2006).

41. Ridley et al. (2006).

42. Ibid.

43. Grabowski (2007).

44. Grabowski and Vernon (2000).

45. Acemoglu and Linn (2004).

46. Finkelstein (2004).

47. Acemoglu et al. (2006).

48. Lichtenberg (2005).

49. Ibid.

50. For example, about 75 percent of pharmaceutical expenditure is publicly financed in Europe (Ess et al. [2003]). In the United States, nearly 70 percent of prescription drug spending was paid for by private insurers and Medicaid in 1998 (Berndt 2002).

51. Ess et al. (2003).

52. Vernon (2005).

53. See, for example, Shyam-Sunder and Myers (1999).

54. Vernon (2005).

55. Giaccotto et al. (2005).

56. Danzon and Chao (2000); Ekelund and Persson (2003).

57. Lu and Comanor (1998); Ekelund and Persson (2003).

58. By contrast, Lu and Comanor (1998) find that a new drug with important therapeutic gains adopts a skimming strategy to launch the new product at a relatively higher price over the existing one, but gradually reduces the price as more competitors enter into the market.

59. Danzon and Chao (2000).

60. Ibid.

61. Grabowski and Wang (2006).

62. Ekelund and Persson (2003); Lu and Comanor (1998).

63. Danzon and Chao (2000).

64. Grabowski (2007).

65. Danzon, Wang et al. (2005).

66. Ibid.

67. Thamer et al. (1998); Lichtenberg (2001).

68. Thamer et al. (1998).

69. Ibid.

70. Gambardella (1995).

71. Cockburn and Henderson (2001).

72. Cockburn and Henderson (1998).

73. Ibid.

74. Murphy and Topel (2006).

75. Jamison (2006, 31).

76. Kremer and Snyder (2003).

77. Between 1999 and 2006, the Bill and Melinda Gates Foundation committed more than US$6 billion in global health grants. A majority of the funds were used to support basic and clinical research to develop new vaccines and drugs in developing countries. A successful example is the foundation's US$47.2 million grant to the Institute for OneWorld Health to complete the development of a drug for visceral leishmaniasis (VL). In August 2006, the Institute for OneWorld Health (2007) received approval for its first drug for VL from the government of India.

78. Shavell and Ypersele (2001).

79. Garber et al. (2006).

80. Comanor (2007).

81. Kremer and Glennerster (2004).

82. Hollis (2007).

83. Ibid.

84. Sloan and Eesley (2007).

85. Drummond (2007).

86. Ridley et al. (2006).

87. Blockbuster drugs are those with annual sales exceeding $1 billion in their fifth year on the market (ibid.).

10

Physician Fees and Behavior: Implications for Structuring a Fee Schedule

Thomas G. McGuire

A fee-based payment to physicians is the dominant form of payment in the United States, Germany, Canada, France, England, and many other countries. In the United States, even when a physician is a member of a group and the group is paid by capitation, individual physicians are generally paid by fees.[1] Fees are the prices paid for physician services, but these prices are not chosen by the individual seller. In public programs in the United States and elsewhere, the fees are set administratively by reported procedures; in Medicare, for example, about seven thousand procedures have their own fees. Private payers also decide fees, often scaling up or down the prices set by Medicare. Negotiation with larger physician groups plays a role in private payments.

Economic research on physician fees has focused on how physicians respond to fee changes. In this chapter, I review some of the literature on physician response to fees, with two purposes: to draw conclusions about what these responses say about physician motivation and economic power; and to draw implications for the design of a fee schedule. Health economics has contributed many studies of the effect of fees on physician behavior and service use. Authors have considered what these studies mean for physician motivation (do physicians pursue a "target income"?) and about physician economic power (can physicians "induce demand" from their patients?). It is less common to consider the meaning of the research for the design of a fee schedule.

This chapter begins with some comments on setting fees in markets versus setting fees by regulation. Although these are not mutually exclusive alternatives, I conclude that some heavy role for regulation is warranted, and to undertake this regulation, some information is needed about how physicians respond to fees. The next section reviews the literature on physician response to fees, and includes coverage of the topics of target income (TI) and physician-induced demand (PID), special to the field of health economics. Then, I turn to the question of what these studies imply for a fee schedule.

Markets and the Regulation of Fees

The first question about fees an economist might ask is, Why set fees administratively? Why not let market forces work out what price should be paid to doctors for their work activities? Scores of physicians compete in most markets to serve many thousands of patients, satisfying at least this structural criterion for a competitive market. Indeed, through the 1980s in the United States, physicians could set their fees, with each physician setting their own prices. The feature of fees that attracted attention in the 1950s was price discrimination: charging higher prices to patients with a greater ability to pay, and lower prices to the poor. Competition among physicians should drive prices to all customers to the marginal cost, eliminating price discrimination. Something else must be going on for price discrimination to be sustained. Reuben Kessel, writing in the inaugural issue of the *Journal of Law and Economics*, argued that a physician conspiracy was behind price discrimination—one orchestrated by the American Medical Association (AMA).[2] According to Kessel, the AMA wielded otherwise-competing physicians into a collusive oligopoly to mimic price discrimination according to a demand elasticity that would have been accomplished by a profit-maximizing monopolist. He supposed that the poor have more elastic demand than the rich. The threat of the loss of hospital privileges kept doctors from cheating on the collusive agreement.

An alternative hypothesis not considered by Kessel (in his still well worth reading social history of medicine during the middle part of the twentieth century) involves a modern microeconomic understanding of the features of physician markets—features that make administrative fees necessary, but problematic. First, individual physicians *face a downward-sloping demand and have market power*. While a well-financed aggressive trade association never did any occupation much harm, physicians do not need coordination by the AMA in order to exercise market power. Health economists nearly universally regard physicians as monopolistically competitive with a downward-sloping demand for their services.[3]

Differentiation can be traced back to information issues. An important service about which I as a patient am highly uncertain puts a premium on a trusted supplier. Patients get attached to physicians, and are not highly sensitive to price or other practice characteristics after having established a relationship with a physician.[4] Individual physician market power means that if patients have insurance, and by the 1960s even the poor and the elderly in the United States were gaining coverage, physicians could exploit this increased willingness to pay by raising prices. This is just what happened in Medicare, and the market-oriented fee schedule policy in Medicare, with fee limits based on historical charges by the physician and those physicians in the same market area, had to be abandoned in the 1980s. Joseph Newhouse argues that market mechanisms to keep supply prices low—either by patients who were mostly covered and had little incentive to shop based on price, or by public and private insurers that sought broad participation by physicians in their plans—were largely ineffective.[5] Setting fees administratively checks the exercise of market power. Market power by itself can explain *high* prices, but more is needed to account for *price discrimination*.

A second relevant feature is that physicians supply a *service that is nonretradable*. This is self-evident. Once sold to one customer, a medical exam, a consultation, or a haircut cannot be resold to another buyer. Arbitrage does not operate in the market for medical services, thus allowing physicians to practice "third-degree" price discrimination across patients, resolving the puzzle addressed by Kessel. Letting markets determine fees would have led to physicians setting high prices due to market power and practicing price discrimination due to nonretradability.

Nonretradability has another implication that relates to a central question in health economics: physician control over the quantity of health care used by patients. Nonretradability implies that physicians can also practice "first-degree" (or "perfect") price discrimination, in effect charging different prices for different units of a service to the same patient. First-degree price discrimination can be thought of in terms of pricing along a demand curve, charging a high price for the first units and lower prices for subsequent units as the valuation falls. An equivalent method for extracting consumer surplus is to make an all-or-nothing offer of a price-quantity pair.[6] The quantity in this case is the same as a perfectly discriminating monopolist would set, and the price is the patient's average valuation.[7] The key point is that physicians can set quantity, and will do so "off the patient's demand curve" in the sense that the quantity set will be beyond the quantity that the patient would demand at the price the physician is charging. This economic model of the profit-maximizing physician accords with experience. Patients are told about the package of services that a physician recommends for a condition, not offered an a la carte menu. The ability to set the quantity follows directly from individual physician market power and service nonretradability. Physicians cannot, of course, control the quantity that patients use; for one, patients often do not fully comply with physician instructions. The literature in health economics would later come to pay a great deal of attention to physician quantity setting under the heading of PID, where the vision was a physician shifting the patient's demand curve rather than simply setting quantity outside of demand due to nonretradability.

Fees and Incentives

Fee-based payment systems, because physicians are paid more for each thing they do, may encourage too much treatment.[8] While this is certainly true in many cases, the problem is not that there are fees but that the fees are set at a level in relation to the marginal cost that encourages too much supply. The relationship of the marginal revenue (the fee) and the marginal cost determines the incentive a physician faces. A low fee would lead to too little care provided. This leads to the natural conception of an ideal fee that is "neutral," neither being too high and encouraging too much care, nor too low and discouraging necessary care.

Economic Neutrality as a Goal

The current fee structures prevailing in the United States can be traced to the work of William Hsiao and his colleagues during the 1980s. Under contract with the U.S. Health Care Financing Administration, the predecessor of today's U.S. Center for Medicare and Medicaid Services, Hsiao undertook a massive effort to measure how much time physicians spent conducting various procedures, using physician expert panels to rate the complexity and effort involved in the work, and supplementing this with survey data on physicians' practice costs.[9] The Resource-Based Relative Value Scale (RBRVS) was promoted as setting fees for procedures based on their relative "cost," taking account of time, subjective effort, and other medical resources. Medicare adopted the RBRVS in a modified form and still uses it as a basis for payment, though many changes have been made over the years.[10]

Medicare's fee schedule is in turn employed by some private insurers and Medicaid programs.

The purpose of the fee reform was to use fees to match revenues and cost, where cost was defined to include physician skill, time, and effort along with material costs. Although these concepts are hard to measure, physician skill and effort are a legitimate element of the economic cost of a labor input. Markets must pay for the skill and efforts of workers.

At a general level, a physician can be regarded as caring about his or her own financial well-being and the health (or possibly economic welfare) of the patient. An economically neutral payment system would take physician self-interest out of the picture by paying exactly cost, so that from the standpoint of the physician's own financial welfare, a physician is indifferent about how much treatment takes place. Then, the only thing left for the physician to worry about is patient welfare, and the choice about treatment would be guided only by what is best for the patient.

Suppose physician utility depends on two arguments: the benefit the patient receives as a function of the quantity of treatment, $B(x)$, and the profit the physician receives, also a function of the quantity of treatment $\pi(x)$: $V(B(x), \pi(x))$. Maximizing V with respect to the choice of quantity leads to the following first-order condition:

$$V_B B' + V_\pi \pi' = 0 \tag{10.1}$$

where subscripts on V represent partial derivatives with respect to the arguments of utility, and B' and π' are derivatives with respect to quantity. The solution to equation (10.1) in general terms involves preferences of the physician for both patient welfare and profit as well as patient benefit itself (the B'). The term π' depends on the relation between costs and revenues. A prospective payment system when payments do not respond to costs is characterized by $\pi' < 0$. A physician's profits would fall with more services provided. A fee-based system when fees exceed costs has $\pi' > 0$, with profits going up as more services are provided.

The economic neutrality of a fee system can be defined as a payment system that sets the marginal revenue equal to the marginal cost. Profit can be any level, but it is invariant to the choice of quantity, and $\pi' = 0$. Therefore, in the case of economic neutrality, equation (10.1) reduces to:

$$B' = 0 \tag{10.2}$$

The physician, even one with a general utility function $V(B(q), \pi(q))$, would choose the quantity to maximize patient benefit.

The Problems with Neutrality in Theory and Practice

Maximizing patient benefit is not the standard for economic efficiency, which requires that costs be considered along with benefits. Economic neutrality leading to marginal benefit $B' = 0$ implies an excess utilization of health care. Since the marginal cost is clearly not 0, setting the marginal benefit of health care at 0 could be understood as the physician choosing quantity to maximize patient health or an accommodation to the patient's demand, subsidized by health insurance.

At an empirical or practical level, administered fees, of which the RBRVS is the most well-known and widely used, have been subject to harsh critique by health economists. Newhouse's *Pricing the Priceless* covers the history and economic research on administered pricing for physicians, hospitals, and health plans, including the problems with an RBRVS-type approach.[11] Among the problems discussed are that an RBRVS is about relative fees, and not the level; the level is driven by budgetary concerns and involves arbitrary elements, including Medicare's built-in adjustments for volume and "sustainable growth" targets; the RBRVS captures the average not the marginal cost; it contains imperfect geographic adjustments; it has a jerry-rigged system of cross-specialty linkages; and inevitably, with estimation errors it will introduce unwanted incentives.

Around the time Medicare's RBRVS-based fee reform was being implemented, Ted Frech convened a conference (published as *Regulating Doctor's Fees*) in 1991 at which Hsiao valiantly defended his methods in the face of withering critiques from physicians and prominent health economists.[12] A sample of the comments follow. Roger Noll: Administered fees are flawed because allocating joint and common costs is arbitrary, we do not measure and cannot anticipate the effects on quality, and we cannot separate opportunity costs from rents. Henry Aaron: A fee schedule is "not an exercise in microeconomics. It is a step in political economy." Clark Havighurst: "It is time to 'jettison the myth that how to pay physicians . . . can be resolved by a magic formula developed by experts sitting around the table.' " Frank Sloan: "Illegitimate sources of variation (e.g., market power) are embedded in fees and should not be taken into account"; "reactions of other payers to Medicare policy need to be taken into account." Jack Hadley: "The fee schedule neglects the role of economies of scale and scope and of value and demand." David Dranove and Mark Satterthwaite: "Administered pricing brings with it a long list of negatives, including the inevitable errors, the poor dynamics when costs change, long run effects on location and specialty choice." Charles Phelps: "Cost is endogenous to the fee"; "Setting a specific fee for a particular service . . . may have as its primary determinant the setting of quality in the market, more than anything else."[13]

Paul Ginsburg and Joy Grossman, in a paper titled "When the Price Isn't Right," recall some of the same points about administered pricing, blaming the inadvertent overpayment for some services for the aggressive expansion of those services contributing to health care cost growth.[14] The underlying data for setting prices are inaccurate, and learning with new procedures renders them "overpriced" after a short period of time. Their idea: have Medicare try to set prices to reflect the cost more accurately—that is, try once more to set "neutral" fees.

If economic neutrality—taking physician financial self-interest out of the picture—is not the right goal, and unattainable anyway, we have to think about how physicians respond when the payments differ from the cost in designing a fee schedule. Physician financial self-interest will inevitably be active in affecting treatment. How should we make use of it? To do so, we need a theory of physician behavior.

Fees, Target Income, and Induced Demand

Largely due to informational issues, health economists regard medical care as being different than most goods and services, and part of the story is that physicians are not expected (or supposed to) behave like other sellers.[15] Empirical researchers in health economics were open to thinking differently about how physicians set prices and quantities. The two most well-known theories in health care are that physicians are motivated by a TI and that physicians have the ability to induce demand for medical services.

Target Income (TI)

In one early study, Victor Fuchs reported that an increased supply of surgeons, controlling for demand factors, *increased* the market price.[16]

Thomas Rice found that lower fees for physician services caused an *increase* in the supply of services.[17] As a possible explanation, Fuchs, Rice, and others propose that physicians pursue a TI.[18] The TI hypothesis was not originally about fees but was used to explain why higher physician-to-population ratios (presumably a measure of supply in relation to demand) were associated with a *higher* price of physician services, not a lower one, as simple price theory would suggest. Suppose physicians only set a price high enough so as to attain some target. They could make more by charging a higher price, but choose not to, perhaps out of concern for patients' welfare. As more physicians appear in a market and patients are spread more thinly among the available suppliers, physicians must raise prices to maintain the TI. TI behavior, in the 1970s, reflected *restraint* in pricing. Physicians were "humanitarian," to use Pamela Farley's term, in not fully exploiting their price-setting power unless they were forced to by competitive pressures.[19]

In the 1980s, when direct fee-setting replaced increased supply as the mechanism used by regulators to limit physician prices, TI was used to explain another empirical anomaly: the negative correlation between fees and the quantity supplied.[20] During the 1980s, writers proposing TI explanations around fee responses linked it to physician-induced demand (PID). Physicians could set quantity because they could induce demand. Interestingly, TI behavior was no longer benevolent. TI frustrated policies designed to contain health care costs. Physicians were using their power to influence patient utilization in their own (the physicians') interests in order to counter well-intentioned fee regulation.

The negative relation between p and q is obvious if the physician sets q to maintain a target where $T = p \times q$. If the price falls, q must go up to maintain the target. The TI hypothesis was taken seriously by health economists and policymakers. The federal government sponsored a conference and published a volume on the supply and pricing issue, titled *The Target-Income Hypothesis and Related Issues in Health Manpower Policy*.[21] The TI hypothesis (along with the perception that physicians could induce demand) worked against physicians at the time of fee reform. The federal government's budget reconciliation act of 1989 dictated that the fee reforms associated with the move to RBRVS fees in Medicare should be "budget neutral," meaning that Medicare should be spending the same in total as it would have spent with the prior fee schedule. To do this, the secretary of the Department of Health and Human Services had to choose a "conversion factor" that set the absolute level of fees.[22] Since the total outlays equal the price times the quantity, projections under the new fee schedule needed to take account of how physicians would change how many procedures they conducted in response to the movement of fees up and down. All the major government agencies bought into the assumption that when fees went down, physicians would bite back and recover 50 percent of their income loss with increased volume, and when fees when up, physicians would simply say "thank you" and not change their volume.[23] This was the fifty-to-zero "volume offset" consensus that cost physicians 6.5 percent of their fees in 1992 (an effect compounded over the years), and that turned out to be wrong.[24]

The most obvious problem with the TI theory is that it does not explain how the target is set. What income is "just right" for physicians? Why should it differ across individuals and change over time?

The TI theory also suffers from a logical flaw. If there is one price and one quantity, $p \times q = T$, the quantity can be found that hits the target (somehow determined) for any price. If, however, as is obviously the case, many prices and quantities contribute to a physician's income target from different procedures and different payers, there is no unique solution for quantities as a function of prices. There is one equation and many unknowns. The equation $p_1 q_1 + p_2 q_2 = T$ cannot be solved for q_1 as a function of prices. When there are many (say, n) quantities, as in the case of Medicare fee reform, if Medicare reduces p_1, even if (and this is a big if) physicians behave according to the TI theory, it does not mean that q_1 needs to go up. Any of $q_2 \ldots q_n$ could change to keep income at the target.

The TI equation is thus incapable of predicting what would happen to quantities following a price change. To be a complete theory, the TI idea needs a model of how a physician makes choices about what combination of quantities to set to achieve a TI. Formalizing the idea of demand inducement is one way to accomplish this.

Physician Induced Demand (PID)

Many empirical studies find that when normal demand-side variables such as demand price, income, and clinical need are controlled for, variables affecting the supply of care such as supply price, physician attitudes, or partnership incentives influence what happens to the patient.[25] How is this to be understood? One answer is: physicians induce demand. The PID hypothesis, associated with Evans, is essentially that physicians engage in some persuasive activity to shift the patient's demand curve in or out according to the physician's self-interest.[26]

At a conceptual level, there is agreement about what constitutes PID. I adopt the following definition from a number of earlier authors: PID exists when the physician influences a patient's demand for care against the physician's interpretation of the best interest of the patient.[27]

It is important to keep two distinctions in mind when applying this definition. The first is the distinction between useful agency and inducement. Fuchs early on defined demand inducement as above, in relation to the consumer's optimal consumption point, leaving open scope for influence in the interest of the patient distinct from inducement.[28] Thus, if a physician influenced a patient to move toward the consumer's optimal point, this would not be inducement, only useful agency. Mark Pauly makes use of the same concept in his definition of a "perfect agent": The physician assists the patient to demand "exactly those quantities of care of various types that the patient would have chosen if he had the same information and knowledge the physician has."[29] The upshot of these definitions is that showing influence is not enough to establish inducement. Quoting Newhouse, the question of PID is not a matter of introspection, of "thinking back on one's last visit."[30] (After all, who has not been influenced by physician recommendations?) PID requires, in essence, a finding of "undue" influence.

The second distinction is between utilization and demand—a distinction that has become more salient with the growth in supply-side cost sharing (physicians bear some of the cost of providing extra services to a patient as under capitalism) and managed care, rationing devices that do not rely on controlling costs by patients decreasing the quantity demanded. A physician can influence utilization without influencing demand. Patients treated in a health maintenance organization (HMO) may receive less treatment than comparable patients in a fee-based plan. This could be interpreted as a PID-type mechanism—a decrease in demand caused by the physician. At the price they were paying and with a fully informed demand, patients would have demanded the extra treatment, but the physician influenced them otherwise and lowered their demand. Alternatively, it could be evidence of rationing. The HMO physicians simply ration the care, not allowing patients to have all they want. The HMO patients have the same demand as the non-HMO ones; it is simply unsatisfied. An empirical finding of an HMO effect, or an effect of prospective payment or managed care, as is now common in the literature, is not sufficient to establish PID in the Fuchs/Pauly sense. Utilization has been affected, but it is not clear that the demand—the function relating the price to the desired quantity—has shifted.

In terms of the economic view of PID, there are theoretical reasons to believe that PID, in the way I have defined it, exists to some degree. Consider a physician who is giving the "optimal" amount of information to a patient, and the patient is using his/her optimal quantity. Around this optimal point, a small increase up or down in quantity has a small impact on consumer welfare, because the consumer is at a point where the marginal benefit of health care is zero (this is how the optimum is defined). The physician, by contrast, may gain or lose money (depending on the payment incentives) from inducing the patient to demand more or less. Whatever particular model we assume about physician motivation, the nature of the trade-off presented to the physician—I can gain income by a change that has a small effect on the welfare of my patient—implies that the physician will be doing some demand inducement. Mark Blaug contends that "it is only the quantitative impact . . . of supplier-induced demand that is a bone of contention among American health economists."[31] As Pauly puts it, "Other things equal, physicians would rather tell the truth, but they would be willing to surrender some accuracy for some amount of money income."[32] Once that trade-off is admitted, it is hard to avoid the conclusion that the physician will be inducing some demand.

Any seller gains from a higher demand, and unless there is some cost to inducement, a physician pursuing net income would induce demand to an infinite extent. It is necessary, therefore, in models of demand inducement to introduce some limit or cost to inducement. Miron Stano takes one direction, making the natural analogy between inducement and advertising.[33] He assumes that inducement has a real resource cost (like advertising) and is limited by the profit calculations of physicians in the presence of diminishing returns. More common are approaches that follow Evans, where inducement is regarded as inherently unpleasant and limited by the psychic costs the physician bears when giving advice to the patient slanted toward their own self-interest.[34] This conception of the cost of inducement fits well with the definitions of inducement that I have been working with. Only influences on demand that push the patient away from the optimal consumption point impose psychic costs on the doctor.[35]

Along with Pauly, I formalize the ideas of Evans and Fuchs in a model intended to draw the implications of PID for physician response to fee changes when there were multiple payers or multiple fees.[36] Inducement is limited by physician disutility. We show in our model that TI is just an extreme case of "income effects." Income effects occur when the marginal utility of income falls as income increases. At a "target," the marginal utility of income decreases at an infinite rate (changing from a positive number to zero). Thus, a general model of physician utility with income effects can encompass pure profit maximization (when the marginal utility of income is constant) and TI (when the derivative of the marginal utility of income is minus infinity at the target). The approach can be used to interpret the effects of a change in the number of patients per doctor as a result of, say, increasing the number of physicians or a change in fees—that is, a change in the margins.

A change in the number of physicians per capita changes physician income, but if the fees remain the same, there is no price or substitution effect. The income effect from a fall in physician income increases the marginal utility of such income. The amount of inducement necessary to bring the return to inducement into equality with this new value must therefore increase. Many studies test this "availability" effect.[37]

Suppose instead we wish to analyze the effect of a fee change. Suppose only one payer (imagine this to be Medicare) reduces its fee. The effect of this can be thought of in two parts: an income effect and a substitution effect, as is customary in the theory of consumer behavior. The income effect of the fee fall increases the physician's marginal utility of income, tending to increase the inducement for all services.[38] There is also a substitution effect that comes about because a reduction in one fee reduces the return to inducement for that service. This effect will tend to reduce the inducement for the service whose fee has fallen and increase it for other services. Thus, the effect of a fee reduction for service on the inducement for that service is ambiguous, depending on income and substitution effects. The net effect, however, is unambiguous for other services. The inducement should increase because income and substitution effects work in the same direction. For small changes in the quality of service, substitution effects can be expected to dominate the income effect—again, just as in consumer theory.

Some studies have used the income and substitution effect framework to organize empirical research. Nguyen and Derrick explore the "overpriced procedures" for which Medicare reduced fees in 1990.[39] Overall, they find no significant volume responses (income effects just balanced by substitution effects), but for the 20 percent of physicians who experienced the largest price reductions, they report a significant negative net income effect on quantity. For these physicians, a 1 percent reduction in price led to an increase in volume of about 0.4 percent. Yip also studies overpriced procedures with data on thoracic surgeons in the states of New York and Washington.[40] She measured the total income impact of a set of Medicare fee reductions, and included this in a series of procedure-level regressions for Medicare and private insurance patients along with measures of procedure price and other covariates. Yip finds evidence that Medicare fee cuts lead to increased volumes by thoracic surgeons to both Medicare and private payers, and that their effect works through the income effect.[41]

Gruber and his colleagues analyze the rates of cesarean section performed on women with Medicaid coverage, finding that substitution effects dominate any income effects, and reductions in the differential between payments for cesarean sections and normal deliveries reduce the rate of cesarean sections.[42] Mitchell and her colleagues find strong cross-price effects for ophthalmologists in Medicare, but no income effects.[43] Nassirim and Rochaix use income and substitution effect ideas to organize findings about physician response to expenditure caps in Quebec.[44] Physicians anticipate hitting ceilings and adjust their intensity recommendations in ways consistent with income effects.

Empirical studies in health economics continue to document the effect of reimbursement changes on health care delivered to patients without interpreting the results in any particular theoretical framework. Reductions in the marginal payment leads to reductions of services used by patients.[45] Jacobson and her colleagues find that higher payments to physicians for providing chemotherapy to Medicare patients leads to proscribing more intensive therapy.[46] The relative fees for breast-conserving surgery and radical mastectomy as treatment for breast cancer affected the rates of these two surgeries received by women in Medicare.[47]

Returning to the Fuchs/Pauly definition of PID, two things must be established for the evidence on physician control or influence to support the PID hypothesis. First, the exercise of control must be in the interest of the physician, not the patient. This criterion, even without a gold standard of what patients ought to get, seems to have been met by the studies reviewed here. Adding up the evidence—on obstetricians doing more cesarean sections, surgeons doing more bypass operations, physicians referring more frequently to their own labs, and other studies— makes a convincing case that physicians can influence quantity and sometimes do so for their own purposes.

The second criterion from the Fuchs/Pauly definition is that the physician exercise quantity control by influencing the patient's demand, not by quantity setting through rationing or via the quantity-setting power available to the monopolistic competitor. Some researchers have attempted to isolate the quantity-setting effect and find some evidence for it, including Martin Chalkley and Colin Tilley among dentists in the United Kingdom, and Hsien-Ming Lien and I among substance abuse counselors in the United States.[48] Most studies, though, do not distinguish the mechanism of quantity control. It could be induced demand in the Fuchs/Pauly sense, quantity setting due to nonretradability, or a reaction of the provider in setting "effort" affecting the demand for the paid-on quantity of care.

Regarding the TI/income effect, there is some evidence for an income effect on physician behavior, but a TI theory is not warranted.[49] Paying physicians a higher fee generally leads to more services per patient. In rare cases, the income effect can dominate the substitution effect, and a negative relation between fees and quantity can arise, but a necessary condition is that the service in question be like potatoes in Ireland in the nineteenth century: a large part of the diet of the physician's practice.

Toward an Optimal Fee Structure

Although there have been many studies in health economics conducting theoretical and empirical analyses of physician response to fees, many fewer have taken on the task of characterizing an optimal fee policy. As noted earlier, a neutral fee is infeasible (and not desirable); thus, physician motivation and economic position must enter in designing an optimal fee policy. Doing so has proved difficult because of a lack of a working model of physician behavior in response to fees in the health economics literature.

This lack is not surprising when we consider the set of features (aka complications) that a working model of physician behavior should be able to handle: physician nonprofit-maximizing behavior, demand-side moral hazard with insurance, physicians' ability to induce demand, the quality of care, fixed and nonconstant costs, and the presence of multiple payers.

The approach I take here is to begin with the simple model of physician behavior, and show that this model calls for a fee below cost. In other words, physicians should be paid by a two-part payment, or a mixed system including a prospective and fee-based component. The fee-based component should *discourage* (not be neutral toward) services at the margin. I then consider these other factors one by one. In each case they either reinforce (or are neutral toward) the argument that fees should be set below the average (and sometimes marginal) cost of providing the care.[50] In sum, a normative economic analysis has something to say about fees, and it is important and operational: physician fees should be set at less than the (average) cost.

Defining an Optimal Fee

Suppose a physician produces quantity of services x, with a cost function $C(x)$. Assume $C' > 0$ and $C'' \leq 0$. The optimal quantity of services for the patient is x^*, defined as the level of x that equalizes the marginal benefit to the marginal cost: $B'(x^*) = C'(x^*)$.[51] An *optimal fee* is the one that leads the physician to supply x^*. Let the fee be f. The optimal fee, leading to x^*, is denoted f^*.[52] I will study the implications of the factors laid out above for choice of f^*.

Physician Regard for Patient's Health Benefit Implies Fees Should Be Less Than Marginal Cost

Let the physician maximize the utility function from earlier, $V(B(x), \pi(x))$, which includes a term for patient benefit as well as profit, both functions of the quantity of services x. Equation (10.1) above was the first-order condition describing the choice of the quantity of services x. Assume patients are nearly or fully insured, and have no direct role in choosing the quantity of services. In order for the physician to choose x^*, the first-order condition needs to be satisfied at this quantity; in other words, equation (10.1') must hold:

$$V_B B'(x^*) + V_\pi \pi'(x^*) = 0 \qquad (10.1')$$

The physician marginal utilities, V_B and V_π are both positive, as is $B'(x^*)$ (since it must equal the positive marginal cost at the optimal level of

x). Thus, for equation (10.1') to hold at x^*, $\pi'(x^*) < 0$, at x^*, physician profit must fall with increases in x.

What fee policy creates a profit function with this feature? Profits *falling* with the quantity implies that the marginal revenue is less than the marginal cost. The marginal revenue is the fee. Thus, for equation (10.1') to hold at x^*, the fee must be *less than* the marginal cost.

A fee set at less than the marginal cost also implies that the fee is less than the average cost, since I have assumed that the marginal cost is nonincreasing. If such a fee were the only revenue, the physician would lose money. To be feasible and acceptable to physicians, the payments must at least cover the costs. We can require the total revenue less the total cost to meet or exceed some minimum profit (which might be 0). To satisfy this requirement, I let the total revenue consist of the fee, f, times the quantity, plus another component of revenue, which I call F, that is independent of the services supplied. Thus, the total revenue is $F + fx$ and the requirement (formally referred to as a participation constraint) is:

$$F + fx - C(x) \geq \pi_0 \tag{10.3}$$

where π_0 is the minimum profit (possibly 0) necessary for the physician to accept the patient.

Satisfying the participation constraint equation (10.3) at the optimal fee, $f^* < C'(x^*)$, requires that $F > 0$. My conclusion is this: To achieve the efficient level of services, a physician must be paid by a mixed system in which a component of the payment should be independent of the services provided and the service-based component should set the fee less than the marginal cost.

The fee-less-than-cost result is not surprising in a model in which the physician values the patient benefit and is the only decision maker. Setting a fee less than the marginal cost serves the function of presenting the decision maker with a cost. Equation (10.1') along with the definition of profit can be used to characterize f^* more precisely. The optimal fee is determined by the physician valuation of the patient benefit in relation to profit. The more the physician values the patient benefit, the greater must be the gap between f^* and the marginal cost to put the brakes on the physician wanting to do more. In the extreme case in which the physician values the patient benefit as much as their own profit—that is, $V_B(x^*) = V_\pi(x^*)$—$f^* = 0$, and the payment to the physician should be fully prospective—that is, all in F. In this case of a "perfect agent," the physicians' utility is identical to the social welfare, and to equate the marginal benefit and the cost when the physician maximizes utility (social welfare), the physician must face the full marginal cost of health care, which is accomplished by a fully prospective payment system. When the physician values the patient benefit some but not so much as the physician's own profit, the fees need to be positive, but they never should be so high as to equal the marginal cost.[53]

Demand-Side Moral Hazard Implies Fees Should Be Less Than Marginal Cost

Patients have a role in deciding quantity, but because they are insured, they tend to demand too much health care.[54] A simple way to incorporate both demand- and supply-side factors determining quantity is to reinterpret physician utility as a function representing the separate interests of patients and physicians, with the weights on the two being the "bargaining power" of the two actors. Maximizing $V(B(x), \pi(x))$ describes the process by which the interest of the patient in the health benefit and the interest of the physician in profit are compromised to determine quantity x.

First-order condition (10.1) would again describe the determination of x, interpreted now as the outcome of bargaining rather than physician utility maximization. Equation (10.1') would still set the requirement on a profit function for the compromise to lead to x^*. Since bargaining weights V_B and V_π are both positive, as is $B'(x^*)$, for equation (10.1') to hold at x^*, f^* must be again less than the marginal cost.

The interpretation here is that patients, because of insurance, will be demanding too much. The payment system to physicians should counter demand-side moral hazard by imposing marginal losses on physicians around the optimal level of treatment. To ensure that the total costs are covered, the optimal f^* less than the marginal cost would have to be coupled with a positive prospective payment F and the physician would have to be paid by a mixed system.

In an alternative interpretation, we could regard the physician and patient as each having desired quantities, and the traded quantity determined by the "short side" of the market. A similar conclusion about the use of the supply-side tool to set the quantity to counter demand-side moral hazard would emerge: we would want the physician to determine the short side and in effect ration care to the insured patient.

In the extreme case, the decision about quantity might be entirely a patient decision, with the physician having no role. (This is the opposite case of the physician being the sole decision maker in the previous section.) So the fee level would have no effect on the quantity, and a model of optimal fee would have to be situated on other grounds. The next several sections could be a basis for the choice of an optimal fee, and they too point in the same direction in terms of the fee in relation to the marginal cost.

Physician Ability to Induce Demand Implies Fees Should Be Set Less Than Marginal Cost

Physicians affect quantity by influencing patient valuation of services. In this chapter's notation, physicians affect the $B(x)$ function in their own interest. The physician would induce demand in the direction in of profits, leading patients to overvalue and demand more than they otherwise would if the physician profits by more services, and conversely, leading patients to demand less than they otherwise would if the physician profits by the patient demanding fewer services.

The ability of the physician to affect patients' demand can be used to counter demand-side moral hazard. For this to work, the physician should move to the left (*re*duce, rather than *in*duce) demand. Models of demand inducement portray the physician as trading off profit against the discomfort (to the physician) of distorting patient preferences or away from those the physician believes would be the most accurate. The optimal fee, f^*, would have to be less than the marginal cost to move the physician to reduce patient demand. Ideally, the fee would be sufficiently less than the marginal cost to convince the physician to shift patient demand to the left just enough to counter the quantity increasing the effects of health insurance.

Physician Services Have a Quality as well as Quantity Component not Directly Covered by Fees

In this case, a prospective component of payment can lead to a socially optimal (efficient) quality level. The quality of physicians' services is a major issue in health policy. Physicians may not recognize illness, always be aware of necessary care, provide services regarded as appropriate for a condition, and explain a condition and its treatment sufficiently to patients so that they will be able to self-manage their care effectively. Policy experiments by private and public payers are ongoing to measure and count the things that physicians are supposed to do (e.g., conduct mamographies for women over fifty), or measure the results of good care (e.g., controlled hypertension) and pay physicians on the basis of counts or the achievement of targets.[55] Rosenthal and her colleagues reported on a survey of commercial HMOs, and found that more than half were using pay for performance in some form in their provider contacts.[56]

Following the literature in health economics, "quality" is a "noncontractible" input into the production of health for the patient.[57] Noncontractibility means the input cannot be used as a basis of payment (cannot be part of the "contract" for payment). It is distinct from observability. Some things a physician can do to improve the quality of a visit are to spend an adequate amount of time with the patient, or pay careful attention to the patient's symptom reports. These activities are observable to a patient, but too ill defined to be able to use as a basis of payment. (How is "time" counted? From the time the patient enters the examining room? The amount of time the physician and patient are together in the room? Less the time the physician is on the phone with other matters?)

One can think concretely about the time a physician puts into an exam or other procedure as the noncontractible input. Some physicians (e.g., psychiatrists) report time-based procedures, but generally physicians are not paid on an explicit report of time. Yet time certainly matters to the quality of most of what a doctor does, and is furthermore observable to patients. Timothy McCall, a physician with an advice book for patients, says, "The amount of time a doctor spends interviewing you, examining you, and explaining things reflects how genuinely concerned that doctor is for your welfare."[58] While time is one concrete candidate for what is meant by noncontractible quality as an input into patient health, diligence, responsiveness, and attentiveness can be thought of in the same category as well.

How should the fee be set if we care about both quality and quantity, but can pay only on quantity? The model just described can be generalized so that now both benefits and costs depend on two inputs—quality denoted as e (for effort) and x: $B(e,x)$, $C(e,x)$. There will now be an e^* as well as an x^*. The revenue function remains $F + fx$, since payment cannot be made on e. Profits and physician utility also now are functions of both e and x. We have regarded x as being determined by the physician, the patient, or both; e is chosen by the physician only.

Within this framework, one can see easily why e would in general, however, be set too low and there would be a "quality problem." Both e and x contribute to physician cost, but only x, through fees, contributes directly to physician revenue. Raising quality raises cost. To induce a physician to devote more time or other elements of noncontractible quality to a visit requires making the patient a more profitable customer. The physician would then be willing to work harder to attract and keep the patient. There are two ways to do this within our payment system: the fee-based part, f, and the prospective part, F. Consider first what happens if we raise f. The physician begins to make profits on the patient. This creates an incentive for the physician to attract patients, and to do so by raising quality, e. The problem with raising f is that the inefficiency of too much x is exacerbated. The quantity of x is likely to go up, exceeding x^* even more.

Suppose a prospective payment F is introduced instead. The prospective payment could be raised just as much as with the increase in fee. The incentive to increase quality would be the same, but absent the exacerbation of the problem of having too much x. An increase in F is clearly a better way to go than an increase in f. Carrying the reason one step further, increasing F while decreasing f permits the creation of incentives to supply more e while supplying less of x for the same total payment from the payer.[59] Thus, the objective of increasing the quality of services implies that a mixed system be employed to give a physician an incentive to attract patients (through setting an F > 0) without exacerbating incentives to oversupply quantity (keeping f less than marginal cost).

Physician Marginal Is Less Than Average Cost, Implying Fees Should Be Less Than Average Cost

Physician fees as figured by Medicare include elements to pay for necessary equipment, malpractice costs, office expenses, and other items that do not vary in proportion to the number of procedures a physician undertakes. My argument that fees should be less than neutral—that is, less than the marginal cost—apply also therefore with respect to the average cost. It would be preferable to pay physicians with a component of revenue, F, independent of the service volume, and reduce fees below the average cost so as to avoid undesirable incentives for too high a quantity.

Changes in costs over time and procedures become more routine. Keeping the marginal payments low can guard against the emergence of excessive fees as learning by doing reduces the costs, but the regulatory process lags behind by years.[60]

Conclusion

The economic theory of physician responses to fees implies that physician fees should be set where possible at a level *below* the cost of the services. This requires that part of the payment be made independent of the quantities of procedures performed. A mix of a prospective and fee-based payment contends with a number of the problems in fee setting that emerge in the theoretical and empirical literature on physician behavior.

Implementing a mixed system for paying physicians by Medicare raises a number of practical problems, challenging the relevance of economic theory for the design of physician payment. A new and different kind of analysis would be necessary in order to give proper consideration to the practical questions. It is worthwhile noting, however, that physician payment systems with these features have emerged in both regulated and market contexts. In Germany, the statutory health insurance system covering 90 percent of the population pays office-based physicians with what amount to two-part payments.[61] A uniform value scale determines the points for each procedure a physician can supply. The total number of points charged in each region can vary, and in a reconciliation period, the payment per point is determined and the payments are finalized. Patients are supposed to enroll with primary care physicians, and although this does not always happen, the payment to physicians is partly based on this enrollment as related to a "fee" associated with this "procedure." The enrollment fees apply to primary care and some specialists, and vary by whether the enrollee is of working age or retired. Table 10.1 reports the top ten procedure codes in terms of payment in the German social insurance system. About 20 percent of total payments are associated with the enrollment fee, rendering this, in effect, a mixed system. Although the fee levels for conventional procedures may be regarded as low, the incentives to please and keep patients can be maintained by the presence of a meaningful enrollment payment. In Israel, which

Table 10.1
Top Ten Procedures by Total Payment for Office-Based Physicians in Germany, Statutory
Health Insurance, 2002

Rank	Procedure	Percent of total payments
1	Basic three-month enrollment	20.8
2	Explanation, planning, and coordination	5.0
3	Consultation fee per three months	4.8
4	Family physician basic payment	2.9
5	Intensive counseling on coping with illness	2.2
6	Home visit	1.9
7	Provision or initiation of lab services	1.9
8	Whole body examination	1.6
9	MRI of head, joints, or extremities	1.5
10	Night, weekend, or holiday fee	1.4
	Total for top ten	44.0

Source: Busse and Riesberg (2004).

also features mandatory enrollment in health plans, some health plan payment to community-based physicians has this feature of a mixed system.

There is some evidence that market forces in the United States would support this kind of mixed payment to physicians. During the 1990s, competition among managed care organizations (MCOs) and medical groups accepting risk in contracts with these MCOs radically transformed the market for health insurance in California.[62] Over the middle part of the decade, health insurance premiums in California were essentially flat, largely due to sharp declines in the rates of hospitalization. Although some of these medical groups organized as Independent Practice Associations subsequently failed after health care costs resumed an upward track at the close of the decade, it is instructive to observe the form of the contracts that emerged in this "market" between the MCOs and the medical groups as well as between the medical groups and the physicians working in the group or as part of the Independent Practice Association.[63] Shared risk was an important part of both sets of contracts. Initially, medical groups were eager for straight capitation contracts.[64] But during the 1990s, the contracts evolved to include more risk sharing in the form of targets and bonuses, and explicit risk sharing over expenditure limits. The contracts between the groups and the physicians also transmitted some but not all of the financial risk to the affiliated physicians.[65] Contracts with mixed system features emerged between the MCOs and the medical groups, and between the groups and the physicians.

Paying physicians by fees for procedures is institutionally embedded in the health care payment system. Fees contribute to the dual problems of "too much quantity" and "too little quality" in health care by creating strong incentives for supplying procedures by payments above the marginal costs while providing no direct payments for elements of quality not counted in the procedures. These problems are related, and a way to deal with both is to reduce the marginal payment for procedures while boosting the payment for attracting patients by a prospective component of payment.

Notes

1. Rosenthal et al. (2002).

2. Kessel (1958).

3. Frech and Ginsburg (1975); Pauly and Satterthwaite (1981); McGuire (1983); Dranove (1988); Dranove and Satterthwaite (1991, 1992, 1999); Getzen (1984); Pauly (1979, 1991); Phelps (1997); Frech (1996); Newhouse (1978); Gaynor (1994).

4. McCarthy (1985).

5. Newhouse (1981).

6. The mathematics of this case are contained in McGuire (2000).

7. See Tirole (1988, 135–137).

8. Ginsburg and Grossman (2005).

9. Hsiao et al. (1988).

10. For a discussion of relative and absolute levels of physician fees, and the processes used to update and modify these, see MedPAC (2006).

11. Newhouse (2002).

12. Frech (1991).

13. Ibid. (381, 137, 135, 71, 73, 70, 129).

14. Ginsburg and Grossman (2005).

15. This section draws on my essay "Physician Agency" (McGuire [2000]).

16. Fuchs (1978).

17. Rice (1983).

18. In this, consider p to be the margin above cost. Speculation about a TI held by doctors can be traced back to Feldstein (1970).

19. Farley (1986).

20. Rice (1983).

21. U.S. Department of Health, Education, and Welfare (1980).

22. U.S. Physician Payment Review Commission (1991, 117–118).

23. Ibid., (121).

24. See Nguyen and Derrick (1997). The regulations are described in the *Federal Register* 56, no. 227, November 25, 1991.

25. See, for example, Gaynor and Gertler (1995).

26. Evans (1974).

27. Some of the more prominent discussions of PID consonant with this definition are Culyer (1989); Eisenberg (1986); Fuchs (1978); Pauly (1980); Williams (1998).

28. Fuchs (1978, 36).

29. Pauly (1980, 5).

30. Newhouse (1978, 60).

31. Blaug (1998, 567).

32. Pauly (1980, 51).

33. Staro (1987).

34. Evans (1974). McGuire and Pauly (1991) take this approach. Peter Zweifel and Friedrich Breyer (1997) assume physician utility depends negatively on the degree of "artificial demand creation."

35. David Dranove (1988) proposed a model of inducement wherein the physician exploits their superior informational position, but is limited by the loss in credibility the physician suffers by being too aggressive in inducing demand. This model is useful for showing that with asymmetrical information, we can expect some inducement. For many purposes we need to go beyond a model that shows there will be demand inducement in equilibrium to address whether the degree of demand inducement changes with changes in the conditions of the market for physician services.

36. McGuire and Pauly (1991). See also an elaboration by Gruber and Owings (1996).

37. See particularly Dranove and Wehner (1994); Gruber and Owings (1996). A recent study applying this methodology to France is Delattre and Dormont (2003), which finds evidence consistent with an availability effect.

38. Even if the income effect was completely dominant and the physician pursued a TI, the TI model does not imply that all income will be recovered from the service experiencing the fee reduction. In general, it will be distributed among all the services a physician supplies.

39. Nguyen and Derrick (1997).

40. Yip (1998). These two states include physician identifiers in these discharge abstract files. Also, thoracic surgeons' practice is primarily hospital based.

41. In a similar study, Ming Tai-Seale and her colleagues also used hospital-level data in Medicare and private insurance to study volume responses to Medicare fee reductions to "overvalued procedures." The directions of effects were generally consistent with the income and substitution effect framework, although there were many data limitations, and many estimated effects were insignificantly different from zero.

42. Gruber, Kim, and Mayzlin (1999).

43. Mitchell, Hadley, and Gaskin (2002).

44. Nassirim and Rochaix (2006).

45. Rosenthal (2000).

46. Jacobson et al. (2006).

47. Hadley et al. (2003).

48. Chalkley and Tilley (2005); Lien et al. (2004).

49. For more comprehensive reviews, see McGuire (2000); Conrad and Christianson (2004).

50. The analysis here draws on and summarizes some of the points made in work I have done with Randy Ellis, Jacob Glazer, and Albert Ma: Ellis and McGuire (1986, 1990, 1993); Ma and McGuire (1997); Glazer and McGuire (2002).

51. Much of the analysis here does not depend on this particular though conventional definition of x^*.

52. This is the same definition of optimal fee employed by Newhouse (2002), and as set out earlier by Pauly (1980). Newhouse shows the fee in an "informed demand" or marginal benefit schedule by a consumer and an upward-sloping marginal cost curve. The intersection, where marginal cost equals marginal benefit defines the optimal fee. In this case, as in a competitive market, this price paid by the seller and buyer would lead to equilibrium and efficiency.

53. As the physician's valuation of the patient's benefit falls to epsilon, a small gap between the fee and the marginal cost will be sufficient to induce the physician to cut back enough to equate the marginal benefit and the marginal cost.

54. The inefficient component of the increase in quantity demanded is caused by the "substitution effect" of the insurance-related price reduction. Insurance also moves purchasing power to the times when a person is ill. Any "income effect" on demand due to this within-person income shift is not inefficient.

55. Rosenthal et al. (2005).

56. Rosenthal et al. (2006).

57. Ma (1994); McGuire (2000).

58. McCall (1996, 52).

59. The production relationship between e and x play a role here too. If e and x are substitutes, a fee less than the marginal cost will give a physician incentives to raise e because it will decrease demand for x. The opposite incentive is created if e and x are complements.

60. I do not include a section here addressing the issues raised by the presence of multiple payers. The general effect of multiple payers in this context will be to weaken the impact of any incentives introduced by one payer (e.g., Medicare). This will not alter the qualitative arguments made here. For a formal analysis of Medicare policy in a multiple-payer context, see Glazer and McGuire (2002). See also Ginsburg and Grossman (2005).

61. Busse and Riesberg (2004). There are two national price schedules, one for the statutory health insurance system that covers most people, and another for the private insurance system. Payment to private practice physicians is a multistep process. Sickness funds negotiate per enrollee payments to regional physician associations. The payment can vary among funds.

62. Casalino and Robinson (1997).

63. Bodenheimer (2000).

64. Casalino and Robinson (1997).

65. Rosenthal et al. (2002).

11

Physician Pay for Performance: Alternative Perspectives

Brian R. Golden and
Frank A. Sloan

People try to use pay as a scalpel. Because it means different things to different people, it's a broad sword at best.

—James Baron and David Kreps, *Strategic Human Resource Management*

In 2006, the Institute of Medicine released the report *Rewarding Provider Performance: Aligning Incentives in Medicare.* Authored by prominent experts in the health care field, the report is both optimistic about the promise of pay-for-performance systems in health care, and also cautious in its recommendations about how to design and implement them. Due to the stature of the committee and the thoroughness of its review, this report will likely, in retrospect, be viewed as seminal. It will also undoubtedly fuel further discussions of how pay-for-performance systems can address the many related ills of health care systems across the developed world, including the overprovision of nonessential care, overutilization of diagnostic technology, inadequate access and quality, and unsafe care.[1]

Given the failure of health systems to adequately address these health system challenges in the past, and the increasing desire to search for a better way, there is a risk that the logic of pay for performance could assume a kind of taken for grantedness among many health system managers and policymakers. Optimism may in part be influenced by the more than one hundred pay-for-performance systems that were in place in the United States by 2005–2007 although rigorous evaluations have been rare.[2]

Even though there is now some support for the notion that compensation systems can be a lever to influence the behaviors and performance of health professionals (e.g., hospital administrators and physicians), it is critical to understand the boundary conditions of effective pay-for-performance systems.[3] More specifically, and in light of several of the chapters presented in this book, it is useful to consider the numerous design and implementation challenges of an effective pay-for-performance scheme.[4]

This chapter provides a perspective to complement recent reviews on pay for performance in health care, many of which suggest that the effects of such systems are mixed or unattractive from a policy standpoint (e.g., possibly decreasing access to those patients with "unincentivized" illnesses).[5] Specifically, this chapter will go beyond the usual explanations that pay-for-performance systems often generate unanticipated and unintended perverse incentives, and suggest the conditions under which pay for performance may be the most and least effective. In the case of the latter, we will suggest alternative mechanisms for controlling health care provider behaviors. The emphasis will primarily be on pay for performance for physicians, whose decisions are estimated to influence approximately 80 percent of health care expenditures, rather than physician groups or health care provider organizations (e.g., multiprofessional clinics or hospitals).[6] The discussion addresses many aspects of health care quality (i.e., clinical effectiveness, efficiency, and patient centeredness).[7]

Synthesizing perspectives from economics, social psychology, and sociology, this chapter extends traditional discussions by suggesting why health care delivery may be an especially difficult sector in which to rely on pay-for-performance systems. Specifically, although no compensation system is neutral in its impacts, or lacks adverse and often unintended side effects, we argue that pay-for-performance systems are likely to influence clinician behaviors in unreliable ways, and that attempts to increase reliability may be prohibitively costly or currently beyond system (e.g., information management and monitoring) capabilities. The health care sector, however, possesses some unique advantages that may mitigate the need to exclusively (or even strongly) rely on pay for performance.

The next section discusses theoretical and empirical research by economists related to pay for performance in health care, including principal-agent problems as they arise in other contexts as well as in health care.[8] Next, we look at empirical evidence on pay for performance in health care, which demonstrates both favorable effects of experience with pay for performance as well as some of its limitations. Scholars in other social science disciplines have studied worker motivations and values to a far greater extent than have economists, although economists have substantially broadened the scope of their inquiries into such topics in recent years. The next section provides a summary of social psychological and sociological concepts as well as empirical research on motivation and professional values. Economic, social psychological, and sociological concepts are used in the following section, which characterizes the heterogeneity in tasks performed in health care in how they are monitored and measured. We then contend that financial incentives cannot possibly succeed without some reliance on professional norms. The final section presents our conclusions about pay-for-performance systems in health care. These systems have some potential to align the incentives of consumers and suppliers of health care. Yet leaders have had an unfortunate proclivity to proclaim one idea as a solution for all of the problems that health care faces. This is a false hope in general and for pay for performance in particular.

Economic Perspectives and Research on Pay for Performance

In the jargon used by economists, pay for performance means creating incentives to reward a desired outcome. The least complex compensation scheme offers payment per unit of output—piece rate compensation. In the absence of strong income effects (higher rates of compensation raising income, which in turn increases the demand for leisure or more generally time away from work), additional output will be forthcoming from an increase in the piece rate.[9] In this simple case with a single objective, the output is easily measured as is the quality of the output. When the quality of the output is difficult for buyers (employers) to measure, there is a possibility that suppliers will reduce the quality to increase the number of pieces sold (e.g., reduce the length of a physician visit). In such instances, other methods of compensation may be more appropriate, such as compensation per unit of input (time-based compensation). But under a time-based compensation, there is a need for the monitoring of worker effort since the worker, at least absent monitoring, has an incentive to shirk.

Physician fee for service is a piece rate compensation system. Alternatives are salary-based payment or a combination of incentives. There is substantial empirical evidence that the level of fees in a fee-for-service system, or whether or not the physician is paid on a fee-for-service, salaried, or other basis, substantially affects physician supply of services and work effort.[10] There is a larger literature in the field of labor economics on the effects of compensation methods, and the levels of compensation on output and effort, indicating that incentives matter.

Another branch of the economics literature focuses on changes in incentives that CEOs have to serve the self-interest of the owners of their enterprises, the shareholders—which is to increase the wealth of the enterprises they lead. Without explicit incentives to maximize shareholder wealth, a CEO paid a salary and perhaps a high one (generating a high demand for leisure time) may not have an adequate incentive to focus on the shareholders' objective. The board of directors could in principle monitor the CEO's effort, discharging the CEO if the effort falls below some acceptable minimum, but such monitoring can be a difficult task for boards, and an even more difficult one for independent financial analysts and shareholders. Thus, firms are increasingly offering stock options and other bonuses that are tied to the company's share price as a means for motivating CEOs to act to maximize the value of the firm.[11]

A problem arises when the incentives of the "agent"—in this case, the CEO—and the "principal"—in this case, the shareholders—are not aligned. In the market for corporate executives, this problem is being solved by offering stock options and performance-based bonuses. Although companies and shareholders can have several goals, the fundamental objective is to make as much money as is feasible.

Principal-Agent Problems

The conflicting objectives between principals and agents have been analyzed in a large number of contexts. The normative focus of theoretical research on the conflicting objectives between principals and agents is how to devise an optimal contract between them—parties in an economic exchange under conditions of uncertainty.[12] The agents are those who perform work for the principal (e.g., the agent manages the principal's assets). The challenge is to design reward systems that align the objectives of both the principal and the agent.

Two assumptions are fundamental. Ideally, agents would act perfectly in the interest of the principals they are supposed to serve. For various reasons, though, they may serve the principals' interests imperfectly. For one, agents have their own personal and professional objectives. Also, agents are likely to be risk averse. Operationalized, they prefer to be compensated for things they can control, such as the amount of effort they put into a task, rather than for the outcomes, which may be a function of both the agents' effort *and* events outside their control. Lawyers for plaintiffs, for example, are often compensated based on the outcome of the legal claim ("contingent fee" compensation). Yet for assuming the risk of receiving no pay in the event that the plaintiff loses the case, their attorneys are well paid if the plaintiff wins.

In health care, a principal is the individual in his or her role as consumer of health care services, policyholder, and taxpayer. The agent is the health care provider. In modern health care systems, public and private insurers are intermediaries with characteristics of both agents and principals: agents for consumers/policyholders/taxpayers in negotiating and overseeing health care financing and delivery, and more like principals in their dealings with providers.

Thus, in publicly funded health systems, the role of a principal may be partly assumed by some body of the state (e.g., the Centers for Medicare and Medicaid Services in the United States, or the Ministries of Health in Canada and the United Kingdom). Their role is to act as steward to the public, and in particular to act on behalf of patients and their families. Private health insurers perform a parallel role in health care systems with private health insurance. At the same time, managers of private insurers organized as for-profit organizations are agents for the firms' owners or shareholders, who are the principals in this context.

Several features of agency theory make it a particularly useful lens through which to understand various principal-agent relationships in health care, including the one we focus on here between purchasers of health care services, such as insurers who purchase care on behalf of the persons they insure (i.e., act as principals), and physicians (agents).[13] Among these, agency theory gives prominent attention to the effect of uncertainty on contract writing and enforcement. "Uncertainty lurks in every corner of the health care field," and is manifest in a host of relationships and settings.[14]

Principal-agent problems abound in relationships between patients and physicians. For example, the cause of a patient's discomfort or illness may be difficult to determine, and making the proper diagnosis may require a substantial effort on the part of the physician. The physician has the opportunity costs of time, however, and does not want to go home at night exhausted from effort expended during the day, and may not be inclined to devote a sufficient amount of time and effort to making the correct diagnosis. In such cases, the interests of patients and physicians are in conflict, and the challenge is how best to align the self-interests of the parties.

Other examples arise once a correct diagnosis has been made. There may be alternative views among physicians as to how to best treat the patient. Some approaches may be more expensive than others even if the alternatives are generally equally effective. A physician may not select the least expensive approach for financial or nonfinancial reasons. While the insurer may desire that the least expensive approach be selected and argue for this, it is always possible that in that particular circumstance, the least expensive option is not medically indicated.

And it is the physician who examines the patient. The insurer may be in a distant location. Matters are more complex when there is no consensus among the experts about which therapeutic approach is the optimal one. And this example assumes that the physician made the proper diagnosis. In the relationship between the physician and the insurer, representing the interests of the patient/policyholder, the insurer may be uncertain about whether or not the physician made a proper diagnosis of the patient, the physician provided quality care, or the care that was provided had a significant impact on the patient's outcome. The insurer may even question whether or not the physician attempted to represent the physician's own interests or those of the patient; in this case, only the physician would know. As these examples reveal, the principal-agent relationship is often characterized by *information asymmetry* in which the agents have greater access to information than the principals, who may have difficulty monitoring the agents or may consider the costs of doing so prohibitively expensive.[15]

As anyone who has ever been a patient knows, office visits tend to be short, reflecting the high opportunity cost of a physician's time. Physicians, like all of us, value nonwork time or leisure, and even during the workday there are many other activities in which physicians can engage than spending time with a patient in an examining room. A particularly vexing problem for principals given the agent's possible desire to shirk is the difficulty of distinguishing between shirking and other factors affecting the patient's outcome. Physicians as agents may engage in "textbook" medicine, and yet a patient's health status may fail to improve. This represents another common form of uncertainty; because agents are presumed to be risk averse, they will be uncomfortable being held accountable for adverse outcomes. On the other hand, imperfect observability creates a condition of moral hazard. In context, moral hazard, a tendency to shirk, arises because of the difficulty the principal has in observing whether or not shirking actually has occurred. The difficulty of observing shirking versus some other reason for a less than perfect outcome, and the lack of relationship between outcomes and shirking, in fact provides a precondition under which shirking can occur.[16]

Fee-for-Service Compensation

To the extent that most physicians are already being paid for performance under the fee-for-service payment system, at first glance it is not apparent why experts would be discussing pay for performance as if this were a new idea. And the general notion that incentives matter is "old hat."

But the principal-agent problem is complex in health care. Monitoring the effort of physicians and other health care providers is, as in other contexts, no simple matter. Patients, as principals, have difficulty in monitoring the effort of their physicians, and health insurers, as intermediaries between patients and providers, have difficulty in doing this as well, for one because they typically work at a considerable distance from where the care is delivered.

The fee-for-service system may be deficient in that physicians are rewarded for a unit of service—such as a visit—whether or not they exercise the level of care that a fully informed patient would demand. There is widespread concern that the current fee-for-service system creates incentives for a high volume of services, yet few for better health.[17] Thus, the notion of compensating physicians for their work in part based on the level of care provided or the outcomes of care obtained (changes in health status) is indeed an attractive one. There is the question of whether or not the pay-for-performance cure is worse or better than the existing piece rate approach to paying physicians, measured in terms of cost versus benefit. Here, the cost includes both outlays on the incentive and the cost of distortions in behavior that arise because of the incentive being offered.

Extrinsic versus Intrinsic Motivation

The focus of economic analysis has been on the effects of financial incentives. Particularly in recent years, there has been some theoretical research on nonfinancial incentives as well.[18] In other work—which

draws on research by psychologists, experts in human resource management, and sociologists—there is a distinction between intrinsic
motivation, the desire to perform a task for its own sake, and extrinsic
motivation, in which explicit rewards, including pay, promotion, and
recognition (e.g., medals for outstanding performance), or fines elicit
the willingness to perform tasks. This body of theoretical research is
based on a substantial amount of experimental and field research by
noneconomists, indicating that extrinsic motivation may crowd out the
effort that would have been forthcoming in the absence of extrinsic
motivators.

For example, offering compensation for a task may suggest to the
agent that the agent is either not motivated to perform the task, absent
the incentive, or faces a high cost of performing a task. In the former
case, offering an incentive makes the agent think that the principal does
not trust their motivations to do the task without a bribe. In the latter
case, the principal knows that the task is arduous and tries to bribe the
agent to undertake it. Absent an explicit incentive, the agent may think
that the task is easy. With the bribe, the agent becomes suspicious that
they are being unduly influenced.[19]

Societies have traditionally relied on professionalism, intrinsic motivation, to achieve desirable outcomes in health care.[20] Professionalism
has been thought to provide a motivation for physicians and other
health professionals to perform in the interests of patients. There is a
risk that offering explicit rewards for good acts will crowd out intrinsic
motivation.

The theoretical research on intrinsic and extrinsic motivation is both
important and interesting. Yet there is virtually no empirical research
in economics on either intrinsic or extrinsic motivation other than
money. The thrust of economic research has been on the individual
rather than on individuals within organizations. There is no research
that is helpful for deciding on the appropriate mix of incentives among
firms, teams within firms, leaders of firms, such as CEOs, and other
personnel.

Pay for Performance in Health Care

While economists have long been concerned about the role of incentives among health professionals, they did not take the lead in advocating pay for performance in health care, perhaps because of an inherent
suspicion that pay for performance leads to unanticipated side effects.

The interest in pay for performance in the United States began to grow markedly in the latter part of the twentieth century as the rise in health care expenditures reached unprecedented—and perhaps unsustainable—levels, coupled with a concern that society was not obtaining sufficient health care benefit from the dollars expended. Both private insurers, whether for-profit or not-for-profit, and Medicare recognized that the dominant fee-for-service model for physicians lacked incentives for cost control and, at least in theory, created incentives for physicians to overtreat their patients. This observation, repeatedly supported in scholarly research, is especially relevant to managed care firms (e.g., health maintenance organizations) whose revenues per insured patient are set ex ante (i.e., before the patient uses the medical care) rather than based on some sort of cost pass-through formula.[21]

This discussion of pay for performance, both among scholars and managed care managers, has been articulated in a variety of system design questions: To whom should pay be targeted—the individual provider, group practices, or the community, for example?[22] How much pay should be at risk?[23] What level of performance is sufficiently meritorious to warrant additional pay?[24] Which outcome measures will be part of the payment scheme, and by implication, which are considered either less important or too difficult to measure reliably?[25] Should rewards be based on exceeding a certain threshold of care or for care improvement?[26] Should rewards be specifically oriented for improving care delivered to underserved populations?[27] What kind of "gaming" is to be expected, and what mechanisms can be designed to prevent or respond to it?[28] Should a bonus-worthy performance be based on absolute levels of performance or improvement?[29] These sorts of questions are precisely the ones that researchers, policymakers, and administrators are now addressing as numerous incentive payment programs have been launched in the past several years.[30] Yet to date, few empirical studies have analyzed the use of pay for performance to improve quality as defined by the Institute of Medicine—that is, care that is safe, effective, patient-centered, timely, efficient, and equitable.[31]

The 2006 Institute of Medicine report evaluated many of those studies.[32] Among the six strongest of the seventeen studies evaluated, and published between 1992 and 2005, some gauge the effect of pay for per-formance on individual physicians, while others examine pay for performance for physician groups.[33] Almost without exception, the methodologically rigorous studies study proxies for quality—that is, the effect of incentives on the *process* than the *outcomes* of care.[34] For instance, Hillman and his colleagues examined the rate of cancer screening, whereas the others evaluated the effect of pay for performance on immunization rates.[35] Across the range of all the studies synthesized by the Institute of Medicine committee, no clear message about the effects of pay for performance emerges. Of the seventeen studies, five revealed positive effects of pay for performance (an improvement) on one of the Institute of Medicine quality indicators, eight revealed partial or mixed effects, three showed no effect, and one identified a negative effect of pay for performance on quality.

Four important studies of pay for performance appeared in 2005–2007 after the Institute of Medicine report was completed and published. Rosenthal and her colleagues address two key questions relative to pay for performance: Should pay for performance be based on relative improvements in performance or on absolute levels, and does pay for performance uniquely contribute to improved performance above and beyond the physician feedback systems (e.g., reminders) typically associated with them?[36] They compare changes in a treatment group before and after the providers were given pay-for-performance incentives with a control group in which the pay-for-performance incentives were not offered in either period. Plan enrollees did have access to indicators of provider performance in both the treatment and control groups. The authors use a difference-in-difference methodology in performance, where the difference in difference is literally the difference of two differences. The first difference is the one in the treatment group performance in the postperiod and preperiod. The second is the difference in control group performance in the postperiod and preperiod. The reason for having the second difference is that other factors affecting performance could have changed after pay for performance was implemented (before the beginning of the postperiod).

The authors study changes in three process of care measures: cervical cancer screening, mammography, and hemoglobin A1c (the final measure, an indicator of diabetes and control of this disease). The only statistically significant improvement in process was for cervical cancer screening, and even for this screening test the treatment group only improved by 3.6 percent relative to the control group; in the preperiod, 39.2 percent of women were screened for cervical cancer. Five quarters later, the rate was 44.5 percent, but since the percent of women screened in the control group increased by 1.7 percent, not all of the increase in screening in the treatment group could be attributed to the pay-for-performance intervention (44.5 − 39.2 = 5.3 − 1.7 = 3.6). Those improvements in performance that occurred were concentrated among providers with relatively poor performance in the preperiod, implying that basing performance on absolute performance is relatively attractive to those who were low performers in the preperiod.

In sum, the authors find positive effects of pay for performance, but only for cervical cancer, and only for physicians in groups that were well below the target goal. Physicians in groups above the target goals improved performance the least. In the introduction to their study, the authors indicate that there were only a few studies demonstrating that pay for performance leads to an improved quality of care; based on their own findings, they conclude that paying clinicians to reach a common, fixed performance target may produce little gain in quality for the money spent.[37]

The United Kingdom spends far less on personal health care services than does the United States. Yet, as in the United States, there is widespread concern about the quality of care that people are getting. Even before pay for performance became widespread in the United States, a narrow pay-for-performance program was introduced in the United Kingdom in 1991, followed by several other initiatives. In 2004, the National Health Service introduced a pay-for-performance contract for family practitioners that increases physician income based on the performance of 146 quality indicators covering care for ten chronic diseases. The pay-for-performance contract permitted physicians to exclude patients from eligibility for specific indicators in the performance calculation—the rationale being that including all patients would cause physicians to engage in cream skimming (i.e., excluding those patients with severe conditions who may not be as responsive to treatment or those who might not be as compliant as others with treatment). Without the exclusion provision, it was feared that pay for performance might unduly disadvantage certain types of patients. One might argue that a noncooperative patient should be excluded, but suppose a lack of cooperation reflects a lack of transportation to visit the physician?

Based on their analysis of this program, Tim Doran and his colleagues report that family practitioners obtained a median of 96.7 percent of the available points for the clinical indicators—much higher than the 75 percent goal set for the program.[38] The higher rate of attainment was good from the standpoint of quality improvement, but as a result the program was much more costly than anticipated. There was no comparison group to permit a judgment of how much the quality of care would have improved in the absence of the pay-for-performance program, yet presumably there would not have been much change in the time span of a year. Fortunately, excluding patients from pay for performance did not prove to be common. But there is a concern that the apparent success of the program could be due to a failure to set the performance targets sufficiently high relative to the cost to the physicians of achieving them.

A third pay-for-performance study by Lindenauer and colleagues compared changes in adherence to ten individual and four composite measures of quality over two years at hospitals with public reports of outcomes at their facilities as well as pay-for-performance incentives— the treatment group versus a control group of hospitals with only public reports of outcomes.[39] Pay for performance was associated with a 2.6 to 4.1 percent improvement over the two-year period from a 1 to 2 percent bonus. The improvement was greater at those hospitals with relatively low performance at the baseline.

A fourth study of the effects of financial rewards for good and the penalties for poor performance for acute myocardial infarction (heart attack) by Glickman and colleagues found no statistically significant improvement in the quality of care and patient outcomes between hospitals offering the incentive and control hospitals.[40] The authors compared their results to those of Lindenauer and his colleagues, noting that the Lindenauer study findings were more favorable to pay for performance than were theirs.[41]

Taken together, the three studies indicate that pay for performance "works" sometimes in that some positive effects could be attributed to the introduction of explicit financial incentives. Yet a lot of the improvement seems to be in bringing the laggards up, and the improvements at least in the U.S. studies were modest. There is a risk that rewards are in effect economic rents—that is, rewards for behavior that would have occurred anyway. The studies thus indicate that pay for performance is not a panacea for cost and quality problems in health care. At best, and when well conceived and executed, pay for performance should be seen as one of several instruments for quality improvement.

Lacking convincing empirical evidence on the positive effects of pay for performance to date, but faced nevertheless with an objective of influencing behavior to achieve socially desirable goals, it is useful to examine the logic of pay for performance—the topic of the next section.

Social Psychological and Sociological Frameworks for Analyzing Pay for Performance in Health Care

Expectancy Theory

The increased attention to pay for performance in health care largely reflects an attempt to change the motivation, and hence the behaviors, of clinicians and health care organizations to achieve improvements in the efficiency of service delivery, clinical outcomes, and patient centeredness. These goals are sometimes conflicting. That is, incentive pay is thought to motivate providers (or their employing organizations) to focus attention and energy on certain objectives, and divert attention away from those goals that, if accomplished, provide a lesser reward.

This characterization of the goals of pay for performance is surely uncontroversial among economists. The analysis, however, needs to be more fully developed in order to understand both the strengths and weaknesses of pay for performance in health care. To this end, we consider two nonmutually exclusive ways of conceptualizing the challenge of influencing physician behavior. One is based on economic principal-agent theory; the other is based on social psychological and sociological theories of motivation and professional socialization.

Social psychologists and sociologists have devoted considerable attention to the study of individual motivation, particularly to the effect of the social context. A complete review of the literature is beyond the scope of this chapter, and would include examinations of equity, goal-setting, leadership, and expectancy theories.[42] One theory that has generated significant attention over several decades, Victor Vroom's expectancy theory, also accords with economists' logic of incentives and the logic of expected utility.[43] Integrated with an examination of professional socialization, it provides a rich understanding of how physicians may view various motivators.

In short, expectancy theory has three components: valence, expectancy, and instrumentality. Valence refers to the importance, attractiveness, desirability, or anticipated satisfaction with outcomes. Expectancy refers to the subjective probability of an action or effort leading to an outcome or performance (e.g., relief of a patient's back pain).

Instrumentality refers to an individual's estimate of his or her probability of obtaining a second-order one (e.g., payment) should the first-order one (e.g., the patient's pain relief) be achieved. In its simplest form, expectancy theory suggests that individuals perform a mental calculus determining how much effort they will expend toward achieving a first-order goal, and this determination of effort is a function of the probability that the effort will lead to accomplishing the first-order goal, the probability that achieving the intermediate goal will result in the second-order reward, and the attractiveness of the reward itself.[44]

Expectancy theory is silent about the value that individuals place on either the intermediate or second-order outcomes. Its proponents, though, are quite clear that the outcomes may be valuable even if they do not have a monetary dimension to them. This is consistent with another stream of motivation research in psychology that differentiates between the extrinsic rewards (e.g., pay, holidays to exotic locations, and earned time off), the type of rewards given prominent attention by economists, and the intrinsic rewards (e.g., the pride one takes from a job well done, overcoming inherent challenges in a difficult job, and the status bestowed on a professional by one's community) more frequently, although not exclusively, examined by other social scientists.[45]

Much empirical research by psychologists has shown that once a minimum level of extrinsic rewards is achieved (a level that varies by individuals), intrinsic rewards may be equally or more strongly motivating.[46] And perhaps counterintuitively, some experimental research has even suggested an inverse relationship between extrinsic and intrinsic rewards. For example, employees who receive substantial intrinsic rewards in their work may be willing to earn fewer extrinsic ones. Increased extrinsic rewards may also devalue intrinsic rewards.[47] Thus, in a large-sample quantitative and qualitative study on several U.S. hospital systems, Janet Dukerich and her colleagues found a negative association between pay and the commitment that physicians had to their hospitals.[48] Rather than being seen as committed partners, they came to view themselves as "hired hands" who merely had a financial relationship with their hospitals and patients.[49]

Many economist readers will see a similarity between expectancy theory and von Neumann–Morgenstern expected utility theory. In expectancy theory, the probabilities represent subjective beliefs.[50] The payoffs in expectancy theory may not be (generally are not) denominated as monetary bets.[51] At least in some variants, expectancy theory recognizes that decision makers are likely to be limited cognitively in the kinds of calculations that underlie decisions and hence employ various decision rules as shortcuts for complex decision problems.

Professional Socialization

To understand which other, nonmonetary outcomes may be of value to physicians, it is useful to turn to the sociological research on professional socialization. As Robert Town and colleagues comment:

Medical education includes one of the most intense socialization processes of any profession, and the products of these programs bring strong professional values to the practice setting. These values include personal responsibility for patients as clients, a strong collegial peer orientation and a strong commitment to patient care regimens based on professional judgment, *unencumbered by organizational imperatives*. Consequently, incentives that are compatible with these professional values may be more influential than incentives that conflict with professional values.[52]

This view accords with initial research on physician training and socialization.[53] One early study, for example, strongly demonstrated that in addition to the technical-clinical knowledge, medical education was also responsible for inculcating long-standing values, including medical responsibility. More specifically, students learn the responsibility of the doctor for the welfare of one's patient, the responsibility one has for the damage one may do to a patient if the doctor performs badly, and conversely, for the good one can do if the doctor performs properly.[54] More recently, in a review of physician compensation systems, James Robinson comments, "In a vivid illustration of the limits of payment incentives, all nations rely heavily on socialization and the inculcation of norms of behavior for physician. While norms and cultural expectations are pervasive across all occupations, medicine seems to be subject to stronger and more explicit codes of conduct."[55]

These comments about the unique values of the medical profession are not likely controversial. Nor, however, are they to suggest that physician behaviors are not affected by payment systems; such a claim would fly in the face of a substantial body of empirical health services and economics research.[56] Rather, our discussion of expectancy theory and medical socialization is intended to complement the prior discussion of agency theory, and suggest that *pay is only one kind of reward and physicians may consider other rewards (e.g., professional pride, recognition, opportunities to do more challenging work) equally or more valuable.*[57] Or as Town and his colleagues observe in their review of incentives, Since financial incentives are only a component of a witches' brew of reinforcers (all incentives) that are related to a physician's decisions, understanding the effect of financial incentives requires understanding how they fit with other reinforcers."[58]

Control Theory

Another relevant social psychological theory is control theory, a synthesis of the agency and organizational theories.[59] Control theory is grounded in the observation that in controlling people's work, only two aspects of that work are revealed: people's behaviors and the outcomes they produce.[60] Agents' preferences, abilities, and their work environments are not typically revealed to principals.

Having presented the principal-agent logic, and how physicians may determine the effort they wish to expend toward a reward and how they may value various rewards, the next step is to begin to develop a model of physician control and monitoring.

Implications for System Design

As in table 11.1, one can array a physician's work in the health system along three dimensions: task programmability, cost-effective behavior

Table 11.1
Variation in Task Programmability and the Ability to Monitor Inputs and Outputs of Care: A Typology

Programmability	Observability	Outcome measurability	
		Low	High
High task	High cost-effective behavior	1 Behavioral controls	5 Behavioral or outcome controls
High task	Low cost-effective behavior	2 Normative controls	6 Outcome controls
Low task	High cost-effective behavior	3 Normative controls	7 Outcome controls
Low task	Low cost-effective behavior	4 Normative controls	8 Outcome controls

observability, and outcome measurability. These dimensions and the relationships among them are presented in the table and discussed below (for now, ignoring the labels in the numbered cells).

Task programmability is a "task's susceptibility to clear definition of the behaviors needed to perform it."[61] It refers to the knowledge of the transformation processes. Here one asks such questions as: Can designers of a pay system specify *in advance* the behaviors a physician ought to perform when identifying an appropriate candidate for bypass surgery, performing the surgery, providing postsurgical care and follow-up, and prescribing appropriate medication? That is, can it be determined—assuming perfect monitoring—whether physicians have engaged in the correct transformation process? If yes, the first necessary condition exists to either reward the physician for engaging in the correct behaviors or withhold rewards (or punish) for the failure to do so. The value of introducing the concept of task programmability to our earlier discussion of agency theory is that agency theorists are typically interested in whether agents achieved a particular outcome (e.g., a patient's improved health), or whether or not they have exerted effort in the interests of the principal. Task programmability provides more precision to the assessment of the latter because it addresses the question, Was the *right* effort exerted?

In general, reward systems based on whether or not agents (e.g., physicians) have engaged in well-accepted practices, rather than based on outcomes, are attractive and not likely to be opposed by agents. This is because the risk to the presumably risk-averse agent is minimized when that agent is evaluated and paid based on whether the appropriate tasks were performed. That is, agents are evaluated based on an activity for which they maintain control. Of course, task programmability is frequently lacking in any profession in which much professional judgment is required and the science is imperfect; medicine is one such profession in which the causal process generating outcomes is (often) poorly understood.[62] Thus, in health care, one can expect to find well-intentioned and expert medical professionals who simply cannot reach a consensus regarding an appropriate care plan for a patient. Task programmability is likewise lacking when patients present with multiple chronic diseases for which accepted care for one disease is at odds with that for another. Finally, the appropriateness of a particular care path for a patient may be debated among competent physicians because they have different interpretations of the patient's condition. Charles Phelps alerts us to this, referring to the job-shape nature of medical practice in which "each patient is unique, at least partly, so it becomes difficult to monitor excessive use of resources or costly activities with precision."[63]

The above conditions present challenges for the designers of pay-for-performance systems. Even when the task programmability is high, however, principals face the additional challenge of monitoring whether or not agents have engaged in the appropriate behaviors. Principals, or those they hire to perform their monitoring of physicians, must be knowledgeable about appropriate processes of care and also devote sufficient resources to monitor these. The options include, but are not limited to, the direct observation of the physician's care for the patient (which is clearly impractical), chart reviews (which are rare other than in instances of suspected negligence), and forced compliance of clinical protocols (which are often opposed by physicians in the name of "professional autonomy").[64]

Not only must the tasks be sufficiently programmable to be amenable to monitoring but the cost versus benefits of monitoring must be justified. As many of the options above suggest, there is a real possibility that monitoring will be impractical or prohibitively costly—at least with the current information and reporting systems.[65] When principals are unable to monitor behaviors cost-effectively, either in real time or retrospectively in a chart review, it is necessary to consider the role of a third dimension of control systems: outcome measurability.

Outcome measurability refers to an outcome's susceptibility to reliable and valid measurement.[66] The challenge for system designers is whether or not they can determine, for example, if the care provided to a patient resulted in an acceptable outcome.

Several important implementation questions are raised in considerations of outcome measurability. First, do insurers *and* physicians agree on the most reliable and valid metrics to assess performance (e.g., whether or not postsurgical infection rates are valid and reliable measures of surgical quality)? If they do not, whether one pay-for-performance metric is selected over another will depend on the power and influence of the interested parties.

Second, can insurers determine whether outcomes are attributable to the medical care provided by the physicians whose behavior will (or will not) be rewarded? As Govindarajan and Fisher suggest, "Good outcomes can result despite poor efforts and poor outcomes can result despite good efforts."[67] That is, patient outcomes are multifactorial—a function of numerous and often interdependent inputs, many of which are not fully controlled by the provider (e.g., a patient's compliance to a clinical protocol, such as what care that persons with diabetes are recommended to, which involves visits to physicians, weight control, taking drugs, etc.). Thus, in the ideal outcome-based control system, outcomes will be *uniquely attributed to the medical care provided* by the physician, rather than being a product of other factors outside the control of the physician.

This condition, and the concern about attributing outcomes to *individual* providers, is one explanation that led the authors of the Institute of Medicine report to raise concerns about the ability to design a pay-for-performance system that rewards cooperative care delivered by clinician teams.[68] These comments imply that uncertainty arises either because of the natural variation in biological processes, the actions of nonagent others (e.g., noncompliant patients), or organizational interdependencies (e.g., a surgical team with a critical care team). Regardless of the cause of the variation in outcomes, physicians as agents may be placed at risk if they are paid based on patient outcomes.

Third, are designers of pay-for-performance systems certain that agents are aware of the metrics used to evaluate and reward them, and do these metrics conflict with each other (e.g., indicators of clinical well-being, cost reduction, and patient satisfaction)? For instance, one can only wonder how physicians in Britain's National Health Service, with its system of 146 quality indicators implemented in 2004, make decisions about how to serve their patients and achieve their targeted pay-for-performance incentives.[69] Expectancy theorists would suggest that the demands of such a mental calculus may be too great to result in predictable outcomes.

The intersection of these three dimensions and recommendations regarding pay for performance is portrayed in cells one through eight in table 11.1. The dimensions are dichotomized for simplicity here, even though of course all three dimensions are realistically continuous measures. What a pay-for-performance system ultimately resembles should be determined by how system designers choose to address the trade-offs associated with both behavior and outcome monitoring. As a guide, work characterized by high task programmability could, *in theory*, be rewarded based on whether physicians engage in behaviors that could be specified ex ante—regardless of outcomes.

For example, it is now well-known that beta-blockers (a medication) should be administered after a heart attack to reduce mortality rates. Yet for the performance of appropriate behaviors to be used as a metric of physician outcomes (success, failure, or somewhere in between), it is necessary for health insurers and other organizations engaged in monitoring on behalf of patients/policyholders/taxpayers to validly measure these behaviors in a cost-effective way. These conditions are found in cell one.

Cell five expands on these conditions. Not only would it be appropriate to reward physicians based on the behaviors in which they engage, one can also reward physicians based on the outcomes of their work. This possibility exists because of the unique intersection of the three dimensions. Specifically, cell five represents those situations in which the outcomes of a physician's work can be *uniquely* attributed to the physician's decisions and actions. This would be the case for a physician who correctly recommends blood tests for a patient suffering from lethargy, and then correctly interprets lab results indicating hypoglycemia (low blood sugar). Because it is well accepted in medicine that this symptom warrants blood testing, and because hypoglycemia is relatively simple to diagnose, risk-averse physicians can sleep easily at night knowing that they are being evaluated under a scheme that does not place physicians' compensation at undue risk. And insurers can appropriately choose to rely on controls and rewards based on behaviors, outcomes, or some combination of the two. The ultimate decision should be based on the *relative* ability to observe behaviors cost-effectively and or the ability to uniquely attribute outcomes to the physician.

Cells six, seven, and eight represent a more limited range of options for the designers of pay-for-performance systems. In these three cells, pay for performance ought to be based on physician outcomes; the task programmability is low (cells seven and eight), and it is difficult to observe behavior cost-effectively (cells six and eight), or both (cell eight). Examples may include hip replacement revision rates or post-surgical infection rates. In these cases, there is legitimate debate about precisely how best to reduce both (i.e., the task programmability is imperfect), or the costs of observing and evaluating these surgical procedures are too high. In the case of an orthopedic surgeon with substantial volume, though, high revision or infection rates would strongly suggest that this surgeon is providing low-quality care.[70]

Many readers familiar with the work of physicians and other health professionals will no doubt have recognized by now, and consistent with many of the concerns identified in the Institute of Medicine report on pay for performance, that given the current monitoring and information systems, there are few conditions for which monitoring is cost-effective, reliable, and valid.[71] It is exceptionally expensive to monitor physician behaviors, either in real time or ex post facto, and decisions about who should bear these costs are the subject of considerable debate.[72] Also, the state of the medical science is sometimes insufficiently developed to be able to specify, with near certainty, the precise behaviors in which physicians ought to engage, especially when patients have multiple chronic conditions. Even when they have familiar ailments, patients may be candidates for a range of care options. For example, a patient suffering from the relatively common lower-back pain may be an appropriate candidate for pain management, bed rest, manual manipulation, or surgery. Whether or not the physician in fact provides the appropriate care is often difficult or expensive to assess. And physicians, under the banner of maintaining professional autonomy and putting the patient first, will probably rail against "micromanaging" by pay-for-performance system designers.[73]

Given these challenges, should pay-for-performance systems be based on outcomes rather than behaviors? Perhaps they should not be based on outcomes—a view that is consistent with the fact that most pay-for-performance systems are process oriented. A focus on outcomes will often be fraught with problems because of the inability to attribute outcomes uniquely to the care of providers. For one, care is often provided in teams, and thus it may be difficult to ascribe success or failure to the acts of physicians. And as discussed above, patients' actions also frequently have a great impact on clinical outcomes. Finally, the stark truth is that patients often fail to recover, or fail to recover as quickly as might be expected, despite being provided the most appropriate care (i.e., behaviors) and absent gross negligence.[74] Thus, holding providers responsible for many outcomes may place undue and unreasonable risk on them. What, then, are we to do?

Normative Controls: Complements for Pay for Performance

As the preceding discussion makes clear, monitoring and rewarding based on behaviors may be overly expensive or impractical to administer, and if based on outcomes may unduly hold providers responsible for outcomes outside their control. Research on control systems, rewards, and motivation suggests an alternative—indeed, one that has always been at the core of professional services, and should not be abandoned or underappreciated: normative controls and values-based motivation.[75] This extends our discussion beyond the self-interested, atomistic physician and allows us to take into account the sociocultural context in which physicians are embedded.[76]

Normative controls are the implicit pressures that encourage all members of society to engage in appropriate, or avoid antisocial, behaviors. William Ouchi referred to control through socialization and the enforcement of established norms as "clan control."[77] Normative control systems proponents, who come mainly from sociological and social psychological traditions, frequently refer to training in the medical and caregiving professions as among the clearest illustrations of normative control systems.[78] Not only do the caregiving professions (e.g., medicine and nursing) attract a particular kind of person but caregiving professionals are socialized in their training and throughout their careers to value certain behaviors and objectives, and reject others.[79]

This is why many readers may have found the discussion above, focused on a physician's responsiveness only to financial rewards, as limited. It leads us to view agents in the health professions as *regularly* attempting to provide less than appropriate levels of care when they are not sufficiently monitored. For many this will not ring true, and given the difficulties described above with gauging provider quality, and monitoring and rewarding physician behaviors or outcomes, it is no wonder that the professions have always relied on normative control systems to ensure that their members "do the right thing."[80]

This ability to count on professional values is tremendously valuable since health professionals can generally be counted on to pursue the interests of patients—despite the absence of reward systems that directly tie pay for performance or the presence of disincentives (or minimal incentives) to do the right thing. This of course does not mean that their behaviors should not be monitored in some way, and for that reason, monitoring is one of the responsibilities of professional societies. Nor does it mean that providers should not receive feedback regarding the outcomes of their care or the administration of their hospitals. This too can improve health care quality.[81]

What it does mean is that we should not be overly concerned that the preceding arguments identify important limitations of pay-for-performance systems in health care. These limitations are entirely consistent with many of the reservations about pay-for-performance systems raised in the broader management literature.[82] Nor do these comments about behavior or outcome-based systems suggest that their consideration ought to be abandoned. Rather, these comments help system designers understand the kinds of work in health care that are amenable to pay-for-performance systems (the world of cells one, five, six, seven, and eight) versus the work for which pay for performance is more problematic (cells two, three, and four). This discussion also suggests the need to enhance task programmability, reduce monitoring costs, and better measure outcomes so that pay for performance can be used more effectively to improve patient care, reduce economic risks to physicians, and lessen total health care costs.

Conclusion: Where Do We Go from Here?

As previous research amply demonstrates, physicians have long shown themselves to be responsive to financial incentives, and thus there are good reasons to critically examine physician pay for performance. Still, it must also be acknowledged that because financial incentives can have such a powerful effect on physician behaviors and decisions, they should be used quite judiciously. Whether health care organizations currently have the system capabilities and knowledge to do so is in doubt.[83] Thus, an alternative to pay for performance must be part of the health policy discourse.

This chapter has identified many challenges concerning the risks borne by physicians under pay for performance deriving from imperfect task programmability, the inability to monitor behaviors cost-effectively, and the difficulties attributing outcomes unique to the decision and behaviors of physicians. Not only will these challenges need to be overcome but a host of other questions must be addressed. For example, Doran and colleagues question whether pay for performance ought to reward for performance improvements or meeting absolute performance thresholds.[84] As they suggest, pay for improvements may create the greatest challenges for physicians who are high performers (prior to the establishment of pay for performance), and may prove to have little incentive benefits or create feelings of injustice. Pay-for-performance systems based on meeting absolute levels may, if the levels are set too high, discourage low-performing physicians from attempting to improve. If the levels are set too low, they will have no effect on current high performers.

Another system design question is whether to implement these systems incrementally (e.g., by service or disease area) or all at once. The authors of the Institute of Medicine report have recommended an incremental approach, in large part so that the necessary information infrastructure can be developed.[85] If implemented incrementally, however, designing incentives in only certain areas initially, the quality and access in nondesignated service and disease areas may suffer. For example, there are suggestions that pay-for-performance plans in Ontario, Canada, for five priority areas (cardiac care, cancer, hip and knee replacement, diagnostic, and cataracts) may be drawing physician attention away from "nonpriority" areas. The authors of the Institute of Medicine report acknowledged this challenge, but offered no approach to addressing it.

As a final illustrative challenge, system designers may question whether it would be more appropriate to reward physician groups rather than individual physicians. This appears to be the direction currently targeted by the U.S. Center for Medicare and Medicaid Services, although this approach would not address the challenges raised here regarding task programmability, cost-effective behavior monitoring, and uniquely attributable outcomes. Rather, these challenges would be masked. This too is noted in the Institute of Medicine report, which acknowledged that the distribution of rewards would be complicated, but the report left this issue for groups themselves to address.

With these questions in mind as well as the challenges about design practical pay for performance systems raised in this chapter, it is useful to consider economists' James Baron and David Kreps comments about pay for performance across a range of industries.[86] They conclude that pay-for-performance systems are less likely to be effective under the following conditions: the more complex the technology of work (the transformation process, which may include making an ill person a healthy person); the more ambiguous the tasks; the more the culture of the organization or profession emphasizes cooperation; the more the system or organization strategy centers on difficult to measure quality or stresses innovation; the more tenuous the connection between inputs and outcomes; the more workforce diversity and/or technological diversity encourages perceptions of inequity or illegitimacy in a pay-for-performance system; the more the general social culture and the specific culture of the workforce militate against "crass monetary distinctions"; and the more one can rely on the intrinsic motivation of the workforce.

When these conditions are present, as many are in health care, one should consider other nonfinancial incentives to influence provider behavior, including "feedback and profiling, peer review, second opinion and utilization management, medico-legal sanctions, and continuing medical education."[87] Finally, even though we may be far from overcoming many of the limitations of pay-for-performance systems raised here and in recent reviews, some unique positive features of health care are worth emphasizing.[88] The systems of selection into the professions and professional socialization in this sector enhance the likelihood that health care providers will generally attempt to do the right thing. Thus, while efforts to develop more effective physician pay-for-performance systems will likely emerge, particularly given the attention that the topic has received, there is reason for confidence that controls based on professional norms will supplement currently imperfect measures to control physician behaviors and outcomes.

In the end, pay for performance is a potentially useful tool, but like many solutions to problems of health care cost and quality, it is no panacea. It should be viewed instead as one of several policy instruments in the toolbox of private and public policymakers. This topic illustrates as well as any other in this book the importance of various academic disciplines working together to solve complex problems in the world's health care sectors. Clearly, no single discipline has the answer to all or even most of the practical issues of health care finance and delivery. It is an encouraging development that in the late twentieth and early twenty-first centuries, scholars from various disciplines concerned with decision making are looking to disciplines other than their own for new perspectives.

Acknowledgments

We would like to acknowledge that valuable feedback of participants in the Oberlin health economics conference.

Notes

1. Robinson (2001); Doran et al. (2006); Leape (1994).

2. Rosenthal et al. (2005).

3. McGuire and Pauly (1991).

4. See chapter 10 in particular.

5. Conrad and Christianson (2004); Institute of Medicine (2006); Rosenthal et al. (2005); Roland (2004).

6. Bohmer (1999). For a complementary discussion of hospital quality, see chapter 12 in this volume.

7. Institute of Medicine (2001, 2006).

8. McGuire (2000).

9. See, for example, Lazear (1999, 2000).

10. Hickson et al. (1987); Sloan et al. (1978); Gaynor and Getler (1995).

11. Jensen and Murphy (1990); Hall and Leibman (1998); Bertrand and Mullainathan (2001); Bebchuk and Fried (2003).

12. McGuire (2000); Milgrom and Roberts (1992); Pratt and Zeckhauser (1985).

13. Kenneth Arrow (1963) devoted considerable attention to the physician (principal)-patient (agent) relationship, although the principal-agent logic applies perfectly well to the insurer (principal)-physician (agent) relationship.

14. Phelps (2003, 5).

15. Town et al. (2004).

16. Eisenhardt (1989); Pauly (1974).

17. Institute of Medicine (2006).

18. Frey (1997); Kreps (1997); Frey and Jegen (2001); Bénebou and Tirole (2003, 2006).

19. See Bénebou and Tirole (2003).

20. Starr (1982).

21. For an overview, see chapter 10 in this volume.

22. Rowe (2006).

23. Institute of Medicine (2006).

24. Rosenthal et al. (2005).

25. Institute of Medicine (2006).

26. Rosenthal and Dudley (2007).

27. Ibid.

28. Conrad and Christianson (2004); chapter 12 in this volume.

29. Rosenthal et al. (2005).

30. Med-Vantage Inc. (2007).

31. Institute of Medicine (2001).

32. Institute of Medicine (2006).

33. The authors of the Institute of Medicine (2006) report graded seventeen evaluations from one (poor) to four (excellent). On individual physicians, see Fairbrother et al. (1999). On physician groups, see, for example, Hillman et al. (1998); Hillman and Ripley (1999); Kouides et al. (1998).

34. The process of care refers to how medical care is conducted; for example, whether or not a test, screening procedure, or preventive care procedure that was indicated by the patient's symptoms or status (e.g., age) was actually ordered.

35. Hillman et al. (1998); Kouides et al. (1998); Hillman and Ripley (1999); Fairbrother et al. (1999).

36. Rosenthal et al. (2005).

37. Thus, their position is consistent with the Conrad and Christianson (2004) contemporaneous review and that of the Institute of Medicine (2006) committee, which concluded that "a robust literature base demonstrating that pay-for-performance strategies lead to improved health outcomes does not yet exist" (36).

38. Doran et al. (2006).

39. Lindenaver et al. (2007).

40. Glickman et al. (2007).

41. Lindenauer et al. (2007).

42. On equity, see Adams (1963); on goal setting, see Locke and Latham (1984); on leadership, see House (1971); on expectancy, see Vroom (1964). For a comprehensive review of research on incentives and compensation in psychology, see Gerhart and Rynes (2003).

43. Vroom (1964); see, for example, Schoemaker (1982).

44. Vroom (1964). Expectancy theory is related to research on self-efficacy, which suggests that individuals must first believe they have the ability to achieve a goal before attempting to reach it (Bandura [1997]). This logic has been used to partially explain physicians' failure to adopt clinical protocols (Cabana et al. [1999]).

45. Thomas McGuire (2000; chapter 10 in this volume) incorporates net patient benefit in his models of physician decision making.

46. Deci et al. (1999a).

47. Compase Pfeffer (1998); Deci et al. (1999b).

48. Dukerich et al. (2002).

49. This issue of a "crowding out effect" (Deci et al. [1999b]) is complicated and far from settled, and its full treatment is beyond the scope of this chapter. One possibility is that the association is due to selection effects. For example, Gaynor and Gertler (1995) found that physicians' with different risk preferences systematically selected physician practices; the more risk-adverse physicians were likely to select practices that spread risk through a greater sharing of revenues.

50. As in several economic studies in recent years; see, for example, Manski (2004).

51. Schoemaker (1982).

52. Town et al. (2004, S85; emphasis added).

53. Blanche et al. (1961); Friedson (1971).

54. Becker et al. (1972).

55. Robinson (2001, 167).

56. Chaix-Couturier et al. (2000); Robinson (2001).

57. Conrad and Christianson (2004).

58. Town et al. (2004, 110–111).

59. Eisenhardt (1985, 1989); Govindarajan and Fisher (1990); Ouchi (1979); Thompson (1967).

60. For an application to health care organizations, see Golden and Ma (2003).

61. Govindarajan and Fisher (1990, 261).

62. Town et al. (2004, 91).

63. Phelps (2003, 198).

64. Cabana et al. (1999). By this we are referring to attempts to force compliance. As an editor has rightly pointed out to one of us, these efforts are frequently unsuccessful, despite incentives designed to "encourage" compliance.

65. Institute of Medicine (2006).

66. Eisenhardt (1985); Ouchi (1979).

67. Govindarajan and Fisher (1990, 262).

68. Institute of Medicine (2006).

69. Doran et al. (2006).

70. Even in this example one can question whether revision and infection rates are uniquely due to surgical quality. Yet if we assume—with large numbers of patients— that noncompliant patients are randomly distributed across surgeons and that the surgeon is responsible for the quality of their team, outcome-based pay may be justified. Of course, it may still be opposed by the risk-adverse surgeon, who may simply prefer to be paid for their effort. Or as Gautam Gowrisankaran (chapter 12, this volume) suggests, the assumption of random unobserved severity of illness is often violated and risk adjustment methodologies are imperfect. Thus, physician risk neutrality cannot be achieved.

71. Institute of Medicine (2006).

72. Ibid.

73. Cabana et al. (1999); Golden et al. (2000).

74. This discussion is not intended to suggest that poor outcomes *only* result from non-compliant patients or factors outside the control of physicians. A well-established literature on patient safety (Institute of Medicine 2006; Leape 1994) shows that not to be the case. Nevertheless, that literature also shows that a substantial portion of medical errors are system errors, and should not be attributed to the gross negligence of a particular individual. When this is the case, this too raises challenges for physician pay-for-performance systems based on patient outcomes.

75. Ouchi (1979); Khatri et al. (2006).

76. Fukuyama (1995); Granovetter (1985).

77. Ouchi (1979).

78. Town et al. (2004); Friedson (1975).

79. Goode (1957); Golden et al. (2000); Friedson (2001). As Hippocrates stated, "In every house where I come I will enter only for the good of my patients, keeping myself far from all intentional ill-doing and all seduction."

80. See chapter 12 in this volume.

81. Monane et al. (1998).

82. For a discussion of the "myths of pay," see Pfeffer (1998).

83. Institute of Medicine (2006).

84. Doran et al. (2006).

85. Institute of Medicine (2006).

86. Baron and Kreps (1999).

87. Bohmer (1999, 4).

88. Rosenthal et al. (2005).

12

Competition, Information Provision, and Hospital Quality

Gautam Gowrisankaran

As health care has begun to be provided in a more market-based setting in the United States since the early 1980s, economic insights have become more relevant to understanding the functioning of the market and the ways in which such functioning can improve. This is particularly true for the hospital sector. Hospital care is of substantial importance, accounting for about 5 percent of the U.S. gross domestic product and 30 percent of U.S. health care spending in 2004.[1] Moreover, the nature of competition in this sector has been substantially transformed in recent years. From 1985 to 2000, hospital closures, mergers, and conversions caused the number of hospitals to drop by 28 percent; the metropolitan-area level Herfindahl index (a common measure of the degree of market concentration with higher values indicating greater concentration and a value of ten thousand signifying a pure monopoly) to rise from about three thousand to four thousand; and the percent of for-profit hospitals to rise from 11.7 to 15.2 percent.[2] The changes in market structure reflect an increased focus on profitability. Hospitals of all types, from for-profit chains to renowned teaching hospitals, have increasingly been forced to consider the economic implications of their pricing, service, and quality decisions.

Crucially, hospitals compete on quality, and yet hospital quality is multidimensional and difficult to measure. Avedis Donabedian defines three domains in which the quality of health care might be assessed: structure, process, and outcome.[3] *Structure* is the mechanism for health care delivery, such as inpatient and outpatient facilities. *Process* is that which is accomplished in the delivery of care—for example, compliance with established guidelines. *Outcome*, such as the probability of survival and the functional status of the patient after being hospitalized, is affected by the use of structure and process. Ultimately, outcome measures are the most important to economists as patient utility depends on outcomes. Data on outcomes are often unavailable, however, and some outcomes are so rare that it is difficult to base reliable assessments on the data.

For some patients, such as Medicare beneficiaries, price is regulated so that competition among hospitals is exclusively over quality and other amenities. Even for other patients, much empirical and anecdotal evidence suggests that quality is a key attribute of hospital care and influential in decisions about the choice of hospital. U.S. medicine traditionally has been suspicious of competition among health care providers, especially physicians, and has seen it as a force that would lower the quality of care as providers use their informational advantage to exploit patients.[4] Some recent industry observers, in contrast, have proposed greater competition as a force leading to higher rather than lower health care quality. In a competitive market, insurers would pay more for higher-quality care.[5]

The primary goal of this chapter is to synthesize and evaluate some of the contributions that economics has made in explaining the determinants of hospital quality, and the links between hospital quality, the provision of information, and competition among hospitals and other health care industry participants, paying particular attention to recent pertinent empirical studies. A second goal is to evaluate the policy implications that can be derived from these contributions of economics. The policy implications typically concern how to design regulations and incentives for the hospital industry to improve its own functioning. Many of these normative issues have not yet been fully addressed by economists—an important subject for future research.

In the remainder of this chapter, I provide a background on the general economics of hospital quality, followed by an evaluation of the contributions of economics in measuring hospital quality. I then discuss empirical findings on the determinants of hospital quality, the effect of information provision regarding hospital and health plan quality, and the effect of competition on hospital quality. Finally, I present some concluding remarks.

Overview of the Economics of Hospital Quality

The quality of hospital care is an output much like hospital quantity, albeit a multidimensional output. Accordingly, economics can be used to define the optimal level of quality. The level of hospital quality is optimal if the marginal cost of additional improvements in quality is equal to the expected marginal benefit of quality to the patient (and others, if there are externalities).

Because economics defines an optimal level of quality, there is the possibility for hospitals to have too high a quality level, as might occur if hospitals take many costly precautions that have only limited impacts on outcomes, or too low a quality level. Assessing the optimal quality level is even more difficult than defining the concept. Evaluating the marginal benefits of quality depends on measuring quality, and then determining the willingness to pay for a unit of quality.

Hospital care is not the only good or service for which quality is difficult to measure. For instance, automobiles vary widely in handling, power, interior room, safety in the event of a crash, and the expected necessity of repairs, all of which are not directly observable (e.g., one cannot determine crash worthiness just by examining the car's appearance). There are a variety of mechanisms to ensure that automobile quality is optimal. These include government regulations (e.g., minimum crash safety standards), reporting requirements (e.g., fuel economy data collected on a uniform basis), and reliability information provided by private organizations (e.g., *Consumer Reports* surveys). Because of these mechanisms, by and large economists do not believe that there is huge market failure in terms of quality for the new car market.

There are parallels between the quality assurance mechanisms for hospitals and automobiles. For instance, there are government regulations regarding hospital quality, including licensure, accreditation, and certificate of need laws. There are a variety of other mechanisms to ensure appropriate quality. Medicare and Medicaid can exclude hospitals that are of low quality. Private health insurers presumably also consider the quality of the hospital when deciding whether or not to include a hospital in its network. Physicians, who are more informed than patients in the medical arena, should also be useful in guiding patients toward a hospital of appropriate quality and are likely more useful than automotive salespeople in this regard. The tort liability system can punish hospitals that skimp on care quality. A variety of report cards rate hospitals in different dimensions.

Nevertheless, economists (and others) worry that there is still a market failure in the provision of hospital quality, in the sense of over- or underinvestment in quality. Market failure may occur for two reasons. First, it is much more difficult to measure hospital quality than automobile quality. Crash testing is a useful way of evaluating the crash worthiness of cars. An analogous mechanism for hospitals would send identical test dummies with cardiac arrest to different hospitals. This is not feasible since cardiac procedures cannot be performed on test dummies and *exactly identical* people with cardiac arrest cannot be found. Survey data can be used to determine accurately which cars have more mechanical problems. In contrast, it is much more difficult to rank hospitals on the basis of outcomes for a variety of reasons discussed below, including patient selection and the multidimensionality of quality measures.

Second, consumers in the hospital market generally do not face incentives that would result in them making optimal decisions. If car A costs $5,000 more to bring to market than car B, then someone buying car A will typically pay $5,000 more to buy car A than car B. But if hospital A provides a treatment that costs $5,000 more than hospital B, it is rare that a patient admitted to hospital A would directly pay this price difference. Medicare patients, for instance, can typically choose any hospital or treatment without facing any sort of pricing differential. This implies that the person would be likely to choose treatment more frequently than would be optimal, as discussed in other chapters in this book.[6]

Yet structuring appropriate incentives is a difficult task; for incentives to be optimal, it would be necessary for people to face the true marginal price of their treatment. This would entail health insurance that paid people lump-sum transfers for illnesses. Lump-sum transfers are common in automobile, property, and life insurance: automobile insurers will typically estimate the cost of damage from a loss and then issue a check to the policyholder, who can choose whether or not to repair the car. Health insurance does not function this way, however, because of the difficulty in assessing the cost of damage. Even if the damage could be assessed, it is difficult to ascertain the optimal lump-sum transfer because sick people may have a different marginal utility of income from the healthy.[7]

Because of perceived inefficiencies in the hospital market and the fact that much of hospital care is paid for by the government, hospital quality has become a public policy issue. Perceived inefficiencies have also led to the continued proposal and implementation of new private mechanisms to try to improve the efficiency of the market by making it more market oriented. For example, consumer-directed health plans, under which enrollees directly pay for much of their care from a special health savings account, have recently been implemented as a tool to make people face incentives that are closer to optimal—at least from the perspective of economic efficiency. Yet there is no consensus about whether any of the potential mechanisms yield outcomes that are closer to optimal. For this reason, there has been much economic research on the measurement of quality, the impact of information, and the relation between quality and competition.

Economics has contributed perspectives to these research questions in at least two broad ways. First, economics provides a framework to analyze the extent to which incentives matter as well as to model the impact of incentives on behavior and equilibrium outcomes. Economists have been willing to apply this type of a framework to settings in which others have typically assumed that decisions are motivated by altruistic behavior (e.g., quality is provided because it is good for people) rather than by incentives. For example, economists have assessed whether certain public policies might cause physicians and hospitals to not accept high-risk patients for treatment and instead admit low-risk patients who may derive relatively little benefit from such care, but whose good outcomes make hospitals *seem* to be effective, and to the extent that such behavior occurs, how it affects the health of patients in equilibrium. By considering these types of incentives, they have arrived at more realistic answers as to the effects of report cards than have previous studies.[8]

Second, economics provides a framework to explain why simple regressions with observational data may yield inconsistent results and how other methods, such as instrumental variables, can be used to address the inconsistency. For this reason, economists are often concerned about the identification of key parameters, and are willing to consider creative solutions to develop more plausibly consistent estimates.

Using these two general insights, economists have generally been willing to tackle a wide variety of issues pertaining to the provision of hospital care. It may not seem natural that economists should measure hospital quality, any more than they should measure automobile quality. Quality issues would seem to be outside the scope of economics, in contrast to such "economic" variables as price. Nevertheless, economists have devised methodologies to deal with complexities such as quality variation within a market. This has occurred largely through the creation of methods that mimic randomized trials in order to provide more plausibly accurate estimates of hospital quality.

Measurement of Hospital Quality and Its Determinants

Estimating hospital quality and its determinants is essential to understanding several important research questions. These include understanding the optimality of hospital quality, how quality affects competition, and how information provision affects quality. More generally, estimating hospital quality is a necessary (though not sufficient) step for making markets work better. Economic studies have found that the diffusion of advanced technologies in the United States over time has yielded benefits—principally improved longevity and health—that are substantially higher than the costs. For example, David Cutler and his colleagues examine treatments for heart attack care from 1983 to 1994.[9] They find that mortality from heart attacks declined substantially over this period, in part because of the increased use of "medically intensive" treatments (sophisticated resource-using therapeutic technologies) such as coronary artery bypass surgery, and in part because of improvements in the quality of these treatments. The mean price of treating heart attack patients increased substantially over this period as well. By assigning a dollar value to the extra life expectancy for heart attack patients, they find that the benefits from the additional treatments were very much worth it. This provides strong evidence that the structural presence of bypass units contributes to the mortality outcome measure of quality of care on average.

In contrast to these findings, several studies associated with the team that assembled the *Dartmouth Atlas of Health Care* have examined variations in practice style across U.S. metropolitan areas.[10] These studies report that areas with more access to advanced technologies do not have higher average risk-adjusted survival probabilities.[11]

One recent study by Jonathan Skinner and his colleagues finds this to be true using longitudinal data from 1986 to 2002, even after including *regional fixed effects*, implying that recent *changes* in technologies are not leading to improved health outcomes.[12] There is also cross-country evidence that more intensive treatments for heart disease do not necessarily lead to higher survival probabilities.[13] Combining these findings, it appears that access to advanced technologies may have resulted in hospitals having substantially better outcomes now than thirty years ago. Yet structural measures of access to advanced technologies by no means necessarily account for all of the differences in outcomes among hospitals at a point in time.

Many process measures of quality seek to evaluate quality according to the extent to which patients are receiving medically appropriate care as contained in the recommendations of practice guidelines. For example, there are a number of medically appropriate care guidelines for treating heart attacks and their aftermaths. These include prescriptions for beta-blockers and immediate reperfusion with angioplasty or thrombolytic (clot-busting) drugs.

Certain longitudinal databases track this type of detail. This allows researchers to uncover the extent to which the care for each patient complies with medically appropriate measures, and to use this to evaluate hospitals according to the care that they provide. Researchers have found that patients' use of medically appropriate measures correlates with other quality measures at the hospital level. For instance, Jersey Chen and his colleagues find evidence that hospitals reported to be the best by *U.S. News and World Report*'s influential list of "America's Best Hospitals" perform better than average on most measures from Cooperative Cardiovascular Project data.[14] Even the top-ranked hospitals were far from perfect, though, using relatively straightforward process of care measures. For example, they provided aspirin to only 96.2 percent of patients for whom it was indicated, and beta-blockers to only 75 percent of the eligible patients.

Despite their advantages, the medically appropriate care measures are somewhat limited as predictors of quality. Many of them are quite straightforward to perform and hence may not offer a complete picture of hospital quality. For example, just giving aspirin to patients when warranted may not be a reliable indicator that the quality of a hospital's surgical care for coronary bypass surgery is high. These measures may also be vulnerable to gaming—a point considered in greater detail below. A hospital may find that administering aspirin is good for its ratings and skimp on aspects of care that do not influence its ratings.

The use of outcome measures of quality can address some of the shortcomings of process measures. Common measures of health outcomes include morbidity, physical functional status, psychosocial functioning, and quality of life.[15] A major difficulty in capturing quality in a single metric is its multidimensionality. As an example, one hospital may be better at preventing deaths from the cardiovascular complications of diabetes, while another one may excel at preventing limb amputations.

Of all the outcome measures, the most widely used is patient mortality. Mortality reflects a definite lack of cure and hence may be related to quality. Moreover, because there are a number of empirical studies that analyze the value of life years, one can translate saved lives into dollar terms, albeit imperfectly. Combining these measures with information on the costs of medical care, one can use mortality outcomes to evaluate the conceptual question of the economically optimal level of quality.

At its simplest level, one can measure hospital quality by examining the mortality rates at different hospitals and ascribing a higher level of quality to hospitals with lower mortality rates. Since patients come to the hospital with more or less severe conditions, it is necessary to account for this in some way, lest we call a hospital that admits a disproportionate number of patients with grave conditions a low-quality one.

Ideally from the vantage point of accounting for differences in the severity of illness of persons admitted to different hospitals, patients would be randomly assigned to hospitals. Yet for ethical and other reasons, it is impossible to implement a randomized clinical trial, which randomly assigns patients to hospitals. Studies that use mortality data to measure the quality of care have thus examined the outcomes of care based on where patients *actually* receive treatment, rather than randomly assigning them to facilities. Data, which may be rich in detail, but for which persons are not randomly assigned to the various groups (in this application, hospitals) in the study, are called "observational data."

With observational data, the mortality rate of a hospital reflects both the quality of the hospital and the severity of illness of the patients who seek treatment at the hospital. To obtain accurate measures of hospital quality, one needs to control for the severity of illness. This process of controlling for the severity of illness using observational data is known as "risk adjustment." Ideally, one would have a patient put a finger on a meter, which would record the patient's severity of illness perfectly and accurately. One would then use this measured severity of illness as a control; the remaining component of mortality (that is not due to the illness severity at the time of admission to the hospital) could then be accurately attributed to hospital quality.

Such a "severity meter" does not exist, of course. Thus, instead, it is necessary to use proxies for illness severity. A typical set of controls for severity includes age, gender, race/ethnicity, and detailed data on diagnoses and other procedures (say, procedures to treat a complication of a foot in a person with diabetes) in an analysis of survival following admission to hospitals of persons with heart attacks. Since these controls are imperfect, part of the severity of illness at admission is unobserved. The underlying assumption that would justify using observational data with a risk-adjustment method is for the unobserved component of the severity of illness to be random across hospitals after the adjustment process.

Unfortunately, there is evidence to suggest that the assumption of random unobserved severity of illness is unlikely to be true even with state-of-the-art risk-adjustment techniques. Hospitals widely considered to be among the best nationally—for example, Johns Hopkins Hospital and the Cleveland Clinic, which are perennially rated among the best by *U.S. News and World Report*—have reported risk-adjusted mortality measures that are higher than those of some other nearby hospitals. One explanation is that these hospitals are not really that good. Another is that people are aware of their reputations as centers of excellence, and hence people with a high (and subtle to the researcher) severity of illness disproportionately flock to these hospitals. Whether or not the first explanation is accurate, the second one seems likely to be true, at least in part. This selection can lead to misleading estimates of hospital quality, wherein hospitals that treat high unobserved severity of illness patients will systematically appear less good than they really are. Ironically, the fact that people respond to incentives in choosing hospitals complicates the economists' task of assessing hospital quality.

Some recent studies by economists, including some by this author, have devised methods that attempt to mimic the randomization of patients across hospitals.[16] The basic idea is to use *patient location* to mimic the randomization of patients. The (identifying) assumption is that unobserved patient severity of illness does not predict where patients live. That is, for example, people live in a rural area and hence distant from a hospital with a sophisticated heart program because they are farmers, not because they have robust hearts. Patient location can then serve as a randomizer, which is uncorrelated with unobserved severity of illness, but that will predict where patients seek treatment, since patients are more likely to choose nearby hospitals.

Figure 12.1 provides a stylized example of how this method works. Panel A shows a hypothetical market with two hospitals and 40 patients. Patient severity of illness is unobserved to the researcher and can be either low or high; the same proportion of high severity of illness patients live near hospital A as near hospital B. By assumption,

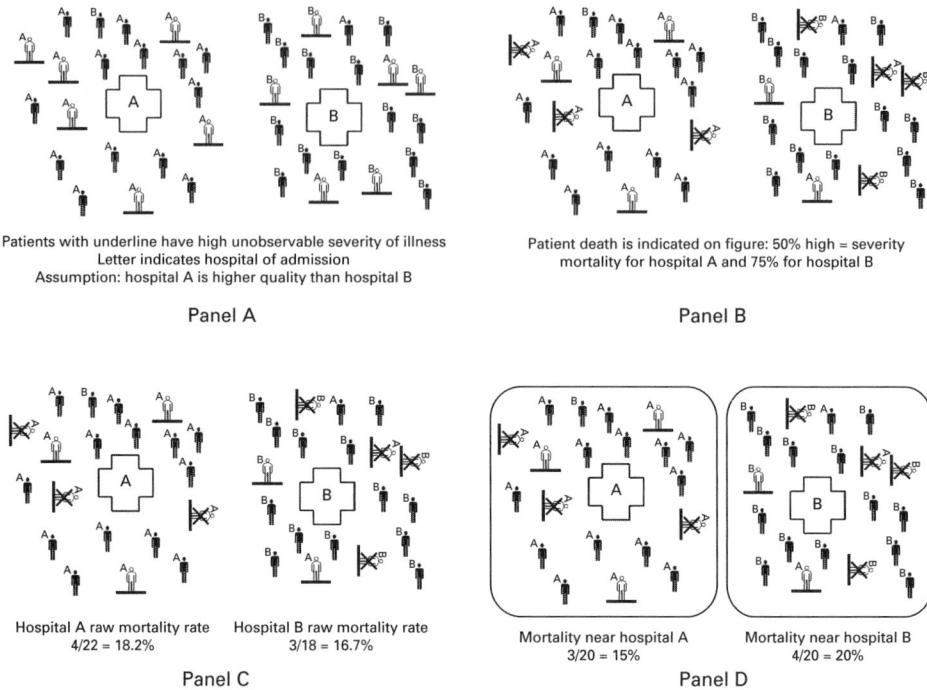

Figure 12.1
Identification of Hospital Quality Using Patient Location: An Example

hospital A is of higher quality than hospital B. High severity of illness individuals are more likely to choose hospital A than hospital B, but patients are also more likely to choose the closer hospital. Panel B shows the outcomes. Hospital A's mortality rate is 50 percent of high-severity illness patients while hospital B's mortality rate for such patients is 75 percent; further, for simplicity, assume that low-severity patients never die from hospital treatment. Panel C shows what would happen if one incorrectly examines quality by using raw mortality rates: hospital A looks worse than hospital B, but this is because it admits a higher proportion of persons with severely ill people than does hospital B, not because it is of worse quality. Panel D then shows an estimator that adequately controls for unobserved selection—one that "identifies" the quality differences: hospital A is found to be better than hospital B, because fewer deaths occur to patients who live near hospital A. While this example is very stylized, the logic from it applies more generally.

McClellan and colleagues use location as a randomizer to evaluate health care quality in the context of evaluating the value of intensive treatments for heart attack patients.[17] More recently, in two studies, my colleagues and I use this method to identify the quality of hospital care for pneumonia.[18] We develop a model in one of these studies consistent with mortality being a discrete 0–1 variable, and implement a *Bayesian statistical analysis.*[19]

The Bayesian analysis provides an efficient way of extracting the signal from the noise, which is important given the low signal-to-noise ratio of mortality data. For example, the suicide rate among psychiatric patients may reflect a hospital's ability to take precautions. But a larger determinant of suicide is likely the underlying agitation and ability of persons to control their own behaviors. These methods can also be used to combine information across time frames, which may be significant. For cancer quality, for instance, the probability that a patient dies within thirty days of being admitted to a hospital is a good gauge of surgical and postoperative care, while longer-term mortality measures will capture the skill of the hospital in eliminating all cancer cells. McClellan and Staiger develop a classical (non-Bayesian) statistical method that combines mortality rates across diseases and times to derive more accurate measures of quality for a given hospital.[20]

There are also critical issues concerning the measurement of the determinants of hospital quality. For instance, many studies investigate the presence of a relationship between surgical volume and mortality outcomes. A statistically significant volume-outcome relationship would be consistent with learning by doing, in which hospital staff learn from treating more patients. Learning by doing is not the only plausible explanation, however; it could be instead that a hospital being high quality, as noted earlier, causes more patients to select the hospital. Luft and colleagues proposed reverse causality, terming it "selective referral."[21]

Gaynor and colleagues and a study that I coauthored have both estimated the extent to which the observed volume-outcome effect is caused by learning by doing and selective referral.[22] These studies assume that the unobserved components of the skill of a hospital staff and patient severity of illness are not clustered based on location. This then implies that one can use random variations in patient flows to understand the extent to which volume causes mortality reductions, in a similar way that the earlier literature used random variations in patient location to estimate hospital quality. This identifying assumption is similar to the earlier literature, but stronger in that the assumption is that both patient severity of illness and a hospital staff's skill are not geographically clustered.

Findings on Determinants of Hospital Quality Outcome Measures

Table 12.1 summarizes methods and findings from a number of economic studies that assess the relationship between hospital quality outcome measures—principally, mortality and ownership types. The studies all risk adjust the mortality rates, but most do not control for patient selection based on the unobserved severity of illness (since these methods are new and complex). While much of the findings have been that different types of hospitals perform similarly, some studies have found mixed evidence to the contrary. For example, Taylor and colleagues find that major teaching hospitals have significantly lower risk-adjusted mortality rates than other hospitals for hip fractures, but not for other conditions.[23] McClellan and Staiger as well as and Picone and colleagues both find that for-profit hospitals have somewhat higher risk-adjusted mortality rates than not-for-profit ones.[24] Sloan and colleagues analyze the impact of ownership type using a instrumental variables approach (a more much common method for seeking to achieve randomization than the methods described above, but one that has come under increasing criticism in recent years as well) with aggregate market characteristics (e.g., state-level measures of the proportions of for-profit and not-for-profit hospitals) as instruments.[25] They find no significant difference in risk-adjusted mortality between for-profit and not-for-profit hospitals.

Importantly, Eggleston and colleagues perform a *meta-analysis* of studies of hospital quality across types of hospitals.[26] They find that overall mortality is significantly (in a statistical sense) higher in public hospitals than in not-for-profit ones, but they find no significant differences between not-for-profit and for-profit hospitals, perhaps reflecting considerable heterogeneity among hospitals within each of the latter ownership categories. The study also performs a detailed meta-analysis of other outcome measures, including mortality from heart diseases and nonmortality outcomes. The relationships among ownership types and outcomes vary among diseases.

Given the discussion of controlling for unobserved selection, it is useful to understand how the results for these models differ from the

Table 12.1
Relation between Ownership Type and Quality

Study	Outcome, sample, and methods	Findings
Chen et al. (1999)	Cooperative Cardiovascular Project care process measures and thirty-day mortality for U.S. heart attack patients in 1994–1995, analyzed with logistic model	Top-ranked hospitals (by *U.S. News*) have about 23% lower mortality than others, 15% more aspirin use, and 28% more beta-blocker prescriptions, but lower rates of immediate reperfusion
Geweke et al. (2003)	Mortality for Los Angeles County pneumonia patients in 1989–1992, analyzed with multivariate probit model that controls for unobserved severity of illness and Bayesian inference	No significant difference between most types of hospitals; weak evidence that mortality at public hospitals is about 15% higher than at other hospitals
McClellan and Staiger (1999a)	Mortality for sample of Medicare heart attack patients in 1985–1994, analyzed with a classical linear probability model that allows for interactions across different mortality measures	In 1994, ninety-day mortality at for-profit and public hospitals is about 10% higher than at not-for-profit hospitals; no significant difference between not-for-profit and teaching hospitals
Picone et al. (2002)	Mortality for sample of Medicare patients in 1982–1994, analyzed with linear probability model with fixed effects	Hospitals that converted from not-for-profit to for-profit had increases in one-year mortality of 35%
Sloan et al. (2001)	Mortality for sample of Medicare patients in 1982–1994 for four diseases (hip fracture, stroke, heart disease, and congestive heart failure), analyzed with instrumental variables	No significant difference between not-for-profit and for-profit hospitals in terms of one-year and shorter-term mortality for these conditions
Taylor et al. (1999)	Survival time for sample of Medicare patients in 1982–1994 for four diseases, (hip fracture, stroke, heart disease, and congestive heart failure), analyzed with Cox proportional hazard model	Major teaching hospitals have 46% lower hazard of death than other hospitals for hip fractures; no significant differences for other conditions

typical findings. Similar to the existing literature, Geweke and his colleagues find that there is no statistically significant difference between the mean quality levels of private not-for-profit, for-profit, teaching, and public hospitals in Los Angeles County.[27] They do find, however, that selection based on the unobserved severity of illness is an important determinant of hospital mortality. Moreover, higher-quality hospitals do indeed attract patients with a higher unobserved severity of illness on average. More generally, their study and other ones also find that differences in the quality among hospitals explain only a small part of the variation in mortality across patients. A far larger portion is explained by patient severity of illness. Patient severity of illness can be broken into observed severity (based on risk adjusters) and unobserved severity. In Geweke and his colleagues' study, unobserved severity was, in turn, far more important than observed severity at explaining mortality.

In contrast to the mixed evidence on performance differences across different types of hospitals, the literature on the relation between hospital volume and quality is more conclusive. Roughly 70 percent of the studies find a positive and significant correlation between volume and outcomes, typically mortality, with hospitals treating more patients for a given disease having lower risk-adjusted mortality rates.[28]

As noted above, this evidence is consistent with both learning by doing and selective referral. Both Gaynor and his colleagues as well as a study I coauthored find evidence in favor of learning by doing, implying that practice does indeed help make perfect.[29] The evidence in favor of learning by doing is probably not surprising given the complexity of many surgeries and the fact that there are no close substitutes to human bodies with which to practice. In our study, we also find some limited support in favor of selective referral for some diseases.[30]

What general implications can we derive from all these studies? Since hospitals of similar types seem to perform similarly, one possible policy recommendation is that there is not too much reason to worry about hospital conversions involving a change in hospital ownership type, most of which have been from not-for-profit to for-profit, in terms of their effect on the quality of care. This policy recommendation is probably not that reassuring, given that we might worry about the effect of conversions on other attributes of hospital care besides quality. For instance, Norton and Staiger document an effect of conversions on the locations of hospitals, implying that conversions of hospitals to for-profit status might limit access to care.[31] Moreover, even if one believed that there is little difference in the mean quality levels between for-profit and not-for-profit hospitals, this does not necessarily imply that a change in ownership status due to changing government regulations would have no impact on quality.

There is a dichotomy, in sum, between the different types of evidence. On the one hand, hospital quality appears to have substantially improved over time. On the other hand, it is hard to find significant or substantial mortality differences for many conditions across a large fraction of current hospitals. Yet hospitals still have substantial room for improvement in terms of simple process measures for cardiac care. We also do not know that much about the relation between process measures of quality and outcome measures. What we do know is that many of the actual determinants of hospital mortality are still unobserved. Thus, another important policy recommendation is to try to better understand the nature of the unobservable component of patient characteristics, which would permit a sounder evaluation of the contribution of quality to mortality.

How can we understand more about the unobservable components of patient characteristics? While economists can derive clever methods to identify parameters of interest from limited sources of variation, we cannot work magic and infer something when the data are insufficient. This suggests the importance of collecting more detailed data on patient characteristics that influence mortality as well as other outcome measures.

A final general recommendation for economic research is to focus on using economic principles in evaluating the quality of economic care— in particular, the marginal cost versus the marginal benefit calculation—rather than simply reasoning that any care with a positive marginal benefit should be provided. Many scholars advocate higher quality without directly addressing the issue of how much quality is provided by the market relative to the efficient level. For instance, David Cutler advocates giving hospitals greater incentives to produce high-quality care, which implicitly assumes that hospital quality is lower than the socially optimal level.[32] A large medical literature on medical errors takes the same approach, without explicitly recognizing that the efficient level of medical errors is likely to be greater than zero.[33]

One study does explicitly examine the question of whether quality is higher than the efficient level.[34] This study examines tort reform that lowers the liability for physicians. It finds that tort reform causes hospitals to perform fewer tests while quality, gauged in terms of mortality, does not suffer. This suggests that hospital quality may be higher than the social optimum in certain dimensions due to malpractice laws. Together, these studies imply that the overall question of where quality stands relative to the efficient level is both interesting and unsettled.

Report Cards for Hospitals

In order for market mechanisms such as competition to cause hospital markets to reflect optimal quality, a crucial precondition is that patients or their physicians must be able to evaluate hospital quality levels for hospitals in their market. For this to be so, the quality must be observable, or at least the patients and their physicians must be able to accurately infer the quality from observable information.

Yet hospital quality is likely to be difficult to observe directly because of the complexity of hospital services and because hospitals provide a multitude of services with different attributes. Moreover, markets for information about quality are often slow to evolve, because information has many aspects of a *public good* and is often hard to value beforehand.[35] Many mechanisms seek to provide information about the quality of health care providers. Physicians are supposed to act as agents for patients in making decisions about hospitals. Nevertheless, physicians may steer patients toward themselves or close colleagues, because of incentives or a lack of complete information.

Over the last decade, several private and governmental organizations have sponsored formal releases of ratings that report performance information directly to consumers. The idea behind this is that it is useful to help consumers to make optimal choices. While existing regulatory mechanisms are likely effective at ensuring basic competency by hospitals, they are not particularly useful at helping to steer consumers to the appropriate level of quality within the set of existing hospitals. Here, I consider the impact of releases of information by third parties, typically government or advocacy organizations. Other studies examine the impact of advertising laws, which regulate the information that providers can publicize.[36]

Table 12.2 summarizes the methods and findings of several economic studies that assess the impact of report cards for health plans and hospitals on demand. One of the earliest and largest releases of hospital report card ratings was from the U.S. government. Between 1986 and

Table 12.2
Impact of Report Cards on Individual Choices

Study	Information release analyzed in study	Findings
Chernew et al. (2007)	Six performance domains for health plans based on HEDIS measures and General Motors' (GM) own information, distributed to salaried GM employees in 1996 and 1997	Information release caused 3% of people to switch toward plans, with a value of information of $20 per enrollee
Dafny and Dranove (2005)	Three performance domains for health plans based on HEDIS and CAHPS measures and disenrollment levels, distributed to Medicare enrollees in 1999 and 2000	In a hypothetical market with three HMOs, four years of report cards would cause high-quality plan to increase market share from 4.7% to 6.5%
Dranove et al. (2003)	Hospital- and/or surgeon-level risk-adjusted mortality rates for hospitals in NY and PA, publicly released in 1990 and 1992, respectively	Costs for coronary artery bypass surgery (CABG) patients in NY and PA fell by $300 relative to control states in the year *prior* to admission; CABGs were being performed on a different, less severely ill population
Jin and Sorenson (2006)	Two performance domains for health plans based on employee satisfaction surveys, distributed to federal annuitants (mostly retired federal employees) in 1998 and 1999	Information release caused about 0.7% of individuals to switch plans, with a value of information of $3.39 per enrollee
Mennemeyer et al. (1997)	Hospital-level risk-adjusted mortality rates released to the public between 1986–1992	A hospital of mean size with a risk-adjusted mortality rate two standard deviations above the mean would see its admissions drop by 35% as a result of the report cards
Peterson et al. (1998)	Same as NY data by Dranove et al. (2003)	Information release caused thirty-day risk-adjusted mortality rate to fall by 14% more than the national trend and the percent of NY State residents who received out-of-state bypass surgery to fall by 9.6%

1992, the Medicare program reported risk-adjusted hospital mortality rates for Medicare patients. Mennemeyer and colleagues examine this release of information and find that adverse mortality outcomes resulted in a small, but statistically significant impact on patient demand: a *doubling* of the mortality rate for a hospital resulted in only one fewer patient per week.[37]

There are many possible reasons why the impact of the Medicare report cards might be so tiny. One likely reason, discussed above, is that the risk-adjusted mortality rates are an inaccurate and biased measure of quality. Another potential reason is that people may not have been adequately informed of the ratings at the time they selected a particular hospital. Managed care plans can be helpful in this regard. For example, United Healthcare, a large managed care plan, identifies patients planning to undergo costly procedures such as organ transplants and provides them with a list of high-quality hospitals.

Pressure from groups concerned about the inaccuracy of these ratings ultimately caused the Medicare program to stop publishing them. State governments, though, started publishing similar information subsequently. For example, New York State started releasing report cards for surgeons and hospitals in late 1989. Like the earlier Medicare report cards, the state report cards were typically based on risk-adjusted mortality rates. Yet unlike Medicare's, the state report cards were generally specific to one condition or procedure. The New York report cards were based on risk-adjusted mortality rates for coronary bypass surgery. Peterson and colleagues analyze the New York data and find that access to bypass surgery in New York increased following the introduction of the report cards; fewer New York residents received out-of-state bypass surgery.[38] The study does not examine whether or not highly rated hospitals within New York increased their market shares. But it does look at the influence of report cards on mortality (see below).

Following its first attempt, in 2005, the U.S. government started publishing hospital ratings on the Web through a database called *Hospital Compare*.[39] Unlike the earlier Medicare ratings, the *Hospital Compare* ones only report process measures of care (e.g., the percent of heart attack patients given reperfusion—a method leading to the restoration of flow to the heart—within two hours of admission), and concern heart attack, heart failure, pneumonia, and surgical infection prevention. I am not aware of any study that has investigated the impact of the *Hospital Compare* ratings due to their recent release.

Report Cards for Health Plans

Many of the released report cards after the year 2000 have informed consumers about the quality of health plans rather than directly about the quality of hospitals. These releases have resulted from earlier complaints with hospital report cards and because health plans are seen as more central to consumer choice than hospitals. Most of these releases of information are based on data aggregated from the Health Plan Employer Data Information Set (HEDIS) and the Consumer Assessment of Health Plan Survey (CAHPS). HEDIS is a set of standardized performance measures for health plans developed by a private not-for-profit organization (the National Center for Quality Assurance) and designed to allow for comparisons across health plans, while CAHPS is a set of standardized consumer survey measures for health plans developed by a public/private partnership with roughly the same goals as HEDIS.[40]

These databases report consumer survey responses such as patient satisfaction, health care delivery measures such as the percent of providers that remain with a plan from year to year, and health care process measures such as the rate of mammographies and immunizations among individuals for whom these procedures are medically appropriate. These databases include some measures of hospital care, such as the percent of patients who receive surgical care following a heart attack. Importantly, they include virtually no outcome measures of hospital performance, perhaps because of the controversy surrounding the earlier Medicare release of risk-adjusted hospital mortality rates.

Several studies consider the impact of ratings information on the choice of health plans. As with hospital report cards, the basic methodology of these studies is to focus on a release of ratings and then examine how the release affected choice behavior. Dafny and Dranove quantify the effect of the largest report card release to date, which was the national release of ratings information on Medicare health maintenance organizations (HMOs).[41] Starting in 1999, the Medicare program mailed all its enrollees a report card with three reported measures of quality, derived from HEDIS and CAHPS data. Dafny and Dranove find that only one of the measures resulted in a significantly positive demand response in which people switched to highly rated plans. This measure, which varied slightly across years, was based on a survey of patient satisfaction with the quality of care of the plan.

Aside from the three reported measures of plan performance, the Medicare program collected other measures that it did not report to enrollees. Dafny and Dranove observe that individuals were already moving toward highly rated plans in the years before 1999, but that report cards amplified that movement, roughly doubling its speed. Nonetheless, the impact of the report cards was moderate, with report cards causing an increased market share for highly rated plans of about 1.8 percent in a simulated market with three plans. Most other studies report similar findings—namely, that report cards cause people to switch toward highly rated health plans, but that the effect is moderate.

Some recent studies have qualified the dollar value that the information provides to consumers, using a formal *Bayesian learning* approach.[42] Chernew and colleagues estimate the value of a release of information from General Motors.[43] This large automaker distributed a HEDIS-based report card to its salaried employees. In the context of a Bayesian learning model, the value of information in utility terms can be quantified as the difference in the *expected utility* of the consumer between the choice that the consumer would have made with and without information.[44] Thus, information is valuable to the extent that it might cause consumers to change their choice of health plan. One can transform the utility units into dollar units by dividing by the marginal utility of an extra dollar of income, which one can derive by estimating the relative willingness to pay for similar plans with different prices.

Chernew and colleagues evaluate the value of the information to consumers from the General Motors report card to be a moderate $20 per enrollee, consistent with the fact that about 3 percent of the employees switched health plans as a result of the report card. They attribute the moderate value of information to ratings that are probably not fully informative and are imprecise relative to prior information about health plans. Similar to Dafny and Dranove, Chernew and colleagues find that individuals value the patient satisfaction survey response measure.[45] Yet they also find that individuals value medical and surgical care measures of quality more than all other reported measures, even though these measures are based only on the rates of performing surgeries rather than surgical or medical outcomes.

Jin and Sorenson examine a release of report card information for retired U.S. government employees; the report cards were constructed from patient satisfaction surveys of these employees.[46] They report a much smaller value of information than Chernew and his colleagues, of only $3.39 per employee, with report cards causing less than 1 percent of employees to switch health plans. Both of these studies base the value of information solely on demand responses, and do not directly measure actual improvements to health that may or may not occur as a result of report cards.

The value of and response to information varies across report card releases. The methodologies used to estimate the value of information are similar across releases with the noted exception that control groups, defined here as people who were not exposed to the ratings, varied substantially across studies. Studies that have added superior controls such as the impact of nonreported measures, however, have found that these controls did not significantly change the conclusions. Thus, the differences across studies are probably due to fundamental differences in the releases. These could include details as to how the performance measures were presented and distributed, the aggregation techniques used to construct the measures, the set of enrollees that the researchers analyzed (employees versus retirees), and the performance domains that were reported to enrollees. Unfortunately, there is little systematic evidence about which of these differences across studies are the most important empirically.

In spite of the differences in the response to information across particular studies, each study mentioned finds that consumers respond to health plan information in a positive way, in the sense of switching toward highly rated plans. Given the assumption that the information is accurate, this implies that report cards create value for consumers. It is somewhat more ambiguous whether or not report cards create value for the insurers, since higher-quality plans may cost more. Nonetheless, the employer or other insurer may also benefit from higher-quality plans to the extent that they lower future health care costs or keep employees more productive. Hence, it would appear worthwhile to distribute this information to the consumer conditional on having collected it.

Whether or not the information is worth more than the cost of gathering it is a different question. To the extent that the information is distributed to a large set of consumers, it is likely to be worth more than the costs. For instance, Jin and Sorenson estimate the cost of collecting HEDIS and CAHPS information to be substantially less than $20 million. This implies that a report card based on these data that is worth $3.70 per enrollee would be worthwhile if it were distributed to six million individuals, which is only 2 percent of U.S. consumers.

In sum, even though these ratings appear to be useful, there is much about them that remains unsatisfactory. The demand response to information conveyed by the ratings, though positive, is variable and weak. The weak response may be because people are fully informed prior to reading the ratings and/or because they trust their physicians to make choices for them. Yet this is contradicted by the fact that individuals report in surveys that they would like to obtain ratings information.[47] It is therefore likely that the response is weak because the report cards are not fully informative.

Supplier Responses to Report Cards

Some recent studies have examined whether or not there is a *provider* rather than just a consumer response to report cards. Economic predictions regarding provider responses to report cards are not clear. For instance, providers might oppose report cards because of the possibility of adverse selection. Many health economists have heard stories of health plans that offered excellent AIDS care in the early 1990s, but that did not want to be identified as such for fear of attracting too many AIDS patients. Even without adverse selection, hospitals may have an interest in keeping the ratings secret, as this may soften price competition.[48]

The hope of policymakers who design report cards is that the report cards cause low-quality providers to improve their quality of care to avoid being shunned by consumers. In this way, provider responses can improve the quality of care for everyone, and hence be even more socially useful than consumer responses. In another context, Jin and Leslie examine report cards for restaurant hygiene quality and finding exactly this pattern.[49] The hygiene report cards caused more people to choose high-hygiene restaurants. But they also caused restaurant hygiene to improve across the board. In aggregate, the report cards caused a large drop in hospitalizations for food-borne illnesses.

Dranove and his colleagues obtain evidence of perverse provider responses to the release of hospital report cards in New York (discussed earlier) and Pennsylvania.[50] Previously, Peterson and colleagues had reported that the New York report card resulted in substantially better outcomes following bypass surgery, and an increase in observable severity of illness indicators, which led to the conclusion that patient access had improved.[51]

Differently than Peterson and colleagues, Dranove and colleagues implement a difference-in-difference identification strategy to evaluate the impact of the report cards on *patients with heart attacks* (not all of whom received coronary artery bypasses), where the experience of neighboring states (e.g., New Jersey) serves as a control group for the states that implement a report card. Dranove and his coauthors find that after the report cards were implemented, persons who received bypass surgery had $300 lower health expenditures *prior* to their bypass surgery relative to the control states. The lower expenditures are an indicator of lower illness severity at the time patients are admitted to the hospital. In contrast, the mean medical expenditures prior to a heart attack for heart attack patients did not change relative to the control states. Their explanation of this pattern is that the report cards caused hospitals to give bypass surgeries to higher proportions of low-risk patients who would not have received the surgery if the report cards had not existed.

Other findings from Dranove and colleagues also support this basic view: the report cards led to a smaller proportion of persons obtaining any cardiac surgery (including diagnostics) within one day of their heart attacks, suggesting that report cards might cause some medical and hospital staff members to withhold immediate treatment due to the risk of poor report card scores. Further, the introduction of the report cards led to a lower use of cheaper substitute technologies such as angioplasties, again indicating the increased use of bypass surgery among low-risk patients. Thus, Dranove and his coauthors' results suggest that Peterson and his colleagues' evidence that report cards resulted in better outcomes in coronary artery bypass surgery patients was misleading; what changed following the introduction of report cards was the case mix of persons undergoing such surgery, not the quality of care provided to patients. The studies in combination imply that the difference in patient mix following the report cards release is based on unobservable factors.

In contrast to the negative impacts just described, Dranove and colleagues also observe that the New York and Pennsylvania report cards caused more high-cost patients to seek care at large academic medical centers. This type of sorting plausibly has a desirable impact: such centers may be more capable of caring for patients with a high illness severity. Overall, then, it is unclear whether the report cards improved or lowered social welfare.

Policy Implications of Report Cards

The research on report cards highlights some important policy implications. First, considering consumer choices, a large release of report card information, such as to Medicare enrollees, is likely to be worthwhile as long as it provides consumers with information that is at least somewhat more accurate than consumers' prior knowledge. The evidence also suggests that more informative report cards would be useful.

Considering the supply response, imprecise report cards may be worse than none at all. Thus, not only is precise information more useful than imprecise information, imprecise information may be worse than no information, because of the *endogeneity* of provider responses.[52] While Dranove and his colleagues analyze report cards based on outcome measures, even process measures are vulnerable to gaming. For example, suppose that a hypothetical health plan report card were to focus exclusively on the mammography rate for the medically appropriate population. Then health plans could "game" this type of measure in at least two ways. First, they could increase the rate by targeting middle-class women who are more likely to obtain mammographies in the absence of any encouragement from the health plan. Second, they could also increase this rate by focusing on mammographies at the expense of other valuable services (e.g., PSA tests for prostate cancer) not reported in the information release.

Because outcome measures are of fundamental importance and because many types of report cards can be gamed, report cards should include outcome measures. Still, it is a challenge for economists and policymakers to design report card mechanisms that are useful to consumers but also not vulnerable to gaming. Toward this end, some of methods to estimate hospital quality that are described above may be useful. Although the specific methods vary in key details, they share a common feature, which is their reliance on patient location as a randomizer. Since individuals are not likely to move in response to releases of information, location-based methods may be useful in constructing a report card that cannot be easily gamed.

Even these methods will be deficient in some respects. One central problem is the imprecision of the underlying data, and methods that are based on unobserved selection will generally be less precise than simpler ones. Report cards are already quite imprecise, and the use of indirect methods such as instrumental variables would make them less precise still. Also, hospitals may object to being judged based on factors that are somewhat outside their control, such as the treatment of patients who are located near them. This may make it difficult on a practical level to implement these methods. It thus remains a difficult task to develop useful report cards.

Effect of Competition on Hospital Quality

Understanding the relation between competition and quality is a central issue in economics in general. Economists are interested in understanding the optimal level of competition in a market. Moreover, the link between competition and quality is central in designing antitrust and other regulatory policies.

In the hospital sector, regulations include basic antitrust statutes that prevent mergers that increase market power, certificate of need laws that regulate entry in about half the U.S. states, and critical access hospital designations that allow for monopoly rents in small markets, among many others.

Health care economists are interested in how the incentives created by competition affect the quality of hospital care. Both quality and prices may change in crucial ways following a change in hospital industry structure. Furthermore, economic theories do not provide an unambiguous prediction of the level of quality provision of a monopolist relative to the social optimum, or even the direction in which consolidation will affect quality. Gaynor, in a survey article, analyzes the relationship between competition and quality.[53] For Gaynor, the simplest context to understand the properties of the equilibrium level of quality provision is one in which the price is fixed, such as by Medicare, and in which quality is perfectly observable. In this case, if the prices are higher than the marginal costs, then quality increases with the degree to which a hospital market is competitive. Even in this simple context, the equilibrium provision of quality may or may not be higher than the socially optimal level.

If prices are not fixed, as in markets in which private health insurers operate, competition may lower prices, making a given consumer more willing to pay for quality due to the income effect (consumers with a given income are not able to buy more hospital care), but the overall impact also depends on consumers' preferences about quality. In general, the change in equilibrium quality provision following a change in competition will depend on the change in the willingness to pay for quality by the "marginal" patient.[54] It is ambiguous whether quality will be over- or underprovided in equilibrium, as the socially optimal quality level depends on the willingness to pay for quality by the *average* patient. Incomplete information about quality adds another level of complication. In this case, firms may credibly signal their quality through price, implying a different force that will affect the quality and price.[55]

Because of the theoretical uncertainties regarding the impacts of competition on quality, empirical evidence is necessarily important in guiding antitrust and other regulatory policies in the hospital sector. Several empirical studies evaluate the impact of competition on quality by regressing measures of competition on quality.

Like hospital quality, competition is measured in various ways. For decades, experts in the economic field of industrial organization have used the structure, conduct, performance (SCP) paradigm, which is roughly parallel to the structure, process, and outcome measures described for hospital quality above.[56] The SCP paradigm derives its name from the fact that it assumes that industry structure (e.g., market concentration) causes firm conduct (e.g., pricing behavior) that then results in a certain level of performance (e.g., welfare relative to the social optimum). Given the SCP framework, government policy can concern itself with industry structure and choose the structure that maximizes performance. To understand the structure that maximizes performance, it is then useful to regress performance on either conduct or industry structure to evaluate the sign and magnitude of the effect that is actually being caused by industry concentration.

Antitrust policy on hospital mergers is generally directly influenced by this type of SCP regression.[57] The chain of causality that is implicit in the SCP paradigm, however, is not necessarily accurate. A central problem is that competition is likely to be endogenous, implying that a regression of quality on competition cannot be used to derive consistent implications of the causal effect of quality on competition. Specifically, the number of firms in an industry—or more broadly, the level of competition—is likely related to unobserved factors that might also affect quality. If a metropolitan area were to contain a hospital or hospital system of great renown (e.g., the Cleveland Clinic), for example, this hospital is likely to both be of high quality and attract many patients, leading to a concentrated market. This would generate a positive correlation of quality with a measure of concentration, but this correlation would not be causal; if laissez-faire antitrust policies resulted in many hospital mergers, this result does not imply that hospital quality is likely to then rise. The endogeneity problem is likely to exist regardless of whether one uses a Herfindahl index as a measure of concentration or a simpler measure, such as the market share of the four largest firms (generally called a four-firm concentration ratio).

Some recent studies have attempted to evaluate the causal impact of competition on quality in a way that controls for the endogeneity problem. Kessler and McClellan use a *predicted* Herfindahl index instead of the actual Herfindahl index.[58] Specifically, they predict the determinants of hospital choice for each patient based on factors that include the distance to a hospital, assuming that people do not locate their residences because they think that they will need a hospital or want a high-quality hospital. But the regression used to predict hospital choice does not include variables likely to be endogenous. Using the coefficients on distance and other measures, they then predict the market shares for a given zip code and sum across zip codes in order to determine the predicted Herfindahl index for each hospital. The predicted Herfindahl indexes do not vary based on whether or not a market contains a hospital of great renown, unlike the regular Herfindahl index (or four-firm concentration ratio), and thus it is not vulnerable to the criticism of endogeneity noted above. The study also incorporates hospital-level fixed effects, implying that it can identify the effects of competition on quality by changes in market structure such as hospital exits that change the predicted Herfindahl index.

Using a sample of Medicare heart attack patients, Kessler and McClellan find that prior to 1991, competition reduced quality, while after 1991, competition increased quality. This change is plausible, given changes in hospital payment practices and the growth of competitive pressures from HMOs that occurred during the 1980s.

Using data from the early 1990s, Robert Town and I also investigate the impact of competition on quality, but we allow for different effects for Medicare, Medicaid, HMO, and fee-for-service and self-pay patients, and separately examine the quality of treatment for pneumonia and heart attack care.[59] We similarly develop a measure of predicted competition that sums the predicted Herfindahl indexes across patients by the likelihood that they choose the hospital. We report similar findings for both diseases, which are that competition for Medicare patients decreased quality but that competition for HMO patients increased quality.

Competition for Medicare and HMO patients is fundamentally different because of the nature of price competition. Since 1984, Medicare reimburses hospitals with a prospective payment system that is based on the diagnosis or procedure, and is largely invariant to the quality of care provided. Thus, an explanation for the Medicare results is that Medicare reimbursements are at a sufficiently low level for our sample that hospitals do not invest in high-quality care when competition is fierce, because they are not that interested in serving Medicare patients. In contrast, it is likely that a high-quality hospital can extract higher prices from an HMO, as including the high-quality hospital in its network would help the HMO obtain enrollees. For instance, most major metropolitan areas contain one or two medical schools, each with an affiliated chain of hospitals. Including these hospitals in a health plan is often seen as necessary for a plan to be high quality. We also note that our results provide an explanation for the change in the effect of competition on quality noted by Kessler and McClellan: the number of HMO patients increased dramatically during the late 1980s and early 1990s. Since competition had a positive effect on quality for HMO patients but a negative effect for Medicare patients, the increased number of HMO patients could have caused the combined impact of competition on quality to switch from negative to positive.

Another study, by Hamilton and McManus, examines the market for in vitro fertilization using data from 1995 to 2001.[60] There is an important observable process measure of quality for in vitro fertilization, which is the number of embryos transferred in each cycle of treatment. More embryos leads to a higher probability of multiple births, and multiple births lead to medical complications and are enormously costly. Similar to the study I coauthored with Town, this study finds that competition leads to higher-quality treatments in the sense that clinics in competitive markets transfer less embryos on average.

If the higher-quality care attributable to increased competition is socially optimal, these results suggest that the dual forces of competition and managed care help move hospital markets toward the optimal level of quality. Although some prominent scholars such as Cutler advocate moving toward higher quality, the above studies do not provide any systematic evidence that high-quality care is better from a point of view of achieving the social optimum.[61]

Some recent studies attempt to analyze the cost-benefit trade-off of hospital competition, allowing for the fact that competition has an effect on both the quality and price. Vivian Ho and her colleagues examine a relatively rare and complex surgery for pancreatic cancer called the Whipple with the aim of understanding the optimal level of market concentration.[62] They find that higher concentration leads to higher prices but also to higher volumes, which leads to better outcomes from learning by doing. By combining the price increase with a dollar value of life figure, they estimate that consolidation of Whipple facilities to a monopoly would be optimal, but that half of the mortality gains are taken away by the higher prices resulting from consolidation. Yaa Akosa Antwi and her colleagues develop a modified version of the Herfindahl index that accounts for the fact that hospitals are differentiated products, where distance is a central component of the differentiation.[63]

More generally, these studies are limited in their usefulness because they are based on a Herfindahl index. The use of a predicted Herfindahl index alleviates some of the endogeneity problems with using a regular Herfindahl index. Yet even a predicted Herfindahl index is a summary measure of competition that misses many important facets of competition. For instance, the notion that volume might benefit outcomes, as developed by Ho and her colleagues, cannot be captured by any simple index, since an index typically measures only concentration, not volume.[64] It is difficult for this reason to evaluate how or whether these models would be robust to different medical technologies and policy environments. Thus, these models are probably best used to understand relatively short-term antitrust policy implications.

Although it is difficult to specify, estimate, and identify models of hospital competition, some studies have made progress toward modeling hospital behavior in a framework that allows for endogenous choices of quality and pricing decisions by hospitals. Town and I provide a dynamic model of competition in the hospital industry in which hospitals can compete on prices and invest to improve their quality.[65] We use the model to evaluate the impact of changes in Medicare policy, and the implementation of universal health insurance on price, quality, and welfare levels for different consumer groups.

Abigail Tay estimates a structural model of demand for hospital services, in which quality, measured by mortality, enters into the utility function for patients.[66] This study can potentially be used in conjunction with a supply-side model to analyze the incentives of firms to provide quality care.[67]

In my opinion, there are concerns about the model and identification strategies for this literature that limit its immediate usefulness in an antitrust policy setting. Nevertheless, this type of analysis provides a promising direction in which research should progress for economists to be able to understand the impact of competition and competition policies on hospital quality.[68] The use of more sophisticated methods together with better data should allow researchers to come closer to the difficult goal of evaluating the impact of competition on quality.

What overall implications can we obtain from the literature? One important implication is that competition appears to improve quality, and the effect is potentially large. Another implication is that the impact of quality may vary based on whether the market is one with a fixed, regulated price (such as Medicare) or one where hospitals with higher quality can charge higher prices. Apart from that, there is no real consensus on the effect of hospital competition on quality or the optimal regulatory policies toward hospital competition. The reason why there may be no consistent impact may not be because these studies are not measuring competition or quality accurately but rather because they are examining the impact of quality at different times for different procedures, and these impacts are likely to vary across time and procedures.

Conclusion

This chapter has provided an evaluation and synthesis of the contribution of some of the economics literature on the measurement of hospital quality, and the link between hospital quality, the provision of information, and hospital competition. Hospital quality has improved substantially since the 1970s. Yet it is difficult to characterize many of the factors that result in a high-quality hospital, and it is difficult to estimate hospital quality from outcome data such as mortality.

To foster competition among health care providers, many recent governmental and private organizations have provided formal information to consumers in the form of report cards. Consumers modify their choices of hospitals and health plans based on this information. There is little evidence, however, that the information is accurate, and there is evidence that report cards cause providers to game the system—

for instance, by providing surgeries to individuals who would otherwise not have received surgeries. The evidence on competition and quality is even more mixed. Studies have found that competition can affect quality, but the direction appears to depend on the type of reimbursement system and other specifics of the quality measure.

Unlike some other fields considered in this book, notably health capital (chapter 3) and innovation (chapter 9), there is no unified model of the hospital industry on which to base an evaluation of the nature of competition, quality, and information provision. For this reason, each of the studies and insights mentioned here examine different pieces of the big puzzle of how to improve performance for this large and critical segment of the economy. Progress in understanding the industry will be useful. A whole host of government and private sector policies influence this sector. To date, many of the policies that have been implemented have had unintended effects or in other ways are far from optimal.

Notes

1. Smith et al. (2006).

2. American Hospital Association (2002); Gaynor (2006). The Herfindahl index is the sum of the ratio of the share of each firm's output in the total output in the market squared, multiplied by ten thousand. This measure yields an index that varies from zero (perfect competition) to ten thousand (pure monopoly).

3. Donabedian (1985).

4. For instance, the *Flexner Report* of 1910, which led to the establishment of modern medical education, argued that business ethics are incompatible with socially useful medical education.

5. See Cutler (2004).

6. See, for example, chapters 4 and 5.

7. Nyman (1999b) details this point further.

8. See, for example, Dranove et al. (2003).

9. Cutler et al. (1998).

10. See <http://www.dartmouthatlas.org> (accessed November 19, 2006).

11. See, for example, Wennberg et al. (2002).

12. Skinner et al. (2006). By regional fixed effects, I mean that the study completely controls for non-time-varying regional differences in outcomes by allowing for a separate dummy variable to capture the base outcome in each region.

13. See TECH Research Network (2001).

14. Chen et al. (1999). The Cooperative Cardiovascular Project, which began in 1992, followed persons admitted to hospitals with a heart attack. An exception to the general finding of a correlation between "Best Hospitals" and adherence to guidelines for heart attack care was in the percent of patients receiving immediate reperfusion.

15. Donabedian (1985).

16. These methods are based on the same statistical idea as instrumental variables, although some of them use more complicated econometric tools necessary to address the peculiarities of the hospital quality estimation problem.

17. McClellan et al. (1994).

18. Gowrisankaran and Town (1997); Geweke et al. (2003).

19. Geweke et al. (2003). There are two types of statistical analyses: Bayesian and frequentist (classical). Bayesian analysis is based on Bayes law, formalized in the eighteenth century by Thomas Bayes.

20. McClellan and Staiger (1999b).

21. Luft et al. (1987).

22. Gaynor et al. (2005); Gowrisankaran et al. (2006).

23. Taylor et al. (1999).

24. McClellan and Staiger (1999a); Picone et al. (2002).

25. Sloan et al. (2001).

26. Eggleston et al. (2006). A *meta-analysis* is a study that combines the results of several studies to derive more precise, overall results.

27. Geweke et al. (2003).

28. Halm et al. (2002). For pneumonia, Geweke et al. (2003) find more mixed evidence: that the smallest and largest hospitals, measured in terms of number of beds, have the highest mean quality.

29. Gaynor et al. (2005); Gowrisankaran et al. (2006).

30. Gowrisankaran et al. (2006).

31. Norton and Staiger (1994).

32. Cutler (2004).

33. See, for example, Zhan and Miller (2003).

34. Kessler and McClellan (1996).

35. A public good is one that is nonrival (my knowledge of quality does not impinge your knowledge) and nonexcludable (it is hard to prevent the sharing of information).

36. For an analysis of the optometry market, see Rizzo and Zeckhauser (1990). For evidence on the effects of pharmaceutical advertising and the associated public policy issues, see chapter 7 in this volume.

37. Mennemeyer et al. (1997).

38. Peterson et al. (1998).

39. See <http://www.hospitalcompare.hhs.gov> (accessed January 20, 2007).

40. See <http://www.ncqa.org/programs/hedis/> and <http://www.cahps.ahrq.gov/default.asp>, respectively, for details.

41. Dafny and Dranove (2005).

42. Bayesian learning models are formal, rational models of information acquisition based on Bayes law.

43. Chernew et al. (2002).

44. Expected utility means the average utility level that will accrue to the consumer.

45. Dafny and Dranove (2005).

46. Jin and Sorenson (2006).

47. Hibbard and Jewett (1996).

48. Andrew Daughety and Jennifer Reinganum (2006) show that firms can have this type of incentive in equilibrium.

49. Jin and Leslie (2003).

50. Dranove et al. (2003).

51. Peterson et al. (1998).

52. This means that provider responses may adjust in response to the report card environment.

53. Gaynor (2006).

54. The marginal patient here is the one who requires just the level of quality provided by the hospital to select that hospital. Nonmarginal patients would select the hospital if it offered a lower level of quality. The average willingness to pay for a particular quality level reflects the willingness to pay of marginal as well as nonmarginal patients.

55. See Daughety and Reinganum (2006).

56. See Bain (1956).

57. Capps et al. (2003).

58. Kessler and McClellan (2000).

59. Gowrisankaran and Town (2003).

60. Hamilton and McManus (2005).

61. Cutler (2004).

62. Ho et al. (2005).

63. Akosa Antwi (2006).

64. Ho et al. (2005).

65. Gowrisankaran and Town (1997).

66. Tay (2003).

67. Although chapter 3 in this volume concerns the production of health capital rather than hospital quality and demand, these models are also similar to those analyzed in that chapter, in that both estimate the fundamental parameters behind endogenous health care decisions.

68. This is also an issue for the studies discussed in chapter 3 of this volume.

13

Summing Up

Frank A. Sloan and
Hirschel Kasper

This concluding chapter is organized around the three themes of theory, empirical evidence, and public policy. Reflecting the empirical orientation of the health economics field, much of the evidence on incentives and their effects presented in this book has been empirical. Economic theory is the basis for reliable empirical research; but empirical findings have implications not only for the analysis of health care but also for theoretical issues in many other contexts. Although improving public policy decision making is an ultimate goal of empirical research on incentives, most scholars in the field of health economics focus on obtaining empirical evidence, which has relevance to policy formulation. The task of actually choosing and implementing public policies is properly left to others.

Theoretical Issues

Decision Making in Health Care: Are People and Institutions Rational and Forward-Looking?

A key assumption in economic analysis is that people, as individual and household decision makers as well as decision makers for organizations, are rational and forward-looking. By rationality, economists mean that decision makers take account of all information available to them at the time that decisions are made in making choices.

The rationality assumption is critical to most economic analysis, but as we have seen, economists employ it in differing contexts. At one pole is the notion that each person always acts rationally, or at least the working assumption of rationality is generally quite satisfactory; at the other pole is the notion that people can be caught up in what others are doing and abandon their rationality for a variety of singular events.

Many economists interpret the rationality assumption to imply that people act rationally collectively or on average; individuals may not act fully rationally but their behavior as a group or market is consistent with what would be expected, more or less, from rational behavior.

This does not eliminate the possibility that new information pertinent to the decision-making process becomes available over time. Choices depend on preferences, the costs associated with alternative options, and the decision maker's opportunity set. In terms of the mechanics of optimization, rationality involves seeking to make oneself as well-off as possible given such constraints as one's financial budget and available time (see chapter 4). Welfare economics involves comparisons of various alternatives in terms of their effects on individuals' well-being, given the available resources. As Aaron notes in chapter 2, inference about whether one choice is to be preferred over another in welfare economics is based on the assumption that individuals have well-defined and stable preferences.

Much of health economists' research on incentives has involved the assumptions of rationality and forward-looking behavior. A case in point is Grossman's model of health capital, described by Gilleskie in chapter 3. To establish a theoretical framework for studying the effects of important incentives such as changes in price on the quantity demanded, the standard economic framework suffices. The standard (to economics) framework for analyzing pharmaceutical company investment decisions used by Sloan and Hsieh in chapter 9 seems to do a good job in explaining investment decisions. It seems unlikely that the companies themselves would find this analytic framework implausible.

In several chapters, the assumption of rational and forward-looking behavior and as well as the stability of preferences is challenged. Some go so far as to question whether more choice is really better than less choice, if the many alternatives generate confusion.

To the extent that people are limited or bounded in their decision-making power, having more choice may be worse than less choice. As Aaron argues in chapter 2, at a minimum, under these circumstances, having more choice should increase the costs of reaching decisions. Are people really better off with more rather than fewer health insurance plans among which to choose? As Newhouse and Sinaiko observe in chapter 4, with nontrivial deliberation costs, rather than evaluate the present discounted value of utility associated with every possible option, decision makers may simply adhere to rules of thumb or heuristics in making choices, especially in complex situations. These heuristics may result in the individual failing to maximize utility. On the other hand, in spite of dire predictions that elderly persons would not be able to decide among the many alternatives presented to them by the Medicare Part D (prescription drug) program, most people choosing a Part D plan found their way through all the permutations to an appropriate provider. Economists traditionally have generally favored more over fewer options.

A new branch of economics, behavioral economics, questions the standard assumptions of the discipline. As discussed by Newhouse and Sinaiko in chapter 4, the field of behavioral economics studies the ways in which the decision making of economic agents deviates from rationality. Several chapters in this book apply behavioral economic concepts to incentives in health and health care. Often, there is a plea for additional research since currently, there is only a limited body of empirical evidence on health and health care to suggest that behavioral economics will improve more conventional economic models of decision making in the health field. Neuroeconomics, an even newer movement than behavioral economics, seeks to examine the biological foundations of behavior operating through the functioning of the brain to understand the biology behind choices.

Psychologists tend to view the world quite differently from economists, favoring the view that people are myopic rather than forward-looking, swayed by how alternative options are framed, and if rational, boundedly rational at best. Rather than being made on cold, calculating basis, choices are often influenced by emotions. Self-control problems make it difficult for people to actually execute their plans. Neither the pure economic nor the pure psychological views are likely to be correct all of the time, and it may depend on whether and how quickly people learn the results of their decisions, and can change.

In no single area has the assumption of rational and forward-looking behavior been challenged more than in the use of addictive substances, although even here, standard economic models exist, as Cawley's discussion in chapter 7 of the Becker-Murphy rational addiction model illustrates.[1] A common observation of persons who are addicted, or perhaps not biologically addicted but prone to consume goods that are not beneficial to future health, such as delicious desserts, is what one might term a "mañana effect."

"I will quit smoking tomorrow," or "I will start my diet tomorrow." More formally, it is as if people have two discount rates. Between today and tomorrow, people are highly impatient, preferring consumption today; but between tomorrow and the next day and the next day and the day after that, people are patient, considering the downstream effects of tomorrow's consumption on well-being the day after tomorrow and so on. This phenomenon is termed "hyperbolic discounting," described by Newhouse and Sinaiko in chapter 4 and Cawley in chapter 7. As Cawley notes, time-inconsistent preferences are useful for understanding what would otherwise appear to be irrational behavior, such as when smokers say they want to quit smoking tomorrow, but when tomorrow comes, smokers often or even generally put off quitting for later. In a sense, people with time-inconsistent preferences have a principal-agent problem with their future selves, and must find ways to precommit their future selves to the course of action that will require short-run sacrifices in order to maximize long-run utility.

The empirical evidence accumulated to date on hyperbolic discounting, however, is not nearly as strong as the intuition. This is clearly a topic for future theoretical, econometric (to identify the two discount rates econometrically), and empirical research.

Various chapters in this book point to fruitful areas for future research on behavioral economics. The field is still in its infancy. On the other hand, much of the research by psychologists, although voluminous, has involved small samples on specialized populations such as college students. Research with larger nationally representative samples, combining economic and psychological concepts, is needed as well as a recognition of any difference between whether things worked out well for almost everyone or just worked out on average for anyone.

Adverse Selection and Moral Hazard

The problems created by moral hazard are well illustrated by the provisions of health insurance for at least two reasons. First, all insurers face exceptional hurdles in monitoring the benefits of use of covered services, given the patient-provider relationship, the importance of maintaining confidentiality, the heterogeneity of patients and patients' illnesses, coupled with professional norms. Also, health insurance is sufficiently widespread that experiences with this type of insurance are not easily overlooked as anomalous. The research contributions on moral hazard in the nearly four decades since Pauly wrote his article have largely been empirical to gauge the magnitude of this problem.

Pauly's conclusion in chapter 5 that adverse selection in private health insurance markets, especially in unregulated ones, is a "paper tiger," meaning that it not really a significant issue, will come as a surprise to many. He is careful, however, not to negate the issue in its entirety but rather to stress the importance of institutional arrangements, including regulatory practices as well as whether or not insurance is provided to groups or individuals.

Principal-Agent Issues: Target Income Hypothesis and Supplier-Induced Demand

In other sectors, consumers, the principals, rely on others, the agents, for advice on consumption decisions. Often, the agent stands to gain when there is a transaction. Car salespersons and real estate agents are cases in point. Even department store salespersons have a role in advising consumers about their options. In these instances, the agent has a self-interest that may run counter to the self-interest of the principal. These arrangements persist, perhaps because of widespread faith in the notion that market pressures from competition among agents will in the end force agents to act in the principals' interest. At least in the long run, if an agent mainly acts in the agent's own interest without sufficient regard to the principal's interest, the agent will lose business to more forthcoming competitors. In the case of cars, there are alternative sources of information. Consumers can read magazines, which rate cars and talk with recent buyer. And real estate offerings can be found in newspapers and more recently on the Internet.

There are situations in which the relationship between the principal and the agent may be even more asymmetric than in the above examples. If a person, say, is charged with a felony and retains a lawyer, the person can only hope that the lawyer is a good one and represents that person's interests. While the client can appeal to the state bar or perhaps ask for a retrial, the transactions cost of addressing failed representation can be substantial. Further, if a person is diagnosed with cancer, given the trauma of the diagnosis and frequently the immediate need for treatment, the principal can only hope that the agent will take the principal's best interests to heart. Some but not all medical care falls into this category. Even if physician decision making is not fully motivated by financial self-interest, it may depend on adherence to practices learned from mentors or some other factor with the result that care may not fully be in the patient's interest.[2]

As explained by McGuire in chapter 10, two related hypotheses about principal-agent behavior in markets for physicians' services have appeared in the economic literature: the target income (TI) hypothesis and the physician-induced demand (PID) hypothesis.

TI and PID have been discussed and debated among economists in the health field for decades. In large part, this discourse has generated more heat than light. Flaws in the theories have been identified. For example, as McGuire notes, the TI theory does not specify how the target is set; it is silent about whether or not the physician should raise the price or quantity—and if both, in which combinations—to achieve the income target. In an important paper, McGuire and Pauly formalized PID theory, with one implication being that the TI theory is a special case of PID.[3] In their framework, the anomalous behaviors in the market for physicians' services arise from strong income effects on physician effort. But there is no empirical evidence to support the view that the income effects are that large.

In the end, a strong dose of competition is what many economists would recommend to offset these principal-agent problems. For example, if there is substantial competition among cancer centers for health plan enrollees and patients, including good information about the options, physicians at any one center may be less well positioned to induce demand. But as seen in the next subsection, the theoretical issues are more complicated than this.

The Effect of Competition on the Quality of Care

That greater competition in a market leads to a higher quality and/or variety of goods or services in general cannot be deduced theoretically. Moreover, this is an unsettled issue in the economic literature on industrial organization more generally. Gowrisankaran briefly discusses the conceptual issues in chapter 12 in the context of competition among hospitals. He acknowledges that not only do we not know whether competition raises the quality of hospital care but we also do not know how these changes compare to the normative benchmark of socially optimal care. In other words, it is possible that competition among the sellers of health care services raises quality, but quality may be increased to a level even above that at which the marginal social benefit equals the marginal social cost. A major insight of economics is that higher quality in any single good is not always better. It can be too high as well as too low.

Health economics can make progress in this area, but progress is also dependent on theoretical and empirical research in the industrial organization literature more generally. Studies are needed in several areas before economists will be able to generalize about this important relationship, which has significant implications for not only health services delivery but antitrust policy as well.

Monopoly, Competition, and Innovation

Whether or not competition increases the quality of care assumes a constant level of technological knowledge. In the health sector, as in others, ranging from agriculture to computer software and hardware, technological change is an extremely critical source of productivity gains. Much technological change is plausibly endogenous rather than exogeneously caused—that is, by trial and error, someone discovers that the earth is round. As Aaron notes in chapter 2 and discussed more fully below, the question of how to promote investment in knowledge poses a well-understood dilemma. Once knowledge is developed, the marginal cost of using it is zero or nearly so. Efficiency requires that the price of the product be set at marginal cost. But developing knowledge is costly. Nonaltruistic producers cannot be expected to allocate scarce resources to knowledge development voluntarily without expecting an adequate financial return. In part, the fixed cost of knowledge development has been paid by grants from governments and foundations that support basic research because the outcome *might* generate such great advantages.

The main approach for encouraging applied research and development is to stand ready to award a temporary monopoly in the form of patent protection to investors to stimulate applied research and development. Patented products can generate economic profits from current sales to cover the fixed costs of research and development, but monopoly pricing leads to lower levels of consumption of the patented products than would be socially optimal, *given* that the knowledge has been developed. This is a deadweight loss—making society worse off in this crucial sense.

Here, then, static efficiency calls for a different price than does dynamic efficiency, which considers incentives to produce a socially optimal rate of knowledge production. We need not only be concerned with a socially optimal output of a product that is produced given a knowledge base (static efficiency) but also that those investments for which the ex ante social benefit exceeds the ex ante social cost are undertaken. Obviously, making calculations ex ante is no easy task, but venture capital companies make these types of decisions all the time, of course, comparing anticipated private returns with private cost.

A case can be made then that monopoly is the market structure that the economist doctor should order. There are alternatives to patents, however, which are discussed by Sloan and Hsieh in chapter 9 as well as in a briefer form in a section below. As Sloan and Hsieh emphasize, the key policy challenge is how to achieve an appropriate balance between static efficiency that considers short-term benefits from greater price competition and dynamic efficiency that considers long-term benefits from appropriate incentives for innovation.

Empirical Issues

The Effects of Price on the Consumer Use of Health Services and Health

We now know more about price incentives as determinants of demand for medical care and health behaviors more generally than about any other empirical topic in the health care field. In large part, this is due to the RAND Health Insurance Experiment (HIE), a randomized control trial to estimate the effects of cost sharing on health and the demand for health care services.

That price influences demand does not come as a shock, at least to anyone who had a course in microeconomics. As Aaron states in chapter 2, the law of demand is after all a *law*. The solution of Grossman's optimization model yields an individual demand for health that is negatively related to its price (chapter 3).

The research question is about price elasticities, not about directions of effect. Aaron adds that economists' interest in price is not only limited to the out-of-pocket price consumers pay, net of what health insurance pays on account of plan deductibles, coinsurance, copays, and stop-loss provisions; also included in price are the costs associated with waiting times, travel distance and hassle, and red tape. Evidence that nonmonetary costs, such as travel time, influence demand is no less clear-cut.

As Newhouse and Sinaiko report, key results from the HIE were that relative to free care (complete health insurance coverage), the total spending on medical care, including insurance payments, was about

30 percent lower and one to two fewer visits annually when the insurance plan included a large deductible, and about 20 percent lower when the plan specified a 25 percent coinsurance rate combined with a stop-loss provision. The coinsurance rate is the part of the total bill that the patient bears out of pocket; the stop-loss is a ceiling on out-of-pocket spending, which the HIE made a function of the person's income. For most services, the elasticity seems similar—0.2 in absolute value (chapter 5). The HIE looked for differences in the elasticity of demand for households with different incomes and did not find that low-income families were much more responsive to price.

The HIE researchers examined whether the reductions in use with increased cost sharing come out of a lower use of beneficial or needed care, or alternatively, out of care that was not needed. They found that increased cost sharing reduced both. This is a disturbing result and, to some, a sufficient condition to oppose increases in cost sharing. Economists, however, are uncomfortable with the concept of "need," or in second-guessing how people ought to behave.[4] Do families with two children need a four-bedroom home or need to take each child to the doctor twice a year? Likewise, a person with the flu who places a high value on not missing work may obtain medical care, when a person in the same condition who places on lower value on this outcome may not. People who are especially sensitive to pain may benefit from painkillers while people who place a high value on avoiding the adverse side effects of painkillers may not demand such medication. Practitioners are not always well positioned to value the benefit of services to consumers.

The HIE researchers found surprisingly little effect of cost sharing on health, perhaps because the elderly were not included in the study and the time period covered by the study was only three to five years. Perhaps more important than the results on the relationship between the extent of coverage and health outcomes, the HIE developed procedures and methods to measure health outcomes that continue to this day.

As Aaron along with Newhouse and Sinaiko emphasize, times have changed since the HIE was completed more than a quarter century ago. Health spending is much higher now in real terms. Some areas of medicine are entirely new. Many product innovations have occurred. There have been significant changes in health care financing in the United States. Since governments and foundations are now much less likely to provide financial support for large-scale experiments like the HIE, it seems likely that the HIE will be a one-of-a-kind study for a long time to come.

The Effects of Price on Harmful Behaviors

A major contribution of empirical economics is the demonstration that behaviors that are often or even generally harmful to people who engage in them are responsive to changes in price. As Cawley documents, a large number of economic studies have found that smoking is negatively correlated with the price of cigarettes. This price is substantially influenced by state and federal government excise taxes. Cawley pegs the price elasticity of smoking participation (the decision to smoke or not smoke) at around –0.48. Similarly, almost every study that estimates the price elasticity of demand for alcohol finds that the use of alcohol falls with price increases. Cawley cites a study that shows that even sexual activity responds to price. As in the analysis of demand for health care services, economists consider travel time or the hassle needed to acquire addictive substances, the probability of being arrested and convicted, and the fines or jail sentences associated with convictions to be elements of the price paid. The nonprice costs also influence the demand for addictive and harmful goods and services. Interestingly, Cawley reports that price is a greater deterrent to heavy drinking than to light smoking.

The Supply Response to Changes in Price

Economists distinguish between short- and long-run responses. In the short run, at least one factor of production is fixed. In the analysis of the market for physicians' services, it is useful to distinguish between long-run responses—which involve decisions to enter the profession of medicine as well as specialty, location, and retirement—and short-run decisions—which involve output, hours of work, and other practice choices.

As we note in chapter 1 and Nicholson observes in chapter 8, the high internal rates of return on medical education in general along with the high returns to training in some specialties plausibly reflect a combination of entry barriers and compensating wage differentials for the nonfinancial aspects of work, perhaps even fewer work years. In addition, however, since it takes a long time to add to medical school capacity and for students to be attracted to a field offering high financial returns to training, some differentials in compensation may persist for a long time. In other words, even in the absence of entry barriers, this is a market that takes a long time to clear. As Nicholson reports, there is some empirical evidence that students do consider financial returns when deciding on whether or not to apply to a medical school. Yet the evidence that compensation differences among physician specialties influence the choice of specialty is mixed. Thus, some other mechanism, perhaps government direction, may be more effective in allocating medical talent.

Given the substantial front-end investment in any new pharmaceutical product, this choice too is a long-run decision. Overall, the empirical studies provide consistent evidence that incentives affect firms' investments in pharmaceutical research and development (chapter 9). This may seem like an obvious finding to economists, but a widespread view is that such firms earn substantial economic rents and that equally productive innovations can be realized by offering pharmaceutical companies appreciably lower returns than they enjoy currently.

The analysis of short-run supply responses to changes in price is more complex, and the empirical evidence is less clear. McGuire summarizes this research in chapter 10. As explained above, substantial reductions in the prices paid to physicians may increase effort and output, and some empirical research suggests that this is so (see chapter 10). In the long run, though, reductions in price may lead to increased exits in the form of earlier retirements and losses of physicians from patient care to other medical pursuits.

As Golden and Sloan emphasize in chapter 11, pay is only one type of reward for services provided. Other rewards take the form of professional pride, recognition, opportunities to do challenging work, regular hours of work, and supportive colleagues. In fact, the theory of compensating wage differentials (see chapter 8) predicts that high nonfinancial rewards should substitute for pay. Some of Golden and Sloan's earlier research goes further than this in chapter 8, arguing that increased extrinsic rewards, such as higher financial rewards, may devalue intrinsic awards. By this they mean, for example, that professionals may be willing to provide some services for altruistic reasons, but once an explicit price is attached to these services, their value is diminished to some extent.

An alternative to attaching prices to a unit of service, as has been a common practice for physician and hospital services, have been proposals to pay for performance—that is, to pay higher prices to reward better performance (chapter 11). This raises the question of whether performance should be based on certain care processes being performed (e.g., whether certain medications are prescribed after a heart attack) or outcomes of care (e.g., rates of survival or health indicators at a certain period after a heart attack. In chapter II, Golden and Sloan contend that physicians and hospitals would prefer to be paid on process rather than outcomes, on the grounds that they are risk averse and outcomes also depend importantly on factors outside the control of the provider. Moreover, there are questions about the validity and reliability of specific outcome indicators as measures of performance. In the end, health care is heterogeneous. Pay for performance provides a better fit for some types of services than for others, along dimensions that Golden and Sloan list.

Consumer Information and Information Provision

The lack of adequate and asymmetric information between patients and providers underlies many of the market failures in health care. Not surprisingly, economists and others have, in principle, viewed public policies that involve the dissemination of information as welfare improving. As a practical matter, however, many supporters are aware that the actual effects depend on the details of policy implementation.

One approach has been to encourage the dissemination of information on the performance of hospitals in the form of report cards (chapter 12). The problem is not with the concept but with the implementation details. When report cards are based on few indicators, as is inevitable to a certain extent, there is an incentive for providers to game the system—that is, to perform well on the indicators that are measured, possibly at the cost of poorer performance on the indicators that are not measured. When report cards are based on outcome measures, there is an incentive for hospitals to accept less severely ill patients for treatment, thus creating access barriers for more severely ill patients. Further, some hospitals are too small so that the sample sizes on the outcomes are too small to generate reliable measures of their performance.

For better or worse, patients may not attach much weight to report cards. For one, they may not be sufficiently empowered to choose hospitals, given the role of physicians in the referral decision, but consumers also may have information on the dimensions of quality that is not monitored. The empirical evidence reviewed by Gowrisankaran in chapter 12, moreover, does not make a clear case that consumer welfare has been improved by report cards, at least to date.

Another information provision policy, unique to the United States and New Zealand, is the direct-to-consumer advertising (DTCA) of branded pharmaceutical products (chapter 6). Advocates of DTCA stress its importance in empowering health care consumers in their roles as decision makers about their own personal health care. Critics, on the other hand, argue that DTCA has increased the demand for recently introduced products that offer few clinical advantages over older ones and therefore have increased expenditures on pharmaceutical products without markedly improving the public's health.

Critics of advertising in general argue that advertising creates artificial distinctions among rival products, and gives incumbent firms, especially those with large advertising budgets, more market power relative to their competitors. Economists generally have not been particularly sanguine about advertising since it often does not convey that much information about product attributes, rather eliciting images to affect the advertised products' emotional appeal (e.g., cigarette ads with the Marlboro Man or Joe Camel). It is also asserted that much advertising involves market stealing from competitors in a zero-sum game that leaves consumers no better off. Yet such contentions run counter to economists' propensity to assume that preferences are exogenous and not subject to second guessing.

If such DTCA as for the "Purple Pill" (Nexium) indeed represent attempts by manufacturers to win over consumers from cheaper, effective products, the general objections to advertising would apply to pharmaceutical DTCA as a whole. Nonetheless, the evidence on DTCA, which is reviewed by Berndt and Donohue in chapter 6, suggests that its main effect is to encourage people with specific chronic ailments such as high cholesterol, high blood pressure, and diabetes to visit their physicians. At the visit, physicians seem to be open to a number of drug therapeutic alternatives. Thus, the main effect of DCTA appears to improve consumer awareness of their illnesses and encourage them to seek care. In this sense, DTCA overall seems welfare enhancing.

While some forms of advertising, such as DTCA of pharmaceutical products, have some useful informational content, there is empirical evidence that people gain knowledge about alternatives on their own.

Two examples from this book illustrate this type of learning. In chapter 3, Gilleskie describes the study by Gregory Crawford and Matthew Shum that examines the learning about alternative anti-ulcer drugs.[5] Drugs have various therapeutic and adverse side effects that differ among individuals, but by trial and error people learn which drug works best for them. Heterogeneity among patients means it is unlikely that one drug works best for all individuals with a given illness. Second, Nicholson finds that medical students' estimates of physician earnings increase in accuracy during the time they spend in medical school (chapter 8).[6]

The Structural Approach, and Natural and Social Experiment Approaches

One analytic approach, which is gaining popularity among applied microeconomists, is the "structural approach" (see chapter 3). In specifying structural models, economists develop a formal economic model of individual optimization subject to constraints and then use the available data to estimate the parameters of the determinants in the models. Rational expectations and forward-looking behavior are generally assumed, in contrast to the models of behavioral economists.

An alternative approach uses data from natural or social experiments. An example of a natural experiment is a change in policy in one state that is not changed in the same way at the same time in other states, which therefore may be regarded as a control group. The HIE was a social experiment. In chapter 3, Gilleskie describes four papers in which the structural approach has been used in the field of health economics. A fifth study that uses a structural approach is briefly reviewed by Gowrisankaran in chapter 12.

An advantage of the structural approach is that the models' estimates can be used to perform counterfactual policy experiments. Yet to date, the little policy analysis has been based on structural models. In part, the lack of use in public policy making reflects the paucity of studies. Structural models are difficult to estimate, although estimation has become much more feasible as computing power has increased. The structural approach is gaining popularity in other applied microeconomic fields, especially in empirical industrial organization. The close relationship between the underlying economic theory and empirical analysis is an attractive feature of the structural approach. Economics is at its best when it is open to the use of alternative analytic approaches where techniques developed in one field of economics support new research in other fields.

Public Policy

An objective of theoretical and empirical analysis in economics is to guide public policy decisions. Yet in the real world of politics, public policies are advocated and opposed for many reasons, including the private interests of the groups affected positively or negatively by a policy change. In this section, we explore a few of the public policy options indicated by the theoretical and empirical analyses of incentives.

The direct control approach has become as unpopular in U.S. health policy as it now is in other sectors of the U.S. economy. In recent years, price incentives are "in." Regulatory approaches are not as dominant as they once were but they are still much honored in some situations. Price incentives take the form of increased cost sharing and the use of other financial incentives to control health spending (see chapter 2), and financial incentives to encourage the provision of high-quality care, as embodied in pay for performance (chapter 11).

Even advocates for increasing cost sharing argue that this is efficient only up to a point. Increased cost sharing is good up to the point where the decrease in welfare due to the increased expenditure risk equals the welfare gain from the reduced misallocation of scarce resources (chapter 5).

The case for raising excise taxes on cigarettes and alcohol is stronger unless one values the additional expenditure risk such taxes impose on addicts and other heavy users of these goods. There is a concern that high excise taxes may lead to bootlegging and smuggling, especially if state taxes vary greatly. But it is surprising that in view of the high social cost of smoking and heavy drinking, the excise taxes on these products are not higher than they are.[7] Admittedly, this is a complex issue, but certainly one that is not all that conceptually complex. How much one should raise excise taxes depends on whether or not the harmful effects on others within the household are considered to be external or internal costs, and whether or not excise taxes should only be based on externalities or reflect internalities as well. Also, because demand is price inelastic, higher taxes imply greater expenditure; families thus have less money to spend on other goods and services.

More specifically, to the extent that hyperbolic discounting can be shown to be an important phenomenon empirically, an experimental tax increase this not only would show the limits of the rationality assumption but would have crucial policy implications as well since the case for raising the excise tax on addictive and other harmful goods would be even stronger than if the users are rational and forward-looking. That is, one would want to consider the internal as well as external costs in setting excise taxes on harmful products.

Paradoxically, as some economists have come to question rational behavior as a universal phenomenon, there has been a decline in reliance on consumer deference to professionalism and professional norms, and a corresponding increased reliance on market forces to achieve socially desirable outcomes from health care. The growing influence of DCTA and report cards on provider performance are examples of approaches that place a greater reliance on consumers as decision makers, or at least view them as having an increased role in the decision-making process (chapters 6 and 12).

Times change as do the most fashionable public policy approaches. While a government-run, single-payer approach to financing health care in the United States has not received public widespread support to date, and has encountered plenty of public opposition from certain stakeholders such as organized medicine, sentiments could change, particularly as expenditures and pressures on public budgets increase. Further, in spite of its reputation as a privately run health care system, about half of the spending of personal health care services is from public sources, and this fraction is likely to increase with the aging of the U.S. population.

Medicare is a huge public program, larger in budgetary terms than the national health services in other countries. The problems it faces are immense. Even with reliance on market forces, Medicare pays differentially fixed fees to physicians. Changes in these fees are likely to have important effects on physicians' input and output decisions in ways that are not fully understood. Setting administered prices is a messy business, and unfortunately, the empirical evidence from economic research to date, some of which is summarized in chapter 10 by McGuire, offers a bit of two-handed advice—"the on the one hand and on the other hand" types of advice that economists are sometimes criticized for giving. For example, if Medicare cuts the fees it pays for services provided to Medicare beneficiaries, the quantity of services that Medicare beneficiaries receive may increase or decrease. Put more positively, economists warn policymakers that the direction of effect of this type of policy change cannot be deduced on the basis of logic alone. Careful empirical studies are needed.

Technological change in pharmaceuticals and vaccines has been an important source of improvements in health, both in the United States and other countries. The major incentive for innovation in this sphere as well as in medical devices has been patent protection. In a world without patents, the rates of innovation would undoubtedly be much lower than they have been (chapter 9). Yet patents have problems of their own. Not only is there the deadweight welfare loss due to monopoly pricing but in addition, even with monopoly protection, the financial returns to some innovations are insufficient for companies to make the requisite investments. These include some potentially effective vaccines as well as drugs used to treat diseases that are most common in low-income countries. As a result, economists have proposed alternative incentive schemes to patents. Several of these alternatives—advance-purchase commitments, optional rewards, and priority review vouchers—were described in chapter 9. Each of these alternatives has both pluses and minuses. And whatever their merits, implementing alternative incentive arrangements will face political challenges. The patent system is known and well entrenched, and there likely would be fierce opposition to an alternative approach that even gives the appearance of threatening it. In the United States, any approach that gives the appearance that the government is directly involved in setting the prices of pharmaceutical products also set off political opposition.

Final Comment

As the chapters in this book indicate, we have come a long way in understanding the role of incentives in health care and health decision making, but there is much more progress to be made. In the end, choices about the allocation of resources are made by markets, either private or public "markets." All research can do is to identify the likely effects of various policy decisions and the policy trade-offs. Economics presents a useful framework and methodology for assessing these policy effects and trade-offs, both before the policies are implemented, and after to reconsider their relative social benefits and costs to society.

Notes

1. Becker and Murphy (1988).

2. See the discussion in chapter 2 on this point.

3. McGuire and Pauly (1991).

4. See Pauly's commentary on this issue in chapter 5.

5. Crawford and Shum (2005).

6. Nicholson (2005).

7. On smoking, see Sloan et al. (2004).

References

Aaron, Henry J., and William B. Schwartz. 1984. *The Painful Prescription: Rationing Hospital Care*. Washington, DC: Brookings Institution Press.

Aaron, Henry J., William B. Schwartz, and Melissa Cox. 2005. *Can We Say No? The Challenge of Rationing Health Care*. Washington, DC: Brookings Institution Press.

Acemoglu, Daron, David M. Cutler, Amy Finkelstein, and Joshua Linn. 2006. Did Medicare Induce Pharmaceutical Innovation? *American Economic Review* 96 (2): 103–107.

Acemoglu, Daron, and Joshua Linn. 2004. Market Size in Innovation: Theory and Evidence from the Pharmaceutical Industry. *Quarterly Journal of Economics* 119 (3): 1049–1090.

Acton, Jan Paul. 1975. Nonmonetary Factors in the Demand for Medical Services: Some Empirical Evidence. *Journal of Political Economy* 83 (3): 595–614.

Adams, J. Stacy. 1963. Toward an Understanding of Inequity. *Journal of Abnormal Psychology* 67: 422–436.

Agency for Health Care Research and Quality, Center for Financing, Access, and Cost Trends. 2003. Population Characteristics. *Medical Expenditure Panel Survey* HC-064:P7R3–P8R1.

Ahituv, Avner, V. Joseph Holz, and Tomas Philipson. 1996. The Responsiveness of the Demand for Condoms to the Local Prevalence of AIDS. *Journal of Human Resources* 31 (4): 869–897.

Ainslie, George. 1991. Derivation of "Rational" Economic Behavior from Hyperbolic Discount Curves. *American Economic Review* 81 (2): 334–340.

———. 1992. *Picoeconomics: The Strategic Interaction of Successive Motivational States*. New York: Cambridge University Press.

Akerlof, George A. 1991. Richard T. Ely Lecture: Procrastination and Obedience. *American Economic Review* 81 (2): 1–19.

Akosa Antwi, Yaa O. D., Martin Gaynor, and William B. Vogt. 2006. A Competition Index for Differentiated Product Oligopoly with an Application to Hospitals. Mimeo, working paper.

Alexander, G. Caleb, Lawrence P. Casalino, and David O. Meltzer. 2005. Physician Strategies to Reduce Patients' Out-of-Pocket Prescription Costs. *Archives of Internal Medicine* 165 (6): 633–636.

Altman, Lawrence K. 1982. Prescription Drugs Are Advertised to Patients, Breaking with Tradition. *New York Times*, February 23, 1.

American Hospital Association, ed. 2002. *Hospital Statistics, 2002 Edition*. Health Forum. Chicago: American Hospital Association Company.

American Medical Association. 2003. *Physician Socioeconomic Statistics*. Chicago: American Medical Association.

———. 2006. *Physician Characteristics and Distribution in the U.S.* Chicago: American Medical Association.

Angell, Marcia. 2004. *The Truth about Drug Companies*. New York: Random House.

Argys, Laura M., and Daniel I. Rees. 2006. Searching for Peer Group Effects: A Test of the Contagion Hypothesis. Department of Economics, University of Colorado at Denver.

Arrow, Kenneth J. 1963. Uncertainty and the Welfare Economics of Medical Care. *American Economic Review* 53 (5): 941–973.

Association of American Medical Colleges. 2006. *AAMC Data Book*. Ed. James Youngclaus, Kendra Campbell, Sarah Schoolcraft, and Aleya Horn. Washington, DC: Association of American Medical Colleges.

Avorn, Jerry, Milton Chen, and Robert Hartley. 1982. Scientific versus Commercial Sources of Influence on the Prescribing Behavior of Physicians. *American Journal of Medicine* 73 (1): 4–8.

Bagwell, Kyle. 2007. The Economic Analysis of Advertising. In *Handbook of Industrial Organization*, ed. M. Armstrong and R. Porter. Amsterdam: Elsevier.

Baicker, Katherine, and Amitabh Chandra. 2004. Medicare Spending, the Physician Workforce, and Beneficiaries' Quality of Care. Health Affairs: W184–197. Available of <http://www.healthaffairs.org>.

Bain, Joe S. 1956. *Barriers to New Competition*. Cambridge, MA: Havard University Press.

Baker, Dean, J. Bradford DeLong, Paul R. Krugman, N. Gregory Mankiw, and William D. Nordhaus. 2005. Asset Returns and Economic Growth/Comments and Discussion. *Brookings Papers on Economic Activity* (1): 289–315.

Bandura, Albert. 1997. *Self-Efficacy: The Exercise of Control*. New York: W. H. Freeman and Company.

Baron, James N., and David M. Kreps. 1999. *Strategic Human Resource Management*. New York: John Wiley and Sons.

Barro, Robert, and Xavier Sala-i-Martin. 2004. *Economic Growth*. 2nd ed. Cambridge, MA: MIT Press.

Basara, Lisa Ruby. 1992. Direct-to-Consumer Advertising: Today's Issues and Tomorrow's Outlook. *Journal of Drug Issues* 22 (2): 317–330.

Bazzoli, Gloria J. 1985. Does Educational Indebtedness Affect Physician Specialty Choice? *Journal of Health Economics* 4 (1): 1–19.

Bebchuk, Lucian Arye, and Jesse M. Fried. 2003. Executive Compensation as an Agency Problem. *Journal of Economic Perspectives* 17 (3):71–92.

Becker, Gary S. 1962. Irrational Behavior and Economic Theory. *Journal of Political Economy* 70 (1): 1–13.

———. 1965. A Theory of the Allocation of Time. *Economic Journal* 75 (299): 493–517.

Becker, Gary S., and Kevin M. Murphy. 1988. A Theory of Rational Addiction. *Journal of Political Economy* 96 (4): 675–700.

———. 1993. A Simple Theory of Advertising as a Good or Bad. *Quarterly Journal of Economics* 108 (4): 941–964.

Becker, Howard S., Blanche Geer, and Stephen Miller. 1972. Medical Education. In *Handbook of Medical Sociology*, ed. Howard E. Freeman, Sol Levine, and Leo G. Reeder. Englewood Cliffs, NJ: Prentice Hall.

Bell, Robert A., Michael S. Wilkes, and Richard L. Kravitz. 2000. The Educational Value of Consumer-Targeted Prescription Drug Print Advertising. *Journal of Family Practice* 49 (12): 1092–1098.

Bénebou, Roland, and Jean Tirole. 2003. Intrinsic and Extrinsic Motivation. *Review of Economic Studies* 70 (244): 489.

———. 2006. Incentives and Prosocial Behavior. *American Economic Review* 96 (5): 1652.

Benham, Lee. 1972. The Effect of Advertising on the Price of Eyeglasses. *Journal of Law and Economics* 15 (2): 337–352.

Berndt, Ernst R. 2002. Pharmaceuticals in U.S. Health Care: Determinants of Quantity and Price. *Journal of Economic Perspectives* 16 (4): 45–66.

———. 2005. To Inform or Persuade? Direct-to-Consumer Advertising of Prescription Drugs. *New England Journal of Medicine* 352 (4): 325–328.

———. 2006. The United States' Experience with Direct-to-Consumer Advertising of Prescription Drugs: Perspective. In *Promoting and Coping with Pharmaceutical Innovation: An International Perspective*, ed. Frank A. Sloan and Chee-Ruey Hsieh. Cambridge: Cambridge University Press.

Berndt, Ernst R., Ashoke. Bhattacharjya, David Mishol, Almudena Arcelus, and Thomas Lasky. 2002. An Analysis of the Diffusion of New Antidepressants: Variety, Quality, and Marketing Efforts. *Journal of Mental Health Policy and Economics* 5 (1): 3–17.

Berndt, Ernst R., David M. Cutler, Richard G. Frank, Zvi Griliches, Joseph P. Newhouse, and Jack E. Triplett. 2000. Medical Care Prices and Output. In *Handbook of Health Economics*, ed. Anthony J. Culyer and Joseph P. Newhouse. Amsterdam: Elsevier.

Bernheim, B. Douglas, and Antonio Rangel. 2004. Addiction and Cue-Triggered Decision Processes. *American Economic Review* 94 (5): 1558–1590.

Bertrand, Marianne, and Sendhil Mullainathan. 2001. Are CEOs Rewarded for Luck? The Ones without Principals Are. *Quarterly Journal of Economics* 116 (3): 901–932.

Bhattacharya, Jayanta. 2005. Specialty Selection and Lifetime Returns to Specialization within Medicine. *Journal of Human Resources* 40 (1): 115–143.

Blanche, Geer, Everett S. Hughes, Anselm Strauss, and Howard Saul Becker. 1961. *Boys in White: Student Culture in Medical School*. Chicago: University of Chicago Press.

Blaug, Mark. 1998. Where Are We Now in British Health Economics? *Health Economics* 7: 563–579.

Blumenthal, David. 2006. Employer-Sponsored Insurance: Riding the Health Care Tiger. *New England Journal of Medicine* 355 (2): 195–202.

Bodenheimer, Thomas. 2000. California's Beleaguered Physician Groups: Will They Survive? *New England Journal of Medicine* 342 (14): 1064–1068.

Bohmer, Richard, and Melanie Harshbarger. 1999. Note on Physician Compensation and Financial Incentives. Harvard Business School. Abailable at <http://www.harvard business.org>.

Bolin, Kristian, and Björn Lindgren. 2002. Asthma and Allergy: The Significance of Chronic Conditions for Individual Health Behaviour. *Allergy* 57 (2): 115–122.

Bonaccorso, Silvia N., and Jeffrey L. Sturchio. 2002. For and Against: Direct to Consumer Advertising Is Medicalizing Normal Human Experience: Against. *British Medical Journal* 324 (April): 910–911.

Bosworth, Barry, Susan M. Collins, Steven N. Durlauf, and Jeffrey A. Frankel. 2003. The Empirics of Growth: An Update/Comments and Discussion. *Brookings Papers on Economic Activity* (2): 113–206.

Burstein, Philip L., and Jerry Cromwell. 1985. Relative Incomes and Rates of Return for U.S. Physicians. *Journal of Health Economics* 4 (1): 63–78.

Busse, Rienhard, and Annette Riesberg. 2004. Health Care System in Transition: Germany. Copenhagen: World Health Organization Regional Office for Europe on behalf of the European Observatory on Health Systems and Policies.

Cabana, Michael D., Cynthia S. Rand, Neil R. Powe, Albert W. Wu, Modena H. Wilson, Paul-Andre C. Abboud, and Haya R. Rubin. 1999. Why Don't Physicians Follow Clinical Practice Guidelines? A Framework for Improvement. *JAMA* 282 (15): 1458–1465.

Cady, John F. 1976. An Estimate of the Price Effects of Restrictions on Drug Price Advertising. *Economic Inquiry* 14 (4): 493–510.

Cameron, A. Colin, and Pravin K. Trivedi. 1998. *Regression Analysis of Count Data*. New York: Cambridge University Press.

Cameron, A. Colin, Pravin K. Trivedi, Frank Milne, and John Piggott. 1988. A Microeconomic Model of the Demand for Health Care and Health Insurance in Australia. *Review of Economic Studies* 55 (181): 85.

Capps, Cory, David Dranove, and Mark Satterthwaite. 2003. Competition and Market Power in Option Demand Markets. *RAND Journal of Economics* 34 (4): 737–763.

Cardon, James H., and Igal Hendel. 2001. Asymmetric Information in Health Insurance: Evidence from the National Medical Expenditure Survey. *RAND Journal of Economics* 32 (3): 408–427.

Carlton, Dennis W., and Jeffrey M. Perloff. 2005. *Modern Industrial Organization.* 4th ed. Boston: Pearson Addison-Wesley.

Carnes, Patrick, J. 2001. *Out of the Shadows: Understanding Sexual Addiction.* 3d ed. Center City, MN: Hazelden.

Casalino, Lawrence P., and James C. Robinson. 1997. The Evolution of Medical Groups and Capitation in California. Oakland: Henry J. Kaiser Foundation and California HealthCare Foundation.

Case, Anne C., and Lawrence F. Katz. 1991. The Company You Keep: The Effects of Family and Neighborhood on Disadvantage Youths. National Bureau of Economic Research working paper.

Cawley, John, and Donald S. Kenkel, eds. 2007. *The Economics of Health Behaviors.* Northampton, MA: Edward Elgar.

Cawley, John, Sara Markowitz, and John Tauras. 2004. Lighting Up and Slimming Down: The Effects of Body Weight and Cigarette Prices on Adolescent Smoking Initiation. *Journal of Health Economics* 23 (2): 293–311.

Chaix-Couturier, Carine, Isabelle Durand-Zaleski, Dominique Jolly, and Pierre Durieux. 2000. Effects of Financial Incentives on Medical Practice: Results from a Systematic Review of the Literature and Methodological Issues. *International Journal for Quality in Health Care* 12 (2): 133–142.

Chalkley, Martin, and Colin Tilley. 2005. The Existence and Nature of Physician Agency: Evidence of Stinting from the British National Health Service. *Journal of Economics and Management Strategy* 14 (3): 647–664.

Chaloupka, Frank J., Michael Grossman, and John Tauras. 1999. The Demand for Cocaine and Marijuana by Youth. In *The Economic Analysis of Substance Use and Abuse*, ed. Frank J. Chaloupka, Michael Grossman, Warren K. Bickel, and Henry Saffer. Cambridge, MA: National Bureau of Economic Research.

Chaloupka, Frank J., and Kenneth E. Warner. 2000. The Economics of Smoking. In *The Handbook of Health Economics*, ed. Anthony J. Culyer and Joseph P. Newhouse. Amsterdam: Elsevier.

Chassin, Mark R., Jacqueline Kosecoff, Rolla Edward Park, Constance M. Winslow, Katherine L. Kahn, Nancy Merritt, Joan Keesey, Arlene Fink, David H. Solomon, and Robert H. Brook. 1987. Does Inappropriate Use Explain Geographic Variations in the Use of Health Care Services? A Study of Three Procedures. *JAMA* 258 (18): 2533–2537.

Chen, Jersey, Martha J. Radford, Yun Wang, Thomas A. Marciniak, and Harlan M. Krumholz. 1999. Do "America's Best Hospitals" Perform Better for Acute Myocardial Infarction? *New England Journal of Medicine* 340 (4): 286–292.

Chernew, Michael, Gautam Gowrisankaran, and A. Mark Fendrick. 2002. Payer Type and the Returns to Bypass Surgery: Evidence from Hospital Entry Behavior. *Journal of Health Economics* 21 (3): 451–474.

Chernew, Michael, Gautam Gowrisankaran, and Dennis P. Scanlon. 2006. Learning and the Value of Information: Evidence from Health Plan Report Cards. National Bureau of Economic Research working paper.

Chou, Shin-Yi, Michael Grossman, and Henry Saffer. 2004. An Economic Analysis of Adult Obesity: Results from the Behavioral Risk Factor Surveillance System. *Journal of Health Economics* 23 (3): 565–587.

Church, Jeffrey, and Roger Ware. 1999. *Industrial Organization: A Strategic Approach.* New York: Irwin McGraw-Hill.

Cochrane, John H. 1995. Time-Consistent Health Insurance. *Journal of Political Economy* 103: 445–473.

Cockburn, Iain M., and Rebecca M. Henderson. 1998. Absorptive Capacity, Coauthoring Behavior, and the Organization of Research in Drug Discovery. *Journal of Industrial Economics* 46 (2): 157–182.

———. 2001. Scale and Scope in Drug Development: Unpacking the Advantages of Size in Pharmaceutical Research. *Journal of Health Economics* 20 (6): 1033–1057.

Cogan, John F., R. Glenn Hubbard, and David P. Kessler. 2005. Making Markets Work: Five Steps to a Better Health Care System. *Health Affairs* 24 (6): 1447–1457.

Cohen, Wesley M., Richard R. Nelson, and John P. Walsh. 2002. Protecting Their Intellectual Assets: Appropriability Conditions and Why U.S. Manufacturing Firms Patent (or Not). Cambridge, MA: National Bureau of Economic Research.

Colman, Greg, Michael Grossman, and Ted Joyce. 2003. The Effect of Cigarette Excise Taxes on Smoking before, during, and after Pregnancy. *Journal of Health Economics* 22 (6): 1053–1072.

Comanor, William. 2007. The Economics of Research and Development in the Pharmaceutical Industry. In *Pharmaceutical Innovation: Incentives, Competition, and Cost-Benefit Analysis in International Perspective*, ed. Frank A. Sloan and Chee-Ruey Hsieh. Cambridge: Cambridge University Press.

Conrad, Douglas A., and Jon B. Christianson. 2004. Penetrating the "Black Box": Financial Incentives for Enhancing the Quality of Physician Services. *Medical Care Research and Review* 61 (3): S37–S68.

Cook, Philip J., and Michael J. Moore. 2000. Alcohol. In *The Handbook of Health Economics*, ed. Anthony J. Culyer and Joseph P. Newhouse. Amsterdam: Elsevier.

———. 2001. Environment and Persistence in Youthful Drinking Patterns. In *Risky Behavior among Youths: An Economic Analysis*, ed. Jonathan H. Gruber. Chicago: University of Chicago Press.

Cooper, Richard A., Thomas E. Getzen, Heather J. McKee, and Prakash Laud. 2002. Economic and Demographic Trends Signal an Impending Physician Shortage. *Health Affairs* 21 (1): 140–154.

Costa, Dora L. 2000. Understanding the Twentieth-Century Decline in Chronic Conditions among Older Men. *Demography* 37 (1): 53–72.

Costa, Dora L., and Matthew E. Kahn. 2004. Changes in the Value of Life, 1940–1980. *Journal of Risk and Uncertainty* 29 (2): 159–180.

Cragg, John G. 1971. Some Statistical Models for Limited Dependent Variables with Application to the Demand for Durable Goods. *Econometrica* 39 (5): 829–844.

Crawford, Gregory S., and Matthew Shum. 2005. Uncertainty and Learning in Pharmaceutical Demand. *Econometrica* 73 (4): 4.

Cremieux, Pierre, Denise Jarvinen, Genia Long, and Phi Merrigan. 2007. Pharmaceutical Spending and Health Outcomes. In *Pharmaceutical Innovation: Incentives, Competition, and Cost-Benefit Analysis in International Perspectives*, ed. Frank A. Sloan and Chee-Ruey Hsieh. Cambridge: Cambridge University Press.

Crimmins, Eileen M., Yasuhiko Saito, and Sandra L. Reynolds. 1997. Further Evidence on Recent Trends in the Prevalence and Incidence of Disability among Older Americans from Two Sources; The LSOA and the NHIS. *Journal of Gerontology: Social Sciences* 52B (2): S59–S71.

Cropper, M. Lynne. 1977. Health, Investment in Health, and Occupational Choice. *Journal of Political Economy* 85 (6): 1273–1294.

Culyer, Anthony J. 1989. The Normative Economics of Health Care Finance and Provision. *Oxford Review of Economic Policy* 5 (1): 34–58.

Culyer, Anthony J., and Joseph P. Newhouse, eds. 2000. *Handbook of Health Economics*. 2 vols. Amsterdam: Elsevier.

Currie, Janet, and Brigitte C. Madrian. 1999. Health, Health Insurance, and the Labor Market. In *Handbook of Labor Economics*, ed. Orley Ashenfelter and David Card. Amsterdam: Elsevier.

Cutler, David M. 2004. *Your Money or Your Life*. New York: Oxford University Press.

Cutler, David M., and Ernst R. Berndt. 2001. *Medical Care Output and Productivity (National Bureau of Economic Research Studies in Income and Wealth)*. Chicago: University of Chicago Press.

Cutler, David M., and Adriana Lleras-Muney. 2006. Education and Health: Evaluating Theory and Evidence. National Bureau of Economic Research working paper 12352.

Cutler, David M., and Mark McClellan. 2001. Is Technological Change in Medicine Worth It? *Health Affairs* (September–October): 11–29.

Cutler, David M., Mark McClellan, Joseph P. Newhouse, and Dahlia Remler. 1998. Are Medical Prices Declining? Evidence from Heart Attack Treatments. *Quarterly Journal of Economics* 113 (4): 991–1024.

Cutler, David M., and Sarah J. Reber. 1998. Paying for Health Insurance: The Trade-off between Competition and Adverse Selection. *Quarterly Journal of Economics* 113 (2): 433–466.

Cutler, David M., Allison B. Rosen, and Sandeep Vijan. 2006. The Value of Medical Spending in the United States, 1960–2000. *New England Journal of Medicine* 355 (9): 920–927.

Cutler, David M., and Richard J. Zeckhauser. 2000. The Anatomy of Health Insurance. In *The Handbook of Health Economics*, ed. Anthony J. Culyer and Joseph P. Newhouse. Amsterdam: Elsevier.

Dafny, Leemore, and David Dranove. 2005. Do Consumer Report Cards Tell Consumers Anything They Don't Already Know? National Bureau of Economic Research working paper 11420.

Danzon, Patricia M. 2000. Liability for Medical Malpractice. In *Handbook of Health Economics*, ed. Anthony J. Culyer and Joseph P. Newhouse. Amsterdam: Elsevier.

Danzon, Patricia M., and Li-Wei Chao. 2000. Does Regulation Drive out Competition in Pharmaceutical Markets? *Journal of Law and Economics* 42 (2): 311–357.

Danzon, Patricia M., Sean Nicholson, and Nuno Sousa Pereira. 2005. Productivity in Pharmaceutical-Biotechnology R & D: The Role of Experience and Alliances. *Journal of Health Economics* 24 (2): 317–339.

Danzon, Patricia M., and Mark V. Pauly. 2002. Health Insurance and the Growth in Pharmaceutical Expenditures. *Journal of Law and Economics* 45: 587–613.

Danzon, Patricia M., Y. Richard Wang, and Liang Wang. 2005. The Impact of Price Regulation on the Launch Delay of New Drugs: Evidence from Twenty-Five Major Markets in the 1990s. *Health Economics* 14: 269–292.

Dardanoni, Valentino, and Adam Wagstaff. 1990. Uncertainty and the Demand for Medical Care. *Journal of Health Economics* 9 (1): 23–38.

Daughety, Andrew F., and Jennifer F. Reinganum. 2006. Imperfect Competition and Quality Signaling. Mimeo. Department of Economics, Vanderbilt University, WP05–W20.

Davis, Karen. 2004. Consumer-Directed Health Care: Will It Improve Health System Performance? *Health Services Research* 39 (4): 1219–1233.

Davis, Karen, Michelle M. Doty, and Alice Ho. 2005. How High Is Too High? Implications of High Deductible Health Plans. Commonwealth Fund, April. Available at <http://www.commonwealthfund.org/publications/publications_show.htm?doc_id=274007>.

Davis, Morris A., and E. Michael Foster. 2005. A Stochastic Dynamic Model of the Mental Health of Children. *International Economic Review* 46 (3): 837–866.

Deci, Edward L., Richard Koestner, and Richard M. Ryan. 1999a. A Meta-Analytic Review of Experiments Examining the Effects of Extrinsic Rewards on Intrinsic Motivation [see comment]. *Psychological Bulletin* 125 (6): 627–668.

———. 1999b. The Undermining Effect Is a Reality After All—Extrinsic Rewards, Task Interest, and Self-Determination: A Reply to Eisenberger, Pierve, and Camerson (1999) and Lepper, Henderlong, and Gingras (1999). *Psychological Bulletin* 125 (6): 692–700.

DeCicca, Philip, Donald Kenkel, and Alan Mathios. 2002. Putting Out the Fires: Will Higher Taxes Reduce the Onset of Youth Smoking? *Journal of Political Economy* 110 (1): 144.

———. 2005. The Fires Are Not Out Yet: Higher Taxes and Young Adult Smoking. In *Substance Use: Individual Behaviour, Social Interactions, Markets, and Politics*, ed. Björn Lindgren and Michael Grossman. New York: Elsevier.

DeCicca, Philip, Donald S. Kenkel, Alan D. Mathios, Yoon-Jeong Shin, and Jae-Young Lim. 2006. Youth Smoking, Cigarette Prices, and Anti-Smoking Sentiment. NBER Working Paper 12458. Cambridge, MA: National Bureau of Economic Research.

Delattre, Eric, and Brigitte Dormont. 2003. Fixed Fees and Physician-Induced Demand: A Panel Data Study on French Physicians. *Health Economics* 12 (9): 741–754.

della Vigna, Stefano, and Ulrike Malmendier. 2004. Contract Design and Self-control: Theory and Evidence. *Quarterly Journal of Economics* 119 (2): 353–402.

de Meza, David. 1983. Health Insurance and the Demand for Medical Care. *Journal of Health Economics* 2 (1): 47–54.

DeWalque, Damien. 2005. How Does the Impact of an HIV/AIDS Information Campaign Vary with Educational Attainment? Evidence from Rural Uganda. Development Research Group, World Bank.

Dills, Angela K., Mireille Jacobson, and Jeffrey A. Miron. 2005. The Effect of Alcohol Prohibition on Alcohol Consumption: Evidence from Drunkenness Arrests. *Economics Letters* 86 (2): 279–284.

DiMasi, Joseph A., Ronald W. Hansen, and Henry G. Grabowski. 2003. The Price of Innovation: New Estimates of Drug Development Costs. *Journal of Health Economics* 22 (2): 151–185.

DiNardo, John, and Thomas Lemieux. 2001. Alcohol, Marijuana, and American Youth: The Unintended Consequences of Government Regulation. *Journal of Health Economics* 20 (6): 991–1010.

Donabedian, Avedis. 1985. *The Methods and Findings of Quality Assessment and Monitoring: An Illustrated Analysis*. Vol. 3. Ann Arbor, MI: Health Administration Press.

Donohue, Julie M., and Ernst R. Berndt. 2004. Effects of Direct-to-Consumer Advertising on Medication Choice: The Case of Antidepressants. *Journal of Public Policy and Marketing* 23 (2): 115–127.

Donohue, Julie M., Marisa Cevasco, and Meredith B. Rosenthal. 2007. A Decade of Direct-to-Consumer Advertising of Prescription Drugs. *New England Journal of Medicine* 357 (7): 673–681.

Doran, Tim, Catherine Fullwood, Hugh Gravelle, David Reeves, Evangelos Kontopantelis, Urara Hiroeh, and Martin Roland. 2006. Pay-for-Performance Programs in Family Practices in the United Kingdom. *New England Journal of Medicine* 355 (4): 375–384.

Dorfman, Robert, and Peter O. Steiner. 1954. Optimal Advertising and Optimal Quality. *American Economic Review* 44 (5): 826.

Dranove, David. 1988. Demand Inducement and the Physician-Patient Relationship. *Economic Inquiry* 26 (2): 281–299.

Dranove, David, Daniel Kessler, Mark McClellan, and Mark Satterthwaite. 2003. Is More Information Better? The Effects of "Report Cards" on Health Care Providers. *Journal of Political Economy* 111 (3): 555–588.

Dranove, David, and Mark A. Satterthwaite. 1991. The Implications for Resource-Based Relative Value Scales for Physicians' Fees Income and Specialty Choices. In *Regulating Doctors' Fees: Competition, Benefits, and Controls under Medicare*, ed. H. E. Ted Frech. Washington, DC: AEI Press.

———. 1992. Monopolistic Competition When Price and Quality Are Imperfectly Observable. *RAND Journal of Economics* 23 (4): 518–534.

———. 1999. The Industrial Organization of Health Care Markets. In *Handbook of Health Economics*, ed. Anthony J. Culyer and Joseph P. Newhouse. Amsterdam: Elsevier.

Dranove, David, and Paul Wehner. 1994. Physician-Induced Demand for Childbirths. *Journal of Health Economics* 13 (1): 61–73.

Drummond, Michael. 2007. Using Economic Evaluation in Reimbursement Decisions for Health Technologies: Lessons from International Experience. In *Pharmaceutical Innovation: Incentives, Competition, and Cost-Benefit Analysis in International Perspective*, ed. Frank A. Sloan and Chee-Ruey Hsieh. Cambridge: Cambridge University Press.

Dukerich, Janet M., Brian R. Golden, and Stephen M. Shortell. 2002. Beauty Is in the Eye of the Beholder: The Impact of Organizational Identification, Identity, and Image on the Cooperative Behaviors of Physicians. *Administrative Science Quarterly* 47 (3): 507–533.

Dupas, Pascaline. 2006. Relative Risks and the Market for Sex: Teenagers, Sugar Daddies, and HIV in Kenya. Department of Economics, Dartmouth College.

Eggleston, Karen, Yu-Chu Shen, Joseph Lau, Christopher H. Schmid, and Jia Chan. 2006. Hospital Ownership and Quality of Care: What Explains the Different Results? Cambridge, MA: National Bureau of Economic Research.

Ehrlich, Isaac, and Hiroyuki Chuma. 1990. A Model of the Demand for Longevity and the Value of Life Extension. *Journal of Political Economy* 98 (4): 761–782.

Eisenberg, Daniel. 2004. Peer Effects for Adolescent Substance Use: Do They Really Exist? Unpub. ms., University of Michigan.

Eisenberg, John M. 1986. Doctors' *Decisions and the Cost of Medical Care*. Ann Arbor, MI: Health Administration Press.

Eisenhardt, Kathleen M. 1985. Control: Organizational and Economic Approaches. *Management Science* 31 (2): 134–149.

———. 1989. Agency Theory: An Assessment and Review. *Academy of Management Review* 14 (1): 57–74.

Ekelund, Mats, and Bjorn Persson. 2003. Pharmaceutical Pricing in a Regulated Market. *Review of Economics and Statistics* 85 (2): 298–306.

Ellis, Randall P., and Thomas G. McGuire. 1986. Provider Behavior under Prospective Reimbursement: Cost Sharing and Supply. *Journal of Health Economics* 5 (2): 129–151.

———. 1990. Optimal Payment Systems for Health Services. *Journal of Health Economics* 9 (4): 375–396.

———. 1993. Supply-Side and Demand-Side Cost Sharing in Health Care. *Journal of Economic Perspectives* 7 (4): 135–151.

Ellison, Sara Fisher, Iain Cockburn, Zvi Griliches, and Jerry Hausman. 1997. Characteristics of Demand for Pharmaceutical Products: An Examination of Four Cephalosporins. *RAND Journal of Economics* 28 (3): 426–446.

Elster, Jon. 1999. Introduction to *Addiction: Entries and Exits*, ed. Jon Elster. New York: Russell Sage Foundation.

Elster, Jon, and Ole-Jorgen Skog. 1999. Introduction to *Getting Hooked: Rationality and Addiction*, ed. Jon Elster and Ole-Jorgen Skog. New York: Cambridge University Press.

Ess, Silvia M., Sebastian Schneeweiss, and Thomas D. Szucs. 2003. European Healthcare Policies for Controlling Drug Expenditure. *Pharmacoeconomics* 21 (2): 89–103.

Evans, Robert G. 1974. Supplier-Induced Demand: Some Empirical Evidence and Implications. In *The Economics of Health and Medical Care*, edited by Mark Perlman. London: Macmillan.

Evans, William N., and Matthew C. Farrelly. 1998. The Compensating Behavior of Smokers: Taxes, Tar, and Nicotine. *RAND Journal of Economics* 29 (3): 578–595.

Fairbrother, Gerry, Karla L. Hanson, Stephen Friedman, and Gary C. Butts. 1999. The Impact of Physician Bonuses, Enhanced Fees, and Feedback on Childhood Immunization Coverage Rates. *American Journal of Public Health* 89 (2): 171–175.

Farley, Pamela J. 1986. Theories of the Price and Quantity of Physician Services: A Synthesis and Critique. *Journal of Health Economics* 5 (4): 315–333.

Farrelly, Matthew C., Jeremy W. Bray, Gary A. Zarkin, and Brett W. Wendling. 2001. The Joint Demand for Cigarettes and Marijuana: Evidence from the National Household Surveys on Drug Abuse. *Journal of Health Economics* 20 (1): 51–68.

Feather, Ken R. 1997. Oral History Interview with Ken Feather. Rockville, MD: U.S. Food and Drug Administration.

Fein, Rashi, and Gerald I. Weber, eds. 1971. *Financing Medical Education: An Analysis of Alternative Policies and Mechanisms*. New York: Carnegie Commission on Higher Education and the Commonwealth Fund.

Feldstein, Martin S. 1970. The Rising Price of Physicians' Services. *Review of Economics and Statistics* 52 (2): 121–133.

Feldstein, Paul J. 1999. *Health Care Economics*. Albany, NY: Delmar Publishers.

Fendrick, A. Mark, and Michael E. Chernew. 2006. Value-Based Insurance Design: A "Clinically Sensitive" Approach to Preserve Quality and Contain Costs. *American Journal of Managed Care* 1 (January): 18–20.

Fendrick, A. Mark, Dean G. Smith, Michael E. Chernew, and Sonali N. Shah. 2001. A Benefit-Based Copay for Prescription Drugs: Patient Contribution Based on Total Benefits, Not Drug Acquisition Cost. *American Journal of Managed Care* 7 (9): 861–867.

Fineberg, H. V., R. Bauman, and M. Sosman. 1977. Computerized Cranial Tomography. Effect on Diagnostic and Therapeutic Plans. *JAMA* 238 (3): 224–227.

Finkelstein, Amy. 2004. Static and Dynamic Effects of Health Policy. *Quarterly Journal of Economics* 119 (2): 527–567.

Finkelstein, Amy, and Kathleen McGarry. 2003. Private Information and Its Effect on Market Equilibrium: New Evidence from Long-Term Care Insurance. National Bureau of Economic Research working paper 9957.

Fisher, Elliott S., David E. Wennberg, Therese A. Stukel, Daniel J. Gottlieb, F. Lee Lucas, and Etoile L. Pinder. 2003a. The Implications of Regional Variations in Medicare Spending, Part 1: The Content, Quality, and Accessibility of Care. *Annals of Internal Medicine* 138 (4): 273.

———. 2003b. The Implications of Regional Variations in Medicare Spending, Part 2: Health Outcomes and Satisfaction with Care. *Annals of Internal Medicine* 138 (4): 288.

Fogel, Robert W. 1997. Secular Trends in Nutrition and Mortality. In *Handbook of Population and Family Economics*, ed. Mark R. Rosenzweig and Oded Stark. Amsterdam: Elsevier.

Forster, Martin, and Andrew M. Jones. 2001. The Role of Tobacco Taxes in Starting and Quitting Smoking: Duration Analysis of British Data. *Journal of the Royal Statistical Society: Series A (Statistics in Society)* 164 (3): 517–547.

Frank, Richard G. 2001. Prescription Drug Prices: Why Do Some Pay More Than Others Do? *Health Affairs* 20 (2): 115.

———. 2004. Behavioral Economics and Health Economics. National Bureau of Economic Research working paper WP10881.

———. 2006. Behavioral Economics and Health Economics. In *Economic Institutions and Behavioral Economics*, ed. Peter Diamond and Hannu Vartiainen. Princeton, NJ: Princeton University Press.

Frech, H. E. Ted, III. 1975. Imposed Health Insurance in Monopolistic Markets: A Theoretical Analysis. *Economic Inquiry* 13 (1): 55–70.

———. 1991. *Regulating Doctors' Fees: Competition, Benefits, and Controls under Medicare.* Washington, DC: AEI Press.

———. 1996. *Competition and Monopoly in Medical Care.* Washington, DC: AEI Press.

Frech, H. E. Ted, III, and Paul B. Ginsburg. 1975. Imposed Health Insurance in Monopolistic Markets: A Theoretical Analysis. *Economic Inquiry* 13 (1): 55–70.

Frederick, Shane, George Loewenstein, and Ted O'Donoghue. 2002. Time Discounting and Time Preference: A Critical Review. *Journal of Economic Literature* 40 (2): 351–401.

Freedman, Vicki A., and Linda G. Martin. 1998. Understanding Trends in Functional Limitations among Older Americans. *American Journal of Public Health* 88 (10): 1457–1462.

Frey, Bruno S. 1997. *Not Just for the Money: An Economic Theory of Personal Motivation.* Cheltenham, UK: Edward Elgar.

Frey, Bruno S., and Reto Jegen. 2001. Motivation Crowding Theory. *Journal of Economic Surveys* 15 (5): 589–611.

Friedman, Milton. 1953. *Essays in Positive Economics.* Chicago: University of Chicago Press.

———. 1991. Gammon's Law Points to Health Care Solution. *Wall Street Journal,* November 12, A20.

Friedman, Milton, and Simon Kuznets. 1945. *Income from Independent Professional Practice.* New York: National Bureau of Economic Research.

Friedson, Eliot. 1971. *The Professions and Their Prospects.* Beverly Hills, CA: Sage.

———. 1975. *Doctoring Together: A Study of Professional Social Control.* Chicago: University of Chicago Press.

———. 2001. *Professionalism: The Third Logic.* Chicago: University of Chicago Press.

Fuchs, Victor R. 1978. The Supply of Surgeons and the Demand for Operations. *Journal of Human Resources* 13: 35–56.

———. 1982. Time Preference and Health: An Exploratory Study. In *Economic Aspects of Health*, ed. Victor R. Fuchs. Chicago: University of Chicago Press.

Fukuyama, Francis. 1995. *Trust: The Social Virtues and the Creation of Prosperity*. London: Hamish Hamilton.

Galbraith, John Kenneth. 1958. *The Affluent Society*. Boston: Houghton-Mifflin.

Gambardella, Alfonso. 1995. *Science and Innovation: The U.S. Pharmaceutical Industry during the 1980s*. New York: Cambridge University Press.

Garber, Alan M., Charles I. Jones, and Paul M. Romer. 2006. Insurance and Incentives for Medical Innovation. National Bureau of Economic Research working paper 12080.

Gardner, Eliot L., and James David. 1999. The Neurobiology of Chemical Addiction. In *Getting Hooked: Rationality and Addiction*, ed. Jon Elster and Ole-Jorgen Skog. New York: Cambridge University Press.

Gaviria, Alejandro, and Steven Raphael. 2001. School-Based Peer Effects and Juvenile Behavior. *Review of Economics and Statistics* 83 (2): 257–268.

Gaynor, Martin. 1994. Issues in the Industrial Organization of the Market for Physician Services. *Journal of Economics and Management Strategy* 3 (1): 211–255.

———. 2006. What Do We Know about Competition and Quality in Health Care Markets. Cambridge, MA: National Bureau of Economic Research.

Gaynor, Martin, and Paul Gertler. 1995. Moral Hazard and Risk Spreading in Partnerships. *RAND Journal of Economics* 26 (4): 591–614.

Gaynor, Martin, Harald Seider, and William B. Vogt. 2005. Volume-Outcome and Antitrust in U.S. Health Care Markets. *American Economic Review Papers and Proceedings* 95 (2): 243–247.

Gerdtham, Ulf G., and Bengt Jönsson. 2000. International Comparisons of Health Expenditure: Theory, Data, and Econometric Analysis. In *Handbook of Health Economics*, ed. Anthony J. Culyer and Joseph P. Newhouse. Amsterdam: Elsevier.

Gerhart, Barry, and Sara L. Rynes. 2003. *Compensation: Theory, Evidence, and Strategic Implications*. Thousand Oaks, CA: Sage.

Gertler, Paul, Manisha Shah, and Stefano M. Bertozzi. 2005. Risky Business: The Market for Unprotected Commercial Sex. *Journal of Political Economy* 113 (3): 518–550.

Getzen, Thomas E. 1984. A "Brand Name Firm" Theory of Medical Group Practice. *Journal of Industrial Economics* 33 (2): 199–215.

Geweke, John, Gautam Gowrisankaran, and Robert J. Town. 2003. Bayesian Inference for Hospital Quality in a Selection Model. *Econometrica* 71 (4): 1215–1238.

Giaccotto, Carmelo, Rexford E. Santerre, and John A. Vernon. 2005. Drug Prices and Research and Development Investment Behavior in the Pharmaceutical Industry. *Journal of Law and Economics* 48 (1): 195–214.

Gibson, Diane. 2003. Food Stamp Program Participation Is Positively Related to Obesity in Low Income Women. *Journal of Nutrition* 133 (7): 2225–2231.

Gibson, Teresa B., Ronald J. Ozminkowski, and Ron Z. Goetzel. 2005. The Effects of Prescription Drug Cost Sharing: A Review of the Evidence. *American Journal of Managed Care* 11 (1): 730–740.

Gilleskie, Donna B. 1998. A Dynamic Stochastic Model of Medical Care Use and Work Absence. *Econometrica* 66 (1): 1–44.

Gilleskie, Donna B., and Thomas A. Mroz. 2004. A Flexible Approach for Estimating the Effects of Covariates on Health Expenditures. *Journal of Health Economics* 23 (2): 391–418.

Gilleskie, Donna B., and Koleman S. Strumpf. 2005. The Behavioral Dynamics of Youth Smoking. *Journal of Human Resources* 40 (4): 822–866.

Ginsburg, Paul B., and Joy M. Grossman. 2005. When the Price Isn't Right: How Inadvertent Payment Incentives Drive Medical Care. *Health Affairs* 24: W376–W384.

Glazer, Jacob, and Thomas G. McGuire. 2000. Optimal Risk Adjustment in Markets with Adverse Selection: An Application to Managed Care. *American Economic Review* 90 (4): 1055–1071.

———. 2001. Why Don't Private Employers Use Risk Adjustment? Conference Overview. *Inquiry* 38 (3): 242–244.

———. 2002. Multiple Payers, Commonality, and Free-Riding in Health Care: Medicare and Private Payers. *Journal of Health Economics* 21: 1049–1069.

Glickman, Seth W., Fang-Shu Ou, Elizabeth R. DeLong, Matthew T. Roe, Barbara L. Lytle, Jyotsna Mulgund, John S. Rumsfeld, W. Brian Gibler, E. Magnus Ohman, Kevin A. Schulman, and Eric D. Peterson. 2007. Pay for Performance, Quality of Care, and Outcomes in Acute Myocardial Infarction. *JAMA* 297 (21): 2373–2380.

Golden, Brian R., Janet M. Dukerich, and Frances H. Fabian. 2000. The Interpretation and Resolution of Resource Allocation Issues in Professional Organizations: A Critical Examination of the Professional-Manager Dichotomy. *Journal of Management Studies* 37 (8): 1157–1187.

Golden, Brian R., and Hao Ma. 2003. Mutual Forbearance: The Role of Intrafirm Integration and Rewards. *Academy of Management Review* 28 (3): 479–493.

Goldman, Dana P., Geoffrey F. Joyce, Jose J. Escarce, Jennifer E. Pace, Matthew D. Solomon, Marianne Laouri, Pamela B. Landsman, and Steven M. Teutsch. 2004. Pharmacy Benefits and the Use of Drugs by the Chronically Ill. *Journal of the American Medical Association* 291 (19): 2344–2350.

Goode, William J. 1957. Community within a Community: The Professions. *American Sociological Review* 22 (2): 194–200.

Govindarajan, Vijay, and Joseph Fisher. 1990. Strategy, Control Systems, and Resource Sharing: Effects on Business-Unit Performance. *Academy of Management Journal* 33 (2): 259–285.

Gowrisankaran, Gautam, Vivian Ho, and Robert Town. 2006. Causality, Learning, and Forgetting in Surgery. Mimeo, working paper, University of Minnesota.

Gowrisankaran, Gautam, and Robert J. Town. 1997. Dynamic Equilibrium in the Hospital Industry. *Journal of Economics and Management Strategy* 6 (1): 45–74.

———. 2003. Competition, Payers, and Hospital Quality. *Health Services Research* 38 (6): 1403–1422.

Grabowski, Henry G. 2007. Competition between Generic and Branded Drugs. In *Pharmaceutical Innovation: Incentives, Competition, and Cost-Benefit Analysis in International Perspective*, ed. Frank A. Sloan and Chee-Ruey Hsieh. Cambridge: Cambridge University Press.

Grabowski, Henry G., and John M. Vernon. 2000. Effective Patent Life in Pharmaceuticals. *International Journal of Technology Management* 18 (1–2): 98–99.

Grabowski, Henry G., and Y. Richard Wang. 2006. TRENDS: The Quantity and Quality of Worldwide New Drug Introductions, 1982–2003. *Health Affairs* 25 (2): 452–460.

Granovetter, Mark. 1985. Economic Action and Social Structure: The Problem of Embeddedness. *American Journal of Sociology* 91 (3): 481–510.

Grossman, Michael. 1972a. *The Demand for Health: A Theoretical and Empirical Investigation.* New York: Columbia University Press.

———. 1972b. On the Concept of Health Capital and the Demand for Health. *Journal of Political Economy* 80 (2): 223–255.

———. 1982. The Demand for Health after a Decade. *Journal of Health Economics* 1 (1): 1–3.

———. 2000. The Human Capital Model of the Demand for Health. In *Handbook of Health Economics*, ed. Anthony J. Culyer and Joseph P. Newhouse. Amsterdam: Elsevier.

———. 2001. The Economics of Substance Use and Abuse: The Role of Price. In *The Economic Analysis of Substance Use and Abuse*, ed. Michael Grossman and Chee-Ruey Hsieh. Northampton, MA: Edward Elgar.

———. 2004. The Demand for Health, 30 Years Later: A Very Personal Retrospective and Prospective Reflection. *Journal of Health Economics* 23 (4): 629–636.

Grossman, Michael, and Frank J. Chaloupka. 1998. The Demand for Cocaine by Young Adults: A Rational Addiction Approach. *Journal of Health Economics* 17 (4): 427–474.

Gruber, Jonathan H. 2000. Health Insurance and the Labor Market. In *Handbook of Health Economics*, ed. Anthony J. Culyer and Joseph P. Newhouse. Amsterdam: Elsevier.

Gruber, Jonathan H., John Kim, and Dina Mayzlin. 1999. Physician Fees and Procedure Intensity: The Case of Cesarean Delivery. *Journal of Health Economics* 18 (4): 473–490.

Gruber, Jonathan H., and Botond Köszegi. 2001. Is Addiction "Rational"? Theory and Evidence. *Quarterly Journal of Economics* 116 (4): 1261–1303.

———. 2004. A Theory of Government Regulation of Addictive Bads: Tax Levels and Tax Incidence for Cigarette Excise Taxation. *Journal of Public Economics* 88 (9–10): 1959–1987.

Gruber, Jonathan H., and Sendhil Mullainathan. 2005. Do Cigarette Taxes Make Smokers Happier? *Advances in Economic Analysis and Policy* 5 (1): 1–45.

Gruber, Jonathan H., and Maria Owings. 1996. Physician Financial Incentives and Cesarean Section Delivery. *RAND Journal of Economics* 27 (1): 99–123.

Haas-Wilson, Deborah. 2003. *Managed Care and Monopoly Power*. Cambridge, MA: Harvard University Press.

Hadley, Jack, Jeanne S. Mandelblatt, Jean M. Mitchell, Jane C. Weeks, Edward Guadagnoli, and Yi-Ting Hwang. 2003. Medicare Breast Surgery Fees and Treatment Received by Older Women with Localized Breast Cancer. *Health Services Research* 38 (2): 553–574.

Hall, Brian J., and Jeffrey B. Liebman. 1998. Are CEOs Really Paid Like Bureaucrats? *Quarterly Journal of Economics* 113 (3): 653–691.

Hall, Robert E., and Charles I. Jones. 2007. The Value of Life and the Rise in Health Spending. *Quarterly Journal of Economics* 122 (1): 39–72.

Halm, Ethan A., Clara Lee, and Mark R. Chassin. 2002. Is Volume Related to Outcome in Health Care? A Systematic Review and Methodologic Critique of the Literature. *Annals of Internal Medicine* 137 (6): 511–552.

Hamermesh, Daniel S., and Neal M. Soss. 1974. An Economic Theory of Suicide. *Journal of Political Economy* 82 (1): 83.

Hamilton, Barton, and Brian McManus. 2005. Competition, Insurance, and Quality in the Market for Advanced Infertility Treatment. Mimeo. John M. Olin School of Business, Washington University, St. Louis.

Hammitt, James K., Jin-Tan Lui, and Jin-Long Lui. 2000. Survival Is a Luxury Good: The Increasing Value of a Statistical Life. Mimeo, Harvard University.

Harris, Richard. 1964. *The Real Voice*. New York: Macmillan.

Hay, Joel. 1991. Physicians' Specialty Choice and Specialty Income. In *Econometrics of Health Care*, ed. Gérard Duru and Jean H. P. Paelinck. Amsterdam: Kluwer Academic Publishers.

Heckman, James J. 2000. Causal Parameters and Policy Analysis in Economics: A Twentieth Century Retrospective. *Quarterly Journal of Economics* 115 (1): 45–97.

Heidenreich, Paul, and Mark B. McClellan. 2000. Trends in Heart Attack Treatments and Outcomes, 1975–1995: A Literature Review and Synthesis. In *Medical Care Output and Productivity*, ed. Ernst R. Berndt and David M. Cutler. Chicago: Chicago University Press.

Hellerstein, Judith K. 1998. The Importance of the Physician in the Generic versus Trade-Name Prescription Decision. *RAND Journal of Economics* 29 (1): 108.

Herring, Bradley, and Mark V. Pauly. 2006. Incentive-Compatible Guaranteed Renewable Health Insurance Premiums. *Journal of Health Economics* 25 (3): 395–417.

Hibbard, Judith H., and Jacquelyn J. Jewett. 1996. What Type of Quality Information Do Consumers Want in a Health Care Report Card? *Medical Care Research and Review* 53 (1): 28–47.

Hickson, Gerald B., William A. Altemeier, and James M. Perrin. 1987. Physician Reimbursement by Salary or Fee-for-Service: Effect on Physician Practice Behavior in a Randomized Prospective Study. *Pediatrics* 80 (3): 344–350.

Higgins, Stephen T., Sheila M. Alessi, and Robert L. Dantona. 2002. Voucher-Based Incentives: A Substance Abuse Treatment Innovation. *Addictive Behaviors* 27 (6): 887–910.

Hillman, Alan L., and Kimberly Ripley. 1999. The Use of Physician Financial Incentives and Feedback to Improve Pediatric Preventive Care in Medicine. *Pediatrics* 104 (4): 931.

Hillman, Alan L., Kimberly Ripley, Neil Goldfarb, Isaac Nuamah, Jonathan Weiner, and Edward Lusk. 1998. Physician Financial Incentives and Feedback: Failure to Increase Cancer Screening in Medicaid Managed Care. *American Journal of Public Health* 88 (11): 1699–1701.

Ho, Vivian, Robert J. Town, and Martin Heslin. 2005. Regionalization versus Competition in Complex Cancer Surgery. Mimeo. International Health Economics Association 5th World Congress, Barcelona, Spain.

Hollis, Aidan. 2007. Drugs for Neglected Diseases: New Incentives for Innovation. In *Pharmaceutical Innovation: Incentives, Competition, and Cost-Benefit Analysis in International Perspective*, ed. Frank A. Sloan and Chee-Ruey Hsieh. New York: Cambridge University Press.

Holmer, Alan F. 1999. Direct-to-Consumer Prescription Drug Advertising Builds Bridges between Patients and Physicians. *JAMA* 281 (4): 380–382.

———. 2002. Direct-to-Consumer Advertising: Strengthening Our Health Care System. *New England Journal of Medicine* 346 (7): 526–528.

House, Robert J. 1971. A Path Goal Theory of Leader Effectiveness. *Administrative Science Quarterly* 16 (3): 321–328.

Hsiao, William C., Peter Braun, Douwe Yntema, and Edmund R. Becker. 1988. Estimating Physicians' Work for a Resource-Based Relative-Value Scale. *New England Journal of Medicine* 319 (13): 835–841.

Hsieh, Chee-Ruey, Kuang-Ta Lo, Yichen Hong, and Ya-Chen Shih. 2007. Pharmaceutical Innovation and Health Outcomes: Empirical Evidence from Taiwan. In *Pharmaceutical Innovation: Incentives, Competition, and Cost-Benefit Analysis in International Perspective*, ed. Frank A. Sloan and Chee-Ruey Hsieh. Cambridge: Cambridge University Press.

Hsu, John, Mary Price, Richard Brand, G. Thomas Ray, Bruce Fireman, Joseph P. Newhouse, and Joseph V. Selby. 2006a. Cost-Sharing for Emergency Care and Unfavorable Clinical Events: Findings from the Safety and Financial Ramifications of ED Copayments Study. *Health Services Research* 41 (5): 1801–1820.

Hsu, John, Mary Price, Jie Huang, Richard Brand, Vicki Fung, Rita Hui, Bruce Fireman, Joseph P. Newhouse, and Joseph V. Selby. 2006b. Unintended Consequences of Caps on Medicare Drug Benefits. *New England Journal of Medicine* 354 (22): 2349–2359.

Hurley, Jeremiah E. 1991. Physicians' Choices of Specialty, Location, and Mode. *Journal of Human Resources* 26 (1): 47–71.

———. 2000. An Overview of the Normative Economics of the Health Sector. In *Handbook of Health Economics*, ed. Anthony J. Culyer and Joseph P. Newhouse. Amsterdam: Elsevier.

Huskamp, Haiden A., Patricia A. Deverka, Arnold M. Epstein, Robert S. Epstein, Kimberly A. McGuigan, and Richard G. Frank. 2003. The Effect of Incentive-Based Formularies on Prescription-Drug Utilization and Spending. *New England Journal of Medicine* 349 (23): 2224–2232.

Huskamp, Haiden A., Patricia A. Deverka, Arnold M. Epstein, Robert S. Epstein, Kimberly A. McGuigan, Anna C. Muriel, and Richard G. Frank. 2005. Impact of 3-Tier Formularies on Drug Treatment of Attention-Deficit/Hyperactivity Disorder in Children. *Archives of General Psychiatry* 62 (4): 435–441.

Iizuka, Toshiaki. 2004. What Explains the Use of Direct-to-Consumer Advertising of Prescription Drugs? *Journal of Industrial Economics* 52 (3): 349–379.

Iizuka, Toshiaki, and Ginger Zhe Jin. 2005a. Direct to Consumer Advertising and Prescription Choice. Owen Graduate School of Management, Vanderbilt University.

———. 2005b. The Effect of Prescription Drug Advertising on Doctor Visits. *Journal of Economics and Management Strategy* 14 (3): 701–727.

IMS Health. 2005. *Top-line Industry Data: Total U.S. Promotional Spending by Type.* Available at <http://imshealth.com/ims/portal/front/articleC/0,2777,6599_78084568_78152318,00.html> (accessed August 22, 2006).

Institute of Medicine. 1999. *To Err Is Human.* Washington, DC: National Academies Press.

———. 2001. *Crossing the Quality Chasm: A New Health System for the Twenty-First Century.* Washington, DC: National Academies Press.

———. 2004. *Insuring America's Health: Principles and Recommendations.* Washington, DC: National Academies Press.

———. 2006. *Rewarding Provider Performance: Aligning Incentives in Medicare.* Washington, DC: National Academies Press.

Institute for OneWorld Health. 2007. Visceral Leishmaniasis Fact Sheet. Available at <www.oneworldhealth.org/pdf/leishmaniasis%20Fact%20Sheet.pdf>.

Ippolito, Pauline M., and Alan D. Mathios. 1995. Information and Advertising: The Case of Fat Consumption in the United States. *American Economic Review* 85 (2): 91.

Irons, Richard, and Jennifer P. Schneider. 1996. Differential Diagnosis of Addictive Sexual Disorders Using the DSM-IV. *Sexual Addiction & Compulsivity* 3: 7–21.

Jacobson, Lena. 2000. The Family as Producer of Health: An Extended Grossman Model. *Journal of Health Economics* 19 (5): 611–637.

Jacobson, Mireille, A. James O'Malley, Craig C. Earle, Juliana Pakes, Peter Gaccione, and Joseph P. Newhouse. 2006. Does Reimbursement Influence Chemotherapy Treatment for Cancer Patients? *Health Affairs* 25 (2): 437–443.

Jamison, Dean T. 2006. Investing in Health. In *Disease Control Priorities in Developing Countries,* ed. Dean T. Jamison, Joel G. Breman, Anthony R. Measham, George Alleyne, Mariam Claeson, David B. Evans, Prabhat Jha, Anne Mills, and Philip Musgrove. Oxford: Oxford University Press.

Jensen, Michael C., and Kevin J. Murphy. 1990. Performance Pay and Top-Management Incentives. *Journal of Political Economy* 98 (2): 225–264.

Jin, Ginger Zhe, and Phillip Leslie. 2003. The Effect of Information on Product Quality: Evidence from Restaurant Hygiene Grade Cards. *Quarterly Journal of Economics* 118 (2): 409–451.

Jin, Ginger Zhe, and Alan T. Sorensen. 2006. Information and Consumer Choice: The Value of Publicized Health Plan Ratings. *Journal of Health Economics* 25 (2): 248–275.

Kahneman, Daniel, Ilana Ritov, and David Schkade. 1998. Economists Have Preferences, Psychologists Have Attitudes: An Analysis of Dollar Responses to Public Issues. Princeton University working paper 0-8330-0782-3.

Kaiser Family Foundation and Health Research Education Trust. 2005. *Employer Health Benefits 2005 Annual Survey, September, Section 9a.* Available at <http://www.kff.org/insurance/7315/index.cfm> (accessed July 27, 2006).

Kakalik, James S., and Nicholas M. Pace. 1986. *Costs and Compensation Paid in Tort Litigation.* Santa Monica, CA: Institute for Civil Justice, RAND.

Kallen, Alexander, Steven Woloshin, Jennifer Shu, Ellen Juhl, and Lisa Schwartz. 2007. Marketwatch: Direct-to-Consumer Advertisements for HIV Antiretroviral Medications: A Progress Report. *Health Affairs* 26 (5): 1392.

Keeler, Emmett B., Joseph P. Newhouse, and C. E. Phelps. 1977. Deductibles and the Demand for Medical Care Services: The Theory of a Consumer Facing a Variable Price Schedule under Uncertainty. *Econometrica* 45 (3): 641–655.

Kenkel, Donald S. 1991. Health Behavior, Health Knowledge, and Schooling. *Journal of Political Economy* 99 (2): 287–305.

Kersh, Rogan, and James Morone. 2002. The Politics of Obesity: Seven Steps to Government Action. *Health Affairs* 21 (6): 142.

Kessel, Reuben. 1958. Price Discrimination in Medicine. *Journal of Law and Economics* 1: 20–53.

Kessler, Daniel P., and Mark B. McClellan. 1996. Do Doctors Practice Defensive Medicine? *Quarterly Journal of Economics* 111 (2): 353–390.

———. 2000. Is Hospital Competition Socially Wasteful? *Quarterly Journal of Economics* 115 (2): 577–615.

Khatri, Naresh, Alok Baveja, Suzanne A. Boren, and Abate Mammo. 2006. Medical Errors and Quality of Care: From Control to Commitment. *California Management Review* 48 (3): 113–141.

Khwaja, Ahmed. 2001. Health Insurance, Habits, and Health Outcomes: A Dynamic Stochastic Model of Investment in Health. Ph.D. diss., University of Minnesota.

———. 2006. A Life Cycle Analysis of the Effects of Medicare on Individual Health Incentives and Health Outcomes Mimeo. Fuqua School of Business, Duke University. Working paper (no number).

Kihlstrom, Richard E., and Michael H. Riordan. 1984. Advertising as a Signal. *Journal of Political Economy* 92, no. 3 (June): 427–450.

Kirigia, Joses M., and Lenity H. Kainyu. 2000. Predictors of Toilet Ownership in South Africa. *East African Medical Journal* 77 (12): 66–67.

Kolata, Gina. 1983. Prescription Drug Ads Put FDA on the Spot (Legal and Ethical Complications). *Science* 220 (April 22): 387–389.

Kouides, Ruth W., Nancy M. Bennett, Bonnie Lewis, Joseph D. Cappuccio, William H. Barker, and F. Marc LaForce. 1998. Performance-Based Physician Reimbursement and Influenza Immunization Rates in the Elderly: The Primary-Care Physicians of Monroe County. *American Journal of Preventive Medicine* 14 (2): 89–95.

Kravitz, Richard L., Ronald M. Epstein, Mitchell D. Feldman, Carol E. Franz, Rahman Azari, Michael S. Wilkes, Ladson Hinton, and Peter Franks. 2005. Influence of Patients' Requests for Direct-to-Consumer Advertised Antidepressants: A Randomized Controlled Trial. *JAMA* 293 (16): 1995–2002.

Kreling, David H., David A. Mott, and Joseph B. Wiederholt. 2001. *Prescription Drug Trend: A Chartbook Update.* Henry J. Kaiser Family Foundation. Available at <http://www.kff.org/rxdrugs/upload/Prescription-Drug-Trends-A-Chartbook -Update-Chartbook.pdf> (accessed July 27, 2006).

Kremer, Michael. 1993. The O-Ring Theory of Economic Development. *Quarterly Journal of Economics* 108 (3): 551.

Kremer, Michael, and Rachel Glennerster. 2004. *Strong Medicine: Creating Incentives for Pharmaceutical Research on Neglected Diseases.* Princeton, NJ: Princeton University Press.

Kremer, Michael, and Christopher M. Snyder. 2003. Why Are Drugs More Profitable Than Vaccines? Cambridge, MA: National Bureau of Economic Research.

Kreps, David M. 1997. Intrinsic Motivation and Extrinsic Incentives. *American Economic Review* 87 (2): 359–364.

Kutty, Nandinee K. 1998. *The Production Function by the Elderly: A Household Production Function Approach.* Social Science Research Network. Available at <http://papers.ssrn .com/5013/papers.cfm?abstract_id=133332#paperdownload> (accessed February 21, 2007).

Laibson, David. 1997. Golden Eggs and Hyperbolic Discounting. *Quarterly Journal of Economics* 112 (2): 443–477.

Landon, Bruce E., Sharon-Lise T. Normand, Richard Frank, and Barbara J. McNeil. 2005. Characteristics of Medical Practices in Three Developed Managed Care Markets. *Health Care Organizations and Their Environments* 40 (3): 675.

Lazear, Edward P. 1999. Personnel Economics: Past Lessons and Future Directions. *Journal of Labor Economics* 17 (2): 199.

———. 2000. Performance Pay and Productivity. *American Economic Review* 90 (5): 1346–1361.

Leape, Lucian. 1994. Error in Medicine. *JAMA* 272 (23): 1851–1857.

Lee, Chulhee. 2005. Wealth Accumulation and the Health of Union Army Veterans, 1860–1880. *Journal of Economic History* 65 (2): 352–385.

Lee, Thomas H., and James J. Mongan. 2006. Are Health Care's Problems Incurable? One Integrated Delivery System's Program for Transforming Its Care. Brookings Institution. Available at <http://www.brookings.edu>.

Leffler, Keith B. 1978. Physician Licensure: Competition and Monopoly in American Medicine. *Journal of Law and Economics* 21: 165–186.

Leibenstein, Harvey. 1950. Bandwagon, Snob, and Veblen Effects in the Theory of Consumers' Demand. *Quarterly Journal of Economics* 64 (2): 183–207.

Levin, Richard C., Alvin K. Klevorick, Richard R. Nelson, Sidney G. Winter, Richard Gilbert, and Zvi Griliches. 1987. Appropriating the Returns from Industrial Research and Development; Comments and Discussion. *Brookings Papers on Economic Activity* (3): 783–820.

Levine, Philip B. 2001. The Sexual Activity and Birth-Control Use of American Teenagers. In *Risky Behavior among Youths: An Economic Analysis*, ed. Jonathan H. Gruber. Chicago: University of Chicago Press.

Levy, Douglas E., and Ellen Meara. 2006. The Effect of the 1998 Master Settlement Agreement on Prenatal Smoking. *Journal of Health Economics* 25 (2): 276–294.

Levy, Helen, and David Meltzer. 2004. What Do We Really Know about Whether Health Insurance Affects Health? In *Health Policy and the Uninsured*, ed. Catherine G. McLaughlin. Washington, DC: Urban Institute Press.

Lichtenberg, Frank R. 2001. The Effect of New Drugs on Mortality from Rare Diseases and HIV. Cambridge, MA: National Bureau of Economic Research.

———. 2003. Pharmaceutical Innovation, Mortality Reduction, and Economic Growth. In *Measuring the Gains from Medical Research: An Economic Approach*, ed. Kevin M. Murphy and Richard H. Topel. Chicago: University of Chicago Press.

———. 2005. Pharmaceutical Innovation and the Burden of Disease in Developed and Developing Countries. *Journal of Medicine and Philosophy* 30 (6): 633–690.

Lien, Hsien-Ming, Ching-to Albert Ma, and Thomas G. McGuire. 2004. Provider-Client Interactions and Quantity of Health Care Use. *Journal of Health Economics* 23 (6): 1261–1283.

Lindenauer, Peter K., Denise Remus, Sheila Roman, Michael B. Rothberg, Evan M. Benjamin, Allen Ma, and Dale W. Bratzler. 2007. Public Reporting and Pay for Performance in Hospital Quality Improvement. *New England Journal of Medicine* 356 (5): 486–496.

Lindsay, Cotton M. 1973. Real Returns to Medical Education. *Journal of Human Resources* 8 (3): 331–348.

Localio, A. Russell, Ann G. Lawthers, Troyen A. Brennan, Nan M. Laird, Liesi E. Hebert, Lynn M. Peterson, Joseph P. Newhouse, Howard H. Hiatt, and Paul C. Weiler. 1991. Relation between Malpractice Claims and Adverse Events Due to Negligence. Results of the Harvard Medical Practice Study III. *New England Journal of Medicine* 325 (4): 245–251.

Locke, Edwin A., and Gary P. Latham. 1984. *Goal Setting: A Motivational Technique That Works*. Englewood Cliffs, NJ: Prentice Hall.

Lopez-Casasnovas, Guillem, Berta Rivera, and Luis Currais, eds. 2006. *Health and Economic Growth: Findings and Policy Implications*. Cambridge, MA: MIT Press.

Lowenstein, George. 1999. A Visceral Account of Addiction. In *Getting Hooked: Rationality and Addiction*, ed. Jon Elster and Ole-Jorgan Skog. New York: Cambridge University Press.

Lowes, Robert. 2003. Malpractice: Do Other Countries Hold the Key? *Medical Economics* 80: 58–69.

Lu, Z. John, and William S. Comanor. 1998. Strategic Pricing of New Pharmaceuticals. *Review of Economics and Statistics* 80 (1): 108–118.

Lucas, Robert E., Jr. 1976. Economic Policy Evaluation: A Critique. Paper presented at the Carnegie-Rochester conference series on public policy.

Lueck, Sarah, and Jane Zhang. 2006. Give Us Your Sick . . . Thanks to a Shift in Medicare Policies, Insurers Are Seeking Out Those They Once Avoided. *Wall Street Journal*, October 21, R5.

Luft, Harold S., Sandra S. Hunt, and Susan C. Maerki. 1987. The Volume-Outcome Relationship: Practice-Makes-Perfect or Selective-Referral Patterns? *Health Services Research* 22: 157–182.

Lundborg, Petter. 2006. Having the Wrong Friends? Peer Effects in Adolescent Substance Use. *Journal of Health Economics* 25 (2): 214–233.

Lussier, Jennifer Plebani, Sarah H. Heil, Joan A. Mongeon, Gary J. Badger, and Stephen T. Higgins. 2006. A Meta-Analysis of Voucher-Based Reinforcement Therapy for Substance Use Disorders. *Addiction* 101 (2): 192–203.

Ma, Ching-to Albert. 1994. Health Care Payment Systems: Cost and Quality Incentives. *Journal of Economics and Management Strategy* 3 (1): 93–112.

Ma, Ching-to Albert, and Thomas G. McGuire. 1997. Optimal Health Insurance and Provider Payment. *American Economic Review* 87 (4): 685–704.

Maddala, G. S. 1983. A Survey of the Literature on Selectivity Bias as It Pertains to Health Care Markets. In *Advances in Health Economics and Health Services Research*, ed. Richard M. Scheffler and Louis F. Rossiter. London: JAI Press.

Madison, Kristin M. 2005. The Residency Match: Competitive Restraints in an Imperfect World. *Houston Law Review* 42: 759–836.

Madrian, Brigitte C., and Dennis F. Shea. 2001. The Power of Suggestion: Inertia in 401(K) Participation and Savings Behavior. *Quarterly Journal of Economics* 116 (4): 1149–1187.

Manning, Willard G., Linda Blumberg, and Lawrence H. Moulton. 1995. The Demand for Alcohol: The Differential Response to Price. *Journal of Health Economics* 14 (2): 123–148.

Manning, Willard G., Emmett Keeler, Joseph P. Newhouse, Elizabeth Sloss, and Jeffrey Wasserman. 1991. *The Costs of Poor Health Habits*. Cambridge, MA: Harvard University Press.

Manning, Willard G., and M. Susan Marquis. 1996. Health Insurance: The Trade-off between Risk Pooling and Moral Hazard. *Journal of Health Economics* 15 (5): 609–639.

Manning, Willard G., and John Mullahy. 2001. Estimating Log Models: To Transform or Not to Transform? *Journal of Health Economics* 20 (4): 461–494.

Manning, Willard G., Joseph P. Newhouse, Naihua Duan, Emmett B. Keeler, Arleen Leibowitz, and M. Susan Marquis. 1987. Health Insurance and the Demand for Medical Care: Evidence from a Randomized Experiment. *American Economic Review* 77 (3): 251.

Mansfield, Edwin. 1986. Patents and Innovation: An Empirical Study. *Management Science* 32 (2): 173–181.

Manski, Charles F. 2004. Measuring Expectations. *Econometrica* 72 (5): 1329–1376.

Manton, Kenneth G., and XiLiang Gu. 2001. From the Cover: Changes in the Prevalence of Chronic Disability in the United States Black and Nonblack Population above Age 65 from 1982 to 1999. *Proceedings of the National Academy of Sciences* 98 (11): 6354–6359.

Marder, William D., and Richard J. Willke. 1991. Comparisons of the Value of Physician Time by Specialty. In *Regulating Doctor's Fees*, ed. H. E. Frech. Washington, DC: American Enterprise Institute Press.

Markel, Howard. 2006. Dr. Osler's Relapsing Fever. *JAMA* 295 (24): 2886–2887.

Markowitz, Sara, and Michael Grossman. 2000. The Effects of Beer Taxes on Physical Child Abuse. *Journal of Health Economics* 19 (2): 271–282.

Markowitz, Sara, and John Tauras. 2006. Even for Teenagers, Money Does Not Grow on Trees: Teenage Substance Abuse and Budget Constraints. National Bureau of Economic Research working paper 12300.

Marschak, Jacob. 1953. Econometric Measurements for Policy and Prediction. In *Studies in Econometric Methods*, ed. William Hood and Tjalling Koopmans. New York: John Wiley.

Maryland Department of Health and Mental Hygiene. 2004. *Student Winners Announced in Stop Smoking Public Service Announcement Campaign.* Available at <http://www.dhmh .state.md.us/publi-rel/html/pr032604.htm> (accessed April 5, 2006).

Mathios, Alan D. 2000. The Impact of Mandatory Disclosure Laws on Product Choices: An Analysis of the Salad Dressing Market. *Journal of Law and Economics* 43 (2): 651–677.

Maurer, Stephen M. 2007. When Patents Fail: Finding New Drugs for the Developing World. In *Pharmaceutical Innovation: Incentives, Competition, and Cost-Benefit Analysis in International Perspective*, ed. Frank A. Sloan and Chee-Ruey Hsieh. Cambridge: Cambridge University Press.

McCall, Timothy B. 1996. *Examining Your Doctor: A Patient's Guide to Avoiding Harmful Medical Care.* Secaucus, NJ: Citadel Press.

McCarthy, Thomas R. 1985. The Competitive Nature of the Primary-Care Physician Services Market. *Journal of Health Economics* 4 (2): 93–117.

McClellan, Mark, Barbara J. McNeil, and Joseph P. Newhouse. 1994. Does More Intensive Treatment of Acute Myocardial Infarction in the Elderly Reduce Mortality? Analysis Using Instrumental Variables. *JAMA* 272 (11): 859–866.

McClellan, Mark, and Douglas O. Staiger. 1999a. Comparing Hospital Quality at For-Profit and Not-for-Profit Hospitals. Cambridge, MA: National Bureau of Economic Research.

———. 1999b. The Quality of Health Care Providers. Cambridge, MA: National Bureau of Economic Research.

McCormack, Lauren A., Peter D. Fox, Thomas Rice, and Marcia L. Graham. 1996. Medigap Reform Legislation of 1990: Have the Objectives Been Met? *Health Care Financing Review* 18 (1): 157.

McGlynn, Elizabeth A., Steven M. Asch, John L. Adams, Joan Keesey, Jennifer Hicks, Alison H. DeCristofaro, and Eve A. Kerr. 2003. The Quality of Health Care Delivered to Adults in the United States. *New England Journal of Medicine* 348 (26): 2635.

McGuire, Thomas G. 1983. Patients' Trust and the Quality of Physicians. *Economic Inquiry* 21 (2): 203–223.

———. 2000. Physician Agency. In *Handbook of Health Economics*, ed. Anthony J. Culyer and Joseph P. Newhouse. Amsterdam: Elsevier.

———. 2003. Physician Agency. In *Handbook of Health Economics*, ed. Joseph P. Newhouse and Anthony J. Culyer. Amsterdam: Elsevier.

McGuire, Thomas G., and Mark V. Pauly. 1991. Physician Response to Fee Changes with Multiple Payers. *Journal of Health Economics* 10 (4): 385–410.

McNeil, Barbara J., and S. James Aldestein. 1976. Determining the Value of Diagnostic and Screening Tests. *Journal of Nuclear Medicine* 17: 439–448.

MedPAC. 2006. Report to Congress: Medicare Payment Policy. Washington, DC: Medicare Payment Advisory Committee.

Med-Vantage. 2007. National P4P and Incentive Survey for 2006. Available at <http://survey.medvantageinc.com/2006Survey/>.

Meer, Jonathan, and Harvey S. Rosen. 2004. Insurance and the Utilization of Medical Services. *Social Science and Medicine* 58 (9): 1623–1632.

Mello, Michelle M., and Troyen A. Brennan. 2002. Deterrence of Medical Errors: Theory and Evidence for Malpractice Reform. *Texas Law Review* 80 (7): 1595.

Mennemeyer, Stephen T. 1978. Really Great Returns to Medical Education? *Journal of Human Resources* 13 (1): 75–90.

Mennemeyer, Stephen T., Michael A. Morrisey, and Leslie Z. Howard. 1997. Death and Reputation: How Consumers Acted Upon HCFA Mortality Information. *Inquiry* 34: 117–128.

Milgrom, Paul, and John Roberts. 1986. Price and Advertising Signals of Product Quality. *Journal of Political Economy* 94, no. 4 (August): 796–821.

———. 1992. *Economics, Organization, and Management*. Upper Saddle River, NJ: Prentice Hall.

Mintzes, Barbara. 2002. For and Against: Direct to Consumer Advertising Is Medicalizing Normal Human Experience: For. *British Medical Journal* 324 (April): 908–909.

Miron, Jeffrey A., and Jeffrey Zwiebel. 1991. Alcohol Consumption during Prohibition. *American Economic Review* 81 (2): 242.

Mitchell, Jean M., Jack Hadley, and Darrell J. Gaskin. 2002. Spillover Effects of Medicare Fee Reductions: Evidence from Ophthalmology. *International Journal of Health Care Finance and Economics* 2 (3): 171–188.

Monane, Mark, Dipika M. Matthias, Becky A. Nagle, and Miriam A. Kelly. 1998. Improving Prescribing Patterns for the Elderly through an Online Drug Utilization Review Intervention: A System Linking the Physician, Pharmacist, and Computer. *JAMA* 280 (14): 1249–1252.

Mongan, James J., Robert E. Mechanic, and Thomas H. Lee. 2006. Transforming U.S. Health Care: Policy Challenges Affecting the Integration and Improvement of Care. Brookings Institution. Available at <http://www.brookings.edu>.

Monheit, Alan C., Joel C. Cantor, Margaret Koller, and Kimberley S. Fox. 2004. Community Rating and Sustainable Individual Health Insurance Markets in New Jersey. *Health Affairs* 23 (4): 167–175.

Morone, James. 2002. Morality, Politics, and Health Policy. In *Policy Challenges in Modern Health Care*, ed. David Mechanic, Lynn B. Rogut, and David C. Colby. Piscataway, NJ: Rutgers University Press.

Mullan, Fitzhugh. 2003. The Future of Medical Education: A Call for Action. *Health Affairs* 22 (4): 88–93.

Murphy, Kevin M., and Robert H. Topel. 2003. The Economic Value of Medical Research. In *Measuring the Gains from Medical Research: An Economic Approach*, ed. Kevin M. Murphy and Richard H. Topel. Chicago: University of Chicago Press.

———. 2006. The Value of Health and Longevity. *Journal of Political Economy* 114 (5): 871–904.

Muurinen, Jaana-Marja. 1982. Demand for Health: A Generalized Grossman Model. *Journal of Health Economics* 1 (1): 5–28.

Nassirim, Abdelhak, and Lise Rochaix. 2006. Revisiting Physicians' Financial Incentives in Quebec: A Panel System Approach. *Health Economics* 15 (1): 49–64.

National Resident Matching Program. 2006. Results and Data: 2006 Match. Washington, DC: Association of American Medical Colleges.

Nelson, Philip. 1970. Information and Consumer Behavior. *Journal of Political Economy* 78 (2): 311.

———. 1974. Advertising as Information. *Journal of Political Economy* 82 (4): 729.

Neslin, Scott A. 2001. ROI Analysis of Pharmaceutical Promotion (RAPPP). Unpublished paper, Amos Tuck School of Business, Dartmouth College.

Newhouse, Joseph P. 1978. *The Economics of Medical Care: A Policy Perspective*. Reading, MA: Addison-Wesley.

———. 1981. The Erosion of the Medical Care Marketplace. In *Advances in Health Economics and Health Services Research*, ed. Richard M. Scheffler and Louis F. Rossiter. Greenwich, CT: JAI Press.

———. 1989. Measuring Medical Prices and Understanding Their Effects. *Journal of Health Administration Education* 7 (1): 19–26.

———. 2002. *Pricing the Priceless: A Healthcare Conundrum*. Cambridge, MA: MIT Press.

———. 2006. Reconsidering the Moral Hazard–Risk Aversion Trade-off. *Journal of Health Economics* 25 (5): 1005–1014.

Newhouse, Joseph P., and the Insurance Experiment Group. 1993. *Free for All? Lessons from the RAND Health Insurance Experiment*. Cambridge, MA: Harvard University Press.

Newhouse, Joseph P., Willard G. Manning, Carl N. Morris, Larry L. Orr, Naihua Duan, Emmett B. Keeler, Arleen Leibowitz, Kent H. Marquis, M. Susan Marquis, Charles E.

Phelps, and Robert H. Brook. 1981. Some Interim Results from a Controlled Trial of Cost Sharing in Health Insurance. *New England Journal of Medicine* 305 (25): 1501–1507.

Nguyen, Nguyen Xuan, and Frederick William Derrick. 1997. Physician Behavioral Response to a Medicare Price Reduction. *Health Services Research* 32 (3): 283–299.

Nicholson, Sean. 2002. Physician Specialty Choice under Uncertainty. *Journal of Labor Economics* 20 (4): 816–847.

———. 2003. Barriers to Entering Medical Specialties. Cambridge, MA: National Bureau of Economic Research.

———. 2005. How Much Do Medical Students Know about Physician Income? *Journal of Human Resources* 40 (1): 100–114.

Nicholson, Sean, and Nicholas S. Souleles. 2001. Physician Income Expectations and Specialty Choice. Cambridge, MA: National Bureau of Economic Research.

Nordhaus, William. 2003. The Health Nations: The Contribution of Improved Health to Living Standards. In *Measuring the Gains from Medical Research: An Economic Approach*, ed. Kevin M. Murphy and Robert H. Topel. Chicago: University of Chicago Press.

Norton, Edward C., Richard C. Lindrooth, and Susan T. Ennett. 1998. Controlling for the Endogeneity of Peer Substance Use on Adolescent Alcohol and Tobacco Use. *Health Economics* 7 (5): 439–453.

Norton, Edward C., and Douglas O. Staiger. 1994. How Hospital Ownership Affects Access to Care for the Uninsured. *RAND Journal of Economics* 25 (1): 171–185.

Nozick, Robert. 1977. *Anarchy, State, and Utopia*. Cambridge, MA: Harvard University Press.

Nyman, John A. 1999a. The Economics of Moral Hazard Revisited. *Journal of Health Economics* 18 (6): 811–824.

———. 1999b. The Value of Health Insurance: The Access Motive. *Journal of Health Economics* 18 (2): 141–152.

———. 2004. Is "Moral Hazard" Inefficient? The Policy Implications of a New Theory. *Health Affairs* 23 (5): 194–199.

O'Donoghue, Ted, and Matthew Rabin. 1999a. Doing It Now or Later. *American Economic Review* 89 (1): 103.

———. 1999b. Incentives for Procrastinators. *Quarterly Journal of Economics* 114 (3): 769.

———. 2001. Risky Behaviors among Youths: Some Issues from Behavioral Economics. In *Risky Behavior among Youths: An Economic Analysis*, ed. Jonathan H. Gruber. Chicago: University of Chicago Press.

Oeppen, Jim, and James W. Vaupel. 2002. *Demography*: Enhanced: Broken Limits to Life Expectancy. *Science* 296 (5570): 1029–1031.

Organization for Economic Cooperation and Development. 2006. *OECG Health Data: 2006, June*. Available at <http://www.oecd.orgdocument/30/0.2340_34631_12968734_1_1_1,00.html> (accessed June 22, 2006).

Osterberg, Lars, and Terrence Blaschke. 2005. Drug Therapy: Adherence to Medication. *New England Journal of Medicine* 353 (5): 487.

Ouchi, William G. 1979. A Conceptual Framework for the Design of Organizational Control Mechanisms. *Management Science* 25 (9): 833–848.

Pacula, Rosalie L., Michael Grossman, Frank J. Chaloupka, Patrick M. O'Malley, and Matthew C. Farrelly. 2001. Marijuana and Youth. In *Risky Behavior among Youths: An Economic Analysis*, ed. Jonathan H. Gruber. Chicago: University of Chicago Press.

Pauly, Mark V. 1968. The Economics of Moral Hazard: Comment. *American Economic Review* 58 (3): 531–537.

———. 1974. Overinsurance and Public Provision of Insurance: The Roles of Moral Hazard and Adverse Selection. *Quarterly Journal of Economics* 88 (1): 44–62.

———. 1979. The Ethics and Economics of Kickbacks and Fee Splitting. *Bell Journal of Economics* 10 (1): 344–352.

———. 1980. *Doctors and Their Workshops: Economic Models of Physician Behavior*. Chicago: University of Chicago Press.

———. 1983. More on Moral Hazard. *Journal of Health Economics* 2 (1): 81–85.

———. 1991. Fee Schedules and Utilization. In *Regulating Doctors' Fees: Competition, Controls, and Benefits under Medicare*, ed. H. E. Ted Frech. Washington, DC: AEI Press.

———. 1997. *Health Benefits at Work*. Ann Arbor: University of Michigan Press.

———. 2005. Effects of Insurance Coverage on Use of Care and Health Outcomes for Nonpoor Young Women. *American Economic Review* 95 (2): 219.

———. 2006. Moral Hazard Meets Evidence-Based Cost Sharing. University of Pennsylvania, Wharton School. Working Paper.

Pauly, Mark V., and Philip J. Held. 1990. Benign Moral Hazard and the Cost-Effectiveness Analysis of Insurance Coverage. *Journal of Health Economics* 9 (4): 447.

Pauly, Mark V., Howard Kunreuther, and Richard Hirth. 1995. Guaranteed Renewability in Insurance. *Journal of Risk and Uncertainty* 10 (2): 143–156.

Pauly, Mark V., Olivia Mitchell, and Yuhui Zeng. 2004. Death Spiral or Euthanasia? The Demise of Generous Group Health Insurance Coverage. National Bureau of Economic Research working paper 10464.

Pauly, Mark V., and Mark A. Satterthwaite. 1981. The Pricing of Primary Care Physicians Services: A Test of the Role of Consumer Information. *Bell Journal of Economics* 12 (2): 488–506.

Pepall, Lynne, Daniel J. Richards, and George Norman. 2002. *Industrial Organization: Contemporary Theory and Practice*. 2nd ed. Cincinnati, OH: South-Western.

———. 2005. *Industrial Organization: Contemporary Theory and Practice*. 3rd ed. Cincinnati, OH: South-Western.

Peterson, Eric D., Elizabeth R. DeLong, James G. Jollis, Lawrence H. Muhlbaier, and Daniel B. Mark. 1998. The Effects of New York's Bypass Surgery Provider Profiling on Access to Care and Patient Outcomes in the Elderly. *Journal of the American College of Cardiology* 32 (4): 993–999.

Petry, Nancy M., and Bonnie Martin. 2002. Low-Cost Contingency Management for Treating Cocaine- and Opioid-Abusing Methadone Patients. *Journal of Consulting and Clinical Psychology* 70 (2) (April): 398–405.

Pfeffer, Jeffrey. 1998. *The Human Equation*. Boston: Harvard Business School Press.

Phelan, Michael J. 2000. Timing and Scope of Emission Reductions for Airborne Particulate Matter: A Simplified Model. *Environmetrics* 11 (6): 627–649.

Phelps, Charles E. 1968. On Second-Best National Saving and Game-Equilibrium Growth. *Review of Economic Studies* 35 (2): 185–199.

———. 1986. Induced Demand: Can We Ever Know Its Extent? *Journal of Health Economics* 5: 355–365.

———. 1997. *Health Economics*. 2nd ed. Boston: Addison-Wesley.

———. 2000. Information Diffusion and Best Practice Adoption. In *Handbook of Health Economics*, ed. Anthony J. Culyer and Joseph P. Newhouse. Amsterdam: Elsevier.

———. 2003. *Health Economics*. Boston: Addison-Wesley.

Philipson, Tomas. 2000. Economic Epidemiology and Infectious Disease. In *Handbook of Health Economics*, ed. Anthony J. Culyer and Joseph P. Newhouse. Amsterdam: Elsevier.

Physicians' Working Group for Single-Payer National Health Insurance. 2003. Proposal of the Physicians' Working Group for Single-Payer National Health Insurance. *JAMA* 290 (6): 798–805.

Picone, Gabriel A., Shin-Yi Chou, and Frank A. Sloan. 2002. Are For-Profit Hospital Conversions Harmful to Patients and to Medicare? *RAND Journal of Economics* 33 (3): 507–523.

Picone, Gabriel A., Frank A. Sloan, and Justin G. Trogdon. 2004. The Effect of the Tobacco Settlement and Smoking Bans on Alcohol Consumption. *Health Economics* 13 (10): 1063–1080.

Pines, Wayne L. 1999. A History and Perspective on Direct-to-Consumer Promotion. *Food and Drug Law Journal* 54 (4): 489–518.

Posner, Richard A. 1994. *Sex and Reason*. Cambridge, MA: Harvard University Press.

Pratt, John W., and Richard Zeckhauser. 1985. Principles and Agents: An Overview. In *Principles and Agents: The Structure of Business*, ed. John W. Pratt and Richard Zeckhauser. Boston: Harvard Business School Press.

Reeves, Kelly N. 1998. Direct-to-Consumer Broadcast Advertising: Empowering the Consumer or Manipulating a Vulnerable Population. *Food and Drug Law Journal* 53 (4): 661–679.

Reichert, Steven, Todd Simon, and Ethan A. Halm. 2000. Physicians' Attitudes about Prescribing and Knowledge of the Costs of Common Medications. *Archives of Internal Medicine* 160 (18): 2799–2803.

Reiffen, David, and Michael R. Ward. 2005. Generic Drug Industry Dynamics. *Review of Economics and Statistics* 87 (1): 37–49.

Reinhardt, Uwe. 2007. The Pharmaceutical Section in Health Care. In *Pharmaceutical Innovation: Incentives, Competition, and Cost-Benefit Analysis in International Perspective*, ed. Frank A. Sloan and Chee-Ruey Hsieh. Cambridge: Cambridge University Press.

Relman, Arnold S. 2003. *Direct-to-Consumer Advertising: What Are the Consequences? Testimony before the U.S. Senate Special Committee on Aging, July 22.* Available at <http://aging.senate.gov/index.cfm?Fuseaction=Hearing.Detail&HearingID-26> (accessed September 2, 2003).

Rice, Thomas H. 1983. The Impact of Changing Medicare Reimbursement Rates on Physician-Induced Demand. *Medical Care* 21 (8): 803–815.

Ridley, David B., Henry G. Grabowski, and Jeffrey L. Moe. 2006. Developing Drugs for Developing Countries. *Health Affairs* 25 (2): 313–324.

Ried, Walter. 1996. Willingness to Pay and Cost of Illness for Changes in Health Capital Depreciation. *Health Economics* 5 (5): 447–468.

Rizzo, John A., and Richard J. Zeckhauser. 1990. Advertising and Entry: The Case of Physician Services. *Journal of Political Economy* 98 (3): 476–500.

Robertson, William J. 1981. Pediatric Manpower. *Pediatrics* 68 (6): 912–913.

Robinson, James C. 2001. Theory and Practice in the Design of Physician Payment Incentives. *Milbank Quarterly* 79 (2): 149–177.

Roemer, Milton I., Carl E. Hopkins, Lockwood Carr, and Foline Gartside. 1975. Copayments for Ambulatory Care: Penny-Wise and Pound-Foolish. *Medical Care* 13 (6): 457–466.

Roland, Martin. 2004. Linking Physicians' Pay to the Quality of Care: A Major Experiment in the United Kingdom. *New England Journal of Medicine* 351 (14): 1448–1454.

Rosen, Allison B., Mary Beth Hamel, Milton C. Weinstein, David M. Cutler, A. Mark Fendrick, and Sandeep Vijan. 2005. Cost-Effectiveness of Full Medicare Coverage of Angiotensin-Converting Enzyme Inhibitors for Beneficiaries with Diabetes [See Comment]. *Annals of Internal Medicine* 143 (2): 89–99.

Rosen, Sherwin. 1986. The Theory of Equalizing Differences. In *Handbook of Labor Economics*, ed. Orley Ashenfelter and Richard Layard. Amsterdam: Elsevier.

Rosenthal, Meredith B. 2000. Risk Sharing and the Supply of Mental Health Services. *Journal of Health Economics* 19 (6): 1047–1065.

Rosenthal, Meredith B., Ernst R. Berndt, Julie M. Donohue, Arnold M. Epstein, and Richard G. Frank. 2003. Demand Effects of Recent Changes in Prescription Drug Promotion. In *Frontiers in Health Policy Research*, ed. Alan M. Garber. Cambridge, MA: MIT Press.

Rosenthal, Meredith B., and R. Adams Dudley. 2007. Pay-for-Performance: Will the Latest Payment Trend Improve Care? *JAMA* 297 (7): 740–744.

Rosenthal, Meredith B., Richard G. Frank, Joan L. Buchanan, and Arnold M. Epstein. 2002. Transmission of Financial Incentives to Physician by Intermediary Organizations in California. *Health Affairs* 21 (4): 197–206.

Rosenthal, Meredith B., Richard G. Frank, Zhonghe Li, and Arnold M. Epstein. 2005. Early Experience with Pay-for-Performance: From Concept to Practice. *JAMA* 294 (14): 1788–1793.

Rosenthal, Meredith B., Bruce E. Landon, Sharon-Lise T. Normand, Richard G. Frank, and Arnold M. Epstein. 2006. Pay for Performance in Commercial HMOs. *New England Journal of Medicine* 355 (18): 1895–1902.

Ross, Lee, and Richard E. Nisbett. 1991. *The Person and the Situation: Perspectives of Social Psychology.* New York: McGraw-Hill.

Rothschild, Michael, and Joseph Stiglitz. 1976. Equilibrium in Competitive Insurance Markets: An Essay on the Economics of Imperfect Information. *Quarterly Journal of Economics* 90 (4): 629–649.

Rowe, John W. 2006. Pay-for-Performance and Accountability: Related Themes in Improving Health Care. *Annals of Internal Medicine* 145 (9): 695–699.

Russ, Benjamin. 1812. *Medical Inquiries and Observations, upon the Diseases of the Mind.* Philadelphia: Kimber and Richardson.

Russell, Louise B. 1998. Prevention and Medicare Costs. *New England Journal of Medicine* 339 (16): 1158–1160.

Saffer, Henry, and Frank J. Chaloupka. 1999. Demographic Differentials in the Demand for Alcohol and Drugs. In *The Economic Analysis of Substance Use and Abuse,* ed. Frank J. Chaloupka, Michael Grossman, Warren K. Bickel, and Henry Saffer. Cambridge, MA: National Bureau of Economic Research.

Salkever, David. 2000. Regulation of Prices and Investment in Hospitals in the U.S. In *Handbook of Health Economics,* ed. Anthony J. Culyer and Joseph P. Newhouse. Amsterdam: Elsevier.

Sandier, Simone. 1989. Health Services Utilization and Physician Income Trends—International Comparison of Health Care Financing and Delivery: Data and Perspectives. *Health Care Financing Review* 10: 33–48.

Santry, Heena P., Daniel L. Gillen, and Diane S. Lauderdale. 2005. Trends in Bariatric Surgical Procedures. *JAMA* 294 (15): 1909–1917.

Saul, Stephanie. 2005. Senate Leader Calls for Limits on Drug Ads. *New York Times,* July 2, C13.

Schaffer, Amanda. 2006. A President Felled by an Assassin and 1880s' Medical Care. *New York Times,* July 25, 2005: F5.

Schmalensee, Richard L. 1978. A Model of Advertising and Product Quality. *Journal of Political Economy* 86: 485–503.

Schoemaker, Paul J. H. 1982. The Expected Utility Model: Its Variants, Purposes, Evidence, and Limitations. *Journal of Economic Literature* 20 (2): 529–563.

Selby, Joseph V., Bruce H. Fireman, and Bix E. Swain. 1996. Effect of a Copayment on Use of the Emergency Department in a Health Maintenance Organization [See Comment]. *New England Journal of Medicine* 334 (10): 635–641.

Shapiro, Irving, Mathew Shapiro, and David Wilcox. 1999. Quality Improvement in Health Care: A Framework for Price and Output Measurement. *American Economic Review* 89: 333–337.

Shavell, Steven, and Tanguy-van Ypersele. 2001. Rewards versus Intellectual Property Rights. *Journal of Law and Economics* 44 (2): 525–547.

Shrank, William H., Henry N. Young, Susan L. Ettner, Peter Glassman, Steven M. Asch, and Richard L. Kravitz. 2005. Do the Incentives in Three-Tier Pharmaceutical Benefit Plans Operate as Intended? Results from a Physician Leadership Survey. *American Journal of Managed Care* 11 (1): 16–22.

Shyam-Sunder, Lakshmi, and Stewart C. Myers. 1999. Testing Static Tradeoff against Pecking Order Models of Capital Structure. *Journal of Financial Economics* 51 (2): 219–244.

Simon, Herbert A. 1982. *Models of Bounded Rationality.* Cambridge, MA: MIT Press.

Skinner, Jonathan S., Douglas O. Staiger, and Elliott S. Fisher. 2006. Is Technological Change in Medicine Always Worth It? The Case of Acute Myocardial Infarction. *Health Affairs*: W34–W47.

Sloan, Frank A. 1970. Lifetime Earnings and Physicians' Choice of Specialty. *Industrial and Labor Relations Review* 24: 47–56.

———. 1971. The Demand for Higher Education: The Case of Medical School Applicants. *Journal of Human Resources* 6 (4): 466–489.

———. 1976. Real Returns to Medical Education: A Comment. *Journal of Human Resources* 11 (1): 118–126.

———, ed. 1995. *Valuing Health Care.* New York: Cambridge University Press.

Sloan, Frank A., and Charles Eesley. 2007. Implementing a Public Subsidy for Vaccines. In *Pharmaceutical Innovation: Incentives, Competition, and Cost-Benefit Analysis in International Perspective*, ed. Frank A. Sloan and Chee-Ruey Hsieh. Cambridge: Cambridge University Press.

Sloan, Frank A., Penny B. Githens, Ellen Wright Clayton, and Gerald B. Hickson. 1993. *Suing for Medical Malpractice.* Chicago: University of Chicago Press.

Sloan, Frank A., Janet Mitchell, and Jerry Cromwell. 1978. Physician Participation in State Medicaid Programs. *Journal of Human Resources* 13: 211–245.

Sloan, Frank A., Jan Ostermann, and Derek Brown. 2006. The Rising Cost of Medicare and Improvements in Survival and Functioning among the U.S. Elderly, 1985–2000. In *Frontiers in Health Policy Research*, ed. David M. Cutler and Alan M. Garber. Cambridge, MA: MIT Press.

Sloan, Frank A., Jan Ostermann, Gabriel A. Picone, Christopher J. Conover, and Donald H. Taylor Jr. 2004. *The Price of Smoking.* Cambridge, MA: MIT Press.

Sloan, Frank A., Gabriel A. Picone, Donald H. Taylor, and Shin-Yi Chou. 2001. Hospital Ownership and Cost and Quality of Care: Is There a Dime's Worth of Difference? *Journal of Health Economics* 20 (1): 1–21.

Smith, Cynthia. 2004. Retail Prescription Drug Spending in the National Health Accounts. *Health Affairs* 23 (1): 160–167.

Smith, Cynthia, Cathy Cowan, Stephen Heffler, and Aaron Catlin. 2006. National Health Spending in 2004: Recent Slowdown Led by Prescription Drug Spending. *Health Affairs* 25 (1): 186–196.

Soumerai, Stephen B., Thomas J. McLaughlin, and Jerry Avorn. 1989. Improving Drug Prescribing in Primary Care: A Critical Analysis of the Experimental Literature. *Milbank Quarterly* 67 (2): 268–317.

Soumerai, Stephen B., Thomas J. McLaughlin, Dennis Ross-Degnan, Christina S. Casteris, and Paola Bollini. 1994. Effects of Limiting Medicaid Drug-Reimbursement Benefits on the Use of Psychotropic Agents and Acute Mental Health Services by Patients with Schizophrenia. *New England Journal of Medicine* 331 (10): 650.

Soumerai, Stephen B., Dennis Ross-Degnan, Jerry Avorn, Thomas J. McLaughlin, and Igoi Choodnovskiy. 1991. Effects of Medicaid Drug-Payment Limits on Admission to Hospitals and Nursing Homes. *New England Journal of Medicine* 325 (15): 1072.

Stano, Miron. 1987. A Further Analysis of the Physician Inducement Controversy. *Journal of Health Economics* 6 (3): 227–238.

Starr, Paul. 1982. *Social Transformation of American Medicine: The Rise of a Sovereign Profession and the Making of a Vast Industry*. New York: Basic Books.

Stigler, George J. 1968. Price and Non-Price Competition. *Journal of Political Economy* 76 (1): 149–154.

Sturm, Roland. 2003. Increases in Clinically Severe Obesity in the United States, 1986–2000. *Archives of Internal Medicine* 163 (18): 2146–2148.

Suh, Jesse J., Helen M. Pettinati, Kyle M. Kampman, and Charles P. O'Brien. 2006. The Status of Disulfiram: A Half of a Century Later. *Journal of Clinical Psychopharmacology* 26, no. 3 (June): 290–302.

Sunstein, Cass R., and Richard H. Thaler. 2003. Libertarian Paternalism Is Not an Oxymoron. *University of Chicago Law Review*. 70 (4): 1159–1202.

Suranovic, Steven M., Robert S. Goldfarb, and Thomas C. Leonard. 1999. An Economic Theory of Cigarette Addiction. *Journal of Health Economics* 18 (1): 1–29.

Sutton, John. 1991. *Sunk Costs and Market Structure: Price Competition, Advertising, and the Evolution of Concentration*. Cambridge, MA: MIT Press.

Tai-Seale, Ming, Thomas H. Rice, and Sally C. Stearns. 1998. Volume Responses to Medicare Payment Inductions with Multiple Payers: A Test of the McGuire-Paul Model. *Health Economics* 7: 199–219.

Tamblyn, Robyn, Rejean Laprise, James A. Hanley, Michael Abrahamowicz, Susan Scott, Nancy Mayo, Jerry Hurley, Roland Grad, Eric Latimer, Robert Perreault, Peter McLeod, Allen Huang, Pierre Larochelle, and Louis Mallett. 2001. Adverse Events Associated with Prescription Drug Cost-Sharing among Poor and Elderly Persons. *JAMA* 285 (4): 421.

Tatsioni, Athina, Deborah A. Zarin, Naomi Aronson, David J. Samson, Carole R. Flamm, Christopher Schmid, Joseph Lau, Mark Helfand, Sally Morton, and Eliseo Guallar. 2005. Challenges in Systematic Reviews of Diagnostic Technologies. *Annals of Internal Medicine* 142 (12): 10048–10055.

Tauras, John A., and Frank J. Chaloupka. 2001. Determinants of Smoking Cessation: An Analysis of Young Adult Men and Women. In *The Economic Analysis of Substance Use and Abuse*, ed. Michael Grossman and Chee-Ruey Hsieh. Northampton, MA: Edward Elgar.

Tauras, John A., Sara Markowitz, and John Cawley. 2005. Tobacco Control Policies and Youth Smoking: Evidence from a New Era. In *Substance Use: Individual Behaviour, Social Interactions, Markets, and Politics,* ed. Björn Lindgren and Michael Grossman. New York: Elsevier.

Tay, Abigail. 2003. Assessing Competition in Hospital Care Markets: The Importance of Accounting for Quality Differentiation. *RAND Journal of Economics* 34 (4): 786–814.

Taylor, Donald H., David J. Whellan, and Frank A. Sloan. 1999. Effects of Admission to a Teaching Hospital on the Cost and Quality of Care for Medicare Beneficiaries. *New England Journal of Medicine* 340 (4): 293–299.

Technological Change in Health Care (TECH) Research Network. 2001. Technological Change around the World: Evidence from Heart Attack Care. *Health Affairs* 20 (3): 25–42.

Temin, Peter. 1980. *Taking Your Medicine: Drug Regulation in the United States.* Cambridge, MA: Harvard University Press.

Temple, Jonathan. 1999. The New Growth Evidence. *Journal of Economic Literature* 37 (1): 112–156.

Thaler, Richard H., and Shlomo Benartzi. 2004. Save More Tomorrow (TM): Using Behavioral Economics to Increase Employee Saving. *Journal of Political Economy* 112 (S1): S164–S187.

Thaler, Richard H., and Hersh M. Shefrin. 1981. An Economic Theory of Self-Control. *Journal of Political Economy* 89 (2): 392–406.

Thamer, Mae, Niall Brennan, and Rafael Semansky. 1998. A Cross-National Comparison of Orphan Drug Policies: Implications for the U.S. Orphan Drug Act. *Journal of Health Politics, Policy, and Law* 23 (2): 265–290.

Thompson, James D. 1967. *Organizations in Action.* New York: McGraw-Hill.

Thornbury, John R., Denis G. Fryback, and Word Edwards. 1991. Likelihood Ratios as a Measure of Diagnostic Usefulness of Excretory Urogram Information. *Radiology* 26: 829–835.

Tirole, Jean. 1988. *The Theory of Industrial Organization.* Cambridge, MA: MIT Press.

Todd, Petra, and Kenneth L. Wolpin. 2003. Using a Social Experiment to Validate a Dynamic Behavior Model of Child Schooling and Fertility: Assessing the Impact of a School Subsidy Program in Mexico. Penn Institute for Economic Research working paper 03-022. Available at <http://pier.econ.upenn.edu/Archive/03-022.pdf> (accessed February 17, 2007)

Town, Robert, Douglas R. Wholey, John Kralewski, and Bryan Dowd. 2004. Assessing the Influence of Incentives on Physicians and Medical Groups. *Medical Care Research and Review* 61 (3): S80–S118.

Trajtenberg, Manuel. 1990. *Economic Analysis of Product Innovations: The Case of CT Scanners.* Cambridge, MA: Harvard University Press.

Transportation Research Board, Institute of Medicine of the National Academies. 2005. *Does the Built Environment Influence Physical Activity? Examining the Evidence.* Washington, DC: National Academies Press.

Troesken, Werner, and Patty Beeson. 2003. The Significance of Lead Water Mains in American Cities: Some Historical Evidence. In *Health and Labor Force Participation over the Life Course*, ed. Dora L. Costa. Chicago: University of Chicago Press.

Tu, Ha T., and Paul B. Ginsburg. 2006. Losing Ground: Physician Income, 1995–2003. In *Center for Studying Health System Change Tracking Report.* Washington, DC: Center for Studying Health System Change.

U.S. Department of Health, Education, and Welfare. 1980. *The Target-Income Hypothesis and Related Issues in Health Manpower Policy.* Washington, DC: Bureau of Health Manpower.

U.S. Food and Drug Administration, Department of Health and Human Services. 1969. Regulations for the Enforcement of the Federal Food, Drug, and Cosmetic Act, and the Fair Packaging and Labeling Act. *Federal Register.* 34. 7802.

———. 1985. Direct-to-Consumer Advertising Moratorium for Prescription Drugs Ended. *Federal Register* 50 (36677).

———. 1997. Draft Guidance for Industry: Broadcast Advertising of Prescription Drugs.

———. 2006. *CDER NDAs Approved in Calendar Years 1990–2004 by Therapeutic Potential and Chemical Type.* Available at <http://www.fda.gov/cder/rdmt/pstable.htm> (accessed July 16, 2006).

U.S. Physician Payment Review Commission. 1991. *Annual Report to Congress.* Washington, DC: U.S. Government Printing Office.

Van De Voorde, Carine, Eddy Van Doorslaer, and Erik Schokkaert. 2001. Effects of Cost Sharing on Physician Utilization under Favourable Conditions for Supplier-Induced Demand. *Health Economics* 10 (5): 457–471.

Variyam, Jayachandran N., and John Cawley. 2006. Nutrition Labels and Obesity. National Bureau of Economic Research working paper 11956.

Veblen, Thorstein. 1899. *The Theory of the Leisure Class.* New York: Penguin Books.

Vernon, John A. 2005. Examining the Link between Price Regulation and Pharmaceutical R & D Investment. *Health Economics* 14: 1–16.

Viscusi, W. Kip, and Josephy E. Aldy. 2003. The Value of a Statistical Life: A Critical Review of Market Estimates throughout the World. National Bureau of Economic Research working paper W9487.

Vroom, Victor H. 1964. *Work and Motivation.* New York: Wiley.

Waters, Teresa M., and Frank A. Sloan. 1995. Why Do People Drink? Tests of the Rational Addiction Model. *Applied Economics* 27 (8): 727–736.

Weeks, William B., Amy E. Wallace, Myron M. Wallace, and H. Gilbert Welch. 1994. A Comparison of the Educational Costs and Incomes of Physicians and Other Professionals. *New England Journal of Medicine* 330 (18): 1280–1286.

Weissman, Joel S., David Blumenthal, Alvin J. Silk, Michael Newman, Kinga Zapert, Robert Leitman, and Sandra Feibelmann. 2004. Physicians Report on Patient Encounters Involving Direct-to-Consumer Advertising. *Health Affairs:* W219–233.

Wennberg, John. 2004. Perspective: Practice Variations: Connecting the Dots. Review of Reviewed Item. *Health Affairs*. Available at <3http://content.healthaffairs.org/cgi/content/full/hlthaff.var.140/DC2>.

Wennberg, John E., Elliott S. Fisher, and Jonathan S. Skinner. 2002. Geography and the Debate over Medicare Reform. *Health Affairs* (February): W96–W114. Available at <http://www.healthaffairs.org>.

Wennberg, John, and Alan Gittleson. 1973. Small Area Variations in Health Care Delivery. *Science* 182: 1102–1108.

Williams, Alan. 1998. Medicine, Economics, Ethics, and the NHS: A Clash of Cultures? *Health Economics* 7 (7): 565–568.

Woloshin, Steven, Lisa M. Schwartz, and H. Gilbert Welch. 2004. The Value of Benefit Data in Direct-to-Consumer Drug Ads. *Health Affairs*: W234–245.

Woodcock, Janet. 2003. *Director, Center for Drug Evaluation and Research, Food, and Drug Administration. Statement to the U.S. Senate Special Committee on Aging, July 22.* Available at <http://aging.senate.gov/index.cfm?Fuseaction=Hearings.Detail&HearingID=26> (accessed September 2, 2003).

Yang, Zhou, Donna B. Gilleskie, and Edward C. Norton. 2006. Prescription Drug Use, Medical Care Utilization, and Health Outcomes: A Model of Elderly Health Dynamics. National Bureau of Economic Research, working paper 10964.

Yaniv, Gideon. 2004. Insomnia, Biological Clock, and the Bedtime Decision: An Economic Perspective. *Health Economics* 13 (1): 1–8.

Yip, Winnie C. 1998. Physician Response to Medicare Fee Reductions: Changes in the Volume of Coronary Artery Bypass Graft (CABG) Surgeries in the Medicare and Private Sectors. *Journal of Health Economics* 17 (6): 675–699.

Zeckhauser, Richard J. 1970. Medical Insurance: A Case Study of the Trade-off between Risk Spreading and Appropriate Incentives. *Journal of Economic Theory* 2 (1): 10–26.

Zhan, Chunliu, and Marlene R. Miller. 2003. Excess Length of Stay, Charges, and Mortality Attributable to Medical Injuries during Hospitalization. *JAMA* 290 (14): 1868–1874.

Zweifel, Peter, and Friedrich Breyer. 1997. *Health Economics*. New York: Oxford University Press.

Zweifel, Peter, and Willard G. Manning. 2000. Moral Hazard and Consumer Incentives in Health Care. In *Handbook of Health Economics*, ed. Anthony J. Culyer and Joseph P. Newhouse. Amsterdam: Elsevier.

Index